Sociology

UNDERSTANDING SOCIETY

Sociology

UNDERSTANDING SOCIETY

Peter I. Rose

Sophia Smith Professor of Sociology and Anthropology,
Smith College

Penina M. Glazer

Dean of the Faculty and Professor, The School of Social Science,
Hampshire College

Myron Peretz Glazer

Professor of Sociology and Anthropology,
Smith College

Consultants

Gary R. Borum, McGavock High School, Nashville, Tennessee
Michael C. Erickson, Bella Vista High School, Fair Oaks, California
Jerry L. Gillett, Holt High School, Holt, Michigan
John Soper, R.L. Thomas High School, Webster, New York

PRENTICE HALL, INC., Needham Heights, Massachusetts

SOCIOLOGY Understanding Society   THIRD EDITION

Peter I. Rose, Penina M. Glazer, and Myron Peretz Glazer

We dedicate this book to our children:

Lies and Dan Rose, and Joshua and Jessica Glazer

Supplementary Material

TEACHER'S RESOURCE HANDBOOK

Printed in the United States of America

013-823253-9
            9 96 95 94 93 92

Permissions

Page 30 excerpt from *The Hidden Dimension* by Edward T. Hall, copyright © 1966 by Edward T. Hall, reprinted by permission of Doubleday & Company, Inc.; **32** "OK, Tribesmen, Now Hear This," by Henry Morgan, reprinted with the permission of Henry Morgan, 1982; **38** excerpt from "The Odd Practice of Neck Binding," by Lance Morrow, copyright 1978, Time, Inc., all rights reserved, reprinted by permission from *Time;* **40** "Totemism and the A.E.F." by Ralph Linton, reproduced by permission of the American Anthropological Association from *American Anthropologist* 26(2):296–300, 1924; **42** reprinted from *Black Nationalism*, pages 212–219, by E. U. Essien-Udom by permission of the University of Chicago Press; **50** excerpt from "Body Ritual Among the Nacirema," by Horace Miner, *American Anthropologist* 58(3)503–505, reproduced by permission of the American Anthropological Association; **52** excerpt from "From a Young Burmese Girl's Notebook," *The UNESCO Courier,* March 1975; **57** from *A Death in the Sanchez Family,* by Oscar Lewis, copyright © 1969 by Oscar Lewis, reprinted by permission of Random House, Inc.; **75** Kingsley Davis, *Human Society,* pages 204–205, Macmillan 1948; **88** E. E. LeMasters, *Blue-Collar Aristocrats,* pages 141–142, The University of Wisconsin Press, 1975; **116** Melvin M. Tumin, *Patterns of Society,* Little, Brown and Company 1973; **215** Roberta Simmons, Florence Rosenberg, and Morris Rosenberg, "Disturbance in the Self-image at Adolescence," *ASR,* vol. 38, 1973; **216** Phyllis LaFarge, "An Uptight Adolescence," Thomas Cottle, "The Connections of Adolescence," in *Daedalus, Journal of the American Academy of Arts and Sciences,* Fall 1971; **216** Alice de Rivera, "On Desegregating Stuyvesant High," from *Sisterhood Is Powerful,* Robin Morgan, ed., Random House, 1970; **218** Karen Durbin, "On Hating and Loving Being Single," *Mademoiselle,* July 1975, reprinted by permission of Karen Durbin, c/o International Creative Management, copyright 1975 by Karen Durbin; **219** Charlotte Leon Mayerson, ed., *Two Blocks Apart,* © 1963 by Holt, Rinehart and Winston, reprinted by permission of Holt, Rinehart and Winston, Publishers; **225** Matina S. Horner, "Fail: Bright Women," *Psychology Today,* November 1969, reprinted by permission, copyright © 1969 Ziff-Davis Publishing Company; **242** Martin Oppenheimer, "The Unionization of the Professional," *Social Policy,* January/February 1975, reprinted with permission of *Social Policy,* published by Social Policy Corporation, copyright 1975 by Social Policy Corp.; **244** William H. Whyte, Jr., *The Organization Man,* copyright © 1956 by William H. Whyte, Jr., reprinted by permission of Simon & Schuster, a division of Gulf and Western Corporation; **254** Kenneth L. Woodward, "Growing Old Happy," from *Newsweek,* February 28, 1977, page 56, copyright 1977 by Newsweek, Inc., all rights reserved; **255** Judith Wax, "It's Like Your Own Home Here," *The New York Times Magazine,* reprinted by permission of the Sterling Lord Agency, Inc., copyright © 1976 by Judith Wax; **267** Earl C. Gottschalk, Jr., "A Place Apart," *The Wall Street Journal,* August 8, 1975, reprinted with permission of *The Wall Street Journal* © Dow Jones & Company Inc., 1975, all rights reserved; **275** based on "Steel Axes for Stone Age Australians," by Lauriston Sharp, in *Human Problems in Technology,* edited by Edward Spicer © 1952 by the Russell Sage Foundation, reprinted by permission of the publisher; **289** Herbert Gans, *The Urban Villagers: Group and Class in the Life of Italian-Americans,* copyright © 1962 by the Free Press of Glencoe, copyright © 1982 by Herbert J. Gans; **291** condensed by permission of Random House Inc. from Jane Jacobs, *The Death and Life of Great American Cities,* copyright © 1961 by Jane Jacobs; **343** from Pierre van den Berghe, "Research in South Africa," in *Ethics, Politics, and Social Research,* Gideon Sjoberg, ed., © 1967 Schenkman Publishing Co., Inc., Cambridge, Mass.; **345** copyright 1951 by Langston Hughes, reprinted from *Selected Poems of Langston Hughes,* by Langston Hughes, by permission of Alfred A. Knopf, Inc.; **355** abridged from pages 99–115 in *From Many Lands* by Louis Adamic, copyright 1940 by Louis Adamic, by permission of Harper and Row Publishers, Inc.; **363** Lee Dirks, "Poverty Is a Simple Issue, Complex Problem," in *The National Observer,* January 27, 1964, reprinted with permission from *The National Observer,* copyright 1964, Dow Jones Company, Inc., all rights reserved; **366** Harry M. Caudill, *Night Comes to the Cumberlands: A Biography of a Depressed Area,* copyright 1962, 1963 by Harry M. Caudill, by permission of Little, Brown and Company in association with the Atlantic Monthly Press; **372** John B. Parrish, "Is the United States Really Filled With Poverty?" reprinted from *U.S. News and World Report,* September 4, 1967, copyright 1967, U.S. News and World Report, Inc.; **387** Richard Rettig, Manuel J. Torres, and Gerald R. Garrett, *Manny: A Criminal Addict's Story,* © 1977 by Houghton Mifflin Company, used by permission; **402** from *Child of the Dark* by Carolina Maria de Jesus, translated by David St. Clair, copyright © 1962 by E. P. Dutton & Co., Inc., and Souvenir Press Ltd., reprinted by permission of the publisher E. P. Dutton, Inc.; **434** reprinted from *Street Corner Society,* by William F. Whyte, by permission of the University of Chicago Press.

Illustration Credits

Page 12 John Curtis/Off-Shoot Stock; **15** Steve Vidler/Leo De Wys; **16** Russ Schleipman/Off-Shoot Stock; **20** (top) Jim McHugh/Sygma; (bottom) Momauuk Eastcott/Woodfin Camp and Associates; **21** Marc and Evelyne Bernheim/Woodfin Camp and Associates; **22** John Des Jardins/DPI; **23** (top) Carol Lee/The Picture Cube (bottom) E.A. Heiniger/Photo Researchers, Inc.; **27** (top) Johan Elers/International Stock Photo; (bottom) David E. Dempster/Off-Shoot Stock; **29** David E. Dempster/Off-Shoot Stock; **30** (left) Robert Frerck/Odyssey Productions; (right) Jacques Jangoux/Peter Arnold; **31** C. Wilfang/Leo de Wys; **33** (top) Fred Bodin/Off-Shoot Stock; **36** F. Schrieder/Photo Researchers, Inc.; **37** (top left) Daniel Zirinsky/Photo Researchers, Inc. (bottom left) Waltes H. hodge/Peter Arnold; (top right) Mathias Oppersdorff/Photo Researchers, Inc.; **39** (top left) Michael Abramson/Woodfin Camp and Associates; (top right) Jan Reis/Woodfin Camp and Associates; **41** Augustis Upitis/Shostal Associates; **47** J. Gerard Smith; **48** Farrell Grehan/Photo Researchers, Inc.; **49** Chris Reeberg/DPI; **50** Brownie Harris/Stock Market; **52** Kal Muller/Woodfin Camp and Associates; **56** Michael Heron/Woodfin Camp and Associates; **57** David Strickler/Monkmeyer; **58** Eric Kroll/Taurus Photos; **60** Frances Laping/DPI; **62** Paolo Koch/Photo Researchers, Inc.; **64** Robert McElroy/Woodfin Camp and

(continued on page 468)

CONTENTS

CASE STUDIES

GRAPHS, CHARTS, AND TABLES

TO THE STUDENT

The purpose of the third edition of *Sociology*, like that of the first two, is most simply stated in its subtitle: *Understanding Society*. From the beginning of our work on the volume, the three of us hoped to offer you a lively, interesting, and challenging introduction to the ways sociologists investigate, describe, and analyze social life. We wanted not only to convey the concepts and techniques of sociology but also to provide a feeling of the excitement and significance of sociological research.

To set lofty goals is one thing; to achieve them is quite another. We were especially gratified by the favorable response of teachers and students across the country to our first editions —and by their comments and suggestions. We have retained many features of the first editions, but we have also added many new elements, including new unit and chapter introductions and expanded chapter reviews.

The vivid photos, graphs, charts, and drawings; the many sociological studies, documented in a reference section; the readings (noted throughout by a grey margin line); and the wide variety of activities are designed to give you a sense of the discipline of sociology. As in the first editions, stimulating thought questions are interspersed throughout the text (indicated by a blue question mark). Review and application questions follow each numbered section, and a chapter review offers a "recap," a list of key terms, further applications, an extended readings section (readings can be found in local libraries or distributed by your teacher), and social studies and critical thinking skills questions.

This edition of *Sociology: Understanding Society* is presented in six units, each containing two to four chapters and concluding with a featured unit application.

The first unit introduces you to the field of sociology and to many of the core concepts used in analyzing social life. The second unit—on social structure—deals with social interaction, roles and relationships, and the ways societies are divided and stratified. Unit Three begins with a chapter on the family and continues with discussions of other major social institutions: religion, education, government, and economic systems.

Using concepts introduced earlier, the fourth unit covers the process of socialization, showing how both males and females learn cultural patterns and social norms as children, adolescents, and adults. Unit Five discusses continuity and change, examining the character of community, the effects of urbanization, and the changes brought about by social movements. The sixth and final unit explores social problems, including prejudice and discrimination, poverty, crime, and problems of mass society, such as population pressures, urban growth and decay, alienation, pollution, and social conflict.

An appendix called "The Research Process" summarizes the methods of social research. We hope that you will find it not only informative but also useful as a guide to carrying out investigations of your own. A glossary includes important sociological terms, which are defined in the text and italicized where they first appear. "Some Significant Sociologists" contains capsule biographies of scholars who have made valuable contributions to the field. We have also provided a guide to careers for those of you whose interest in sociology may have been stimulated by this course.

We have designed *Sociology: Understanding Society* as a comprehensive introduction to a field in which we have spent many rewarding years as students, researchers, and teachers. It is our sincere wish that those who study its lessons will come away with an appreciation of the value of sociology that matches our own.

Peter I. Rose
Penina Migdal Glazer
Myron Peretz Glazer

SOCIETY AND CULTURE

Unit Focus

Sociology is about people—how they act, react, and interact both in their everyday lives and under extraordinary circumstances. It is about their thoughts, feelings, and ideas. And sociology is about the social contexts— groups, neighborhoods, cities, even whole societies—in which these thoughts, feelings, and ideas are formed. Sociology is about social life itself.

In a sense, everyone knows some sociology. To function in society, everyone must learn to follow certain rules and play appropriate parts in the groups to which he or she belongs. Sociologists are trained to explain why people do what they do, like what they like, and think what they think. They **observe, describe, analyze,** and, sometimes, **predict** people's behavior. Throughout this book, on the first page of each chapter, in the section "Using Sociologists' Tools", you will also have an opportunity to observe, describe, analyze, and predict human behavior in various situations.

Applying Sociology

- With what groups do you interact on a daily basis?
- What rules must you observe?
- What patterns exist in your daily, monthly, and yearly routine?

A group of teens playing volleyball is of interest to the sociologist, who studies the ways in which people interact and change.

What Is Sociology?

Chapter Preview

- **Before you read,** look up the following key terms in the glossary to become familiar with their definitions:

sociology
social facts
socialization

hypothesis
culture

biological differences
social differences

- **As you read,** think about answers to the following questions:

1. What practices make sociology a scientific study of society?
2. Why do sociologists study not only characteristics shared by all people but also traits of individuals and groups that are different?
3. In what specific ways does sociology differ from psychology and biology?

Sections in this Chapter

1. The Sociological Approach
2. Human Similarities and Differences
3. What Sociologists Study

Chapter Focus

Why has the size of the average American household continually shrunk in the past 50 years? Why do Americans marry on the basis of love instead of arrangements made by family? Why do young Americans often seek approval from their peers than from their elders, as in some cultures? Why do many Americans look up to movie stars and sports figures rather than to political and military figures?

Giving us answers to these questions and hundreds of others like them so that we can understand ourselves and other people and nations is the primary occupation of sociologists. In studying American and other societies, sociologists have found that everyday life is far more complex than most of us realize. This chapter examines the sociological approach to human similarities and differences.

Using Sociologists' Tools

- **Observe** the behavior and traits of your classmates and yourself.
- **Describe** several characteristics that make you similar to some of your classmates and also different from them.
- **Analyze** whether the differences you noted are inherited or learned characteristics.
- **Predict** what would happen if eye or hair color were the basis for making distinctions between people rather than, for example, gender.

How and why people behave the way they do are basic questions that sociologists try to answer.

1 The Sociological Approach

If you asked most people why they do or think certain things, they might answer, "That's just the way I am." Or they might give you a "common-sense" answer that could very well be wrong. For example, some of the following statements sound like common sense. Which do you think are true and which do you think are false?

1. Families living in large cities are more isolated from friends, neighbors, and relatives than families in small towns.
2. Poor people have more stable marital relationships—with less divorce, fewer separations, and so on—than wealthy people.
3. Many people with strong racial prejudices tend to be obedient and respectful toward their superiors, to demand complete obedience from those below them, and to admire power.

4. Female infants cry more, sleep less, and are more demanding than male infants, who are more passive and content.
5. People's opinions of themselves depend largely on the way others think of them.
6. Second marriages tend to be more successful than first marriages.

If you answered that items 3 and 5 are true and that the others are false, your answers agree with the results of sociological studies. Each of the statements was tested through careful research by sociologists who did not rely on commonly held beliefs but instead tried to find the answers in a scientific way.

Many people are not really aware of why they act and think as they do. But students of sociology have a chance to look beneath the surface. In doing so, they may learn that

15

Sociologists study all aspects of a society, including the ways in which people make their living and bring up their children. What might family life be like for nomadic people such as these Bedouin merchants, who ply their trade in the Sahara?

things are not what they seem. The error of basing beliefs on common sense lies in the fact that conclusions are drawn from appearances. This is an uncritical and unscientific approach to learning.

The sociological approach is different. *Sociology,* a word coined by the nineteenth-century French philosopher Auguste Comte, means "the study of society." Sociology is concerned with groups—how they are formed and how they change—and with the actions of individuals within groups.

The Influence of Social Facts

Sociologists study the interactions among persons in social situations, seeking patterns in those interactions. By observing how cer-

tain forms of behavior are consistently repeated, sociologists try to predict behavior in similar situations. Sociologists regard the personality traits, values, and rules that govern our behavior as socially determined.

For example, suppose that you are a devoutly religious person. You pray and attend worship services. You believe that God watches over you and is pleased by some of your actions and displeased by others. Your religious beliefs are highly personal. You practice the beliefs and values of your religion by choice. Yet, from the sociologist's point of view, an important link exists between your personal beliefs and other facts. The geographic region you come from; whether you live in an urban, rural, or suburban environment; your parents' religion; and the teachings of your church—all these *social facts* have influenced your choice.

A social fact is any social activity or situation that can be measured or observed. Patterns of religious affiliation, marriage rates, percentages of white- and blue-collar workers, crime patterns, divorce rates, and levels of academic achievement are all social facts. Emile Durkheim, an early sociologist, saw the importance of social facts in understanding society. He first introduced the concept in his book *The Rules of Sociological Method* (1895).

Some of Durkheim's most important work concerned suicide. In research conducted in France early in this century, Durkheim studied and compared marital status, religion, and economic conditions with rates of suicide. He found that among those who committed suicide there was a higher percentage of divorced persons than married, of Protestants than Catholics, and of persons undergoing change in economic condition than of those living in a stable economic situation, even poverty.

In summary, Durkheim found that while suicide is a highly individual act, it is influenced by a variety of social facts. Durkheim concluded that even such a personal act as suicide could best be understood in terms of the social situation in which a person lives. Those with the closest bonds to others, those

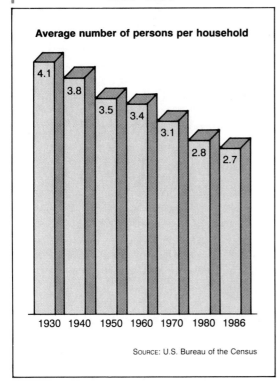

SHRINKING AMERICAN HOUSEHOLDS 1930–1986

Average number of persons per household

4.1 3.8 3.5 3.4 3.1 2.8 2.7

1930 1940 1950 1960 1970 1980 1986

SOURCE: U.S. Bureau of the Census

GRAPH SKILL   Sociological information often provides the basis for economic and political decisions. A sociological fact with many implications is the decrease in size of the average American household. What changes in housing and manufactured products might result from the tastes and needs of smaller families?

most at home in their societies, were the least likely to take their own lives.

If such personal matters as religious belief and the act of suicide can be viewed from the sociologist's point of view, so can an issue that affects a whole society—for example, the relative social positions of women and men. In many societies, women have long been viewed as inferior to men. They have been thought of as more emotional, more dependent, less intelligent, and less able to succeed in business or politics. They were thought to be naturally inclined to do housework, raise children, gossip, and provide emotional support and comfort for their families.

Over the centuries, many people, both men and women, have held this view. After all, haven't many women acted in ways that fit this description? Observations seemed to provide the proof. From a sociologist's point of view, however, this conclusion is too simple. To explain human behavior more fully, sociologists analyze certain aspects of society. In this case, they would study *socialization,* the process by which all of us learn to become members of society. More specifically, sociologists study the beliefs, values, and ways of behaving that males and females are taught in their societies.

According to this kind of analysis, women are not born weak, submissive, or gossipy. If some women have these traits, that is because they have been taught to behave as they do. Their observed behavior neither proves nor disproves their natural inferiority to men. It proves only that they have been socialized into the roles their society considers right for them.

You can see that common sense is inadequate to explain society because it is often based on prejudice. If its conclusions support beliefs that we already hold, we usually don't look further. Sociology teaches us to test our beliefs by using scientific methods and by considering different points of view. It teaches us to question our common sense.

A Systematic Study

Sociology, the study of society, has also been defined as the systematic study of human social behavior. At first glance, this definition of sociology may appear simple, but it is more complex than it seems. "Human social behavior" refers to everything related to the interaction of human beings in groups. Thus, sociologists study people's beliefs, values, and rules as well as their ways of organizing families, educational systems, religions, and so on. They also look at the positions and roles people assume within these systems.

Sociologists tackle all kinds of topics, from the way pairs of people—such as friends, employer and employee, or husband

and wife—interact with each other to the interaction of mobs, crowds, and audiences. They are interested in the daily lives of welfare recipients and in the power struggles of nations. They are concerned with social movements such as the civil-rights movement and with complex organizations such as large corporations. In fact, every aspect of group activity is a potential subject for the sociologist.

All in all, there's a lot to study. The study would be unmanageable—even impossible—unless it was systematic. "Systematic" means that, like all scientists, sociologists use scientific methods to study the things in which they are interested. Such methods involve identifying problems, working out hypotheses, and collecting and analyzing data.

The sociologist begins by concentrating on a problem or set of problems. For exam-

GRAPH SKILL   One way sociologists obtain information about group attitudes is through surveys. In recent years, some observers have concluded that the American family is in trouble, perhaps because some social trends, such as more divorces and fewer children, seem to indicate less emphasis on family life. According to the graph, what two factors do the greatest percentage of families rank as most important? As least important? What do these rankings indicate about the values of the Americans who were polled?

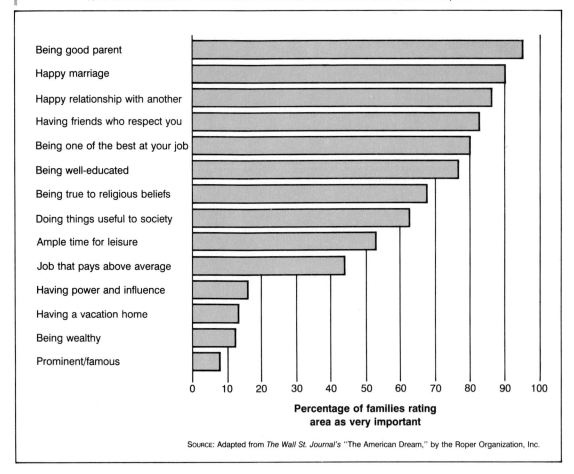

WHAT AMERICAN FAMILIES RANK AS MOST IMPORTANT, 1987

Percentage of families rating area as very important

Source: Adapted from *The Wall St. Journal's* "The American Dream," by the Roper Organization, Inc.

ple, let's suppose that you are interested in education, specifically in the relationship between schoolwork and sports activity. This is the problem you have chosen to study.

Next you work out a *hypothesis*—a hunch, or educated guess—about how two or more things are related. In this case, you believe that students who are active in sports do not do as well in school as students who don't participate in athletics. So you state a hypothesis: "Athletes get lower grades in school than nonathletes." You define "athlete" as someone who takes part in school sports competition—football games, basketball games, tennis matches, swimming meets, and so on—on a regular basis.

To test your hypothesis, you must now collect data. You decide to gather information on grade averages from a certain number of athletes and an equal number of "nonathletes." Then you determine the average scholastic record for each group. Is there a significant difference? If the nonathletes get better grades, you may have at least some evidence to support your hypothesis. You will learn more about this method in the Appendix, "The Research Process."

REVIEW AND APPLICATION

1. IDENTIFY: Sociology, social facts, socialization, hypothesis.
2. What factors did Durkheim consider in his analysis of suicide?
3. List the steps by which a sociologist attempts to reach a conclusion about a common but unproven belief.

CRITICAL THINKING: On page 17 you read that women are viewed as inferior to men in many societies. What traits does the text imply are valued highly in these societies? What activities does the text imply are less valued? Suppose, in a certain society, men are considered inferior to women, but roles are the same as in the first societies. How do you think the values in this hypothetical society differ from the values discussed above?

---

2 Human Similarities and Differences

Three questions are basic to sociology: How much of human behavior is inherited? How much of human behavior is learned? How is each individual unique? These questions offer clues to the nature of human beings and help sociologists understand the various ways humans live. They explain why even identical twins raised together often display personal differences that enable people who know them well to tell them apart.

A similar way of approaching human similarities and differences is to ask: In what ways am I like all other human beings? In what ways am I like some others? In what ways am I like no others?

Divide a sheet of paper into three columns. At the top of the columns write the headings "Like All Others," "Like Some Others," and "Like No Others." List several items under each column. For example, in the first column, you might write, "I have two arms, two legs," and so on; in the second, you might say, "I am a Baptist, a Democrat, a woman"; and, in the last, "I look different and think differently from everyone else in the world." What do your answers suggest about the extent to which human beings are influenced by others, such as parents, teachers, and friends?

Like All Others

In listing ways in which you are like all others, you may have noted certain physical traits and biological needs. Normally, a person has two arms, two legs, two ears, two eyes, a nose, and so on. Like all animals, human beings, to survive as a species, must

Identical twins, even when dressed alike, can be told apart by people who know them well. Every human being has some unique characteristics.

They can think things over and decide whether to do something right away or at some future time. They can decide to deposit ten dollars in the bank to help pay for a bicycle next month or pass up pizza for lunch so they can have birthday cake after dinner. They can put off satisfying immediate wants in anticipation of greater pleasure later.

Most important, human beings can develop and use elaborate communication systems. Through languages, gestures, and signs of all sorts, people exchange ideas, learn better ways of doing things, and teach the young the rules of their society.

Like Some Others

While human beings all do certain things that set them apart from other animals, the way they do them often varies from group to group or from place to place. For instance, human beings all need some sort of shelter, but they live in a wide variety of dwellings, from igloos to steel-and-glass apartment buildings. While all human beings wear clothing for protection, the type of clothing varies from animal skins to business suits.

All societies celebrate big events like marriage. These Polish women prepare for a traditional wedding.

satisfy certain drives and needs: to eat, to eliminate wastes, to protect themselves, to reproduce.

Most animals have little choice in how they go about satisfying their basic drives and needs; they follow their instincts. But people are not limited to following instincts. They can—and do—make choices. For instance, human beings can live in a variety of climates and organize their lives in a variety of ways. They can devise means of satisfying their most basic needs, from inventing clothing for protection to using fire for cooking and warmth.

Since humans can think creatively, they develop elaborate belief systems that offer explanations for the unknown. Only humans have the ability to ponder such questions as the meaning of life. As the psychologist Erich Fromm once wrote, "Man is the only animal for whom his own existence is a problem which he has to solve and from which he cannot escape."

Humans have the unique ability to live in the past and in the future. They can tell you about their great-great-grandfathers, about ancient wars, or about last summer's vacation. They can also say what they hope they will be doing in a year or in ten years.

Because they have a sense of the future, human beings are able to delay gratification.

Climate, custom, and geographical location affect the ways in which humans meet their basic needs for clothing and shelter. The stilt houses pictured here are built on a lagoon in Tiagba in the Ivory Coast, Africa. What does the clothing of the people tell you about the climate?

Sociologists are concerned with the many *social differences* people exhibit—the variations they learn in their societies. Other variations that make people "like some others" have to do with gender, size, and skin, hair, and eye color. These *biological differences* are mainly inherited, not learned, although people are often taught the socially defined meanings of various biological differences.

Some obvious social differences we learn as we grow up are the use of a particular language and a preference for certain kinds of food or clothes. Do you speak English? Do you like steak and potatoes? Do you wear jeans? What about people who live in Malaysia or Malawi or Morocco? Do they speak English? Do they like steak and potatoes? Do they wear jeans?

People similar to "us" do certain things our way, things like speaking, eating, praying, working, and playing. Other people—"they"—do things differently. They too speak, eat, pray, work, and play, but they do these things their way, not ours. Sometimes we are amazed at how easily a seemingly difficult language is learned by a native of the country where it is spoken. Mark Twain is reported to have said, "Imagine, in Paris, even the children speak French!"

Muslims, Jews, and Christians all have ideas of God, but their ideas are very different. Elephant herders, berry pickers, and nuclear physicists all work, but the work they do is very different. Communism, socialism, and capitalism are all ways of organizing the economy, but they are very different ways. Democracy is only one of a number of

American society is highly complex, and Americans pursue an enormous variety of interests. Here balloonists gather to enjoy their sport.

the things they consider good or bad, right or wrong, and pleasurable or painful.

Most of us share many characteristics with fellow Americans. Foreigners are particularly aware of how "American" we are when they visit the United States. We make the same discovery about ourselves when we travel abroad. Our American culture makes us like other Americans in various ways and quite different from people of other cultures. So, too, do German, Pygmy, Eskimo, and Japanese children grow up in cultures that make them like others in their societies but unlike Americans.

Like No Others

Despite many similarities to all others and to some others, each of us is an individual—one of a kind. Individual differences may be accounted for in a variety of ways. Some are purely genetic; except for identical twins, each person inherits a unique combination of genes from his or her parents.

People are unique in other ways as well. Every person has had and will have experiences that are not shared by anyone else. Think how different people are from their brothers or sisters, who were born of the same parents and raised in the same environment. While you share many basic traits with all humans and many others with all other Americans, there are many things that make you unique. You're you.

political systems. Baseball is only one of many recreational activities. And a Western symphony orchestra sounds quite different from African drums or an Indian sitar.

Often biological and social differences are combined. In many societies, women are treated differently from men, and members of certain racial groups are treated differently from others. Can you think of other examples?

So, while we are like all other people in our general needs and talents, we tend to differ from many others because of the manner in which we are brought up—because of our particular *culture*. The word "culture," as used by sociologists, refers to the ways in which a particular group of people lives. Culture includes the rules that members of a society set for themselves, the general ideas around which they organize their lives, and

---

REVIEW AND APPLICATION

1. *IDENTIFY:* Social differences, biological differences, culture.
2. What questions do sociologists ask about human behavior?
3. How do social differences differ from biological differences?

CRITICAL THINKING: On page 20 the kinds of shelters in different cultures are compared. Why do you think the dwellings of Eskimos living in Alaska and people living in New York City vary so widely? Cite a number of factors.

3 What Sociologists Study

While all scientists share basic principles and methods, their approach must be fitted to the subject of their study. The biologist, the psychologist, and the sociologist all study human beings. But because each studies different aspects of human life, each of these scientists puts a different stress on the balance among the three categories "like all others," "like some others," and "like no others."

Biologists study the physical characteristics and life processes that all human beings share. Therefore, they emphasize "like all others." Psychologists, while concerned with group influences, often focus on the unique personality traits of an individual. Arguing that individual experiences can never be duplicated, psychologists tend to emphasize "like no others." Sociologists study the roles of society and culture. They emphasize "like some others."

Understanding cultural and societal variations is an important part of the sociologist's work—and of this course. As a practice exercise in sociology, try analyzing the behavior of the people in the two pictures shown on this page.

You know what the scene in picture A is because it is familiar. First of all, they are like people you've seen many times before, people who wear certain clothes and who do certain things with certain objects. You can observe the manner in which they sit and use their hands, and you can understand what each is doing. You might say these are "typical Americans," not rich, not poor, "just plain folks." The scene depicts a particular aspect of American life.

Now look at picture B. What about these people? Again, what does the picture "say"? What is going on? What are the people doing?

If you aren't sure, that isn't surprising. The scene is unfamiliar. The activities seem strange. You have probably never shared these particular experiences. They are far removed from what you know. This picture shows a Shinto wedding celebration honoring the bride and groom.

A

B

REVIEW AND APPLICATION

1. Why is it difficult to explain the picture of the Shinto wedding celebration?

CRITICAL THINKING: The top picture shows "typical Americans," but it is not a representative sample of all Americans. List three reasons why.

CHAPTER 1 REVIEW

Recap

Sociology is the study of society and of the interactions within society's many groups. By examining social facts—observable, measureable conditions in people's lives—sociologists draw conclusions about social behavior. Sociologists are also concerned with the processes of socialization, by which people learn the values, beliefs, and rules of behavior in their culture. Using a scientific approach, sociologists study social differences. They seek to understand the variations among cultures and to uncover the ways in which human beings are "like some others."

Key Terms

Define the following:

sociology	hypothesis	biological differences
social fact	social differences	culture
socialization		

Applying Sociology

1. Consider a country other than the United States that you have read about or studied. Jot down some ways in which you would be different if you had grown up there.

2. If possible, interview a recent arrival from that or another country and ask him or her what you might be like today if you had grown up in that country instead of in the United States. How would you behave toward your family and friends? What would you do in your spare time? What subjects would you study in school? How would you qualify for schooling beyond high school? How would you act toward your teachers and parents? If the person or persons on whom you depended for a livelihood were to die, who would support you?

3. Cultures differ not only from place to place but also from time to time. Talk to someone who grew up forty to sixty years ago in the United States about how his or her upbringing was different from that of young people today. Summarize your findings in a few paragraphs.

4. Our society is a particularly varied one. Many other societies do not have the variety that we see all around us. This may be one of the reasons that the United States is such an interesting place for sociologists to study. In the United States, one can find almost every form of social life and almost every sort of person. Make a list of topics that you as a sociologist might want to investigate to examine similarities and differences within American society.

Wendy Joi Rohr, "Are You Too Concerned With Being Liked?," *Teen,* May 1987, p. 22, 116.

1. How important is it to recognize your interests, feelings, strong points, and weaknesses?
2. What might happen if you try to change your behavior to meet other people's expectations?

Peter L. Berger, *Invitation to Sociology: A Humanistic Perspective,* Doubleday, 1963, p. 8.

Extended Readings

1. In what ways is sociology different from other fields of study?
2. From what perspective is the sociologist most interested in society?

Clive Wood, "The Character of Personality," *Psychology Today,* March 1987, p. 8, 10.

1. Briefly explain Zuckerman's theory of personality.
2. How is Zuckerman's theory different from that of Hogan?

Social Studies Skills

Testing a hypothesis

If you had a hunch regarding a certain idea, chances are you'd want to prove your hypothesis. Suppose you wanted to test the following hypothesis: "Each month teenage girls read more magazines than teenage boys." What kind of data would you need to support the hypothesis? How would you collect this data?

Writing a detailed description

Observation is an important skill to develop. Test your powers of observation by studying the photograph on page 21. Then write a paragraph describing the scene pictured there. Include enough details so that a sociologist could use your description to draw conclusions about how the people of Tiagba meet their basic needs.

Critical Thinking

1. *Evaluating Cause and Effect:* What factors caused the general decline in household size as shown on the graph on page 17?

2. *Identifying Assumptions:* What are the unstated assumptions in this statement? "These people are backward. Only 4 people out of 100 have television sets."

The Nature of Culture

Chapter Preview

● **Before you read,** look up the following key terms in the glossary to become familiar with their definitions:

archaeologist	ethnocentric	symbolic communication
ethnologist	proxemics	instinctive communication
culture trait	culture	arbitrary communication

● **As you read,** think about answers to the following questions:

1. How do a *cultural item* and a *culture trait* differ?
2. What factors do sociologists take into consideration in differentiating between cultures?
3. What are the major ways a culture transmits its knowledge, beliefs, values, and ways of behaving?
4. What are the most significant symbols of human communication?

Sections in this Chapter

1. Culture Clues
2. Cultural Complexity
3. Transmitting Culture
4. Signs and Symbols

Chapter Focus

Baseball, hot dogs, apple pie, and Chevrolet.
They go together in the good old U.S.A.

This jingle from a television commercial for an American car can be easily understood by most Americans. The advertiser hopes viewers will connect three popular aspects of American culture with a particular brand of car and will regard the car as equally popular.

Even if people from other countries understood what the words in the jingle meant, they might find the combination of these four things confusing. Why can Americans grasp the meaning of the commercial so easily when others can't? We aren't born loving baseball, hot dogs, or apple pie. We learn about them just as we learn about thousands of other aspects of our culture.

This chapter explores how individual elements can serve as clues to the nature of a culture, emphasizing that every culture is a complex whole.

Using Sociologists' Tools

● **Observe** the way your friends greet each other.
● **Describe** what actually happens when close friends meet.
● **Analyze** the signals people in this culture give off to indicate how they feel about someone.
● **Predict** what you think would happen if you went to school in Japan and gave a "high-five" or a bear hug to a new aquaintance.

Cultures may be easy or hard to detect. Above, a group of beaded and plumed Australian aborigines stands out vividly against the backdrop of lower Manhattan.

1 Cultural Clues

Archaeologists are scientists who study the life and culture of ancient peoples, such as the Aztecs of Mexico and the ancient Greeks. Archaeologists try to re-create an accurate picture of the society they are studying. Everything they can find—inscriptions, clothing, jewelry, pots, tools, and even human bones—they regard as clues.

Ethnologists are scientists who study living cultures. They look for clues in billboards, newspapers, styles of furniture and dress, topics of discussion at political meetings, and even television jingles. Ethnologists have one great advantage over archaeologists: they can communicate with the people they are studying.

All the clues that archaeologists and ethnologists study are *culture traits*. A culture trait is the smallest element in a culture. It can be a material object, an act, or a belief. Some sociologists think that no aspect of a

This pretzel vendor and her sidewalk stand offer a number of clues about American culture that an ethnologist would find useful.

FRESH BAKED
SOFT
PRETZELS $1.00

27

culture, even the crudest material object, is without meaning. They consider all cultural objects significant. Look at the objects pictured here and write down what each of them is:

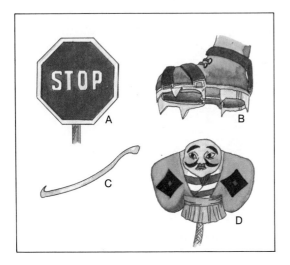

The identity of object A is obvious. It is a stop sign. You know it because of its shape and because of what it says. Object B is less familiar. It is a set of crampons, spiked platforms that mountain climbers attach to their boots to enable them to cross ice fields. Object C is even more difficult to identify. You've probably never seen one, except per-

haps in a magazine. It is a womera, a kind of spear thrower used by Australian aborigines. And object D? It looks like a tiny idol, but in fact it is an ornament found on the end of the cord that ties the traditional purse used by Japanese men and women. It is called a netsuke.

Nine more objects are pictured at the bottom of this page. What are they? How do you know? Are you able to identify any of the objects? Without knowing anything about them, you might not recognize one or two. Here is what they are: E, a jew's-harp; F, Greek worry beads; G, a tire iron; H, a symbol for the eye of God; I, handcuffs; J, a die; K, a menorah, a candelabrum for use during the Jewish festival of Hanukkah; L, a cone of fiber; M, a wine flask.

These objects become recognizable as soon as they are put in the context of a particular culture. Such material culture traits—objects that can be seen, handled, and used—are often called *cultural items*. Try analyzing the cultural item described here.

Imagine that it is the year 4000. You are a member of a team of archaeologists trying to uncover the mysteries of ancient civilizations. You arrive at a barren wasteland reported to have been the site of a great nation some two thousand years ago. After weeks of searching, one of your group finds a single

object, a copper disk. Both sides of the disk are pictured here:

Since you are the specialist in reading and interpreting ancient symbols, you are given the disk. From this object alone, what are you able to say about the culture from which it came? Be careful about making unsupported guesses. For example, you may assume it is a coin. But perhaps it is a religious medal.

All the objects you were asked to identify earlier are cultural items. So are the tables, chairs, and dishes in the dining-room scene in Chapter 1. But not all culture traits are material objects. Some are ideas, beliefs, or accepted practices.

For example, imagine that you are studying football players in the United States. You might identify as material culture traits the uniforms and equipment of the players. As nonmaterial traits you might name the pre-game pep talk by the coach and the belief that players should play to win.

Other nonmaterial culture traits of our society include shaking hands, compulsory education, and freedom of religion. As you study culture traits, you will begin to notice patterns among them. These patterns will enable you to make observations, not about isolated traits, but about a culture itself.

REVIEW AND APPLICATION

1. *IDENTIFY:* Archaeologist, ethnologist, culture traits, cultural items.
2. What are the differences in methods used by archaeologists and ethnologists?

CRITICAL THINKING: On Pages 28 and 29, you read about an imaginary group of archaeologists looking for clues to an ancient civilization. What assumption do the archaeologists seem to make about the origin of the copper disk that they find? What further discoveries would support this assumption?

2 Cultural Complexity

Describing an entire culture, especially one rather different from your own, is never an easy job. While a coin, a carving knife, or a certain belief may tell us much about a particular society, a single trait does not make a culture. *Culture,* as anthropologist Edward B. Tylor noted, is a complex whole that includes "knowledge, belief, art, morals, law, custom, and any other capabilities and habits acquired by man as a member of society."

Cultures consist of a combination of factors that, taken together, form understandable patterns. Sociologists must put the pieces together. Often they begin by trying to "decode" the symbols, as you have just done with a penny, in order to figure out their meaning in a particular context.

Describing a Culture

Imagine that you are an official in the State Department. You have been assigned to visit a remote island in the Pacific where a small group of people has been found. Most of them are descendants of British sailors who were shipwrecked there in 1757. The people have had no contact with the outside world since then. Their homes, their clothes, and their language, though changed in some ways, are more like those of the 1750s than the 1980s or 1990s.

A number of the islanders seem to have a rare disease. It has been decided that they should be offered the chance to come to the United States for treatment. They are not

All cultures are complex, and the nature of a culture cannot be determined by studying only a single trait. People living in different cultures often meet their needs in similar ways. The Hispanic girl at left and the African woman at right are performing the same function, but with different results.

sure what this means, for they have never heard of the United States. After much talk, the mayor of Bristol Town, as they call their settlement, agrees to allow the sick islanders to travel by ship to San Francisco. But he asks that they be prepared for what he is beginning to see is a whole new world.

The voyage to San Francisco will take about two weeks. Your assignment is to go on board the ship to prepare the people for life in the United States. Think about how you would go about it. Remember that these people are of English descent and still speak English, though, to your ear, their language sounds strange. Besides this, they have little in common with modern Americans. In two weeks, you must give them an introduction to American society and culture.

Where would you begin? What would you tell them? Which elements would you emphasize? Would you mention beliefs in such values as equality of opportunity, the importance of work, and pride in country? Would you talk about democracy and free enterprise? Would you describe baseball and football, jazz and rock? Would you mention the flag or the Constitution or the Fourth of July? Would you describe typical aspects of our "material" culture, such as superhighways, shopping centers, ranch houses, pocket calculators, and hamburgers? And how would you explain them?

? Make a list of about twenty American culture traits that would serve as a basis for helping the Bristol Town islanders understand life in the United States. Arrange your list in two columns: "English Traits," those that might have existed in England in 1757 in the same, or slightly different, form; and "New Traits," things unknown in England in 1757.

Different World Views

Cultures differ in basic world views as well as in items, traits, and beliefs. For example, people in different cultures have various attitudes toward such concepts as space. In his book *The Hidden Dimension*, anthropologist Edward T. Hall discusses *proxemics,* the study of social-spatial relationships, and applies this concept to the Japanese.

The Japanese I have known prefer crowding, at least in certain situations. They feel it is congenial to sleep close together on the floor, which they refer to as "Japanese style" as contrasted with "American style." It is not surprising, therefore, to discover that . . . there is no Japanese word for privacy. Yet one cannot say that the concept of privacy does not exist among the Japanese but only that it is very different from the Western conception.

While a Japanese may not want to be alone and doesn't mind having people milling around him, he has strong feelings against sharing a wall of his house or apartment with others. He considers his house and the zone immediately around it as one structure. This free area, this sliver of space, is considered to be as much a part of the house as the roof. Traditionally, it contains a garden, even though tiny, which gives the householder direct contact with nature.

Just as attitudes toward space vary from one society to another, so do ideas about time. In American society, time is often viewed as a commodity; we save time, buy time, and use time. Each day is parceled into time slots, and most of our activities are related to where we have to be and when. In many other societies, however, people do not live by the clock, and time is not central to their daily lives. This is hard for us to imagine.

It is even harder for us to imagine a society in which the members have no conception of time whatsoever. The humorist Henry

Traditional Japanese culture differs from typical American culture in many ways, reflecting different tastes in housing, food, music, and personal and home decoration.

Morgan portrayed such a society in a hypothetical interview that is a spoof of field research. An American researcher interviews a member of an imaginary society called the Marsuppis.

Interviewer: First, I want to thank you for taking the time for this interview.

Marsuppi: What that mean, "time"?

Interviewer: Well, time, like. I mean if you want to go from here to over there it takes time. A couple of minutes, anyway. We all live by the clock, see. It's a [thing] that tells us what time it isn't yet, so we don't have to be there until later. Now is, well, *now,* see. Later is when it gets dark. So that takes time, the difference between now and then, see.

Marsuppi: Why do you care?

Interviewer: Well, that's how we do it. Suppose I want to see a fellow in some other place and I want to get there when he gets there. Okay, so we set a time. So we arrive together.

Marsuppi: How? If one man arrive first, other man arrive second. What first man do?

Interviewer: He waits.

Marsuppi: Then what good is the time? We don't have time. We wait anyway.

Interviewer: Look. A day has twenty-four hours. We split it up into twenty-four parts.

Marsuppi: Why?

Interviewer: Because. That's why. Each part is an hour, each hour has sixty minutes, and each minute has sixty seconds.

Marsuppi: You like that?

Interviewer: Sure I like it. You don't even know when it's Thursday.

Marsuppi: That bad?

Interviewer: Sure that's bad. How can you get anything done? How do you expect to accomplish anything if you don't know when it is?

Marsuppi: I know when it is. What I don't know is what is when?

Interviewer: Well, when is when you don't know when it is, like. . . . Suppose I ask you to do something for me, but not right now. All right, then the question is, when?

Marsuppi: If I like you I do it anyway. What you care about when?

Interviewer: Because I have to go away sometime, see. I have to go back to where I came from. All right, I have to know when. It's a week from Wednesday as a matter of fact.

Marsuppi: Okay. Goodbye.

This imaginary interview uses humor to make two points. First, it shows how *ethnocentric* we are—that is, how firmly we believe in the superiority of our own culture. Second, it demonstrates that while there are different ways of living and acting, one way is not necessarily better than another. Culture is a concept that explains differences, not one that condones or condemns them.

American Subcultures

Having lived in the United States, you know that there are cultural differences within societies as well as among them. Our society is a broad and complex one containing peoples from all parts of the world. Every nationality brings along its own "cultural baggage." And though much of it is lost or replaced, a lot is kept. This is why it's not surprising to find, for instance, that the favorite foods of many Hispanic Americans are different from those of Irish Americans and Swedish Americans.

In addition to differences based on nationality, Americans differ in religious beliefs and practices. Catholics, Protestants, Jews, and those who believe in other religions worship in different ways. Many Americans don't worship at all.

The place where we were born or raised creates differences, too. City children may enjoy playing stickball. Those who live in the country may prefer fishing. People from different cities or different parts of the country—New York and Los Angeles, for example, or the South and the Midwest—exhibit regional differences. Their clothes, food preferences, or ways of speaking may set them apart from one another. Sometimes they have different outlooks on life and different attitudes toward people.

Because all the special qualities based on nationality, religion, and place of residence are variations of the basic American culture, we refer to them as subcultural variations. *Subcultures* are cultural patterns that characterize particular groups within a larger culture. They combine mainstream ideas with traditional or local customs. For example, Columbus Day is an American holiday, but it has special meaning for Italian Americans. Likewise, an annual rodeo might be very important to children in Tucson or Albuquerque but mean little to New Yorkers or Bostonians.

People within the same culture often have different preferences based on the region in which they live. These high school students in Massachusetts are playing ice hockey; the students in Arizona are taking part in a rodeo.

REVIEW AND APPLICATION

1. IDENTIFY: Culture, subcultures, ethnocentric, proxemics.

CRITICAL THINKING: "The Japanese attitudes toward space are the result of Japan's small area and large population." Do you agree with this statement of cause and effect? What assumptions are being made? Explain your answer.

3 Transmitting Culture

No society could survive for more than a single generation without some means of transmitting to others its knowledge, beliefs, values, and ways of behaving. This transmission takes many forms, from helping youngsters imitate their elders to lecturing in a classroom. No matter what is being taught or shared, some form of communication—some way of transmitting ideas from one person to another—must be used.

What Is Communication?

Communication is a fascinating and complex process. The ability to communicate requires both inborn potential and the ability to take in, store, and use information. While all animals communicate, most do so only at a very basic level. Humans, on the other hand, can engage in highly developed forms of communication because the human brain has a greater capacity than that of any other animal. But people must learn to communicate just as they learn almost everything else—through contact with their environment and with those who socialize, or teach, them.

Experts suggest that there are different types of communication. Some communication is purely instinctive. *Instinctive communication* is based on a natural, almost automatic response to a stimulus. For example, most people cringe when they hear loud noises and shield their eyes in bright sunlight. The meaning of these actions can be understood by people from any culture.

Other communication patterns are less automatic. Words, sounds, and gestures, for instance, are assigned arbitrary meanings. They can be understood only when one has the key to the cultural "code" for the language, sounds, and gestures of the people using them. For example, "apple" is the English word assigned to represent a particular fruit with a certain shape, size, taste, and texture. As children learn the English language, they are taught to associate the word "apple" with this fruit.

Words, sounds, and gestures are examples of *arbitrary communication*. While they are not natural in the sense that instinctive communication is, they often seem second nature. Sometimes we forget that we have learned them. But learn them we have.

At a very young age, most children have learned to express themselves appropriately. For example, they may sulk when scolded or smile when pleased. But because so much of communication is based on cultural expectations, the manner of sulking or expressing delight varies from one society to another. Americans are not usually surprised by children who stamp and shout or cry when scolded. However, we may be puzzled by children who respond by staring stoically into space.

? Think of your own daily life. Do you communicate in ways that are truly instinctive and therefore the same in all cultures? List any forms of instinctive communication you use.

Communication is central to the learning process. Words, gestures, and other *symbols,* or things that stand for other things, are used to transmit ideas through *symbolic communication*. Only human beings have the ability to develop and use symbols with which to communicate. This ability enables humans to learn ideas from others and to teach them to new generations. Culture, that combination of ideas, inventions, and objects, is both understood and transmitted because of this ability to communicate.

Facial expressions and the ways people move their bodies are the gestures that make up *body language*. Think for a moment about touching others. At first it might appear that there are no social patterns in this activity. Yet various studies clearly demonstrate that there are such patterns. A recent study, for example, reports that patterns of touching others indicate important differences in power relationships in our culture. Those in authority, such as employers, doctors, teachers, and police officers, do far more touching of those "beneath them" than the other way around. Workers, patients, students, and suspects are generally very reluctant to touch those in positions of authority over them.

Language

Alfred L. Kroeber, an anthropologist, once quipped that "animals do not talk because they have nothing to say." He was referring to nonhuman animals, of course, for people are very talkative once they learn how to speak. However, while all human beings have the ability to communicate through language, languages differ from one society to another, and any language is unintelligible to those who have not learned it. For example, can you read the following?

ΟΤΚ ΕΣΤΙ ΓΛΩΣΣΑ ΑΛΛΗ ΗΙΗ
ΕΛΛΗΝΙΚΗ

If you are thinking, "It's Greek to me," you're right. It *is* Greek. Translated into English it means, "There is no language other than Greek." If you'd been raised in Greece, you would have understood this sentence easily.

Since our language is English, we use its symbols to communicate. We know our ABCs. We know how to put them in a particular order to form words. "Ngorinca," "gug," and "nov shmos kapop" mean nothing to us. But we understand "road," "drive," and "stoplight."

Even the same language can take various forms. If we assume that the only way to write English is with letters, we are wrong. For instance, here are the three familiar words "road," "drive," and "stoplight" written in Morse code:

●■● ■■■ ●■ ■●●

■●● ●■● ●● ●●●■ ●

●●● ■ ■■■ ●■■● ●■●● ●● ■■● ●●●● ■

These words might also have been written in Braille or some other system of symbols.

Words, however they are spelled out, suggest meanings in our minds. Think of what flashes into your head when you read the word "automobile." Next think of that same word with a modifier, such as "antique." Do you see a Model T or a Model A Ford, or does your antique automobile look more like something from the 1940s?

What does the phrase "sports car" make you think of? Do you see a boxy old MG or a new Porsche? Is it red or blue—or didn't you "color" it until you read the words symbolizing these colors?

While the knowledge of a common language helps us communicate, simply knowing the words isn't enough. Some words and phrases have different meanings in societies that use the same language. Such words and phrases are known as idioms. For instance, if a man were to ask a waitress in a British pub for the bathroom, she would probably be quite surprised. Even if she could understand what he meant, she might grin and say: "A bathroom is where you bathe, luv. What you want is the gents'."

Consider some other examples of British usage, all related to automobiles and driving: "boot," "bonnet," "mudguard," "roundabout," and "lorry." If you identified them as the equivalent of our "trunk," "hood," "fender," "traffic circle," and "truck," you scored 100 percent. How did you do?

Of course, a similar test with examples from American English might be given to British students. What do you think they would make of words like "turtleneck" or

There are many forms of communication. In Morse code, which is used in telegraphy, letters are represented by dots and dashes, or short and long sounds. In the Braille alphabet, devised by Louis Braille in the nineteenth century, characters are formed by patterns of raised dots that are felt with the fingers.

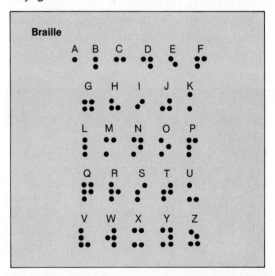

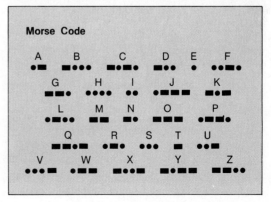

"vest"? Would they understand that they mean exactly the same as their own words "roll-collar" and "waistcoat"?

Gestures

Sometimes words cannot fully express meaning without the help of gestures. Try, for example, to explain the meaning of "spiral staircase" without using your hands. Difficult, isn't it?

Besides being useful in the communication of ideas, gestures are an important aspect of culture. For example, the Japanese "say" hello and goodbye with a bow. Most Westerners use a handshake. At certain times the significance of symbolic gestures can become painfully apparent, as when you extend your hand to another person and get no response. How embarrassing it is to stand there with your hand in the air!

In certain situations, kissing serves the same function as handshaking. Have you ever gone to a wedding and been introduced to a distant aunt? Suddenly neither of you knew whether to shake hands (too formal?) or kiss (too intimate?). Did you end up trying to hide your discomfort at being placed in such an awkward position?

Many other gestures have special meanings. Examine the picture of the woman on the following page. What is the woman doing? You say she is praying, but how do you know? You can tell from the position of her hands and the angle of her head.

Look at the picture on this page. What are the people doing? They are eating. They are Bedouins gathered in a tent in Jordan for a traditional meal. But instead of sitting on chairs at a table, these nomadic Arabs sprawl on rugs. Instead of using knives, forks, and spoons, they make a practice of eating from a large common bowl, using their hands to scoop up the food. Note how these gestures differ from your own.

Salutes have long been a symbol of respect and loyalty. A Roman soldier saluted by touching his fist to his heart before and after

People of all religions pray. Upper left: Jews praying at the Wailing Wall in Jerusalem. Above: A Hindu man praying at the Ganges, a river sacred to all Hindus. Lower left: A woman praying in front of a Zojoji Buddhist temple in Tokyo on Buddha's birthday.

addressing an officer; so did Roman senators when they spoke to Caesar. A medieval knight saluted by lifting the visor of his helmet. Some modern military salutes are modified versions of this gesture that involve touching one's forehead with the back, front, or side of one's open hand.

In many cultures, the open hand is a sign of peace and friendship. Indeed, the handshake is said to have originated from the need to assure others that the right hand held no weapon. In the 1960s, some Americans symbolized their desire for peace and their opposition to the Vietnam war with a V-shaped, two-fingered salute. The same gesture had been popularized by Winston Churchill, the British prime minister, during World War II. It stood for "victory."

REVIEW AND APPLICATION

1. *IDENTIFY:* Instinctive communication, arbitrary communication, symbolic communication, body language.
2. By what method is symbolic communication accomplished?

CRITICAL THINKING: Saluting shows respect for authority. What value does each of the following gestures reflect: saying "thank you", folding hands in prayer, and singing the national anthem?

4 Signs and Symbols

In addition to language and gestures, certain objects, signs, and acts also function as important communicative devices and cultural symbols. Some signs have great emotional significance. Think, for example, of the Jewish Star of David, the Christian cross, the Nazi swastika, or the communist hammer and sickle.

Other signs are strictly useful. Traffic lights, for example, use color to indicate whether one should go or stop. Some signs, such as those shown on this page, are more pictorial. The deer-crossing sign is from the United States, the cattle-crossing sign from Mexico, and the kangaroo-crossing sign from Australia.

In many places throughout the world, artisans indicate their wares with pictorial signs, such as giant spectacles in front of an optometrist's office or a boot over a shoe-repair shop. Sometimes the origins of such oc-

cupational signs are obscure, although they usually have historical meaning. The red-and-white barber pole is a good example. Barbers used to do bloodletting, which was thought to cure many ills; the red and the white represent blood and bandages. We are surrounded by signs that provide shorthand clues to the nature of occupations, social movements, and gender. Can you name some?

Many signs represent *status,* or social standing or prestige. They may be carried, like the baton of a conductor, or worn, like the vestments of a minister, or parked in front of the house, like the limousine of a business executive. Such status symbols carry a message; they, too, are vehicles for the transmission of cultural ideas.

Clothing

Clothing is another group of objects invested with special cultural meaning. For example, consider the significance of the necktie, as described by journalist Lance Morrow:

> The necktie—that vestigial[1] bib, that morning noose—is a strange and sinister article of clothing. When a man feels ill, the first thing to do is loosen his tie; it is, after all, pressing against the carotid arteries, impeding the flow of blood to the brain. Practically, the necktie is as supererogatory[2] as those little belts and buckles that used to adorn the backs of men's trousers. The tie has no function except to clean eyeglasses, and even that it does badly. . . .
>
> But it would be wrong to say that the tie is useless or pointless. Dress is language. The tie has many meanings, many symbolic and psychological uses. . . . Worn with full business suit, it can be a form of armoring, a defense and an assertion of power. It can also be a gesture of compliance. . . .

[1]describing a trace of something that once existed

[2]beyond the degree required

Road signs are common symbols in many countries.

Dress is a form of symbolic language. The necktie, for example, may signal one's membership in white-collar society, or proclaim a willingness to honor societal norms. Here the language of dress is spoken by marketing executives at a work session in Minnesota (left) and by a newspaper publisher in Ithaca, New York (right).

Often, the tie is a uniform signaling solidarity among certain kinds of men, a semaphore[1] announcing that "we all speak the language." It gives men a feeling of security, a certain formality, a necessary distance. Although the tie may be physically uncomfortable, they take psychic comfort from it.

Ties differentiate social classes, kinds of jobs. They can be flags of social ordering. The difference between blue collar and white collar has almost always meant the difference between no tie and tie on the job. While some men in, say, the professional classes go tieless, wearing blue work shirts under their tweed jackets, plenty of factory workers aspire to jobs that involve ties. . . .

Neckties also represent a gesture of respect. A lawyer always advises his client to appear in court wearing a coat and tie. It shows that you have the deference to make yourself uncomfortable. Several years ago, a Florida judge cited a lawyer for contempt of court when the lawyer

[1]an apparatus for signaling

showed up wearing a gold medallion around his neck instead of a tie.

Dress codes in clubs, restaurants, and schools are a form of social discipline resting on the premise that certain kinds of dress will preclude certain kinds of behavior and, of course, certain kinds of people. Reluctantly, some of the nation's fancier restaurants have started admitting the tieless. But [one owner says]: "If you give in on ties, people will start showing up without jackets. Next you will have shirts with short sleeves, or unbuttoned to the navel, with hairy chests and gold chains all over the place. That would be intolerable."

? What signs, symbols, or gestures are popular in your school? Do you use them? Why or why not?

Totems

We are all somewhat familiar with totem poles. The sort of totem pole we think of—a tall post carved and painted with bird, fish, animal, and human figures—is used by certain Native American groups of the Northwest to represent a particular family or group. Anthropologists refer to any item in any culture that has a similar special significance as a *totem*. Many totemic symbols are worn on the body. Many take the form of objects in the natural environment.

Often a family or group descended from a common ancestor has as its symbol an animate or inanimate object, such as a tree, a frog, or a particular bird. These totems take on special, even sacred, meaning for members of the family. A totem is treated as an object with power to protect family members against danger.

A good example of totemism was described by Ralph Linton, an American anthropologist who served in the United States Army in France during World War I. There he observed a peculiar phenomenon in conduct:

> Prior to going overseas into action during World War I, the 42nd Division received the name "Rainbow." The name was arbitrarily chosen by the higher officials and is said to have been selected because the organization was made up of units from many states whose regimental colors were of every hue in the rainbow. Little importance was attached to the name while the division was in America and it was rarely used by enlisted men.
>
> After the organization arrived in France, its use became increasingly common, and the growth of a feeling of divisional solidarity finally resulted in its regular employment as a personal appellation.[1] Outsiders usually addressed division members as "Rainbow," and to the question "What are you?" nine out of ten enlisted men would reply "I'm a Rainbow.". . .
>
> A feeling of connection between the organization and its namesake was first noted in February, 1918, five to six months after the assignment of the name. At this time it was first suggested and then believed that the appearance of a rainbow was a good omen for the division. Three months later it had become an article of faith in the organization that there was always a rainbow in the sky when the division went into action.
>
> A rainbow over the enemy's lines was considered especially auspicious,[2] and after a victory men would often insist that they had seen one in this position even when the weather conditions or direction of advance made it impossible. This belief was held by most of the officers and enlisted men, and anyone who expressed doubts was considered a heretic[3] and overwhelmed with arguments.
>
> The personal use of the divisional name and the attitude toward the rainbow had both become thoroughly established before it began to be used as an emblem. In the author's regiment this phase first appeared in May, when the organization came in contact with the 77th Division, which had its namesake, the Goddess of Liberty, painted on its cars and other divisional property.
>
> The idea was taken up at once, and many of the men decorated the carts and limbers[4] in their charge with rainbows without waiting for official permission. As no two of the painted rainbows were alike, the effect was grotesque and the practice was soon forbidden. Nevertheless it continued, more or less surreptitiously,[5] until after the armistice, when it was finally permitted with a standardized rainbow.

? What did the rainbow represent to the men of Linton's division? According to Linton, the soldiers often claimed to have sighted a rainbow when weather conditions made it impossible. Do you think they really "saw" a rainbow at such times, or did they decide after a successful battle that they must have seen a rainbow before it? If they didn't imagine the rainbow at the time but convinced themselves afterward that they had seen it, why did they make such a claim?

[1]title

[2]lucky

[3]nonbeliever

[4]two-wheeled horse-drawn vehicles that pull field guns

[5]secretly

From November 1979 until January 1981, a number of Americans were held hostage in Iran. During this period, a yellow ribbon tied to a tree became a symbol of caring and support for the hostages. The symbol was borrowed from a popular song of the time about waiting loyally for the return of a loved one.

The American flag may be regarded as a powerful totem. Many Americans wear it as a lapel pin. We all pledge allegiance to it. We have rules about how to handle it, how to fly it, how to fold it, and how to dispose of it when it is worn out. Most of us regard the flag as a general symbol of the American people. We have feelings about it, though we may not want to discuss them openly.

Once, many years ago, a professor tried an experiment with a class of college students who seemed reluctant to admit that a piece of cloth could have near-sacred qualities. He wanted to see what would happen if he violated one of the major rules of flag etiquette in our country: "Old Glory" must never touch the floor. So the professor took a flag from a nearby classroom and walked into his own classroom dragging the Stars and Stripes behind him. Many of the students gasped slightly, swallowed, or stared in disbelief. The professor had made his point that the flag meant more to his students emotionally than they would admit.

In discussing the episode, several of the students stated that, even to make a point, the teacher's action was too extreme. Said one, "I guess it bothered me to see somebody purposely pull the flag across the floor." Said another, "It hit me. That's our flag!" A third said, "You know, it's hard to explain, but I felt a bit sick."

And so did the professor. Like the students in front of him, he found it very difficult to break a rule that had been drilled into him early in life, especially since this rule concerned an important symbol in his society. The flag was a totem in his culture.

Symbolic Acts

Earlier in this chapter you read Edward Tylor's statement that "culture is a complex whole." In the religion of the Black Muslims, symbols and symbolic acts are intertwined as the members perform their daily rituals and participate in religious services. As you read the following excerpts, consider how many symbols come into play during the sacred rituals.

A Muslim daily prayerbook instructs Black Muslims to prepare for prayer by performing the following actions:

Washing the hands to the wrist;
Rinsing the mouth three times;
Cleansing the inside of the nose with water three times;
Washing the face three times;
Washing the arms to the elbows three times (the right arm should be washed first);
Wiping over the head with wet hands;
Wiping the ears with wet fingers;
Wiping around the neck with wet hands; and
Washing the feet (the right one first) to the ankles.

In *Black Nationalism,* E. U. Essien-Udom describes the ceremonies conducted in a Black Muslim temple:

The officer marches briskly down the aisle, comes to a stop, salutes the other guards, and shows the visitor to a seat. Male visitors normally sit on the front rows in the aisle to the right of the speakers' platform, separated from the followers and believers. Female visitors sit immediately behind the male visitors, separated from them by a few rows of empty seats unless there are too many visitors to maintain this separation of the sexes.

The registered Muslim women sit in the center aisle behind the Temple officers, who occupy the front row of this aisle. All male registered Muslims and believers sit in the left aisle. Other men may also sit in the balcony on a crowded day. Women are separated from the men partly because this is the tradition of Islam and partly because undivided attention is required. The Temple is not a place for socializing; mixing the women and men together might cause distractions. . . .

After the prayer, the minister salutes the congregation again, saying, "As-Salaam-Alaikum," to which the followers respond, "Wa-el-Alaikum-Salaam." Frequently the minister asks the congregation, "How do you feel, my dear brothers and sisters?" and makes impromptu remarks to establish rapport. His duty is to bear witness to the teachings of Muhammad and to affirm that "Allah is our God."

REVIEW AND APPLICATION

1. *IDENTIFY:* Status, totem.
2. What are some ways in which clothing is used symbolically? Describe the function of dress codes in a society.

CRITICAL THINKING: Do you think the appearance of a rainbow actually could have affected the performance of the "Rainbow" division in battle? Why or why not?

Recap

Sociologists define culture as the beliefs, values, rules of conduct, and material objects shared by most members of a society. The societies of the world exhibit a wide variety of such cultural elements, and large, complex societies like our own may contain many variations.

No matter how societies may vary, they all share one basic feature: cultural ideas are transmitted from one member to another by means of communication. Humans communicate through symbols—things that stand for other things—which may be sounds, markings, gestures, and clothing or other objects. Language itself is a system of symbols. To study a culture, one must learn its systems of communication.

Define the following:

archaeologist	ethnocentric	symbol
ethnologist	subculture	symbolic
culture trait	instinctive	communication
cultural item	communication	body language
culture	arbitrary	status
proxemics	communication	totem

Applying Sociology

1. Using the charts on page 35, try writing the words "road," "drive," and "stoplight" in Braille. Now try to read the following sentence written in Morse code. Write this same sentence in Braille. Finally, decide on which system—Morse code or Braille—you and a classmate will use. Write him or her a message of at least two or three sentences. Have him or her answer with a reply of similar length.

2. (a) List as many examples as you can of subcultural variations in your community (you will recall that subcultures are cultural patterns of local or traditional groups within the larger society). To what extent are the traits you listed subcultural rather than cultural? That is, how much does each vary from the main cultural pattern? (b) How would foreigners classify the traits you listed? Would they see

•■•• •■ ■• ■■• ••■ •■ ■■• • •• ••• •■ ■•■ • ■•■■

■ ■■■ ■•■• ••■ •■• ■ ••■ •■• •

them as variations of American culture? Would they be surprised to learn that Americans are more different from one another than they imagined?

3. List some gestures that would appear natural to Americans but that might not be understood by people from different cultures (for example, "thumbs up"). If possible, find illustrations from magazines or newspapers that show Americans using gestures. Do you know of any symbols from other cultures that may seem strange to Americans? Draw them if you can.

4. List as many status symbols as you can. Would all groups accept them as desirable to own, wear, or show? Why or why not? Name some "reverse" status symbols (for example, driving a small car to indicate consciousness of energy shortages).

5. Describe in one page a religious ceremony with which you are familiar, such as a service in a church or synagogue. Remember to include the various symbols present and the gestures and other behaviors of the participants.

6. Collect signs and totems used in newspapers and magazine advertisements and write a report on how advertisers use signs and totems to promote a product or service. Public-service advertisements, such as those used in antismoking campaigns, are acceptable. Do the signs and totems set a particular tone or mood? What do they imply about specific values or effects of the product or service? What generalizations can you develop about the use of signs and totems in advertising?

Extended Readings

Wendy Joi Rohr, "Do You Get the Message?," *Teen*, April 1987, p. 20, 24.

1. How do cultural differences affect the meaning of facial gestures?
2. Name a facial gesture that would communicate a positive feeling and one that would communicate a negative feeling.

Horace Miner, "Body Ritual Among the Nacirema," *American Anthropologist*, 58 (1956), pp. 503–507.

1. Can you recognize some of the cultural traits described in the article?
2. To what culture is that of the Nacirema most similar?

"I Get Homesick Every Day," *Today's Immigrants: Their Stories*, Oxford University Press, 1982, pp. 51–52.

1. Discuss several reasons why Americans have discriminated against Vietnamese immigrants.
2. From the information given in the passage, describe the values and ethics practiced by Vietnamese immigrants.

Presenting information visually

Pictures are useful tools for communication across cultural barriers. As you have seen in the chapter, different countries and even different regions of the same country may have traffic hazards that are unfamiliar to visiting motorists. Draw a pictorial sign that clearly warns motorists about each of the following hazards:

    (a) falling rocks in Montana
    (b) a roadside cliff in Ireland
    (c) a sheep crossing in Australia

Writing from an outline

Organizing information is an essential step in the writing process. Study Lance Morrow's description of the necktie's significance on pages 38 and 39. Using this description as a model, outline the special cultural meanings of sunglasses. Then write one or two paragraphs based on your outline.

1. ***Recognizing Values:*** What are the values of the interviewer as shown in the interview on page 32?
2. ***Analyzing Comparisons:*** The totem poles of the Northwest Indians are compared on pages 40–41 to the American flag. Evaluate this comparison—how strong is it?

Conformity and Deviance

Chapter Preview

- **Before you read,** look up the following key terms in the glossary to become familiar with their definitions:

moral orientation	mores	labeling theory
norms	folkways	primary deviance
humanitarianism	anomie	secondary deviance

- **As you read,** think about answers to the following questions:

1. How do societies use values and norms?
2. How are mores and folkways related to values and norms?
3. How do laws differ from other societal norms?
4. What purpose do controlled environments serve?

Chapter Focus

In the ceremony in which they become full-fledged members of the Boy Scouts of America, young Tenderfoots must raise their right hands and recite the Scout Oath: "On my honor I will do my best to do my duty to God and my country, and to obey the Scout Law; to help other people at all times; to keep myself physically strong, mentally awake, and morally straight." In addition, they recite the Scout Law: "A scout is trustworthy, loyal, helpful, friendly, courteous, kind, obedient, cheerful, thrifty, brave, clean, and reverent."

These acts and statements clearly combine cultural symbols —words, gestures, and signs—with values, norms, and behavior within groups. Serving one's country, helping others, and staying physically, mentally, and morally strong are Boy Scout values. This chapter focuses on how societies encourage conformity to norms and the reasons people deviate from them.

Using Sociologists' Tools

- **Observe** your school environment for evidence of its values and norms.
- **Describe** the methods your administration uses to communicate the schools' values and norms.
- **Analyze** the effectiveness of each of the methods you named.
- **Predict** how various groups within the school—teachers, students, administrators—will react to the enforcement of behavioral norms.

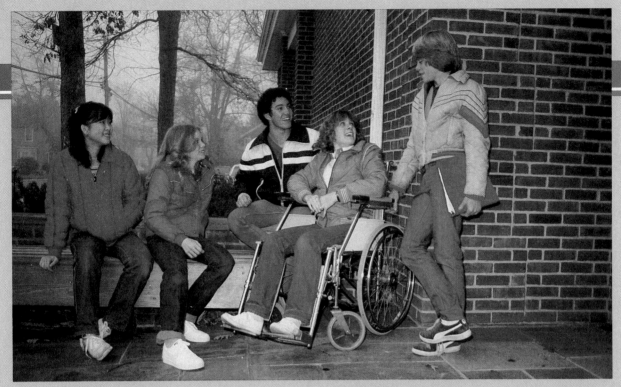

Different as these individuals are, they share a complex set of cultural attitudes on matters of dress, hair style—even what constitutes a good joke.

1 Values and Norms

Values are those ideas and things considered important by a given group of people. They represent ideals, sometimes of an entire society. Values provide goals toward which individuals are encouraged to strive. *Norms* are rules or standards of behavior. They tell people how to act.

Norms, such as those set forth in the Scout Law, the Bill of Rights, and the Ten Commandments, are often based on the common values of a group. All Scouts, all Americans, and all who are part of the Judeo-Christian heritage are expected to subscribe to their group's particular rules. While values and norms are often related in this manner, they are not the same.

All values are important, but norms vary greatly in importance. Some norms are quite rigid, demanding obedience on the threat of punishment; others have less emotional sig-

nificance. This is especially true of rules of behavior that apply in certain places or situations, such as at home, in school, in a place of worship, on the job, or at play. Think of the dress codes at your school, the behavior necessary to get and keep a particular job, or the rules of the games you play in your free time. Other norms—for example, fashions in clothing and the fads people follow because "everybody's doing it"—are still less significant. They suggest rather than require certain ways of doing things.

The things we Americans consider important and the rules we are willing to follow as members of our society or of smaller groups within that society are not ideas that come to us automatically. We know nothing of baseball, hot dogs, apple pie, or Chevrolets before we are taught about them. And we know nothing of good and bad or right and

The Scouts here are expressing values and norms through cultural symbols.

wrong until we are taught our society's values and norms.

Different Cultural Patterns

Many of the values and norms of our society are picked up so naturally that we do not even realize that they are learned rather than inborn. Yet, as we compare our ways of behaving with those of people in other cultures, we can see that much of what we learn is uniquely American and presents a distinct cultural pattern. As you read the following descriptions of behavior in three different cultures, compare the values and norms of each culture with our own American ways.

In the 1930s, anthropologist Ruth Benedict summarized some of her colleagues' field observations about the Dobu of New Guinea, the Kwakiutl of the northwest coast of North America, and the Zuñi of the American Southwest. Benedict was impressed by cer-

tain dominant ideas in each society that governed the behavior of its people. In each society, these dominant ideas formed a unique cultural pattern quite different from those of the other two.

The Dobu, Benedict wrote, lived in a climate of suspicion and treachery. In their society, humiliating others was a mark of distinction, and success was achieved at another person's expense. The Dobu culture emphasized competitiveness and individualism above all other values.

The Kwakiutl were found to be competitive, too, but in a different way. It was not how much one could get away with that counted but how much one could give away. The ritual of the *potlatch,* a practice of lavishing gifts upon others, was a way of glorifying oneself by demonstrating that one was richer than—and therefore superior to—others. At the time of the research, the main gift item was blankets; before that, it was skins; more recently, cases of cola beverages and small transistor radios have become popular.

The third cultural pattern Benedict described was that of the gentle Zuñi, who placed the highest value on self-control and inoffensiveness. Their lives were regulated by numerous ceremonies, and the most intricate details of ritual were invested with extreme significance. More than the Dobu or the Kwakiutl, they lived in a world in which the group as a whole was far more important than the individual.

These three societies had all been called "primitive," but Benedict showed that each had an elaborate social structure based on a unique pattern of culture. Over the years, some scholars have criticized Benedict's interpretation of certain practices, but few have questioned the core idea of her classic work: that values influence conduct and shape the norms by which people live.

Values and Norms in the United States

How did you learn what it means to be an American? How did you learn what to think about yourself, your friends, and your classmates? How did you learn how to behave as a child, as a churchgoer or a party-goer, or as a male or a female? There are bound to be many differences in our complex society. Nevertheless, social scientists have conducted research to try to determine whether there are certain basic values that are held by most Americans.

Sociologist Robin Williams, for example, examined data gathered by many historians and other social scientists and concluded that Americans seem generally agreed on the importance of three core ideas: equality, freedom, and democracy. Helping others, or *humanitarianism,* is also important to a majority of Americans. Humanitarianism is expressed in our concern for the underdog and our willingness to contribute generously to all sorts of charities.

Other American values are personal achievement and success, hard work, faith in progress, efficiency, and practicality. Perhaps most basic of all is what Williams called a *moral orientation,* a tendency to see the world in moral terms—to judge things as right or wrong, good or bad, or ethical or unethical.

Yet, probing more deeply, Williams found that some Americans reveal attitudes that often contradict their statements. While professing to believe in fair play and equality, for example, some Americans reveal racist or sexist opinions.

? Among the people you know, how widespread are the values Williams discussed? Does everyone accept them? Which values are most accepted? By whom is each value accepted—parents, friends, or teachers? How are these values enforced by norms? Who expresses the norms? How important to society is each value?

Since Americans come from many different cultural backgrounds, it is not surprising that members of certain subcultures may have values and norms that are different from those of the majority. Some differences are merely matters of taste. Members of some subcultures

A number of sociologists have found humanitarianism to be an important American value. Helping others and giving to the poor are ways in which Americans show their humanitarian concern.

may favor louder music, brighter colors, and spicier food than the majority. Other differences, such as disagreement about child raising and schooling, are more fundamental. The Amish, for example, refuse to send their children to public schools because Amish values stress religious education. Different subcultures may have different ideas about masculinity and femininity; to be "macho," for instance, appears to be more important to Italian and Mexican Americans than to Jewish and Japanese Americans.

Differences in attitudes and behavior may also be regional or related to class. White farmers in rural Alabama, for example, share some norms with their black farm neighbors that they don't share with wealthy white or black business people living in Los Angeles. Sociologists are interested in these differences. They set out to record, describe, and analyze various cultural elements in an attempt to grasp the significance of a way of life.

Analyzing a Society

In Chapter 2, you imagined that you were an archaeologist who had discovered an American penny, and you tried to decipher the coded messages on both its sides. The symbols you had to decode can tell you a lot about American society. The phrase "In God We Trust" and the word "Liberty" state certain values that the minters of the coin wanted to convey to the American people.

To understand a culture, one must know not only the symbols used to communicate but also the messages carried by those symbols. Such messages frequently are important clues to the values and norms of the culture. When sociologists and anthropologists go "into the field," they often must begin by trying to "decode" symbols.

The selection that follows is from an anthropologist's attempt to capture the essence of a society. As you read Horace Miner's description of several aspects of the daily life of

American society has a wide variety of subcultural groups. Here Italian-Americans are celebrating a religious festival in the "Little Italy" section of New York.

the Nacirema, try to analyze their culture by noting the symbols—both actions and objects—and the values and norms that the symbols portray:

They are a North American group living in the territory between the Canadian Cree, the Yaqui and Tarahumare of Mexico, and the Carib and Arawak of the Antilles.[1] Little is known of their origin, although tradition states that they came from the east. According to Nacirema mythology, their nation was originated by a culture hero, Notgnihsaw, who is otherwise known for two great feats of strength—the throwing of a piece of wampum across the river Pa-To-Mac and the chopping down of a cherry tree in which the Spirit of Truth resided.

Nacirema culture is characterized by a highly developed market economy. . . . While much of the people's time is devoted to economic pursuits, a large part of the fruits of these labors and a considerable portion of the day are spent in ritual activity. The focus of this activity is the human body, the appearance and health of which loom as a dominant concern. . . . While such a concern is certainly not unusual, its ceremonial aspects and associated philosophy are unique.

The fundamental belief underlying the whole system appears to be that the human body is ugly and that its natural tendency is to debility[2] and disease. Incarcerated[3] in such a body, man's only hope is to avert these characteristics through the use of . . . ritual and ceremony. . . . Every household has one or more shrines devoted to this purpose. The more powerful individuals in the society have several shrines in their houses and, in fact, the opulence[4] of a house is often referred to in terms of the number of such ritual centers it possesses. . . .

While each family has at least one . . . shrine, the rituals associated with it are

not family ceremonies but are private and secret. . . .

The focal point of the shrine is a box or chest which is built into the wall. In this chest are kept the many charms and magical potions without which no native believes he could live. . . .

Beneath the charm-box is a small font.[5] Each day every member of the family in succession enters the shrine room, bows his head before the charm-box, mingles different sorts of holy water in the font, and proceeds with a brief rite of ablution.[6] . . .

The Nacirema have an almost pathological horror of and fascination with the mouth, the condition of which is believed to have a supernatural influence on all social relationships. Were it not for the rituals of the mouth, they believe that their teeth would fall out, their gums bleed, their jaws shrink, their friends desert them, and their lovers reject them. . . .

In addition to the private mouth-rite, the people seek out a holy-mouth-man once or twice a year. These practitioners have an impressive set of paraphernalia, consisting of a variety of augers, awls, probes, and prods. The use of these objects in the exorcism of the evils of the mouth involves almost unbelievable ritual torture of the client.

The holy-mouth-man opens the client's mouth and, using the above mentioned tools, enlarges any holes which decay may have created in the teeth. Magical materials are put into these holes. If there are no naturally occurring holes in the teeth, large sections of one or more teeth are gouged out so that the supernatural substances can be applied. In the client's view, the purpose of these ministrations is to arrest decay and to draw friends.

? What clues helped you discover who the Nacirema are? What do you think was the author's purpose in writing this article? What does it say about the norms of the Nacirema?

[1] All the groups mentioned are Native American.

[2] weakness

[3] trapped

[4] luxuriousness

[5] basin

[6] washing

Girls in Burma are trained by their society to appear fragile and feminine. Here a group of young women perform a traditional dance in the formal style they have learned from their elders.

Comparing Norms

You have found that there are some differences in values and norms within our own society. Attitudes on particular issues can, of course, differ still more widely between our society and other modern societies. For example, there are different attitudes about what constitutes the proper behavior for members of each sex. Following is a selection by a Burmese lawyer, Khin Myo Than, in which she describes the behavior of males and females in Burma. As you read, identify some rules of conduct linked with being male or female in Burmese society, and compare them with our own.

The Burmese girl pays great attention to dress and likes to wear her traditional costume. She is very feminine and may appear like a fragile flower. Her status has not changed over the centuries. Is she dominated by men or subdued by tradition, as women in many other countries were and are still? No, and she never has been.

As a little girl, she may play the same games as her young brother. Should a little boy, on the other hand, make garlands of flowers? This is not considered becoming. At the age of five or six, she starts her schooling.

The end for the girls is marked by "nad-win," a sort of "passage rite."[1] . . . on reaching the age of twelve or thirteen, the girl goes through this colorful ceremony during which her earlobes are pierced. Henceforth, she is considered to have reached the "years of discretion." She wears earrings and assumes greater re-

[1] a ceremony marking a person's change in status

sponsibility in the family. Soon she will think of getting married.

For a Westerner, Burmese society may seem prudish. Young girls and boys are not seen kissing and hugging in the streets, and even married couples do not walk arm in arm. Flirtation and dating do not exist. It is only in a very discreet and chaste manner that the Burmese make known their sentiments and feelings. However, this does not mean that a Burmese girl lowers her eyes in front of a man, nor does she stay at home behind closed doors.

Young girls and boys have many occasions to meet: at school or university, but also at pwes (open-air shows that last for three whole nights), at festivals, and even at the pagoda, where one may talk freely, unlike in Christian churches.

What I may call "reserve" in the relationship between young people is equally shared by boys and girls. Young men, having at an earlier age gone through the monastery life,[1] have learned from the monks to become detached from worldly things. They are self-disciplined and respectful towards others. Girls seem more worldly. They like being coquettish and elegant and love to wear jewelry. . . .

With such conceptions, a boy is not surprised should a girl he "courts" (by paying her compliments, composing little poems, or giving small presents) ask him to marry her, if such is his intention. But when a girl asks such a question she is already sure of the answer. . . .

Marriage and, more generally, relations between men and women are based on more equalitarian terms. . . . In France, for instance, a man "gallantly" gives up his seat to a woman and lets her pass before him. Burmese women do not receive such attention from their menfolk. As a matter of fact, in Burma the rules of precedence are based on age and not on sex. Burmese people are very respectful to their elders. Thus, a woman gives precedence to a man older than herself.

On the other hand, French gallantry does not seem to be found in family life. At home after work, a Frenchman seems more preoccupied in getting into his slippers, watching television, or reading his newspapers than helping his wife with the household chores. He finds it natural that his wife, who has also worked the whole day, maybe in a factory or an office, should now do "overtime" on so-called "female duties": looking after the children, cooking, serving at table and washing up, etc.

Though Burmese men, in the eyes of Westerners, may not appear gallant in public, they do not hesitate to share in the family tasks. A Burman is not ashamed nor is he considered "effeminate" when he does the cooking or washes the dishes. It is not uncommon to see a Burman holding his baby in his arms and walking up and down a room humming a lullaby before putting the baby to bed, while his wife may well be reading a newspaper.

Even though the Burman finds it natural to do some of the housework, it is nevertheless the woman who has the responsibility of looking after the home. Generally, she is in charge of the family budget. Traditionally, trade too has long been in the hands of women.

In the markets, smoking their big cheroots (Burmese cigars) or chewing betel nut, women offer their wares or, from an eating stall, sell dishes which were probably prepared by their husbands while they themselves were getting dressed up to go to market.

Young women often run little shops, and thus have many opportunities of meeting young men—and maybe their future husband. . . .

Thus, traditionally, men and women have worked in a complementary way. Nowadays, industrialization has furnished new types of work to which women have quickly adapted themselves. Alongside men, women have taken the road leading to workshops, factories, and offices. They have become teachers, doctors, engineers, lawyers, judges, and even parachutists in the army. . . . Inversely, men may

[1]Burmese boys undergo their passage rite by spending some time in a Buddhist monastery.

be typists or stenographers. In Burma there are no small ads listing "women's jobs." . . .

. . . Burmese women have always been interested in political affairs. Since independence,[1] women have been deputies and ministers, and women flock eagerly to the polling booths. It is estimated that 80 percent of Burma's women [vote].

---

[1]Burma became an independent nation in 1948.

REVIEW AND APPLICATION

1. IDENTIFY: Values, norms, potlatch, humanitarianism, moral orientation.

2. What is the basic cultural pattern of (a) the Dobu; (b) the Kwakiut; (c) the Zuñi? Which is most like the American pattern? Why?
3. According to Robin Williams, what are the most common American values?
4. What are the traditional norms in Burmese society for each sex, according to Khin Myo Than?

CRITICAL THINKING: List everything that you think the groups in each of the following pairs from page 50 have in common: white and black farmers, white and black business people, black farmers and business people, and white farmers and business people. Compare your lists to determine which pair is most similar.

2 Mores and Folkways

Some cultural norms reflect basic values, such as the value expressed in the Golden Rule: "Do unto others as you would have them do unto you." Other norms, though still important, are less essential. They may have to do with dating, getting good grades, wearing the right clothes, or staying out late at night. Still other cultural norms are mere fads, such as wearing leather boots or the way you cut your hair.

Cultural norms fall along a U-shaped line. The norms at the upper ends of the U are strictly enforced. They take the form of *prescriptions,* or rules stating what must be done, and *proscriptions,* or rules forbidding certain behavior. Prescriptions and proscrip-

Cultural norms include prescriptions, or things one must do, and proscriptions, or things one must not do. Preferences include behavior that most people do not feel very strongly about.

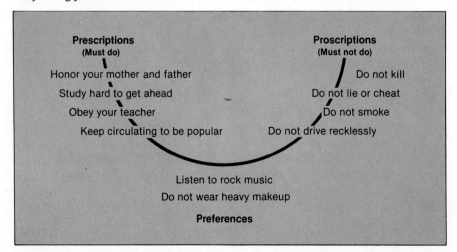

Prescriptions
(Must do)

Honor your mother and father

Study hard to get ahead

Obey your teacher

Keep circulating to be popular

Proscriptions
(Must not do)

Do not kill

Do not lie or cheat

Do not smoke

Do not drive recklessly

Listen to rock music

Do not wear heavy makeup

Preferences

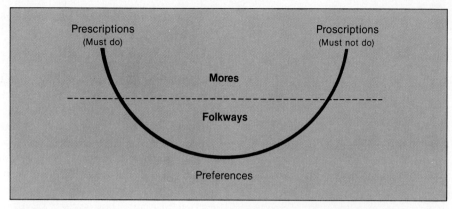

Mores are norms that are related to ideas of right and wrong. Folkways include behavior related less to morality than to personal preferences. However, as the broken line in this diagram indicates, it is sometimes difficult to distinguish between mores and folkways.

tions are referred to as *mores* (pronounced MOR·ayz). The word *mores* is Latin; it is also the root of the English word "morals." Mores are norms that express a society's ideas of right and wrong. They are considered essential to group welfare.

Less strictly enforced standards of behavior that are usually unrelated to morality are called *folkways*. Folkways are preferences rather than demanded or forbidden ways of behaving. For example, in American society it is customary for newly married couples to send thank-you notes for wedding gifts. However, failure to do so would not violate the mores of American culture, only the folkways. On the other hand, paying back borrowed money, keeping promises to friends, and not accepting bribes are mores of American society. Most Americans feel much more strongly about the rightness and wrongness of these activities than they do about getting a thank-you note for a wedding gift.

? Try to sort the following norms into a U reflecting prescriptions, proscriptions, and preferences: (1) don't cheat on your income tax; (2) don't yell "Fire!" in a crowded theater; (3) obey all traffic signs and signals; (4) see good films; (5) be a conscientious, honest worker; (6) do not abuse your children; (7) learn to play chess to develop your mind; (8) read a daily newspaper; (9) don't cross streets without looking; (10) rise for "The

Star-Spangled Banner." Compare your responses to those of a classmate. Is there agreement? If there are differences, how do you explain them?

Cultural Variations

Our everyday lives are guided by prescriptions and constrained by proscriptions. Many of these mores are learned at such a young age that we have no recollection of ever having behaved differently. Our behavior is so deeply ingrained that it is second nature.

People who grow up in particularly religious Christian homes, for example, often begin each meal with a prayer, or grace, and end the day with another prayer. Each Sunday they attend church. They participate in ritual observances, sing hymns, listen to the sermon, and contribute to the collection.

Orthodox Jews begin their days with special prayers, bless their food before eating, and eat only foods that are kosher, or ritually acceptable. Both at home and at work, Orthodox Jewish men keep their heads covered with a small skullcap called a yarmulke. No collection plate is passed at Jewish religious services, but members of the congregation are expected to support the synagogue and, like all Jews, to contribute a portion of their income to charity.

Newcomers to our culture may first adopt its popular images, and then go on to absorb its folkways and mores in a gradual process of assimilation. The photograph shows a restaurant sign in Miami's "Little Havana" neighborhood.

While American Christians and Jews follow different religious practices, they may be similar in other ways. If they are from the same region and have the same social and economic status, they may speak in the same accent, wear the same fashions, watch the same television programs, laugh at many of the same jokes, or engage in the same sports. For example, well-to-do teenagers of both religions may enjoy skiing and sailing, which require expensive equipment. Poorer youngsters of both religions may be enthusiastic about basketball and sandlot baseball, which are not expensive to play. In other words, the mores and folkways that seem so natural are affected by all the elements of culture.

Mores, Folkways, and the Life Cycle

Gender and generation are also important in determining some mores and folkways. In every society there are stages of development, each with its appropriate behavior. Infants, boys and girls, young men and women, the middle-aged, and the elderly all have particular ways of behaving as determined by the values and norms of their cultures. This process, called socialization, is described in Unit Four, which focuses on how people learn the different rules of behavior that apply to the different stages of the life cycle.

Ruth Benedict wrote that, in many societies, what people learn as youngsters—especially about social responsibility, patterns of dominance and submission, and sex roles—has to be unlearned when a new stage is reached. Children learn certain rules of behavior and then must act quite differently when they are suddenly considered grown-up. In the societies Benedict described, there were many important rituals that marked the termination of one stage and the beginning of another. Such rituals are known as *rites of passage*.

Puberty rites, such as the one described in the reading about Burmese sex roles, are rites of passage. In the Western world, we have confirmation ceremonies, bar and bas mitzvahs, debutante balls, coming-out parties, and other such events. The marriage ceremony is another nearly universal rite of passage, when by tradition and law a couple is united, thereby changing the social positions and altering the obligations of both partners. After marriage, the rules of society dictate changes in behavior. Other significant rites of passage in the United States are the first day of school, the first full-time job, and even death.

The rites of passage marking the end of the life cycle are carefully specified. There are many subcultural variations in funeral customs, but the bodies of most Americans are taken to funeral parlors to be embalmed or otherwise prepared for burial. Often they are displayed for a day or so before burial. People come to mourn and express condolences to the family of the deceased. Then a service is held either at the funeral home or in a church, synagogue, or temple, with the casket containing the deceased at the front of the sanctuary.

Pallbearers carry the coffin to a waiting hearse. In a procession to the cemetery, mourners slowly follow the hearse in their cars, with the headlights turned on. At the cemetery, a second ceremony is performed, the coffin is lowered into a grave, and dirt is symbolically thrown on top of it. The mourners may then meet at the home of the deceased to pay their respects.

Funerals are not only rites of passage but, for social scientists, occasions to observe and record the expression of cultural values and norms. Anthropologist Oscar Lewis, for example, studied a death in a poor Mexican family. Here Lewis quotes Roberto Sanchez as he describes the funeral of his maternal aunt Guadalupe. Roberto's description clearly shows the cultural importance of certain mores, folkways, and prescribed rules.

We waited and waited until finally the bus and hearse arrived, with the crowd of curious children who always run ahead of them. Everyone immediately piled into the bus until it was full. Later we brought out my aunt's coffin and I had to break the door frame a little because it wasn't wide enough. My aunt was lifted onto the hearse and I laid her flowers on top of the coffin.

When we had finished loading the hearse, the funeral director asked me, "Who is in charge here?"

"I am, sir."

"Please pay me my money," he said.

"If you wish. It is customary to ask for payment at the cemetery, but if you want it right now you can have it." I still lacked thirty-five *pesos,* but Consuelo got them for me and I paid him the four hundred *pesos.*

The Amish, a Protestant religious group, follow their own strict norms about educational practices, styles of dress, and other behavior. For example, they forbid the use of automobiles, preferring to travel in horse-drawn carriages like the one pictured here.

The rites of passage marking the end of life vary from one society to another. Within a society there may also be subcultural variations. This photograph shows a New Orleans jazz funeral. The musicians play dirgelike music on the way to the cemetery. On the way back, they play joyous music, to symbolize the joy of resurrection.

When we arrived at the Dolores cemetery, I asked the driver to back up and let us off at the chapel. The priest invited us to come in and then he asked us whether we wanted a High Mass with music for thirty-five *pesos,* or a plain mass for fifteen *pesos*.

I took it badly and told him, "I don't have any money, and besides the services should all be the same price." But I said to my brother and sister, "All right, since my aunt hasn't been given the last rites why should we haggle over the last few *centavos* we spend on her?" I told the priest to go ahead and give us the High Mass with the music. And so he gave her the last rites, the ashes, the holy water, the Extreme Unction, and I don't know what else. . . .

When the mass was over, the priest said, "Now may we have an offering for us here?" By this time I was crying, because I felt the last moment had arrived for my aunt. I said, "Here, father, I have only two *pesos* left, but you take them."

"No, son, you keep them. Let the others give something if they want to."

We left and made our way to the spot below the ravine, where we buried my aunt. And so it ended.

REVIEW AND APPLICATION

1. *IDENTIFY:* Prescriptions, proscriptions, mores, folkways, rites of passage.
2. What are some rites of passage you have experienced or will experience?
3. What are some factors that help determine mores and folkways?

CRITICAL THINKING: In the reading about the experiences of Roberto Sanchez, identify several mores that are of special significance to him personally. Which of the mores are prescriptive and proscriptive?

3 The Laws of Society

Many laws reflect the mores of a society and through them its values and norms. In fact, specific behavioral norms are often specified by law. For instance, murder, rape, arson, and theft are illegal in most societies. The laws against them express values that hold that the illegal behavior is wrong. Laws differ from other norms in the methods by which they are enforced. With laws, society has provided formal controls to prevent citizens from breaking them.

Many laws not only codify mores but also specify gradations of "offensiveness." In our criminal codes, for example, a distinction is made between a major crime, or *felony*, and a minor one, or *misdemeanor*. The distinction is often arbitrary; for example, the dividing line between grand theft and petty theft may be set at a figure of, say, one hundred dollars.

Actually, criminal laws form only a small portion of the body of written regulations that limit behavior. Other laws include civil codes, government regulations, and ordinances. Their range is wide, from the requirement that children must attend accredited schools for a fixed number of years to the ruling that all who have incomes above a certain amount must pay taxes at a specified rate.

How Much Regulation?

Freedom of choice is an important American value, but some people feel that more laws are needed to regulate behavior and thus enforce the norms of our society. Others claim that such regulations represent government interference in our lives. They resent what they interpret as a first step toward reducing individual liberty.

For example, practices that affect health and safety are now more strictly controlled than they used to be. Industries cannot dump unlimited amounts of waste into surrounding waters. Factory smokestacks must be of a certain height to protect air quality.

Burning of wastes or leaves is allowed only under certain conditions. The ingredients of foods must be listed on the packages.

Other recent laws protect special groups of people. All government buildings and many privately owned buildings must have appropriate facilities for the handicapped—ramps for wheelchairs, elevators, specially equipped bathrooms, and convenient parking places. Similarly, fair-housing laws forbid real estate agents to discriminate on the basis of race, religion, or creed in renting or selling houses. Such regulations came into being as a result of changing standards and political pressure from concerned groups within our society.

Legislating Morality

What some sociologists refer to as the legislation of morality involves using legal apparatus—the lawmaking and law-enforcing bodies and the judicial system—to influence conduct. While most laws reflect a society's traditional values, some do not. In democratic societies, attempts to legislate morality have had mixed results. For example, in the United States, opposition to liquor in the 1920s led to passage of the Eighteenth Amendment, which prohibited the manufacture, sale, and consumption of alcohol. However, persistent violation of the law by those who rejected its basic premise—that drinking was morally wrong—eventually led to its repeal.

Civil-rights pressures in the 1950s and 1960s led to a series of laws expressing the American value of equality. Later, in the late 1960s and the 1970s, some of these laws required *affirmative action*. Under affirmative action, persons from minority groups are given preferential treatment, through admission and hiring policies, to compensate for discrimination in the past. Some Americans oppose this legislation of mores.

REVIEW AND APPLICATION

1. *IDENTIFY:* Felony, misdemeanor, affirmative action.
2. What is the major difference between laws and other norms in a society?
3. (a) What are the two viewpoints concerning increases in government regulation? (b) Which areas seem to be most affected by new legislation?

CRITICAL THINKING: You have read that freedom of choice is an important value to most Americans. Do you think freedom of choice is important to those Americans who favor laws requiring affirmative action? Why or why not? Do you think freedom of choice is important to those Americans who oppose affirmative action laws? Explain your response.

4 Deviance

Not everyone behaves in ways that society expects or approves. Even children may fail to conform to their parents' values. As adults, they may choose entirely different ways of life. In all societies, there are people who dream of being what they aren't. Sometimes they decide to challenge the system, to push out beyond the limits established by law or tradition.

Political radicals, school dropouts, women who refuse the role of homemaker or mother, and many others are willing to stand up and be counted as opposed to at least some of society's norms. They are willing to risk being labeled nonconformists, troublemakers, oddballs, or, simply, *deviants* because they believe that society's norms should change. Embezzlers, professional thieves, and bank robbers also violate norms, but their deviance is not usually based on a belief that society should change. More often they just want a bigger share of the pie for themselves.

As you can see, the label "deviant" is a broad term. Sociologists define deviance as behavior that violates an essential social norm or set of norms. Deviants are people who go beyond the limits of socially acceptable behavior. Although the definition of deviance is simple, deviant acts in real life are hard to pin down. No single act—not even taking another person's life—is forbidden at all times in every human society.

Deviance, then, is relative. What is deviant behavior in one place or at one time may be acceptable in another place or at another time. For an act to be deviant, it must be considered so by a large number of people or by persons who are powerful enough to force others to conform.

A behavior pattern may be seen as normal, even desirable, by some and as deviant by others. For example, a student who spends a lot of time doing library research may win a teacher's respect and appreciation but be scorned as a "bookworm" by other students. What is normal or desirable to the teacher can be deviant to fellow students.

In the United States, motorcycle gangs are deviant subcultural groups that frequently run afoul of the law.

SOURCE: Drawing by O'Brian; © 1966, The New Yorker Magazine, Inc.

"Well, they can't be all bad."

Some of these students—those who refuse to study—are deviant by the norms of the teacher and of most of society.

At any given time in our society, considerable variety can be found in what is acceptable or unacceptable behavior and what the punishment is for violation of the norm. Such variations are more characteristic of large, advanced societies like ours than of small societies bound by a set of strong, shared traditions. Chapter 16, "Crime," discusses lawbreaking, an obvious form of deviance, and the methods used by society in attempting to control it.

? List several instances of behavior that was considered wrong at one time in our society but is now acceptable. Why do you think such behavior was originally labeled deviant? How do you think the change in definitions came about?

Explanations for Deviance

If all children are socialized to observe the norms of society, why does deviance occur? There is no single satisfactory answer to this question, though sociologists have worked to find one. Three important theories of deviance involve anomie, deviant subcultures, and labeling.

Anomie Emile Durkheim related deviance to modernization. He believed that the variety of norms in an industrialized society combined with the impersonality of such a society weakened the individual's commitment to norms in general. Durkheim spoke of the result as *anomie*—a situation in which either there are no rules for behavior or there are so many rules that no one knows which ones to follow. Anomie, in other words, is normlessness.

Durkheim believed that anomie increased the likelihood that an individual would behave deviantly. That is, he thought that social conditions could lead to higher rates of deviance. But Durkheim wasn't specific about how or why, in the same society, some individuals become deviant and others don't.

Sociologist Robert K. Merton adopted Durkheim's concept of anomie in another attempt to explain deviance. In our society, success is measured mainly by material possessions, and competition is the norm. Many people who have been taught to aspire to success lack the means of achieving it, however. According to Merton, people who cannot reach the goal by acceptable, legitimate means may choose one of four behavior patterns.

1. They may behave acceptably but without hope of success. For them, proper behavior becomes an empty ritual, divorced from the goals to which other members of society link it. An example is a bureaucrat who has given up hope of promotion but remains a stickler for the rules.
2. They may escape through alcohol or drugs. These people retreat from both the social goals and the legitimate means of attaining them.
3. They may accept the goals but try to reach them by disapproved means, such as prostitution, selling hard drugs, theft, dealing in stolen property, and embezzlement.
4. They may turn to rebellion, rejecting the goals, norms, and values of conventional society and substituting their own. Members of communes, radical political groups, and certain religious sects are rebels in one way or another.

Deviant Subcultures Some sociologists believe that deviance grows out of certain subcultures. A subculture, as you have read, is a separate group within the dominant culture. People who live within a certain subculture have been taught its rules and practices.

Some deviant subcultures may be peaceful communities within the dominant culture. This religious sect stresses the harmony of all peoples in its theology. The group is shown seated on Boston Common in Massachusetts.

In the subculture of an urban ghetto, for example, toughness, courage, and contempt for conformity may be the norms. A person who learns such norms may behave acceptably as far as the subculture is concerned but may be viewed as deviant in the larger society, where respect for authority and property are the norms. A person respected in the subculture may be condemned in the larger society as a juvenile delinquent, a vandal, or a drug pusher.

Labeling A third possible explanation of deviance is known as *labeling theory*. To sociologists, "labeling" means describing certain people as deviant because of the things they do. Some sociologists distinguish between two types of deviance: primary and secondary. A person engaged in *primary deviance* violates cultural norms without being discovered. Such a deviant may well consider himself or herself basically normal. The deviance may involve such acts as drug use or occasional shoplifting. The primary deviant is able to justify his or her behavior as harmless or perhaps eccentric.

Once people are labeled deviant, they may become convinced that they are indeed fundamentally different from others in the society. When this happens, they may flee conventional society, perhaps by entering a deviant subculture. They may accept the "deviant" label and increase their deviant behavior. This behavior that follows the discovery by others of a primary deviance is known as *secondary deviance*.

Conforming to Deviant Patterns

Whatever theory of deviant behavior one accepts, sociologists generally agree that certain individuals or groups of individuals are sufficiently different from other members of society to be singled out. Some, such as street-gang members and religious fanatics, often revel in their rebellion. They like the fact that others recognize their difference, and they enjoy the feeling that they are part of a deviant subculture.

In such a subculture, even among rebels and outlaws, certain rules must be learned and obeyed, certain patterns of behavior must be adopted, and certain values must be accepted. Indeed, deviant subcultures often require strict conformity to the norms of the deviant group. Within such a group, those who violate the code are often dealt with severely—as deviants.

In recent years, for example, some young people from conventional homes have left home to join religious groups, where they undergo a period of initiation that prepares them to recruit others. The leaders of these groups demand conformity to the norms they consider right. Parents of such youngsters have sometimes gone to great lengths to find their children and bring them home. Often they are thwarted by leaders who don't want the children to leave or by the children themselves, who fear the punishment that is threatened for leaving.

In the process of reentering society, as in the process of becoming deviant, there is a period of intensive retraining. The individual who has been taught new norms and rules by deviant models must learn to adhere once more to the rules of society. Individual personalities submerged by resocialization must once again be allowed expression.

REVIEW AND APPLICATION

1. *IDENTIFY:* Deviants, anomie, primary deviance, secondary deviance.
2. According to Emile Durkheim, what is a major cause of deviance?
3. How does the labeling theory explain deviance?

CRITICAL THINKING: The text points out on page 62 that some religious sects deviate from societal norms. For example, Amish women and cloistered nuns are rebels compared to typical American women. How do these two groups differ from the rest of society in dress, lifestyle, and outlook? How do they differ from each other? In what ways are they similiar?

5 Forced Conformity in Controlled Environments

Intensive relearning is not limited to joining or leaving a deviant group. It occurs whenever people forsake or are removed from society to live in a special *controlled environment,* or *total environment.* A controlled environment is an organization created for a special purpose and existing apart from regular society. People living in controlled environments are taught new norms and new patterns of behavior.

Some people may find themselves in controlled environments against their will. Examples of such environments are jails and, in some cases, mental hospitals, where the inmates or patients are forced to leave behind their customary freedoms and routines. Some people who enter controlled environments have freely chosen to do so. Their attitudes as participants resemble those of people who voluntarily join an ethnic or other subculture. Those who enlist in the armed forces, some residents in nursing homes, and nuns in convents are examples of voluntary participants in this type of controlled environment. Whether participation is voluntary or involuntary, however, and whatever their purpose, controlled environments have four main features in common.

Some controlled environments, such as the armed forces, are entered voluntarily. Here West Point cadets prepare to fling their caps skyward in celebration during graduation ceremonies.

First, all activities occur in the same place and are under the control of the same authority. In the outside world, most people interact in a variety of settings. It is quite natural there to think of yourself as being at the same time a student in school, a son or daughter at home, a friend at a local hangout, and a worker if you hold a part-time job. All of us like time out from the demands of a particular setting. "Thank God it's Friday," exclaim workers, teachers, and students alike. What they really mean is, "I just want to be away from here, doing different things, seeing other people."

In a controlled environment, this is not possible. The inhabitants eat, work, and sleep in the same place with the same people who are directing their lives. Usually a large number of "inmates" or participants are managed by a small staff operating under a strict chain of command, and the give-and-take of members is carefully regulated.

A second feature of controlled environments is that all aspects of daily life take place in the company of others in the same circumstances. Army recruits, novitiates in a convent, and prisoners in jail have little privacy. They spend most of their days with others in the same position as themselves. Contact with the outside world occurs under conditions set down by those in charge.

Third, in controlled environments, daily activities are set by the authorities. Very often a controlled environment has a formal routine. It determines when you get up and when you go to bed, what you wear, and when and what you eat, what work you do, and what recreation you may enjoy.

Finally, the goal of all activities in a controlled environment is to fulfill the purpose of the organization. Army officers use physical training, strict rules, and limited contacts with the outside world to make civilians into soldiers. A captain on a ship also has a job to do and must direct the crew's activities to get it done.

Of course, not every controlled environment exhibits all four traits to the same degree. There are exceptions to the rules—vis-

CONTROLLED ENVIRONMENTS

Type	Purpose
Homes for the blind, orphaned, elderly, and retarded	To take care of people who cannot take care of themselves
Mental hospitals	To provide help for those who need it and protect the community
Reform schools, jails, prisoner-of-war camps	To remove potentially dangerous people from society
Special-purpose environments, such as armed services and boarding schools	To perform assigned educational functions, such as to train people to fight and to educate students
Monasteries, convents	To serve as retreats from worldly values and to prepare people to enter religious orders

CHART SKILL   *What is the main feature common to all of the controlled environments described in the chart above?*

iting days, passes, vacations, and so on—that ease the control in some environments. Not all norms are enforced equally strictly. In Chapter 16, you will read about the problems of enforcing society's norms inside the walls of penal institutions.

Controlled environments are found in every modern society. Governments seem to have found no way to get along without them. No military establishment in the world would consent to have recruits simply take a few classes and read some books about soldiering and then consider them "combat-ready." Similarly, societies almost always demand that people who are mentally disturbed enough to be considered dangerous to themselves and others be isolated in highly controlled environments.

Sometimes governments confine people strictly for political reasons, as in internment and concentration camps. Societies in which large numbers of citizens are subjected to or threatened by this kind of punishment for political activities are defined as *totalitarian* societies. Democratic societies, on the other hand, must try to balance the value of solving social problems by the use of controlled environments against the value of preserving the civil liberties of those being forcibly re-educated to the society's norms.

REVIEW AND APPLICATION

1. *IDENTIFY:* Controlled environment, total environment, totalitarian.
2. What are the four primary features shared by all controlled, or total, environments?

CRITICAL THINKING: Reread pages 64–65 and find the statements that are based on the following assumptions:

a) Enforcing all rules equally in a controlled environment is undesirable if not impossible.
b) A controlled environment produces better soldiers than purely academic training produces.
c) The principle purpose of mental institutions is to protect and restrain rather than to cure the mentally disabled.
d) Totalitarian societies unjustly imprison many people.

CHAPTER 3 REVIEW

Recap

The values people hold and the norms they follow make up the pattern of their culture. American culture, for example, can be described by identifying the values most Americans consider important and the rules by which they live.

The most important norms are called mores; those less so, folkways. Not all norms are followed by everyone at all times; some apply only to certain groups in society. But norms serve as guides for behavior in every society. Class, gender, and generation operate in determining norms, as do culture and region. Laws are codified norms. An increase in legal regulations is interpreted by some as excessive government interference in American life.

Those who violate society's norms to an intolerable degree are known as deviants. Some theorists consider deviance to be a result of competing values in a large, industrialized society. Others see deviance as a way of achieving goals denied by other means. In any case, deviance is relative to the time and place in which it occurs. Deviant groups have their own strict rules requiring conformity; both joining a deviant group or a controlled environment and rejoining society require a process of reeducation in norms.

Key Terms

Define the following:

values	mores	anomie
norms	folkways	labeling theory
potlatch	rites of passage	primary deviance
humanitarianism	felony	secondary deviance
moral orientation	misdemeanor	controlled environment
prescriptions	affirmative action	total environment
proscriptions	deviant	totalitarian

Applying Sociology

1. Draw a line down the middle of a sheet of paper. On the left side, list ten ways males are expected to behave in American society today. On the right side, write the expected behaviors of females. On the top of the sheet put an "M" or an "F" to indicate your own sex.

   Hand all the papers to one person, who will separate the papers marked "M" from those marked "F." As a class, ana-

LATIN AMERICAN NORMS

Femininity	Masculinity
Gentle and mild	Hard, rough-natured
Sentimental	Cold
Emotional	Intellectual
Intuitive	Rational, analytical
Impulsive, lacking in foresight, frivolous	Orderly, farsighted
Superficial	Profound
Fragile, the weaker sex	Strong
Submissive, docile	Overbearing, authoritarian
Dependent, protected, easily frightened, tearful	Independent, brave, never crying
Timid	Bold
Cautious, prudent	Aggressive, daring
Maternal	Paternal
Flirtatious, seductive, a sex object	Severe, seducer
Fickle, inconstant	Stable
Pretty	Ugly
Lacking in self-confidence	Self-confident
Passive	Active
Self-sacrificing	Self-centered, comfort-loving
Envious	Generous
Curious	Indifferent
Monogamous	Polygamous
Virgin	Expert and experienced in lovemaking
Faithful	Unfaithful
Home-loving	Deeply absorbed by business and public life

SOURCE: Hernan San Martin, "Machismo: Latin America's Myth-Cult of Male Supremacy," *The UNESCO Courier*

lyze the data. List the norms for males in two columns: (a) as chosen by males and (b) as chosen by females. Do the same with norms for females.

Did your study show marked differences in norms as perceived by males and females? If so, what items were listed more frequently by males? What items were listed more frequently by females? What values do these norms reflect? Why do you think this is so?

2. Now analyze Latin American norms concerning masculine and feminine behavior. Sociologist Hernan San Martin asked

men and women in a number of Latin American countries to list the major characteristics that they thought described the sexes in Latin America. In what ways is this list like the one you compiled for North Americans? In what ways is it different?

3. Some people think that there are no guidelines or rules to tell people how to behave in dating relationships. List all the rules you can, even if they are competing sets of rules, that our culture gives us for behavior on dates. Do you feel that there are too many different possibilities to choose from? Why or why not? What would you consider an ideal set of norms for a first date? You might compare your list with those of your classmates.

4. Watch a few hours of commercials on network television. When regular programs come on, switch the dial to find other commercials. Note what people's concerns are in these commercials: their hair, their teeth, their pets, and so on. Do you think the commercials are accurate reflections of American norms? Why or why not?

5. In our society certain activities may be accepted in some circumstances and rejected in others. Name a situation in which each of the following activities would be accepted as "normal" and a situation in which each would be thought of as deviant.

asking for money
singing the national anthem
taking a human life
reading a newspaper
wearing a bathing suit
eating popcorn
hugging and kissing
telling jokes
throwing a person to the ground
drinking beer
carrying a revolver

6. Do a book report on an account of a prison-camp experience, such as *Night*, by Elie Wiesel. Or read *The Diary of Anne Frank* and report on how living in a totalitarian society (in this case, the Netherlands during the German occupation) duplicates some of the conditions of a controlled environment. *Darkness at Noon*, by Arthur Koestler, and *The First Circle* and *Cancer Ward*, by Alexander Solzhenitsyn, describing various conditions in Russia, are other possibilities for reports.

Extended Readings

Robert Levine, "Waiting Is a Power Game," *Psychology Today*, April 1987, pp. 24–33.

1. What values do the lines for buses in Israel demonstrate?
2. What does the story of King Hassan and the British royal family illustrate?

Gregory Jaynes, "This Is Against My Rights!," *Time*, July 6, 1987, p. 42.

1. Why was Ed Lawson arrested?
2. In your judgment, were the police justified in arresting Ed Lawson? Why or why not?

Richard Cohen, "Suddenly I'm the Adult?," *Psychology Today*, May 1987, pp. 70–71.

1. How does the author view "growing up"?

2. List three of the milestones the author mentions in the article.

Social Studies Skills

Distinguishing sociological facts from opinions Informed people are able to distinguish facts from opinions in what they read and hear. Read the following statements and then distinguish the facts from the opinions. Explain how you made the distinctions.

a. Norms are rules or standards of behavior.
b. Americans seem generally agreed on the importance of three core ideas: equality, freedom, and democracy.
c. The Nacimera have an almost pathological horror of and fascination with the mouth.
d. The Burmese girl . . . is very feminine and . . . appear[s] like a fragile flower.
e. Both at home and at work, Orthodox Jewish men keep their heads covered with a small skullcap called a yarmulka.

Obtaining information from a photograph
Not all information comes from written sources. Careful analysis of a photograph can also provide many details. Study the caption and photo on page 57. Then use the details you observe to answer the following questions:

a. How does the clothing that the Amish wear differ from the clothing people in your community wear?
b. Do you think the Amish live in rural or urban areas? Why do you think as you do?
c. What kinds of shops and services in your community probably are not available in an Amish community? What kinds of shops and services would an Amish community have that your community does not?
d. How would you describe Amish norms?

Critical Thinking

1. *Evaluating Cause and Effect:* In this chapter you read a description of norms in Burmese society (pages 52–54). Some norms in Burma are very different from those of other societies, such as our own. For example, Burmese women, not men, propose marriage. Make a list of norms in Burma that are different from those in the United States. Then explain what you think causes those differences.

2. *Recognizing Values:* Identify the values of Roberto Sanchez, the funeral director, and the priest as described on pages 57–58.

UNIT APPLICATION

Here Comes the Bride

The traditional wedding music begins to play. The bride, dressed all in white, walks slowly down the aisle accompanied by her father. The groom escorts her to where the minister is standing. Relatives and friends feel both great joy and a special sadness as they view the changing of old relationships and the beginning of new ones.

Vows are exchanged and, as the ceremony draws to a close, the minister clearly states, "By the authority vested in me by the Commonwealth of Massachusetts, I now pronounce you man and wife." Then he adds, "You may kiss the bride." She lifts her veil, and the couple kiss and walk arm in arm through the smiling congregation.

The ceremony does not end there, however. Everyone walks across the street to a large hotel. After checking their coats, the guests take escalators to the mezzanine where a small ballroom has been prepared with abundant food and refreshments. They dance to the music of a local band hired especially for the occasion, and they toast the newly married couple. Waiters and waitresses keep the plates and glasses filled.

Later on, as the party begins to break up, a rich variety of gifts is found piled high on a table near the hallway—gifts to help the couple set up their new home to begin their new lives.

This brief description of a typical American scene lends itself neatly to careful sociological analysis. For the wedding celebration to be successful, its planners must take into account a great many things, not the least of which are the important symbols, rites of marriage, and prescribed rituals in this particular culture. All these sociologically significant factors had to be meshed successfully to avoid embarrassment and even possible failure. Consider, for example, the significance of such ritualized ceremonies in our society.

Using and Analyzing Concepts

1. (a) What symbols are represented in the ceremony described here? To what extent are they specific to our culture? To what extent are they common to all cultures?
   (b) What rules are being followed here and who sets the standards? Who is involved in the ceremony? What functions do they perform? Why?
   (c) By what authority or authorities does a minister exercise the right to perform marriages?
2. Apply the type of sociological analysis used in question 1 to another occasion with which you are familiar, such as a baptism, a bar mitzvah, or a bridal shower. Subject this occasion to the same step-by-step scrutiny.

3. Collect data from various members of your class about the ways they and their family would deal with a death in the family. Is religion the major factor that explains different forms of behavior? If not, what other factors seem important? What arrangements would be made for the funeral? What symbols would be used to symbolize respect for the dead person? What rituals would seem to be meant to comfort the family?

4. Design a ceremony of your own—for instance, your graduation from high school. Indicate the symbols you think should be important, the significant rituals you would introduce, the important persons you would need, and what they should say.

SOCIAL STRUCTURE

Unit Focus

Like members of all societies, Americans belong to a broad range of social organizations. We all tend to measure ourselves against other people in our own and other groups. We evaluate where we stand in terms of relative social position, prestige, and influence. Our place in this layered structure—this social stratification—can be based on wealth, political power, ethnic background, race, religion, or a combination of these or other criteria. Each society has ways of distinguishing its insiders from its outsiders, those high on the social ladder from those lower down.

Unit One focused on the nature of society and culture. Now you will examine social structure, as you explore the many ways in which society is organized. This unit focuses on the patterned relationships among the groups and communities in which life's dramas are played out.

Applying Sociology

- Of what groups are you a member?
- On what factors is your position in society based?
- Where are you on the social ladder?

The family is the basis of our social structure. It is one of the most important factors which influence who we are and what we become.

Roles, Relationships, and Groups

Chapter Preview

- **Before you read,** look up the following key terms in the glossary to become familiar with their definitions:

ascribed status   reciprocal roles   social categories
achieved status   statistical aggregates   primary group
role conflict   social groups   secondary group

- **As you read,** think about answers to the following questions:

1. Why do people need to have social contact with other people?
2. How do status labels help people to relate to each other?
3. Why are role conflicts inevitable?
4. What is a formal organization?

Chapter Focus

In the play *As You Like It*, William Shakespeare wrote:

All the world's a stage and all the men and women merely players: They have their exits and their entrances; and one man in his time plays many parts.

Shakespeare was an astute sociological observer. He recognized that, in real life as in the theatre, each person has many parts to play.

Think for a moment of how many parts you must play in a typical day. You may start out as a "respectful son or daughter"; then, perhaps, you are a "faithful friend", then . . . As you make your mental list, you will find that you relate to many different people in different ways.

This chapter is about human *relationships*. You will examine how people act, interact, and react in different social settings.

Using Sociologists' Tools

- **Observe** the issues that seem to be important in determining status in your school.
- **Describe** the specific characteristics that appear to be essential in "labeling" classmates.
- **Analyze** the problems you or your classmates may have in determining when one role conflicts with another.
- **Predict** what would happen if your school had an honor system and you saw your best friend cheating.

Much of who we are begins with our status as family members. This close-knit farm family paused to be photographed during the Iowa corn harvest.

1 The Need for Others

To be truly human in a sociological sense, everyone needs others. As the poet John Donne wrote, "No man is an island." Although some people may live apart from formal society, no one can learn to live entirely without others. The few instances in which children have been raised virtually alone provide evidence of the devastating effects of isolation on the human condition.

CASE STUDY: Anna, a Child in Isolation

Anna was an illegitimate child. Her grandfather, who was ashamed that his unmarried daughter had borne a child, decided that Anna must be kept alone in an upstairs room. In a well-known study, sociologist Kingsley Davis analyzed this "case of extreme isolation":

The infant received only enough care to keep her barely alive. She was seldom moved from one position to another. Her clothing and bedding were filthy. She apparently had no instruction, no friendly attention.

When finally found and removed from the room at the age of nearly six years, Anna could not talk, walk, or do anything that showed intelligence. She was in an extremely emaciated[1] and undernourished condition, with skeleton-like legs and a bloated abdomen. She was completely apathetic, lying in a limp . . . position and remaining . . . indifferent to everything. She was believed to be deaf and possibly blind. She of course could not feed herself or make any move in her own behalf. After being discovered and being removed from

[1]thin

75

isolation, Anna was given a good deal of love and attention. . . .

. . . By the time Anna died . . . approximately four and a half years later, she had made considerable progress as compared with her condition when found. She could follow directions, string beads, identify a few colors, build with blocks and differentiate[1] between attractive and unattractive pictures. She had a good sense of rhythm and loved a doll. She talked mainly in phrases but would repeat words and try to carry on a conversation. She was clean about clothing. She habitually washed her hands and brushed her teeth. She would try to help other children. She walked well and could run fairly well, though clumsily. Although easily excited, she had a pleasant disposition. Her improvement showed that socialization, even when started at the late age of six, could still do a great deal toward making her a person.

During Anna's six years of isolation, she had almost no contact with other people. She had no experience in learning how to relate to others. As Davis explained, her condition

[1] tell the difference

People need other people in order to learn to be fully human.

at the time of her discovery showed that the bare necessities of life cannot make a "complete person." In his analysis of Anna, Davis stressed the need to communicate with people. Physical contact alone was not enough. Anna had that—to a limited degree—but she had almost no social contact.

Perhaps the learning process would have speeded up once Anna had learned to talk well. But because of her early death, there is no way of knowing how her development would have progressed as she grew older. Davis also studied another child, however, whose case history provides more data about the importance of social contact in human development.

CASE STUDY: *Isabelle, a Survivor of Isolation*

Davis's second case history was similar:

The other case of extreme isolation, that of Isabelle, helps in the interpretation of Anna. This girl was found at about the same time as Anna under strikingly similar circumstances when approximately six and a half years old. Like Anna, she was an illegitimate child and had been kept in seclusion for that reason. Her mother was a deaf-mute, and it appears that she and Isabelle spent most of their time together in a dark room. As a result Isabelle had no chance to develop speech; when she communicated with her mother it was by means of gestures. . . . Her behavior toward strangers, especially men, was almost that of a wild animal, manifesting much fear and hostility. In lieu[2] of speech she made only a strange croaking sound. In many ways she acted like an infant.

Like Anna, Isabelle was rescued from her life of isolation. She was taken to a public home to be cared for and taught. At first those who worked with her were certain she was retarded. Yet, Davis reports:

The individuals in charge of her launched a systematic and skillful program of training. The task seemed hopeless at first but

[2] place

gradually she began to respond. After the first few hurdles had at last been overcome, a curious thing happened. She went through the usual stages of learning characteristic of the years from one to six not only in proper succession but far more rapidly than normal. In a little over two months after her first vocalization[1] she was putting sentences together.

Nine months after that she could identify words and sentences on the printed page, could write well, could add to ten, and could retell a story after hearing it. Seven months beyond this point she had a vocabulary of 1,500–2,000 words and was asking complicated questions. Starting from an educational level of between one and three years . . . she had reached a normal level by the time she was eight and a half years old. . . . She eventually entered school, where she participated in all school activities as normally as other children.

The cases of Anna and Isabelle show how important it is for people to interact with others. Much behavior that appears to be natural is in fact taught by those with whom a child comes into contact. Parents and other influential persons teach the child how to function as a member of society. This training includes such basic skills as talking and caring for himself or herself, but it also includes much more: what the child should like and dislike, what is good and bad, even what is pleasurable or painful.

We and all other human beings reflect in our behavior and attitudes the ways and views of those close to us. We change as we grow older, meet others, and have new ex-

[1]that is, after she first started to speak

Helen Keller, both deaf and blind, was taught to communicate by Anne Sullivan. Here Helen Keller "listens" to what her teacher is saying by feeling her nose, lips, and throat.

periences. Yet our personalities are largely shaped by those who first teach us how to act.

REVIEW AND APPLICATION

1. Can any rules of behavior be learned without help from other human beings? List those you can think of.
2. What was similar about the lives of Anna and Isabelle before age six? What was similar about their lives after age six?

CRITICAL THINKING: What caused Isabelle to fear and hate men and to act like an infant? What was the result of the systematic program of training she underwent for two years? Why do you think this result was not immediate?

2 The Labels by Which We Are Known

Anna and Isabelle, shut away from society, had almost no social contact. In contrast to these isolated girls, the ordinary child by the age of six has related to many people—father, mother, brothers and sisters, teachers, and others. In each of these relation-ships, the child occupies a certain social position, or *status*.

To sociologists, status means not only prestige but also the position a person occupies in relation to others. A boy of six, for example, has the status of son in relation to his parents, the status of brother in relation to his brothers and sisters, and the status of pupil in relation to his teachers.

Clearly, each of us occupies a number of statuses. The father of the six-year-old boy is also a salesman, a baseball fan, a PTA member, and a Republican precinct captain. The boy's older sister is also a high school student, a tennis fanatic, a collector of rare butterflies, and a friend to many others.

Each status may be thought of as a sort of label. When asked to describe yourself, you often use terms defining status. For example, you might say, "I'm a white, female, Catholic student. I'm a music major, a Young Democrat, and a part-time school librarian." Status labels apply to many spheres of life. The chart on this page shows some in each of several categories.

Why Have Status Labels?

When we ask for information about others, we expect people to describe them in terms of status labels. "Bill Smith? Oh, he's one of the Smiths from Highland Village. About twenty years old, goes to State, plays football. You know him—he was the lifeguard at the pool last summer."

Such labeling is useful for people who want to find out about someone because it tells them what he or she is like. The other person falls into a recognized social category. Status labeling also tells us what to expect in terms of behavior.

"Grandfather," "judge," and "clerk" are all statuses. The names themselves give clues to expected behavior. Grandfathers in our society should show affection toward grandchildren. Judges are supposed to be dignified and impartial. Clerks are expected to be polite and helpful to customers.

Status labels also tell us how we are expected to behave toward others. Some such labels are visible. An officer in the military wears symbols to indicate rank, so that someone of a lower rank knows without a doubt whom to salute. A varsity letter identifies a top athlete and calls for respect from fellow students. A clerical collar indicates a member of the clergy. Similarly, when you see someone standing on a street corner wearing a blue uniform, a badge, and a revolver, you are expected to address him or her as "Officer," not "Hey, you!"

Relatively few people wear such obvious emblems of status; most indications of status

CHART SKILL Social status defines the positions a person occupies in relation to others. Can a person have more than one status label? Cite examples.

STATUS LABELS

Category	Examples of Statuses
Sex	Male, female
Age	Infant, child, adolescent, adult, senior citizen
Kinship	Mother, father, son, daughter, husband, wife, brother, sister, grandparent, cousin, aunt, uncle, mother-in-law, firstborn, middle child
Occupation	Mechanic, doctor, lawyer, merchant, police chief, plumber, mason, secretary, farmer, clerk, manager
Religion	Priest, minister, rabbi, elder, deacon, layperson, parishioner, bishop, communicant
Club or association	President, vice-president, secretary, treasurer, committee chairperson, member
Government	Citizen, legislator, administrator, senator, judge, bureaucrat, commissioner, mayor, governor

A basketball coach has one status in relation to his team. He may have other statuses as a husband, a brother, a son, a father, and a friend.

are more subtle. We often listen or look for clues to tell us how to relate to someone. For instance, a man might introduce himself by saying simply, "Hello, I'm Steve Stern." That doesn't tell us much about him. But notice the difference if he says, "Hello, I'm Dr. Stern," or, "Hello, I'm Mr. Stern, assistant principal," or, "Hello, I'm Steve Stern, the meter reader." Even if he says nothing at all, we are alert for symbols: clothing, jewelry, his way of speaking, even his gestures and hairstyle.

Psychologist Leonard Bickman performed several experiments to measure the effect of dress on the way people respond to others. In one experiment, a dime was left repeatedly in full view in a public phone booth. Each time someone picked up the dime, either a male or a female student dressed in either high-status or low-status clothing tried to reclaim it. What were the results? The sex of the claimant had no effect on response, but the mode of dress did have an effect. Of those approached by a well-dressed student, 77 percent returned the dime, while only 38 percent of those approached by a poorly dressed one did so.

Bickman also performed several experiments to test the influence of uniforms. Here, too, the experimenters' dress made a difference. When experimenters were dressed as security guards, 83 percent of the subjects obeyed aggressive commands such as "Pick up this litter" or "Give that man a dime for the parking meter." When the experimenters were dressed as milkmen or as ordinary citizens, 46 percent obeyed the commands.

You may have heard someone say, "I try to treat everyone alike." From what you have learned so far about relationships between people in different social positions, how successful would such an effort be? What reasons, if any, can you give for treating people differently?

How Status Is Determined

Statuses are determined in two ways. Some are assigned, or given, at birth and are

Both photographs here illustrate achieved status. Above, these participants at a business meeting in a corporate boardroom have each struggled and sacrificed to achieve their positions. Below, two British judges wear emblems of their status to clearly indicate their position and how they are meant to relate to others.

called *ascribed statuses*. We are born male or female. We are born black or white or brown. Other statuses are acquired as we go through life and are known as *achieved statuses*.

There are two types of ascribed status. Some, such as gender, usually cannot be changed. Others, such as religion, social class, and nationality, can be changed under certain conditions.

The example of adoption shows the difference between the two types of ascribed status. Suppose that a girl is born to Chinese parents. Shortly after she is born her parents die in an accident and she is adopted by an American couple, who immediately bring her to the United States. She will grow up speaking English and practicing American customs in her everyday life. But she will always be female, and she will always have East Asian physical characteristics.

Achieved statuses are acquired in a variety of ways. We may fight, work, or study for them. Sometimes we just "fall into" them by luck—by being at the right place at the right time. For example, a company recruiter trying to fill a job opening may need someone with a certain combination of skills, such as knowledge of chemical engineering and the ability to speak French. But no matter how an achieved status is attained, it is not on the basis of birth. One is not born a husband or wife. One is not born an auto mechanic, a club treasurer, or an accountant.

It is true that some persons are more likely to achieve certain positions than others. People who hate public speaking aren't likely to run for student-body president. Those who are afraid of heights don't usually go in for window washing. And sometimes those who do have certain talents never get to use them because of discrimination.

Some achieved statuses are not what we think of as achievements. They may result from bad luck, poor planning, or lack of effort. If a shop owner's business fails and he has to go to work for someone else, he acquires a new achieved status as a salesperson. High school dropout, unemployed bricklayer, and widow are other examples of achieved statuses.

Many statuses in our society and in similar societies require special knowledge or skills. One does not automatically become a high school senior, a Class A skier, or a brain surgeon. Educational opportunities play a part in the kinds of achieved statuses one attains. Family and community background also play a part. For example, a young man who grows up in a family of very religious Jews in an Orthodox Jewish neighborhood is more likely to achieve the status of rabbi than a Jew from a less religious home. A young woman who has lived all her life in a rural farm community is more likely to achieve the status of farmer than a city-bred woman. The talented child of an entertainer may find it easier to become one, too.

REVIEW AND APPLICATION

1. *IDENTIFY:* Status, ascribed status, achieved status.
2. Make a list of ten statuses you hold.
CRITICAL THINKING: In the experiment discussed on page 79, what assumption do you think most of the subjects made about the experimenters in uniform?

Many statuses are the result of educational opportunities. This woman achieved the status of judge through advanced education.

3 Learning And Playing Roles

All of us are supposed to know how to act in each position we occupy. The pattern of behavior linked with any given status is called a *role*. A person's role in any status is a set of expectations for behavior. These expectations are held both by the person who has attained the status and by others. For instance, a person with the status of parent expects to act and is expected to act in certain ways. The positions of brother, daughter, and friend are each associated with a particular set of expectations. So are those of concert pianist, high school sophomore, and police officer.

Everyone plays many roles in a single day, because everyone holds a variety of statuses. One minute you may be playing the role of son or daughter, the next that of student. An hour later you are enjoying the spectator role in the bleachers at the stadium.

Referring again to your list of ten statuses (question 2, above), describe the role connected with each. Now choose another member of your family—a parent, for example. Try to list the roles he or she plays in the course of a day.

When Roles Are Related

Sociologists are concerned with the ways any particular status affects our behavior and attitudes. They are also interested in the ties between people in related statuses in the same spheres of life—for instance, doctors and patients, athletes and coaches, and husbands and wives. Related roles are called *reciprocal roles*.

In the doctor-patient relationship, for example, each person usually has a clear-cut set of expectations about how the other will act. The patient expects the doctor to be well trained and to be able to apply his or her medical knowledge to the treatment of the patient's illness. The patient also expects that the doctor will prescribe only medicine that is necessary and will not be concerned with how much profit a druggist can make on a prescription. The doctor, on the other hand, expects the patient to be respectful of the doctor's expertise and to discuss medical problems frankly. A doctor will often say to a patient, "Without your trust, it is impossible for me to help you." The way in which the person plays the role of patient is largely influenced by the doctor's expectations.

Doctors are also involved in other reciprocal roles in their professional lives. They have to relate to nurses and fellow doctors, among others. Here, too, there are expectations about how each will behave. If a nurse gives more advice than a doctor expects, the doctor may become flustered and angry. Similarly, doctors rarely criticize one another, and when this occurs the doctor under attack may charge his colleague with unprofessional behavior.

Doctor-patient, doctor-nurse, and doctor-doctor relationships are largely controlled by the expectations held by each of the persons involved. It's not necessary to be a doctor, a patient, or a nurse to act the part. Anyone who knows the social situation and the statuses of the persons involved can act the same way.

If you have done role playing in class, you've probably noticed how easily you can begin to act out socially defined roles, even those you have never played before. You probably found that your action depended on the status of the character you were playing and those of the other characters with whom you interacted. You may have identified with your character, feeling to some extent the pain or the joy or the frustration. If in an acting situation we can so readily assume roles that are not usually ours, think of how much more easily we can slip into behavior patterns that are already familiar to us.

? Write down the list of ten statuses you created earlier (question 2, page 81). Opposite each one, list a reciprocal role. For instance, opposite "student" you might write "teacher." Then name three other pairs of reciprocal roles, such as brother-sister or police chief–rookie, and point out some special ways in which these persons are expected to relate to each other.

When Roles Conflict

Suppose you are midway through the most wonderful summer of your life working at a summer camp in New Mexico. You've made new friends and earned some much-needed money, and you've been asked to go hiking in the Rocky Mountains with your new friends when camp ends. A letter from your mother arrives saying that your father has to enter the hospital for a serious operation.

Although you know your mother would never ask you to come home, you are sure

The relationship between doctor and patient depends on roles that are clearly understood.

she would like you to be there. You wonder what you should do. You think about it and then decide to go home. This is an example of a *role conflict*—a situation in which the behavior that is expected of one role comes into conflict with the behavior expected of another role. In this case, the role of friend conflicted with your role of son or daughter.

A role conflict can also consist of conflicting expectations of the same role. For example, a parent who has one child pitching a baseball game at the same time another is starring in a school play can't watch them both. Yet one expectation of the parent's role is to show interest in all of his or her children's activities.

A person is expected to behave differently as a family member, friend, churchgoer, student, consumer, and voter. One is expected to play the role or roles that fits each status. What happens when the roles conflict?

Often such a dilemma is resolved by the *compartmentalization* of behavior—acting under different sets of principles in different situations. Thus one may support the "brotherhood of man" in a house of worship but remain silent at a town meeting when others protest the integration of schools and neighborhoods. A parent may be tough on the job but spoil her children. A student may tell friends that he doesn't care about making high marks in school but eagerly accepts a teacher's suggestion to try out for the honor society. In other words, we may and often do change our behavior—and our stated opinions—to fit various situations. But it isn't always easy. Consider two examples.

A secretary is asked by her boss to type a letter describing his plans to undertake some activities that are not in the interest of the company. One expectation of her role of secretary is loyalty to her supervisor. Another expectation is loyalty to the company. Which expectation of the role comes first?

A newly elected Republican mayor is under strong pressure to replace the present park superintendent with a Republican party worker. She feels that the present superintendent, a Democrat, has done an excellent job and is highly qualified to continue in the job. Which role comes first—the role of chief executive officer of the city or the role of local party leader? What should the mayor do?

Another way of resolving role conflict is to set priorities. We must decide which role comes first—in other words, which of our many selves we want to be at a given time. The mayor, for example, may decide that her role as the town's chief executive officer has priority over her role as local party leader. Thus, she will keep the park superintendent on the payroll, at the risk of antagonizing her fellow Republicans.

Sometimes the pressures are so great that it is difficult to set priorities. Consider the following situation:

Georgia Cummings is a pep-rally leader, the captain of her basketball team, and the chairwoman of the senior class recreation committee. She is one of the most popular girls in her class. Next month the student body is holding an election for sports coordinator, a student selected to work with school administrators in determining how school funds should be spent on athletic programs.

The position, which has always been held by a boy, calls for someone who is well organized, assertive, and good at arithmetic. Georgia thinks she can do a better job than any of the boys who are planning to run. She also thinks the position would give her valuable experience that would help qualify her for a job after graduation.

She has discussed her interest in running with several close friends, both male and female. Her friends have warned her that she will have fewer dates if she wins. Her male friends think the job should go to a boy. However, most of her friends agree that she is well qualified for the job.

Georgia's father has encouraged her to run for the office. He says that, when he was a senior, he held a similar position that taught him a lot about business. As the time to submit her name for the election draws closer, Georgia wonders what to do.

? Why might Georgia's friends oppose her running? What are the expectations of her in the roles of friend, date, and daughter? If you were Georgia, what would your decision be? Why?

Role conflicts confront us often. We usually recognize them, but we rarely analyze them. Studying a fictional case is good practice for analyzing real-life role conflicts.

Judging Relationships

Sociologists often rank social relationships along a line from personal to impersonal. Individuals at the personal end are those to whom we feel closest. Those at the other end are the most distant. In between fall those with varying degrees of closeness or distance. Such a line, extending from one extreme to another, is called a continuum. Most people have many relationships all along the line.

Try judging the quality of relationships by studying the pictures on page 85, each of which shows two or more people interacting. The people seem to belong together. They are persons who have something in common. Visual clues indicate that they share a common culture, our culture. These are typical American scenes. Where on the continuum would you place each interaction?

A number of guesses about the quality of the relationship in each picture come to mind. The bonds between the mother and child are no doubt closer than those among the workers at top right. The teenagers on the front steps seem to be good friends. They may tell one another intimate things, secrets perhaps. We tell our parents intimate things, too, but the relationship is different. A close friend is regarded as an equal; a parent, however loving, is not. What about picture C? The interaction here is more impersonal; the man is picking up material at an airline ticket counter.

The nature of the relationship is different in each of these situations. In studying the quality of relationships, sociologists consider these questions: How strongly do the individuals feel about each other? How long will the relationship last? How general or specific is the relationship?

The parent-child relationship shown in picture D is highly emotional, long-lasting, and very general. It is not limited to a specific situation. On the other hand, the link between the agent at the ticket counter and the customer shown in picture C is without strong feeling, short-term (lasting only a minute or two), and very specific. The former is clearly a personal relationship; the latter, an impersonal one.

The relationships shown in picture E are harder to define. One often has strong feelings about one's friends, and it would not be surprising if you saw such closeness in this picture. Such interaction might be long-lasting or short-lived. The girls and boys gathered on the steps might see each other in many situations or only for certain specific activities.

Picture B portrays a work group in conference. While the members of the group may feel a certain closeness, it is very possible that their degree of personal involvement is limited to on-the-job activities. The relationship could end as soon as one of the workers takes employment elsewhere.

Picture A represents a special relationship, subject to many variables. A grandparent may exert a powerful effect or a weak effect on a grandchild, depending on how near the two live to each other and what the nature of their relationship is when they do meet. Even a rarely seen relative can be influential in a number of ways.

Everyone has relationships with others that range from personal to impersonal.

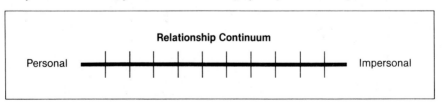

Relationship Continuum

Personal ──────────────────────────── Impersonal

A

B

C

D

E

You have already seen how important close personal relationships are in the development of infants. The first section of this chapter described two children who spent their first six years in isolation. Anna and Isabelle suffered serious emotional and physical damage because they were denied continued interaction with other human beings who truly cared for them.

Another well-known study revealed similar results. René Spitz observed what happened to small children who had been raised in an orphanage. These children got better care than Anna and Isabelle; they were bathed and fed regularly and always had clean clothes. Yet they developed poorly. Some did not live to adulthood. Why?

Spitz concluded that the infants lacked a basic ingredient for healthy development: they had not built a strong personal relationship with an adult. The nursery staff simply lacked the time to play with the children and to show them individual attention. Concern or caring is very important if a child is to adapt successfully to his or her environment.

These conclusions about the importance of personal, intimate relationships for children also apply to adults. Let us look at another example. Why do soldiers fight? Part of the answer lies in their belief in a cause, described by such slogans as "my country right or wrong," "keeping the world safe for democracy," and so on. But there is at least one other vital factor, which was documented by research on the German army during World War II. Investigators found that personal relationships with their buddies encouraged men in combat. Soldiers didn't want to let their friends down, so they kept on fighting long after they might otherwise have given up.

During the same period, the United States Army also recognized this tendency. On the first day of basic training, the drill sergeant had each recruit choose a buddy. When a soldier was in trouble, the buddy became the person to turn to. Forming this kind of personal relationship helped soldiers adapt to the uncertainty of a new situation.

REVIEW AND APPLICATION

1. *IDENTIFY:* Role, reciprocal role, role conflict, compartmentalization.
2. What are the questions sociologists ask when considering the quality of relationships?
3. In the René Spitz study, why did children raised in an orphanage tend to develop poorly?
4. What factor about relationships was uncovered by studies conducted during World War II? What did the United States Army do when they recognized this tendency?

CRITICAL THINKING: Consider the following dilemma: For years, Patrick O'Neill has gone regularly to see his grandparents on Tuesday night. It is an old O'Neill tradition. Then on Saturday Patrick's best friend invites him to a surprise birthday party being held on Tuesday night for Patrick's girlfriend. Patrick decides to go to the birthday party rather than to visit his grandparents. What aspects of his relationships might Patrick have evaluated in making his decision?

4 Groups

In both close and distant relationships, the roles we play and the manner in which we play them are shaped by the groups to which we belong. Understanding role behavior, then, requires an understanding of the varied nature of the groups in modern society. Sociologist Ely Chinoy wrote:

In everyday conversation, "group" is usually applied indiscriminately to many different collections of people . . . members of a ladies' club, a teenage gang in Harlem or the Bronx, a Boy Scout troop, the 60,000 or so workers at the Ford River Rouge plant, the more than a million members of the United Automobile Workers, and the employees of U.S. Steel are all likely to be called "groups.". . . Each nation is frequently identified as a group, as are the innumerable families, clans, societies, and tribes found among primitive peoples. Members of the Catholic Church, Jews, government employees, a movie audience, . . . professors, electricians, bankers, men, women, fans of some popular singer or movie actress, readers of comic books or of sociology texts—each of these is likely to be labeled in ordinary conversation as a group. . . .

This legion of groups is obviously so diversified that it would be difficult, if not impossible, to characterize them in general terms. . . . Sociologists therefore face the task of distinguishing a precise language for their analysis.

Kinds of Collectivities

To sort out this tangled web of different kinds of collectivities, sociologists recognize three main types. They distinguish *statistical aggregates* and *social categories* from *social groups*.

A statistical aggregate consists of individuals who share certain traits but who may have no personal connection and may play dissimilar roles. Those who wear glasses, those who read *Time* magazine, those who earn between $20,000 and $30,000 a year, and those who buy Fords are statistical aggregates.

A social category is made up of people of similar status who play similar roles and may or may not know one another. This would include people in many occupations and professions—police officers, cleaners, assembly-line workers, engineers, and the like. Groups who face discrimination or who are expected by society to act in certain ways also make up social categories. For example, Haitian refugees and migrant laborers belong to this type of collectivity.

The members of a social group, however, are more closely related to one another. Of the pictures you analyzed earlier, the mother and child, the close friends, and the fellow workers illustrate relationships that qualify them as social groups. A social group has three characteristics: its members interact with each other in regular, expected ways; they share similar beliefs and values; and they have a feeling of association with each other.

Many collections of people—friends, families, fraternal orders such as the Elks or Masons, social clubs, professional societies, athletic associations, business organizations, and political parties—have these characteristics. But even among these groups there are significant variations in the degrees to which people share their beliefs, values, and goals. And the sense of belonging and intimacy that members feel also varies greatly.

Primary and Secondary Groups

Sociologists generally classify social groups as either primary or secondary. A *primary group* is one in which the individuals have close, personal, informal relationships. The members have few secrets from each other, and there is almost no limit to the subjects that may be discussed. Close friends form a primary group. A *secondary group* is one in which people have more limited, specialized, and temporary connections with each other. Such clubs as the Rotarians, Civitans, and Y-Teens are secondary groups. Of course, within a secondary group some members may become close friends, thus forming a primary group.

The most striking difference between primary and secondary groups is the closeness and informality of the primary group as contrasted with the distance and formality of the secondary group. Rules for behavior are generally taken for granted when we are with our parents and friends. At work or at school, however, we are constantly aware of the complex rules that define what we are supposed to do, where we are supposed to be, and where we stand in relation to others.

In our daily lives we take part in both primary and secondary groups. Family and friends form primary groups. The work group is usually a secondary group, especially if it is a large corporation or agency.

GROUPS AND COLLECTIVITIES

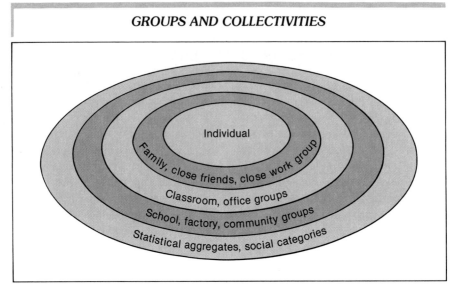

Individual

Family, close friends, close work group

Classroom, office groups

School, factory, community groups

Statistical aggregates, social categories

CHART SKILL   All people belong to many groups and collectivities that vary greatly in terms of intimacy and in the influence they have on the lives of their members. Primary social groups, such as families and close friends, are intimate and lasting. Secondary social groups, such as classroom, office, and community groups, are less personal and tend to be more specialized. Groups may overlap, and their boundaries may change as relationships change. Statistical aggregates and social categories consist of members who share traits, but they are not social groups. What characteristics of social groups do statistical aggregates and social categories lack?

The Importance of Primary Groups

At the beginning of this chapter Shakespeare's observation that "all the world's a stage" was quoted. As Shakespeare knew, in our daily lives we play many roles that imply certain interactions with others. People come to expect certain things of us, just as we learn to expect certain things of them. The following selection shows the importance of role expectations and role reciprocity.

From 1967 to 1972, sociologist E. E. LeMasters conducted a study of a working-class tavern using the method of *participant observation*. The men who went to the tavern were mostly construction workers who spent many of their off-the-job hours relaxing together. As a result of their close relationship, they responded as a primary group in times of stress or grief. The following description of their behavior illustrates this response:

When the family of a regular customer of The Oasis suffers a tragedy, the group responds. Funerals are attended conscientiously, flowers are sent, hospitals are visited, and funds are collected for the family.

One night I stopped in at the tavern and found the people at the bar talking about a man in his forties who had been a regular patron of The Oasis and was reported to be dying of cancer.

One of the men brought a glass jar over and asked me to contribute to a fund for the man's family. "Lee," he said, "put something in this jar. That poor guy is up there in that hospital tonight dying of cancer and his four little kids are sitting down in that . . . house crying."

Another time a popular member of the inner group suffered a disastrous fire, losing his home and almost all of his furniture and personal property. The regular patrons responded to this crisis with help of various kinds.

Another customer was diagnosed as having active tuberculosis and had to be hospitalized for several months. Visits were made to the sanatorium, and handicraft items made by the person while hospitalized were sold at The Oasis.

In a very real sense the inner core of the tavern's patrons functions as a mutual aid society: psychological support is provided in times of crisis; material help is available if needed; children are cared for; cars loaned; and so on. In our vast, impersonal society such support and aid are highly functional.

? Discuss the meaning of the last sentence in the reading above: "In our vast, impersonal society such support and aid are highly functional."

REVIEW AND APPLICATION

1. *IDENTIFY:* Statistical aggregates, social categories, social groups, primary groups, secondary group, participant observation.
2. List some secondary groups to which you belong. Are there any personal relationships that have developed in those groups? Explain.

CRITICAL THINKING: Are the Oasis patrons typical of primary groups in America?

---

5 Formal Organizations

What do the Motor Vehicle Bureau, General Motors, the United States Navy, and the General Association of Regular Baptist Churches have in common? They are all secondary groups, and they are also what sociologists call *formal organizations*. A formal organization is a highly organized group with specific goals or purposes and a clearly defined set of roles.

The system by which people in a formal organization perform their jobs is called a *bureaucracy*. Bureaucracies exist in federal, state, and local governments; in factories, large corporations, and the armed services; and also in hospitals, churches, and sports associations. Even school systems become bureaucracies if they are large enough. In a country as large as the United States, bureaucracies seem to be an inescapable by-product of our rapid growth.

It would be almost impossible to go through life without some contact with a bureaucracy. Whenever you have a question about your income tax or telephone bill, you must deal with a bureaucracy. If your new car is recalled, you are dealing with another bureaucracy. Census taking, taxation, health and welfare services, and the production and distribution of goods to all parts of the country would be impossible without bureaucracies.

Bureaucracies are more than just "red tape." They all have some common features:

1. There is a clear-cut division of labor, with many jobs being highly specialized, as in an automobile-factory assembly line.
2. There is a clearly defined chain of command. The links of authority and responsibility bind each employee to the person directly above and the person directly below. People in bureaucracies are always aware of where they stand in relation to others in the system. Most often the table of organization—the chart depicting these links—looks somewhat like a pyramid, with many workers at the bottom, fewer supervisors in the middle, and even fewer managers at the top.
3. There is a formal system of rules for carrying out activities. Members occupy specific positions, each with a clearly defined role.
4. The people who are employed in a bureaucracy are virtually interchangeable; it is their positions that are important. It doesn't matter much if one person quits and another is hired. The position remains

Small work groups such as this fire department in Marion, New York, may be either primary or secondary groups, depending on the closeness and informality among members of the group.

the same, and each person who fills it must play the same role.

5. Ideally, there is little emotional interaction among role players. Officials are expected to act impersonally, and all employees are supposed to be treated the same. Promotions, raises, and other benefits result from merit and not from special friendships or relationships that have nothing to do with the job. The emphasis is on getting the task done.

☐? In a typical day most of us will confront at least one bureaucratic organization. Which of the formal organizations you come in contact with fit the description of a bureaucracy?

Social Relationships in Bureaucracies

Most relationships within bureaucracies tend to be impersonal, short-lived, and very specific. People generally care less about one another than do the members of primary groups. At least two of the features of bureaucracies are clues to the quality of relationships.

In a bureaucracy, the position is all-important. When one person replaces another in a given role, the work goes on as usual after a few hours, days, or weeks. This is very different from what goes on in a primary group. In a family, for example, the loss of a mother, father, or other family member markedly changes the nature of the group and usually has a significant effect on everyone else in it.

Another feature of bureaucracies is the chain of command. The chain of command tells people to whom they report and who reports to them. They know who has the right to tell them what to do.

Informal Pressures in Bureaucracies

In theory, members of bureaucracies interact on a formal level characteristic of secondary groups. But anyone who has ever worked in a big office or factory knows that this is not entirely true. The group that gets together at coffee break every day or always meets for lunch in the cafeteria resembles a primary group. In bureaucracies many, perhaps most, people have both personal and impersonal relationships.

There are other ways in which bureaucracies depart from the features described earlier. Not everyone performs exactly the tasks assigned, and not everyone always goes through the chain of command to get things done. Say that new workers are supposed to be hired from a waiting list in the order in which they applied. Yet sometimes a supervisor has a friend who "really needs a job." Somehow that name jumps to the top of the list. In your own experience with bureaucracies, how often have you "bent the rules" a little in order to cut through the red tape when trying to get something done in a hurry at school or on the job?

Breaking or bypassing the rules is what one sociologist refers to as "bureaucracy's other face." Impersonal, formal relationships are assumed to be the most important ones in a bureaucracy. However, within most bureaucracies informal pressures give rise to new sets of norms, new channels of communication, and new groups based on shared experiences.

CHART SKILL Organizational charts indicate a strict hierarchy of relationships. Why might the organization below require a clearly defined chain of command?

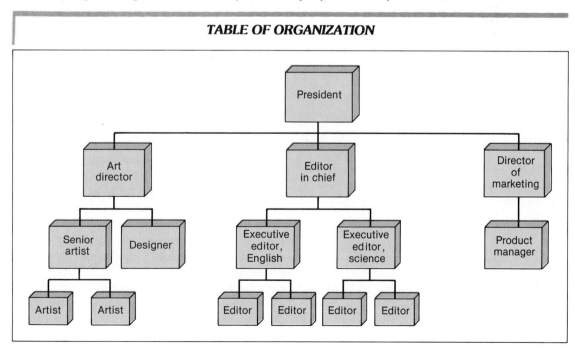

TABLE OF ORGANIZATION

Primary friendship groups often develop within a secondary group. For example, students develop friendship groups within the secondary group of their university.

? Think, once again, of the Motor Vehicle Bureau. What types of personal relationships might the clerk there have on the job?

Case Study: *An Exceptional Bureaucracy*

While most large organizations have the characteristics discussed above in both their formal and their informal aspects, there are exceptions. For example, some large industrial firms in Japan have been described as being more like big, happy families than cold, impersonal organizations. In the following selection, a journalist who spent many years living and working in Japan describes the social structure of one of these large Japanese firms:

The most pampered work force is that of the Matsushita Electric Industrial Company. Japan's largest maker of electronic products (Panasonic and other brands), Matsushita has 54,000 employees at its 120 plants throughout the country. From the time anyone is hired, he has job security until he retires at sixty. He can be fired only for a crime or insanity. . . .

The worker is reassured of management's regard for him by twice-yearly cash bonuses of three months' salary, plus a token present on his birthday. Commuters get transportation allowances, and everyone, from executives to assembly-line workers, eats low-priced meals at the company's cafeterias. If a worker deposits his money in a Matsushita bank, it earns at three times the usual rate. . . .

Every morning and afternoon, the factory work is stopped for fifteen-minute breaks. For the energetic workers, there are mini tennis courts set up near warehouses. For the less ambitious, there are tree-shaded avenues where an employee can relax on the grass by a roadway until it is time to go back to work.

At night many Matsushita employees head not for home but for a company gym or classroom. There, at no charge, they pursue a range of activities that the company offers with the aim of reinforcing a sense of group identification. Men learn judo or fencing; women are taught flower arranging and the intricate tea ceremony. Both sexes may study calligraphy,[1] Buddhism, English, or Spanish. So popular is the program that, a few years ago, some employees opposed the elimination of Saturday work because they feared consequent weekday overtime might make them late for their classes.

If a Matsushita employee wants to marry, a matchmaker in the personnel office will introduce him to a likely mate. If the match works, the couple can be married by a company-hired Shinto priest in a company wedding hall and feted at a company-arranged banquet. Entire cost to the newlyweds: $700, about half what it would otherwise be.

The couple can honeymoon at a company hotel; or if they decide to go abroad,

[1]handwriting as an art

Matsushita's travel bureau will make all arrangements. On their return, they can move into an apartment in one of the thirty company housing projects. When they are ready to build their own home, they can do so on land that the company owns, and finance it with a low-cost company loan.

REVIEW AND APPLICATION

1. *IDENTIFY:* Formal organization, bureaucracy.
2. What are the five features characteristic of bureaucracies?
3. List three ways in which relationships in bureaucracies differ from those in primary groups.
4. How can the chain of command in a bureaucracy be sidestepped?

CRITICAL THINKING: Compare what you know of American norms and values with the norms and values reflected in Matsushita's treatment of its employees. What aspects of Matsushita's system would American workers most likely endorse? Why? Which aspects might they reject? Why?

Some Japanese companies differ markedly from American corporations in the personal and all-encompassing nature of their relationship to their employees. Here Japanese workers participate in a company exercise program.

CHAPTER 4 REVIEW

Recap

With others, and through others, people learn the many roles they are to play in the drama of life. They learn how each role is related to particular positions, or statuses, in the social structure. Some of these statuses are ascribed, and others are achieved.

Some roles, known as reciprocal roles, are related. Doctor and patient, for example, are reciprocal roles. Sometimes the requirements of one role that a person plays conflict with those of another role. For instance, being a good son or daughter may conflict with being a good friend.

Often behavior in these different roles is related to the collectivities to which we belong. Three main types of collectivities identified by sociologists are statistical aggregates, social categories, and social groups. Social groups range from small, intimate, and personal primary groups to large, formal, and impersonal secondary groups.

Most businesses and many other formal organizations qualify as bureaucracies, having formal chains of command and, ideally, little emotional interaction among role players. But even within a large bureaucratic organization, personal relationships often develop. Some Japanese firms exhibit a unique personal involvement with employees, despite the size of the organization.

Key Terms

Define the following:

status	role conflict	primary group
ascribed status	compartmentalization	secondary group
achieved status	statistical aggregate	participant observation
role	social category	formal organization
reciprocal roles	social group	bureaucracy

Applying Sociology

1. Write a mini-drama about a situation involving several players who hold very different statuses. For example, the characters might include a youth who has been caught shoplifting, a juvenile court judge, the arresting officer, and the offender's parents.

2. Pick one formal organization with which you are familiar. (a) Begin by drawing a poster-size table of organization similar to the chart on page 91. List as many positions as possible in the organization. Next to each position place the name of the person who occupies it. Two examples might be "Principal—Jack Klein" and "Guidance counselor—Anne Ling." (b) Choose at least three positions in the table and write a role description of each one. Include chief duties, chief role relationships, and some expected behaviors in these relationships. (c) Now write a paragraph summarizing how, or whether, the bureaucracy you have chosen exhibits the five features of a bureaucracy.

3. Turn back to page 85 and review the pictures. Then cut out from magazines

and newspapers a group of five photographs illustrating role relationships. Label them A, B, C, D, and E. Now evaluate the relationship depicted in each photograph as follows: (a) high or low emotional feeling; (b) long or short duration of relationship; and (c) general or specific nature of relationship. Compare your pictures with those of your classmates. Are your selections similar? Do you agree with their ratings? What might account for any differences?

4. Study the front page of a newspaper and list all the groups, organizations, and collectivities mentioned. Then classify them under the various headings devised by sociologists—statistical aggregate, social category, and so forth.

Extended Readings

Claire Berman, "How Many Friends Are Enough?," *Parents,* January 1987, p. 65–66, 128–130.

1. How do three- and four-year olds choose friends?
2. What social skills do children learn from group interaction?

John Papanek, "Athletes or Role Models?," *Sports Illustrated,* June 15, 1987, p. 84.

1. Does the author think that athletes or celebrities should be role models for young people?

2. What did the author conclude about athletes who use drugs and then return to the sport after treatment?

Carol Simons, "They Get By With a Lot of Help From Their *Kyoiku Mamas,*" *Smithsonian,* March 1987, pp. 44–52.

1. What qualities does the Japanese mother-child relationship foster in children?
2. How does Japanese culture view the role of mothers?

Social Studies Skills

Solving a personal delemma
Study the list of statuses that you created for question 2 on page 81. Rearrange your list according to which roles are most important, less important, and least important to you at this time in your life. (Add the statuses of *student* and *friend* if they are not already on your list.) Now use this list to help resolve the following dilemma: It is a Sunday night. You must finish a sociology report for Monday, but your best friend comes over to discuss problems he is having with his parents. You have a dilemma. Do you do your report or try to cheer up your friend? How did your ranking of statuses affect your choice?

Critical Thinking

1. *Evaluating Cause and Effect:* Suppose someone concluded, based on the two Bickman experiments described on page 79, that people are greatly influenced by the way other people are dressed. Evaluate this causal reasoning.

2. *Evaluating Samples:* Based on the description of the Japanese company on pages 92–93, how reasonable is it to conclude that Japanese companies are very good to their workers? Explain the reasoning behind your decision.

CHAPTER

Social Stratification

Chapter Preview

- **Before you read,** Look up the following key terms in the glossary to become familiar with their definitions:

social stratification   feudal estate system   transitional societies
social mobility   class consciousness   meritocracy

- **As you read,** think about answers to the following questions:

1. What determines a person's status in nonindustrial societies?
2. Why is wealth an important source of status and power in many industrial societies?
3. What social classes exist in the United States?
4. Why is it so difficult to become a member of a higher social class in the United States?

Sections in this Chapter

1. Stratification in Nonindustrial Societies
2. Stratification in Industrial Societies
3. Stratification in the United States

Chapter Focus

"He's a member of the upper crust." "She is so typically middle-class." "I'm just a regular working-class guy." You've probably heard statements like these many times. If you analyze them, they can tell you a lot about American social structure.

If you examine any society, you will note that some people appear to have higher positions than others. There isn't a society in the world where everyone is equal. Social rank is sometimes based on biologically inherited traits, such as gender or race. Sometimes it is based on socially inherited characteristics, such as the position or wealth of one's family. And sometimes rank is based on personal achievement.

Social rank is often determined by a combination of what sociologists call class, prestige, and power. Class is frequently based on possessions; prestige is determined by what other people think; and power is the result of control over others.

Using Sociologists' Tools

- **Observe** the most obvious differences between students in your school who are thought to be rich and those thought to be poor.
- **Describe** the distinguishing characteristics of rich and poor kids.
- **Analyze** how some criteria for determining socio-economic status, such as the style of clothes people wear, may be misleading.
- **Predict** how "class" would be identified if students wore uniforms.

Social rank is often determined by a combination of class, prestige, and power.

1 Stratification in Nonindustrial Societies

The arrangement of individuals and families into graded layers is known as *social stratification*. Studies by sociologists and anthropologists indicate that, while every society has some form of stratification, the bases for ranking people vary considerably. In many premodern, or folk, societies, the primary divisions are based on gender and age. In most small, isolated, traditional societies, men have higher status than women. Older men have the highest status of all.

Many such societies seem to make little use of the main criteria of social standing in industrial societies: economic advantage and political power. One reason is that most men in folk societies do the same kind of work as other men, and most women do the same kind of work as other women. Consider the folk society of the Kung Bushmen of the Kalahari Desert in Africa. In order to survive, the Kung must hunt. Working in groups, the

men search out and kill animals ranging from antelope to giraffes. After the hunters have made several kills, they take the food to the village and divide it equally among the men and women of the village.

Closed Systems

Except for folk societies, most societies today have systems that require increasingly specialized and stratified labor forces. Societies can be placed along a continuum according to the rigidity of their systems of social stratification—that is, the degree to which it is possible to move from one stratum to another. At one end of the stratification continuum are the closed systems, in which social position is determined by birth and there is little chance of moving from one stratum to another. Closed systems are most common in nonindustrial societies. One of

India has a caste system based on the Hindu religion. Under this system, people remain at the same level of wealth, power, and influence as their parents. Those at the bottom of the social system, formerly called the untouchables, are unable to raise themselves from poverty.

the most rigid is the traditional *caste system* of India, which is based on hereditary divisions specified by the Hindu religion.

The Caste System   For centuries, Indian society was divided into four main castes. The Brahmans, members of the highest, or priestly, caste, were assured of wealth, honor, and power for life. Below the Brahmans were the warrior caste, the merchant caste, and

the peasant caste. At the bottom of the social system were the *untouchables,* who were not considered members of any caste.

Untouchables were born to a life of poverty, shame, and powerlessness. They were thought to be so unclean that physical contact with them would pollute the members of the higher castes. If even the shadow of an untouchable touched a Brahman, the Brahman had to perform religious cleansing rites.

As long as the religious system supported the caste rules, the untouchables were doomed to suffer misery and neglect. Yet, despite its injustices, few people challenged the Indian caste system until Mahatma Gandhi led a movement to win India's independence from Britain and to abolish discrimination against untouchables.

In achieving this latter goal, Gandhi was only partially successful. The Indian constitution of 1950 outlawed discrimination against untouchables, but religious and traditional sanctions still keep people in caste divisions. Most of the untouchables, who are now referred to as the "scheduled caste," still occupy the same lowly status as before.

Many societies with racial minorities have the characteristics of a caste system. It has often been suggested that the barriers to movement and other laws directed against blacks in the Republic of South Africa are almost as restrictive as the rules of caste. Broadly speaking, "caste" may be based not only on religion but also on social and economic factors and political beliefs.

The Feudal Estate System   Almost as restrictive as the caste system in limiting the movement of a society's members is the *feudal estate system,* another system in which social position is determined by birth. Under this system, one is born into a certain level and often spends a lifetime as a serf or a peasant or, perhaps, a lord. *Social mobility,* or movement into a different stratum, is difficult but not, as in the caste system, impossible. People may change their "estates," as the levels are called, by obtaining a royal decree, by performing a special service, by joining the priesthood, or by marrying someone of a higher position.

The feudal system existed throughout much of the world for many centuries, and it still remains in certain areas, particularly in parts of the Middle East, Southeast Asia, and Latin America. For example, the Latin American hacienda, consisting of a landlord and peasants, or peons, who work the land, has many feudal characteristics.

In such societies, there is very little change from generation to generation. Landowners, for example, live in fine homes in much the same way as their parents and grandparents. Peasants serve the landowning class in the owners' houses as well as in the fields, just as their ancestors did.

This type of division rests on custom and tradition as well as on the unequal division of power and wealth. In a feudal system many of the poor peons honor the landowners because such people have always been the powerful ones in the society. In a closed, traditional society, people don't ask whether a certain division is fair or whether it can be changed by hard work. They assume that it has to be the way it is and always has been. (See pages 79–80 for a discussion of ascribed statuses.)

Societies with feudal characteristics usually produce only enough to feed and care for their individual members. Since they do not have sophisticated machinery, fertilizers, or modern farming techniques, they rarely produce any extra crops that can be sold or traded for money or other goods. As long as the land yields enough for the owner and the peasants, there is little incentive to increase production.

Societies with closed stratification systems, then, have four major traits:

1. Few changes take place from one generation to another.
2. People rely heavily on tradition for their beliefs and values.
3. Social status is almost always ascribed rather than achieved.
4. People usually produce only enough to satisfy their own communal requirements.

Transitional Systems

Few completely closed systems exist today. Modernization has taken place in almost every area of the world, and even the most feudal societies have undergone some changes. They have been exposed to new ideas by the presence of colonial powers, through contact with foreign armies during wars, and by revolutionary groups seeking to change society. Many formerly closed societies are now *transitional societies*.

In transitional societies, many people still live in much the same way as peasants do in traditional societies. The upper class lives a life of privilege, with little change from generation to generation.

Transitional societies, unlike traditional ones, have a growing middle class and an expanding urban labor force. Many of the workers have formed groups to further their own interests and are active in political parties. Yet large numbers of people are unable to achieve a decent standard of living. Chances for mobility continue to be extremely limited for the masses of poor who are uneducated and unskilled.

In a transitional system such as that of Egypt or the Philippines, income, prestige, and power remain very unevenly divided. The upper class and much of the middle class live well, while large numbers of lower-class people live in dire poverty. The total wealth of a transitional system is often quite limited, leaving little for the members of the lowest strata. If 60 percent of the people have only 20 percent of national income, they are probably living in extreme poverty. Malnutrition, disease, and high rates of infant mortality are common results.

Although class divisions are not quite as clear-cut as in closed societies, people in transitional societies still possess *class consciousness,* or awareness of their position in the social system. In a transitional system, people often associate with others who share their circumstances. Yet, unlike closed systems, transitional systems offer the promise of economic, social, and political change. Many people move from one part of the country to another in search of greater opportunity. Mobility from one class to another is made possible by expanding educational and economic opportunities. Some national governments provide jobs and encourage the belief that all classes will benefit from their programs.

As people in a transitional system see others getting better jobs or homes, their own hopes for improving their lot rise. People in all classes become aware that a greater share of society's wealth might be theirs if they could work together to get it. They no longer accept class divisions as unchanging. This awareness often leads to conflict among classes.

REVIEW AND APPLICATION

1. *IDENTIFY:* Social stratification, caste system, untouchables, feudal estate system, transitional societies, class consciousness.
2. What is a closed system of stratification? Cite examples.
3. (a) How is mobility accomplished in a traditional system? (b) What type of production and distribtuion is characteristic of this system?
4. (a) How does a transitional system differ from a traditional one? (b) What is one possible danger arising from a transitional state of development?
5. Describe the caste system of India. What was Mahatma Gandhi's role in trying to change this system? Were Gandhi's efforts successful? How?
6. Describe the feudal estate system. How might people change their estates?
7. What are the four major traits of societies with closed stratification systems?
8. What are some of the ways in which people in a transitional society can achieve social mobility?

CRITICAL THINKING: Which of the following do you think most people in a transitional society value: tradition, modernity, mobility, stability, service, power, the rural life, or urban opportunities? Explain your response.

2 Stratification in Industrial Societies

Strata exist in industrial societies, but there people have a significant chance of moving from one level to another. In these "open" societies, status is, ideally, achieved rather than ascribed. People who have ambition, skill, and talent are thought to be able to rise above the level into which they were born. In its most open form, this type of system is correctly called a *meritocracy,* because a person's social position is supposed to depend solely on merit, or achievement.

When sociologists analyze how Americans are ranked, they use the term *class.* Sociologists define a social class as a group of people who share a similar rank or place in society, who have similar opportunities, and who share many values and ways of behaving. Class differences appear in the training of children and in the goals parents set for their children. Among the various social classes, one can see differences in life style, values, opportunities, and goals.

Studying the stratification of a social system helps sociologists answer many questions about a society: In any system, who are the rich, respected, and powerful? Who are the in-betweens? Who are the poor, rejected, unemployed, and unemployable? What problems are raised by social stratification? What solutions are offered to these problems?

How is a society divided into social classes? People can be classified into any number of groups, according to the amount of income and the type of jobs they have. Using this as the measure, one can roughly lump together a small group of people who are very rich into a single upper class. The middle class includes owners of small businesses, professionals, managers, and civil servants. The working class is composed mainly of the large number of people doing manual labor in manufacturing, mining, construction, and other industries. The lower class includes poor people who are jobless or who work from time to time at very low-paid service or unskilled jobs.

Knowing someone's social class can help you understand his or her behavior. Imagine that you are a member of a research team made up of a psychologist, a guidance counselor, an educator, and a sociologist. Together you are studying the career goals of

People who work mainly with their hands, whether on their own or for a giant corporation, are usually considered members of the working class. Below, a steelworker (on the left) and a lobsterman (on the right) each bring a feeling of pride to their quite different occupations.

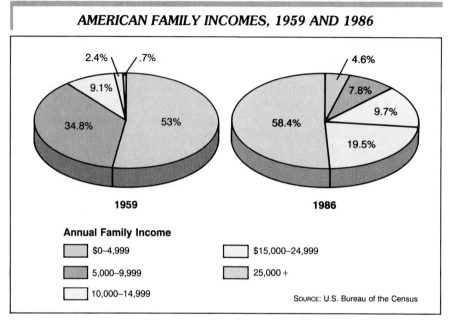

AMERICAN FAMILY INCOMES, 1959 AND 1986

1959

2.4% .7%
9.1%
34.8% 53%

1986

4.6%
7.8%
9.7%
58.4% 19.5%

Annual Family Income

$0–4,999 $15,000–24,999

5,000–9,999   25,000+

10,000–14,999

SOURCE: U.S. Bureau of the Census

GRAPH SKILL   The graphs show the percentage of American families at various income levels in 1959 and 1986. Inflation is responsible for much of the increase in income. Do you see any alterations that might not be due to inflation?

high school students. You want to know why some students choose to attend college while others do not go beyond high school. One member of the team finds that mental ability is only a partial answer. Some excellent students in the group plan to get jobs that require very little training.

The sociologist suggests that social class may be a major factor. Those who come from middle- and upper-class families may be more likely to plan for college than sons and daughters of working- or lower-class families. To verify this, you must be able to identify the social class of each student. Social scientists faced with such a problem often find that a good, if rough, measure of social class is family income.

Wealth

At the beginning of the 1980s, the median family income in the United States was about $17,000. Even allowing for inflation, the overall standard of living for Americans

was rising. The graphs on this page show the distribution of income of families in both 1959 and 1986. The top income group includes very different sorts of families, from families with two wage earners to those whose incomes are above $1 million and derived from stocks, rents, and similar sources.

If income and wealth are used as the measure of social class, the stratification system in the United States can be pictured as a diamond, as in the diagram. It has a relatively small percentage of poor people at the bottom and a very small percentage of rich people at the top. Most people live neither in serious poverty nor in great riches.

In some societies, the wealthy—mainly business owners and landowners—make up a very small percentage of the population but control a large percentage of the wealth. Urban white-collar workers make up a middle class and receive a lesser percentage of the total wealth. Poor urban and rural workers comprise the bulk of the population. Such a stratification system is often shown as a pyramid, as in the diagram on this page. This distribution of wealth exists in many transitional societies.

High income and high prestige tend to go together, as do low income and low prestige. Those who are high on one scale are usually high on the other. In a complex system like our own, however, this is not always true. An owner of a trash-collection business might earn more than a teacher, but the teacher tends to have more prestige because of the nature of the work. Plumbers, electricians, and carpenters often earn as much as or more than some managers, social workers, and librarians. But in our society, skilled workers have less prestige than white-collar workers. In the United States, it is important not only how much one earns but also how one earns it.

？ If you were to try to divide the American population into upper, middle, and lower classes strictly on the basis of family income,

"This is my executive suite and this is my executive vice-president, Ralph Anderson, and my executive secretary, Adele Eades, and my executive desk and my executive carpet and my executive wastebasket and my executive ashtray and my executive pen set and my . . ."

SOURCE: Drawing by H. Martin; © 1974 The New Yorker Magazine, Inc.

what figures would you use in making your divisions? If you have difficulty in deciding where to draw the class lines, what might be the reason?

Prestige

Prestige is the honor or respect that a person is given by others in the community. Income, wealth, job, and power all contribute to one's standing in society. Prestige is often related to the job one holds. Doctors, judges, and scientists have high-prestige positions. Street cleaners, janitors, and ditchdiggers have low-prestige jobs in our society.

Prestige tends to be based on personal judgment, not on census figures or other precise measures. It is based on how most people in a society feel about an activity. One job may have great prestige in one society and very little prestige in another.

The following table shows some of the results of a nationwide survey of prestige rankings. In 1964, sociologists Robert Hodge, Paul Siegel, and Peter Rossi chose a random sample of more than three thousand adults across the United States and asked them to

CHART SKILL   *What are the differences between these two societies?*

DIAGRAMMING SOCIAL STRATIFICATION

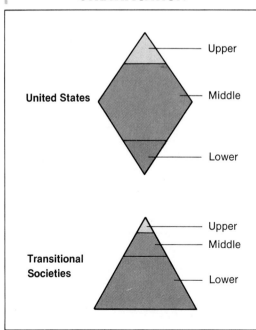

rate ninety occupations commonly found in the United States. (See the Appendix for a discussion of sampling.)

Participants were asked to rate occupations as excellent, good, average, below average, and poor. Researchers tallied the results

CHART SKILL   *Study this list of occupations. Which occupation ranks highest in prestige? Lowest? How does the education required for the five top-ranked occupations differ from that required for the five lowest-ranked occupations?*

OCCUPATIONAL PRESTIGE IN THE UNITED STATES

Rank	Occupation	Rank	Occupation
1.0	U.S. Supreme Court justice	46.0	Newspaper columnist
2.0	Physician	47.0	Police officer
3.5	Nuclear physicist	48.0	Daily newspaper reporter
5.5	State governor	49.5	Radio announcer
8.0	U.S. congressional representative	49.5	Bookkeeper
8.0	College professor	51.5	Insurance agent
11.0	Chemist	53.0	Carpenter
11.0	Lawyer	54.5	Manager of a small store in a city
14.0	Dentist	57.0	Mail carrier
14.0	Architect	57.0	Railroad conductor
17.5	Psychologist	57.0	Traveling salesperson for a wholesale concern
17.5	Minister	59.0	Plumber
17.5	Member of the board of directors of a large corporation	62.5	Barber
17.5	Mayor of a large city	62.5	Factory machine operator
21.5	Priest	62.5	Lunch stand owner-operator
21.5	Airplane pilot	62.5	Garage mechanic
24.5	Banker	67.0	Truck driver
29.5	Accountant for a large business	70.0	Store clerk
29.5	Public school teacher	72.5	Restaurant cook
31.5	Owner of a factory that employs about 100 people	74.0	Nightclub singer
31.5	Building contractor	75.0	Filling-station attendant
34.5	Symphony orchestra musician	77.5	Coal miner
34.5	Novelist	80.5	Restaurant waiter
39.0	Electrician	80.5	Taxi driver
44.0	Farm owner-operator	83.0	Janitor
44.0	Funeral director	83.0	Bartender
44.0	City government welfare worker	87.0	Sharecropper
		88.0	Garbage collector
		90.0	Shoe shiner

SOURCE: Adapted from Robert W. Hodge, Paul M. Siegel, and Peter H. Rossi, "Occupational Prestige in the United States, 1925–1963," *American Journal of Sociology.* Most recent survey conducted.

In the United States, high income and high prestige tend to go together. Corporate executives rank high on any occupational-prestige scale. However, professionals often have greater prestige, even when their incomes are lower than those of corporate executives.

and gave each job a score depending on the number of times it came up in each category. From these data, they ranked the ninety occupations in order of their prestige in American society. The table shows the ranking of some of those ninety occupations. A survey taken in the 1970s roughly confirmed these findings. Except for changes due to the addition of new professions, such as astronaut and computer programmer, a similar poll would probably produce much the same results today.

Sources other than occupation can also contribute to a person's prestige in the community. A very civic-minded person, for example, might be more highly thought of than someone else with the same job. In a small town in Kansas, the owner of a candy and newspaper store was elected mayor. His prestige went up greatly, even though he continued to run the same business and made little extra money. His new public position made him one of the most respected people in that town.

A rich person whose money was inherited or won in a lottery may have high prestige even though he or she does not hold a high-prestige job. On the other hand, wealthy people whose families made their money several generations ago often look down on the "new rich," people who may have as much money as they do but lack the education, the upbringing, or the reputation of the old rich families. Families that are not socially accepted despite their high incomes often make a great effort to send their children to the "best schools" and to expose them to travel, art, music, and the accepted sports. They hope to give their children the kind of upbringing that will make them attractive to the upper circles even if the parents themselves are not.

In some societies, the most religious people have the greatest prestige. Holy men in India, for example, are highly esteemed for leading a holy life with few or no material belongings. Other social systems, such as those of France and Great Britain, honor scholars

Prestige and influence can be based on longstanding wealth and tradition, even when power is not formally exercised. Prince Charles and Queen Elizabeth, as members of the British royal family, have this kind of prestige which often expresses itself through elaborate formal ceremonies and pageants.

and poets. In such countries as Portugal and Argentina, serving in the army brings great prestige and honor.

In the United States, success is often measured in material terms—both in actual income and in possessions conspicuously displayed. Of course, many people receive high salaries because they have jobs that are considered important. Many captains of industry make well over a quarter of a million dollars a year. National television anchorpeople, who also have influential jobs, make more than a million. However, so do some sports figures. Thus, income and prestige may or may not be related to power.

CASE STUDY: *Power: Three Case Studies*

Power is the ability to control, and, along with income and prestige, it is one of the factors affecting social status. In order to understand any stratification system, then, it is necessary to understand the sources and dis-

tribution of power within it. The German sociologist and economist Max Weber identified three major bases of power in any political system: *traditional authority,* which is inherited; *charismatic authority,* which is based on the special personal qualities of particular leaders; and *rational-legal authority,* which is formally delegated to persons in particular positions.

Sources of Power People reach positions of power for a variety of reasons. The following three cases demonstrate this. As you read them, try to identify each person's source of power using Weber's terms.

Maria Swanson is a math teacher in her late forties. Many of her students see her as an exciting teacher who makes the classroom come alive.

"You can't fall asleep when she is at the front of the room," says one.

"She's always challenging you and making you think. Her range of knowledge is really fantastic. I've heard her argue with other teachers. There's no doubt that Ms. Swanson comes out on top," states another student.

"Swanson commands great respect from her fellow teachers," someone observes. "When she gets up to speak at a meeting, people listen. They know her remarks will be right to the point and will help the staff make a wise decision. She's a good person to have around."

? Does Swanson have power? If so, what is the source of her power? Would you call it traditional, charismatic, or rational-legal? Can you think of people you know who also have such power?

Harrison Butterfield is a quiet man, short and balding, who dresses in the conservative suits of a business executive. His schedule is set, and it never varies. Up at 6:00 A.M., he walks two miles each morning before breakfast. He reads the daily papers over coffee and carefully checks the financial news before going to his office.

Arriving exactly at 8:30, Butterfield goes over the mail with his secretary, who knows that he does not take part in the usual office chitchat. At 10:00, one or two of the younger managers report to him on progress or problems. Butterfield listens carefully and freely advises them on what to do. The younger managers have learned from experience that Butterfield expects them to take his advice.

The younger people do not always agree with him, but they respect Butterfield's experience and admit his ability to influence their careers. The people Butterfield likes move up the line. Those who don't work well with him often find themselves looking for other jobs.

? What is the source of Butterfield's power? How does the nature of his power differ from that held by Swanson?

Marjorie Reading holds no formal position, but she is known and welcomed by school and business groups. For several generations, her wealthy family has invested in good business opportunities and made large gifts to worthy projects. Several times a month she meets with college presidents and city officials, who attempt to interest her in their newest ideas to build a sports center, a new language lab, a school to train public health officials, or some other project. Reading always listens and often suggests ways to improve their planning.

? Does Reading have power? If so, what is the source of her power? How does her power differ from that exercised by Swanson and Butterfield? How is her power like that exercised by Swanson and Butterfield?

You will read more about power and authority in political systems in Chapter 8. Personal qualities, such as charm, leadership ability, speaking ability, or special knowledge or skills, can give people power. Other sources of power are vested in certain statuses people hold. Police officer, president, general, and director are a few examples of statuses that give a person power over certain situations and over the people involved with them. Finally, one of the chief sources of power is the possession of wealth.

As you might expect, these sources of power are often linked. For example, a popular senator with good speaking ability holds a powerful position as head of a major committee of the Senate. It is likely that both popularity and position contribute to the senator's power.

Is There a Power Elite? Groups that hold a great deal of social power in a society are known as elites. Directors of large corporations who control vast sums of money and make major policy decisions are an economic

In non-Western societies, power is almost always vested in the status a person holds. Family prestige and wealth from oil have made this Saudi Arabian influential.

Wealth in industrialized societies is often conspicuously displayed through a luxurious style of life and by taking part in expensive leisure activities such as polo.

elite. High-ranking officers and Pentagon officials in the United States armed forces make up a military elite.

? Can you name two other elites in American society? Are there elites in your community and your school?

For a quarter of a century, sociologists have disagreed about the nature of elites in American society. Some sociologists think that one small, powerful group in American society makes almost all the major decisions. They argue that men from similar backgrounds and with similar interests control all the major institutions. Not only do these generals, corporation executives, and high government officials go to the same parties and belong to the same country clubs, but they often move from one position of power to another. Corporation presidents become Cabinet officers or heads of regulatory agencies. In changing jobs, they continue to serve the interests of the businesses they know so well.

Sociologist C. Wright Mills, who coined the term "the power elite," quoted a famous corporation president who later became a Cabinet officer as saying, "What's good for General Motors is good for the country." This, said Mills, showed that a small group of men from the military, industry, and government who make the major policy decisions for the country really believe that the government should have the same interests as major corporations and Pentagon officials. Some observers claim that Mills missed the point of the Cabinet officer's remarks; they say what was meant was that policies that aid big business are good for the American economy in general.

A second group of sociologists, including David Riesman, disagrees with Mills. These sociologists think that many different interest groups compete to make major policy decisions. According to this theory, these groups exercise control by serving as "veto groups." Union elites vie with business elites. Different businesses often have different needs and don't always act in concert. Professional elites hold influence in certain areas and often have very different world views. Movie and TV stars form an elite that sometimes enters the decision-making arena.

REVIEW AND APPLICATION

1. *IDENTIFY:* Class, meritocracy, traditional authority, charismatic authority, rational-legal authority.
2. What criteria do sociologists use when defining a person's class?
3. What are the three major sources of stratification in industrial societies?
4. How does the stratification system of the United States differ from that of transitional societies?
5. What is prestige? What factors contribute to a person's prestige?
6. What are the three bases of power according to Max Weber?
7. How does C. Wright Mills interpret the statement, "What's good for General Motors is good for the country"? How does David Riesman interpret this quotation? Are their interpretations different? What viewpoint do you support?

CRITICAL THINKING: Compare the table of occupations on page 104 with what you have read about prestige in other countries. Which occupations on the table would have the most prestige if the criteria in the United States were the same as in India? if the criteria were the same as in Great Britain?

3 Stratification in the United States

Now let's look at social classes in the United States. As you read about them, note how closely the ways of life described here fit the class structure of your own town or city. What changes would you make in these descriptions to have them reflect your own town or city more accurately?

Social Class

Many people spend all their lives in the same social class. They may have little opportunity to get to know members of other classes. The major social classes in the United States are described here. With which classes have you had any contact?

The Upper Class In our society, a small group of well-to-do families—including owners of large businesses, top executives, and those with large investments—live in the most beautiful homes. Members of the upper class have a life style and a self-image that mark them as VIPs—"very important people." Some of them were born into wealthy families. Through years of luxury, fine education, and travel, they have assumed a style of gracious living that may include collecting art or antiques. Others may have made their money more recently through business or professional work, but they have taken on the values and style of those who were born rich and influential. The upper class is often divided between "old money" and "new money." Those whose families have been well-to-do for generations often look down on families whose wealth has been recently acquired.

Upper-class people serve on boards of directors of corporations, universities, banks, and charities. They are consulted when important decisions are made. Reporters talk about them in the society pages of the newspaper, and they are well known beyond the local community. Their children often go to costly private schools and colleges, where they mix with others of their social class.

G. William Domhoff, a social scientist, has spent years studying this small but important group of people. Domhoff feels that the upper class has the strongest class consciousness of all Americans. Its members think of themselves as part of a special group that makes them different from everyone else. By educating their children in special schools, by vacationing at a few expensive resorts, and most of all by intermarriage, they keep this group feeling alive.

Those families listed in the Social Register, a directory of upper-class American families, typically hold "coming-out" parties to introduce their daughters to society. These students at a private school in South Carolina await their introduction.

Members of the upper class are very powerful in the economy and the government. In spite of their small numbers, they are the single most influential group in corporations, foundations, and institutes that study and advise on public policy. Through these positions they influence the policy of both business and government.

The Upper Middle Class Living near and sometimes among the upper class are people close to the top of the social system. They are professional and business people who generally think of themselves as educated, successful leaders of their local communities. Unlike that of the upper class, their wealth is rarely inherited, and they have no private fortunes. Since their high income comes directly from their work, careers are important to the upper middle class. Their careers in-

fluence their whole way of life. Even outside their jobs, they try to make the right contacts, are very concerned about their reputations, and often take an active part in community affairs. Very often leaders of major social institutions, such as clergy, school board members, and major political figures, are recruited from this group.

Most children of the upper middle class tend to stay in that class. Through education and changes in the economic system, newcomers also join its ranks. Children of upper-middle-class parents must have successful careers or risk downward mobility. Only the very rich can stay idle and still remain members of the same social class.

The children of the upper middle class are brought up to do well in school. Music lessons, summer camps, travel, and stylish clothes are a natural part of their lives. They expect to go to college and choose a career. If they do not do this, the family is disappointed.

The Lower Middle Class Who lives in the modest but well-kept neighborhoods? Shop owners, office workers who do not have high managerial positions, highly paid skilled workers, salespeople, government workers, and those who supervise laborers live there and comprise the lower middle class. Studies have shown that most members of the lower middle class have a high school education, perhaps with some college training. They generally have little influence in community affairs and politics. But they often belong to civic, church, and social groups.

Lower-middle-class people have often been singled out as "respectable." They stress moral values, religion, and working hard to get ahead. They tend to own their own homes, and they spend much time and money caring for their houses. They see themselves as a notch above most manual workers and strive to keep up that distinction.

The women often want to venture outside their family roles, but they resist any commitments that might keep them from meeting their families' needs. They usually seek jobs rather than careers or do volunteer work for organizations such as the PTA, which is geared toward their children's education and supports their main role as mothers.

One study of a middle-class community concluded that lower-middle-class ideas about the family extend to the way they regard government. Lower-middle-class people think government should be like a family—honest and upright; otherwise, it's "just politics." It is mainly for this group, the study maintained, that politicians running for election emphasize their own decency and honesty compared to the supposed immorality of their opponents.

The Working Class In the same neighborhood one finds the working class, the employees of local shops and factories. Assembly-line work and other semiskilled jobs require little formal education. While some workers, especially those who finish high school, may move into the middle class, the rate of upward mobility is not high. Some of their children may move into the middle class, but only a small number of workers are willing or able to give up the security of their weekly paychecks to prepare for better-paying, more highly skilled work.

Workers often belong to unions and believe that their economic advancement depends on collective bargaining with management. Although not all are active in union politics, working-class people are the ones who support the union by paying dues, voting for union-supported political candidates, and, when necessary, going out on strike. Leisure activities vary, but many relax by watching TV, bowling, participating in church-related activities, or following their favorite sports team.

Sociologist Peter Binzen, in a study of the working class, described a typical member as a "steady worker and a family man":

People in the lower middle class often place great value on owning their own homes. Many have moved out of central-city neighborhoods so their children will have a safe place to play.

Some working-class people own their own homes. They take pride in maintaining them and in making additions as their families grow.

High costs make it difficult for members of the working class to afford homes. Many working-class people live in apartments and form communities within cities.

He quit school in tenth grade to get a job. His wife, also a native of the area . . . was a better student than he was. . . . Their house and car are paid for. . . . The house is neat and better furnished than its plain gray exterior would lead one to expect. . . .

The husband described himself and his neighbors as "people who like to pay their own way. . . . compared to other sections, it is a decent place to raise children and to live. . . . Rich people have children that commit suicide, drive like maniacs, and are unruly. Rich people live on high parties and are social climbers. We are honest hard-working people with children we love dearly. . . . We are sick of reading in the paper where looters, arsonists, and murderers are allowed to do whatever they . . . please."

The Lower Class   Although friendships can easily form across different neighborhoods and backgrounds, few of the men and women described so far know the people who live in public-housing projects or in run-down dwellings in poorer areas. Some poor people are new to an area and cannot find steady jobs. They live on whatever low-paying work they can find or on welfare payments. Others are elderly or sick, or they may be single parents trying to raise young children on a very small budget. Lower-class people find it difficult to break out of the vicious circle in which they are caught.

One member of the lower class described his situation this way: "I've been scuffling for five years from morning to night and my kids don't have anything, my wife don't have anything, and I don't have anything. There," he said, gesturing down the hall to a bed, a sofa, a couple of chairs and a television set, all shabby, some broken, "there's everything I have and I'm having trouble holding onto that."

Poor education, poor health, and poor reputations make it hard for lower-class people to get good jobs. Trapped by poverty, some may begin to feel a sense of hopelessness. Since ill luck seems to follow them, they lack the motivation to learn the social and economic skills needed to move up the social ladder. As a result, lower-class neighborhoods are often plagued by street crime. Chapter 15 contains a fuller discussion of the complex causes of poverty and of the groups that are most likely to be affected by it.

Social Mobility

To understand any stratification system, one must analyze how much upward mobility it allows—that is, how much chance there is for individuals to get a larger share of wealth, prestige, and power. We have seen that some Americans have better chances than others to improve their social position. Children of upper-class parents are more likely to stay in the upper class because of better access to education, jobs, and material resources. On the other hand, we have all heard of people who worked their way up from poverty and became rich, powerful, and respected.

Mark Aguirre (left), Magic Johnson (right), and Isiah Thomas (bottom) are professional athletes who have seen the Horatio Alger story come true in their own lives. Here, at a basketball camp, they are helping youths develop their own skills.

Success, American Style At the turn of the century, Horatio Alger, Jr., wrote stories about American boys who went "from rags to riches" through hard work, honesty, and luck. Typically the stories contained dialogue such as the following between a young man and a wealthy woman whom he has saved from the sly tricks of a pickpocket. In this reading, the woman speaks to Ben, the young hero:

> "In this country, the fact that you are a poor boy will not stand in the way of your success. The most eminent men of the day, in all branches of business, and in all professions, were once poor boys. I dare say, looking at me, you don't suppose I ever knew anything of poverty."
>
> "No," said Ben.
>
> "Yet, I was the daughter of a bankrupt farmer and my husband was a clerk in a country store. I am not going to tell you how he came to the city and prospered, leaving me, at his death, rich beyond my needs. Yet that is his history and mine. Does it encourage you?"
>
> "Yes, it does," answered Ben earnestly.

Ben does make it, of course, and the novel ends happily. But are the Horatio Alger stories true to life?

How Mobile Are Americans? Just how much mobility is there in the United States, and how do sociologists measure it? There are no exact measures. However, sociologists have designed several indicators, or approximate measurements, to help them judge the amount of mobility. The chief method is to make an occupational rating scale. The scale compares fathers' and sons' occupations to see how much movement there is between generations from one job category to another.

Study the table on the next page. It gives some information about upward and downward mobility, but it does not tell the whole story. Farmers can be wealthy and influential, middle-class, or very poor. Some business people have great wealth and prestige in society. Others have less than some professionals or highly skilled workers. Still, it is

OCCUPATIONAL MOBILITY IN THE UNITED STATES

Job Categories of Fathers	Percentage of Sons in Each Job Category				
	Upper white-collar	Lower white-collar	Upper manual	Lower manual	Farm
Upper white-collar	52.0	16.0	13.8	17.1	1.1
Lower white-collar	42.3	19.7	15.3	21.9	0.8
Upper manual	29.4	13.0	27.4	29.0	1.1
Lower manual	22.5	12.0	23.7	40.8	1.0
Farm	17.5	7.8	22.7	37.2	14.8

SOURCE: Adapted from Robert M. Hauser and David L. Featherman, "Occupations and Social Mobility in the United States," Institute for Research on Social Poverty, 1976.

CHART SKILL   By examining this table, you can roughly estimate the amount of change in class from one generation to the next. Would you say there is little upward mobility? Moderate upward mobility? Or great upward mobility? What does the table fail to take into account?

possible to make some judgments about the life chances of children of those at the upper and lower ends of the social scale.

Which groups in the table have the greatest percentage of sons staying in the same job category? Which groups have the greatest mobility? Do all groups have a certain amount of upward mobility from fathers to sons? Is there downward mobility in all job categories?

In general, the findings in the table show that there is some mobility, both upward and downward, for every occupational group. But it is much more likely that a person will stay in the job category of his father or move only one notch up or down. It is unusual, though not impossible, to go either from rags to riches or from riches to rags.

REVIEW AND APPLICATION

1. Why does G. William Domhoff feel that the upper class has the strongest class consciousness of all Americans?

2. Describe the importance of a career to members of the upper-middle-class.

3. How do lower-middle-class women often see their roles? How do members of the lower middle class tend to view government?

4. Why might lower-class people be unable to break out of poverty?

5. What does Peter Binzen's study reveal about the way working-class people see themselves?

6. What were the topics of Horatio Alger's writings?

CRITICAL THINKING: In September Martha will start at the same law school that her father attended. Brian plans to work two shifts at a local factory, to save his earnings, and to buy a florist shop. Next week Bill will start his job at a local factory and attend his first union meeting. What assumptions has each of these young people made about getting ahead, and what social class is each aspiring to?

CHAPTER 5 REVIEW

Recap

In every society, there is inequality —that is, some people have higher social positions than others. Sociologists study the different ways in which societies are stratified, or divided into different levels known as strata; how much distance separates these strata; and how readily a person can move from one stratum to the next.

Nonindustrial societies tend to have traditional systems of stratification, such as the caste system of India or the near-feudal systems of some Latin American countries. In contrast to these closed systems, transitional societies allow some degree of social mobility. A growing middle class and class consciousness accompany the changing economy of a transitional society.

In industrialized, open societies, such as that of the United States, wealth, prestige, and power provide bases for stratification. Each social class tends to have a distinct style of life. While people may rise in social rank by means of talent and effort, most remain in the same class as their parents.

Key Terms

Define the following:

social stratification	social mobility	class
caste system	transitional society	traditional authority
untouchable	class consciousness	charismatic authority
feudal estate system	meritocracy	rational-legal authority

Applying Sociology

1. This chapter examined different types of stratification systems: the closed systems —including the caste system and the feudal system; the transitional systems; and our own fairly open system. With modernization taking place all over the world, formerly closed systems are opening up. And even the most open systems could probably become even more open by offering greater equality of opportunity. Most societies, therefore, are neither completely open nor completely closed.

   Comparing systems is a useful way to see characteristics more clearly. Where do you think the United States fits in the following chart? For each characteristic decide whether the United States is (1) very closed, (2) somewhat closed, (3) mixed, (4) somewhat open, or (5) very open.

2. Some of the more technologically advanced societies, such as that of Sweden, have entered a postindustrial phase of development. Research this stage and draw up a list of its advantages and disadvantages. Can any of the disadvantages be prevented?

3. Pick three people in the class to lead a discussion on sources of prestige in your school. Which of the following items are important sources of prestige: popularity, good grades, good looks, nice clothes, participation in sports? Do you think that the sources of prestige your school honors are appropriate ones?

CLOSED AND OPEN SYSTEMS OF STRATIFICATION

Closed	Open
Ascribed statuses, especially one's family or caste, most important in determining one's place in life	Achieved statuses (job, income, education) most important in determining one's place in life
Inequality thought to be permanent and right	Inequality present but subject to change; ideal of equality present
Distinct and long-lasting differences in life styles of classes	Differences in life styles among classes made less obvious by uniformity spread through the mass media and through mass-produced copies of elite styles
Strong class consciousness, with everyone knowing his or her place	Little class consciousness, everyone believing mobility is possible
Belief that fate determines social status and no change is possible	Belief that one's position is determined by accident but can be changed by individual effort
Friendship and socializing among classes disapproved and punished	Friendship and socializing among classes approved and attempted, although achieved only to a limited degree
Mobility disapproved and impossible	Mobility among classes approved, possible, and desirable
Many restraints on upward mobility including permanent imprint of the life style of one's family	Few restraints on upward mobility except lack of resources and being unable to erase marks of lower-class membership

Source: Adapted from Melvin M. Tumin, *Patterns of Society*, Little, Brown

4. Name half a dozen persons who enjoy high status in your community or in the United States chiefly because they exercise power. What seem to be the sources of their power?

5. Name two elites besides business and the military (a) at the national level; (b) at the community level. Is there an elite that has power in student affairs in your school?

6. Conduct a study to determine whether there is a power elite in your community. You might collect information on this topic in the following ways:

(a) Ask a cross section of people to name the most influential people in your community. Are the same people named over and over again?

(b) Study several key decisions recently made in the community—for instance, zoning, selection of candidates for office, or school policy. How many people took part? How many different social groups were represented? Which groups seem to have the power to "get their way"?

(c) Make a list of powerful positions in the community. How many women, minority-group members, and poor people hold such positions? Do you think decisions in your community would be different if members of these groups had more influence?

(d) When there is conflict over issues between major businesses and the town government, what people are involved in the conflict? Who is involved when the conflict is between business and labor? Are any other interest groups involved?

Extended Readings

John Elkins, "Out of Time," *American Way*, December 15, 1987, pp. 16–19.

1. What groups within American society is the author discussing?
2. In what different ways does time affect the economic structure of our society.

Peter I. Rose, "Colonists and Coneheads," *Salt*, August 1987, pp. 6–7.

1. Define the various groups that the author describes in the article.

2. What could a sociologist learn from studying a small town's social stratification?

Elliot Liebow, *Tally's Corner*, Little Brown, 1967, pp. 29–71.

1. Why does the truck driver believe the men do not want to work?
2. What relation does class have to the men's attitude about work?

Social Studies Skills

Completing a chart to compare social classes
Charts are helpful tools for comparing related information at a glance. Create a chart comparing the five major social classes discussed in section 3. Add categories to examine each aspect of each class's social behavior. Complete the chart using facts from pages 109 to 112. Analyze the data in your completed chart. What comparisons can you make?

Critical Thinking

Evaluating Cause and Effect: Low income people tend to vote less frequently than high income people. Explain what you think causes this lower rate of voting.

UNIT APPLICATION

Hacienda for Sale

About twenty years ago, a newspaper in Bolivia carried the following advertisement: "For sale, on the main highway a half hour from the capital city—hacienda with 500 acres of land, 50 sheep, much water, and 20 peons."

Imagine this scenario. Don Pedro, a prospective buyer, reads the ad and goes to view the property. Don Luis, the owner, shows him around and then hands him a paper listing the responsibilities of the peons and those of the owner:

PAYMENTS AND DUTIES OF THE PEONS

Crops	10 percent of harvest
Livestock	10 percent of lambs or other offspring
Field labor in owner's fields	15 days per month
Domestic labor in house	1 week at a time in rotation with other peon families; may be performed by wife or grown daughter
Care of owner's animals	2–4 weeks per year and raising one pig for owner
Transport of owner's crops to market	Total responsibility; if insufficient mules available, peon rents mules and pays with 5–6 days labor
Chopping firewood for owner's use	Total responsibility; usually requires about 10 days per year
Average total days per year worked for hacienda	180 days
Extra services performed by women and children	Weaving and spinning wool; scaring birds away from ripening crops

DUTIES OF THE OWNER

Provide seed for sowing annually

Allow each family to use a small- to medium-sized plot of cultivated land and the use of pasture land

Keep a store on hacienda where peons can exchange crops for food and clothing and get credit against next year's crops

Serve as godfather at baptism of peon's children

Keep a small chapel for religious ceremonies

Keep a cemetery on the grounds

After studying the paper, Don Pedro says, "That looks fair. You offer the peons security and supervision in return for their services and devotion. But what happens if they don't grow the promised amount or if they should try to leave and work for a hacienda that requires less payment?"

"Well," Don Luis replies, "if a lazy or incompetent peon cannot meet his labor or payment obligations, we take objects of value from him. Usually these are blankets, cattle, or pigs. At winter's end when I return from our city home, or from traveling abroad, I usually take an inventory to see who is unable to make the agreed-on payments.

"As for leaving to work for other haciendas, this is very unlikely. Few of the peons know how to read, so they don't learn of other chances. This is the home of their fathers and grandfathers. My cousins who own the neighboring estate use roughly the same system I do. If some of the peons act up, my trusted foreman uses some form of physical punishment. But we do not whip as harshly as Don Reyes, whom you might have heard of. Don Reyes does not know how to manage his peons."

Using and Analyzing Concepts

1. On the basis of the evidence, which of the following statements about the hacienda system are probably true and which are probably false?

   (a) "Master" and "servant" roles characterize the relationship between landlord and peon.
   (b) If peons do not like their treatment, they are free to move away.
   (c) Peons are born into their social class and have almost no chance for upward mobility.
   (d) The landlord sees the peons as people who should be treated fairly and offers them the chance for education and promotion.

2. On the Bolivian hacienda there is no chance that one of the peasants can ever become a landlord. Identify some factors that make it impossible for this to happen.
3. What social class seems to be totally absent?
4. Show that the hacienda society has a closed stratification system by answering these questions about it:

   (a) What social classes are there?
   (b) What factors determine class status?
   (c) Which of these statuses are ascribed rather than achieved?
   (d) Why would the peasants accept such a system even to the point of wanting the landlord to be godfather to their children?

5. Why is there no mention of farm equipment in the ad? How would the use of machinery change the workers' roles on the farm?
6. What is the name of the social system described in this exercise?

SOCIAL INSTITUTIONS

Unit Focus

Sociologists view social institutions—those organizations set up to meet various social needs—as distinct but interrelated systems. This unit examines the five most important social institutions: the family, religion, the educational system, government, and the economic system.

In general, each of these five parts or subsystems performs a specific social function. The family has what sociologists have referred to as a *sustaining function;* it serves to reproduce and nurture the species. Religion and education have *maintaining functions;* they offer explanations for the unknown and teach the things that are knowable. Government and the economic system, on the other hand, have *controlling functions;* they regulate people's activities and influence their political and economic behavior. This unit focuses on the functions of the principal social institutions.

Applying Sociology

- With which social institutions do you have the most interaction?
- What are some of the ways in which your family serves a sustaining function?
- What role does the United States education system play in your life?
- How does the United States economic system affect your life?

The educational system is one of the five major social institutions of our society.

121

CHAPTER

6

The Family

Chapter Preview

- **Before you read,** look up the following key terms in the glossary to become familiar with their definitions:

matrilocal residence   patrilineal descent   matrilineal descent
patrilocal residence   bilateral descent   neolocal descent

- **As you read,** think about answers to the following questions:

1. How has the American family changed in the last 100 years?
2. Why do Americans seem to prefer to marry for love rather than on the basis of arrangements made by family?
3. Are the parental roles of mothers and fathers culturally or biologically determined? Why?
4. Why is the divorce rate in the U.S. higher than in any other country in the world?

Chapter Focus

Many social scientists believe that the biology of human beings makes some kind of family organization necessary. Babies have a lengthy period of dependency, and all societies must protect and socialize their young.

There is an old saying, "You can choose your friends but not your relatives." This is largely true, for we don't choose our parents. Parenthood itself is well defined by norms. The role definition of "parent" usually includes the notion of authority over children; that of "child" includes obeying and being respectful toward parents.

This chapter discusses some historical forces that have affected the structure and functions of the family. It examines courtship, marriage, parenthood, divorce, and other aspects of family life.

Using Sociologists' Tools

- **Observe** the extent to which parents influence their childrens' lives.
- **Describe** the ways some parents might put pressure on their children to behave in particular situations.
- **Analyze** the responses of three of your friends who face parental pressure to get good grades, play sports, or attend the "right" college.
- **Predict** what would happen if parents did not assume the responsibility of leading or guiding their children.

Despite shifts in the size and nature of the family, our need for love and attention from other family members is unchanged.

1 History and Functions of the Family

The family is currently the subject of much scholarly research. Some observers feel that the future of the family is uncertain. Others view changes in the family as characteristic of an institution that has always been subject to historical forces.

Questions about the family tend to stir up strong feelings and controversy. For example, some social analysts see the move today away from the traditional "Father-knows-best," patriarchal family—in which power resides with the husband—as a healthy trend. They argue that the modern American family provides women and children with greater opportunity for growth and development than ever before. Other social critics, however, see such current trends as the increases in divorce and teenage pregnancies as evidence of decadence in a society that increasingly condones self-centeredness and tolerates irresponsible behavior.

? In your opinion, do any aspects of family life seem to be changing? What aspects are likely to remain the same?

Changes in the Family

Certain needs of infants have remained constant throughout the course of human history. So has the need of society to teach the young how to become contributing members as they grow older. While families still fulfill these basic needs, in many parts of the world the functions of the family have changed during the last 150 years.

Some governments have tried to alter the pattern of family life to make it serve changing goals. For example, Soviet and communist Chinese leaders have tried to replace people's traditional family values and norms. Instead of centering their lives around family

123

ties, people were to depend on the community and to dedicate themselves to the state.

The goals of the Soviets and Chinese have not been fully achieved. Certain functions continue to be met in traditional ways in spite of pressures from the authorities. Nevertheless, parents in Russia and China have lost much of their former power and are seen less as guides and more as sources of love. In traditional China, for example, parents chose the marriage partner and wielded great power over daughters and daughters-in-law. Now young couples no longer live with the parents and under their control. Schools and other government-sponsored organizations have become more important in transmitting the values and norms of societies to children.

In American society and in many other industrial nations, change has been less deliberate, although almost as dramatic. The family once served as an economic unit of production. This situation is now rare. The family has gradually become smaller as the average number of children has declined. As the roles of parents and children have changed, other institutions have begun to meet many of the needs formerly filled by the family.

Sociologists have traditionally explained the major changes in family size, structure, and functions that came about in the late eighteenth century as a consequence of industrialization. When most people lived on farms, children contributed their labor to help the family prosper, tending livestock

Earlier in this century, the average American family was much larger than it is today.

and working in the fields. But the invention of new farm machinery meant that fewer people were needed to grow food. Many people abandoned the farms for the cities, where new jobs in manufacturing were opening up. People in small villages began to be influenced by new ideas. Although urban families still kept their ties to relatives, they also had much more contact with people who were not kin.

Other major changes occurred. Within the family, old forms of authority came under challenge. Before industrialization, sons had depended on their fathers to will them land or at least to help them establish themselves on new farms. As families moved to cities and more fathers began to work long hours away from home in factories, their influence over their sons declined. Sons left home and sought their own fortunes. Mobility from one location to another became commonplace.

Children were no longer essential as laborers. As families moved off farms and child-labor laws limited children's participation in the labor market, the young became an expense rather than an economic help. More children lived to adulthood, too, as improvements in medicine and sanitation reduced disease. Thus, it was no longer necessary to have many babies in order to guarantee that some would survive.

At the same time, the growth of medical knowledge about reproduction, the legalization of birth control, and the lessening opposition to birth control by major religious organizations made it possible to choose how many children to have. These changes had important results in the course of this century. For example, as late as 1900, the average woman had 8 pregnancies. In 1980, the average number of pregnancies per woman was 2.2.

? What is the ideal number of children for a family to have today? Why?

Social scientists have long believed that the changes that occurred in England and the United States following industrialization would be repeated wherever industrialization took place. Therefore, the following changes should occur in all industrializing countries:

Many modern families are smaller than those of previous generations.

1. A fall in the death rate
2. A loosening of old kinship ties and ties to the land
3. A decline in the old forms of authority, such as father, church, and community elders
4. Increased mobility, both geographic and social
5. Increasing isolation of parents and children as they cease to share work
6. An increase in individual isolation
7. A shift in the economic function of the family from one of production to one of consumption
8. A greater emphasis on the family as a source of emotional gratification

In some industrializing countries, however, not all these changes have occurred. Although there have been some changes in the family in most such countries, historians now disagree about the causes. Did changes in family size and values follow or precede industrialization? Some evidence indicates that

Today families may no longer share work, as families did in preindustrial societies, but they often share recreation. In the United States, male and female family members may enjoy the same activities.

the trend toward smaller families was not brought about by industrialization. Rather, this and other changes may have resulted from shifts in political and economic institutions, such as altered patterns of land ownership, new religious movements, or technological developments. These shifts, in turn, may have made industrialization possible.

Whether changes in the family come before or after industrialization, however, once they occur, the industrialized society applies pressures for them to continue. Modern society, for example, needs people who can move from place to place easily—people with geographic mobility. They must be able to change locations to find work. For example, an engineer may go to school in southern California, but work first in Seattle, then in Houston, then in North Carolina—wherever the jobs are. The engineer's mobility makes it more difficult for him or her to keep close ties with distant family members.

Family ties may also be weakened by a person's moving up the social ladder—by so-

cial mobility. For example, the engineer may achieve greater wealth, prestige, and power than others in his or her family. The engineer's friends and ways of living are likely to be changed as a result. Brothers, sisters, and cousins may not reach the same level in society, even though they seemed much alike as children.

On the other hand, people may find it even more difficult to keep in touch with old friends. In a mobile, impersonal society, family ties continue to be important. Relatives often travel long distances for weddings, funerals, and important holidays. Parents and children continue to be responsible for one another. Some family norms seem not to have changed.

Support Systems for the Family

One aspect of the family that society's values and norms have continued to support is the traditional union of two people in a marriage. In all societies, marriage, the beginning of a new family, is sanctioned by elders, by representatives of the state, or by religious authorities. The illustration on this page shows some marital residence patterns—the *patrilocal residence*, the *matrilocal residence*, and the *neolocal residence*—that are supported in different societies by norms. *Polyandry*, the practice of having two or more husbands, and *polygyny*, the practice of having two or more wives, are other family structures in some societies. The term *polygamy* is used to describe both these forms of plural marriage.

In the United States, marriage is sanctioned by the state, which grants a license, and usually by a formal religious group as well. Most wedding ceremonies are still performed by the clergy in a manner prescribed by a given religion. In many Christian denominations, marriage is a sacrament, and marital vows have sacred meaning.

Marriage and ancestry together form the base of kinship. Most of the obligations that

Family residence patterns differ among and within societies. In patrilocal residence, the husband and wife live with the husband's family; in matrilocal residence, the couple lives with the wife's family. The pattern is neolocal when a couple lives in a new location.

FAMILY RESIDENCE PATTERNS

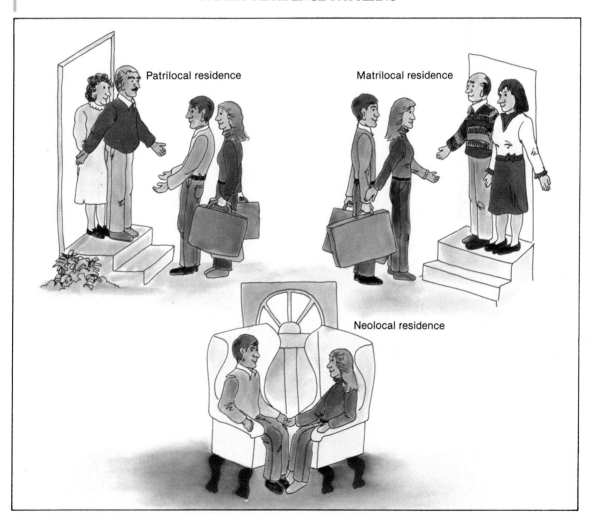

Patrilocal residence

Matrilocal residence

Neolocal residence

go with being a family member are too important to be left to chance, so they are codified, or made into laws. Parents have legal and financial responsibility for their children and to each other. For example, if one partner incurs a debt that he or she is unable to pay, the other partner is responsible for the debt. When a marriage breaks up, a court decides on child custody and support and whether there should be alimony. Family life may seem to be a private affair, but many of its aspects are shaped by cultural norms and are subject to public regulation.

In most Western societies, the family also serves as the means for transmitting property from one generation to another. In-

Research on the family has shown that the loss of a family member through death while children were still young was common in the past. This happens less often today. Here a Hasidic Jew and his grandchild enjoy each other's company. A century ago, the shorter average lifespan might have made such sharing impossible.

heritance, regulated by laws of kinship, usually goes from parent to children or to other close relatives. Kinship is determined by a society's rules of descent. In *bilateral descent,* children trace their ancestry through both parents. Descent that is traced through the father's line is *patrilineal descent.* When it is traced through the mother's line, it is *matrilineal descent.* In the United States, society recognizes parents on both sides, and laws of inheritance follow the bilateral pattern.

Families bequeath more than property. Sociologists have demonstrated that the family plays an important role in determining how far a person will go in life. Education, talent, and opportunity are factors given or transmitted to individuals by the family. Families are the main source of personal development. Through the family, both material benefits and values are passed on from generation to generation.

How important do you think families are in influencing the positions their offspring attain in later life? Recall what you learned in the chapter on social stratification.

Facts and Fictions

It has been commonly accepted that the family in the era of our great-great-grandparents was usually an *extended family*—three generations living under one roof or perhaps in separate houses on the same street. Some say the family of the past was closer, more helpful and loving, than families are today. But are these assumptions true?

Researchers on the family have come up with some unexpected findings. For instance, historians suggest that it was very rare for several generations of a family to live together. Throughout Western history, most people simply did not live to see their grandchildren grow up. One study shows that as recently as a hundred years ago, life expectancy in Massachusetts was about forty-seven years in rural towns; in places with populations of 10,000 or more, it was thirty-seven years for females and forty-one years for males. One out of three children did not live until the age of five.

In fact, even the *nuclear family*—a mother, a father, and their unmarried children—was often disrupted. Many women died in childbirth, which meant that many families had either single parents or stepparents. Although some people did live to be very old, most families in early America suffered the loss of a loved one through death while children were still young.

Evidence also challenges the view that families of the past were more congenial and satisfying for their members. For many women, certainly, this was not true. With little education or economic opportunity and very limited legal rights, they were dependent first on their fathers and then on their husbands. Unmarried women often had to rely on their relatives for a place to live in return for helping around the house; they were usually pitied and patronized.

Social historians are also discovering that some seemingly modern family problems are not new at all. Just as family stability is a concern today, so it was in Puritan New England. In 1679, for example, clergyman Increase Mather convened a group of clergy and lay elders to prepare a report on why their land had suffered devastating wars with the Indians. They believed that these events could be interpreted as God's punishment for their sins. Their report stated, "family government has decayed, and fathers no longer keep their sons and daughters from prowling at night."

While discussions of the contemporary family often concentrate upon conflict and dissolution, it is clear that the family of the past was also faced with problems. Because conditions in the larger society have changed the functions that families serve, the problems facing families have also changed.

REVIEW AND APPLICATION

1. *IDENTIFY:* Patrilocal residence, matrilocal residence, neolocal residence, polyandry, polygyny, polygamy, bilateral descent, patrilineal descent, matrilineal descent, nuclear family, extended family.
2. In what ways is the family supported by society? What functions does the family perform in return?
3. What unexpected facts have been uncovered by new research on family change?
4. What changes have taken place in the American family in the last 150 years?
5. According to sociologists, what social and economic processes were involved in these changes?

CRITICAL THINKING: What are some of the problems facing family stability today that were not present in the past?

2 Courtship and Marriage

Almost every discussion of marriage these days stresses changes and problems. Such discussions may touch on the rising divorce rate, proper roles for husbands and wives, new forms of marriage—or no marriage at all. What are the historical sources of some of our ideas about marriage?

For hundreds of years in Europe, most marriages were arranged by parents. Romantic love had little or nothing to do with marital choice. Instead, families approved marital unions to further their economic interests or to maintain religious and kinship ties. Often the size of the dowry, or financial offering, that the bride's family could give was instrumental in the choice. Frequently the rights and obligations of the bride's and groom's families were spelled out in detailed marriage contracts. The husband and wife might grow to love each other later, but that was a secondary consideration. The interests of the family as a whole were more important.

As time passed, this system underwent many changes. In America, even in colonial times, young people began to have some veto power. The parents still chose, but the bride- or groom-to-be could object if the choice was personally unacceptable.

Children became more and more independent as families moved to cities. There young people met one another in schools and churches and at work. Parental choice was replaced by a proposal: a man first proposed marriage to the woman of his choice and then asked her father for his daughter's "hand." This dual ritual symbolized dual values: the importance of personal choice and the continuing parental concern that a child make the right choice of a marriage partner.

Marital Norms Today

Although marriage for love is the norm in the United States today, parents still exercise some control over their children's choices. For example, they may threaten to discontinue educational or other support, or to change their wills, if a son or daughter marries an unacceptable partner. Parents here and throughout the world still use appeals to family loyalty and other psychological pressures to influence their children's marital choices.

In our own society, those with means send their children to colleges and universities where they will be most likely to meet others at their social level. Religious and ethnic groups bring together young people of marriageable age in social clubs and camps, just as matchmakers and other arrangers used to do.

The opportunities for marriage outside a person's immediate social group, class, or religion have grown in our society over the years. Marriages between individuals of different ethnic and religious backgrounds occur more often than before. Marriage is often a means of social mobility. People of different socioeconomic backgrounds do meet, fall in love, and marry.

Yet the old ideas are not dead. Many parents still do not want their children to marry "beneath them." Religious concerns, educational background, and other factors influence an individual's choice. Interracial marriages, still relatively rare, are accepted in a few communities but condemned in many others.

Some people today follow the older, more traditional rituals of their culture. This Japanese bride and the wedding party are wearing traditional marriage attire.

Courtship normally takes place during late adolescence and early adulthood. Young people have to balance a variety of pressures in choosing a partner. The choice can be quite stressful to young adults. Divorce rates may be rising, but most people still feel that they are making a lifetime choice when they marry. Most people choose marriage partners at an age when they are continuing to grow and change intellectually and emotionally, which makes it difficult to be sure they have made the right choice.

The wedding is a rite of passage. Many weddings follow certain rituals, and the participants conform to customary ways. A white gown and tuxedo, flowers, rice, a gathering of friends and family, and a feast all mark the new status. Gifts of household items—pots and pans, silverware and dishes, linens and blankets—are common recognition that the new couple are setting up their own home.

The new status means new roles. In the past, role expectations were quite specific. Women stayed home or worked a short time until they began having children. Their first obligation was homemaking. Men's first duty was to earn a living. Now expectations of wives and husbands are less well defined.

? Do people in your family and among your friends follow customary rituals when they get married? If so, what do you think are their reasons?

Toward Greater Equality

Just as marriages moved historically from an arranged to a free-choice system, so the nature of marriage has moved from a male-dominated relationship to one that is more evenly balanced. Even in the past, certain women held some power in their marital relationships, by virtue either of their personal qualities or of the wealth or family connections they brought to the marriage. But until recent decades, in most families power resided with husbands. Legal restrictions limited a wife's rights to own property and to exercise custody over her children in case of divorce. Many mores reinforced this legal inequality.

The movement toward more equal relationships began in the mid-nineteenth century, when women reformers led supporters of women's suffrage and equal rights. In the 1850s, feminist Lucy Stone and her husband, Henry Blackwell, drew up their own marriage contract because they believed that a wife should not be forced to swear obedience to her husband, as the traditional ceremony required.

The couple published the following statement: "While we acknowledge our mutual affection by publicly assuming the relationship of husband and wife, yet, in justice to ourselves and a great principle, we deem it a duty to declare that this act on our part implies no sanction of, nor promise of voluntary obedience to, such of the present laws of marriage as refuse to recognize the wife as an independent, rational being, while they confer upon the husband an injurious and

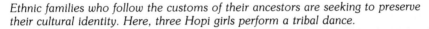

Ethnic families who follow the customs of their ancestors are seeking to preserve their cultural identity. Here, three Hopi girls perform a tribal dance.

VIEWS OF WOMEN ON THE IDEAL WAY OF LIFE

Way of Life Chosen	1975 (%)	1980 (%)	1985 (%)
Married with children	76	74	74
With full-time job	32	33	38
With no full-time job	44	41	34
Married with no children	9	10	9
With full-time job	6	6	6
With no full-time job	3	4	3
Unmarried with full-time job	9	8	9
Not sure	6	8	10

Source: Gallup Poll

CHART SKILL   Polls conducted in 1975, 1980, and 1985 showed that about 75 percent of American women wanted to be married and to have children. How have women's attitudes on the ideal lifestyle changed from 1975 to 1985?

Mother and breadwinner, this woman reflects a social change of circumstance. In contrast to the norm of thirty years ago, a majority of women now hold jobs outside the home and must balance work and family roles.

unnatural superiority, investing him with legal powers which no honorable man would exercise, and which no man should possess."

As women attained legal and political rights, more education, and employment outside the home, the psychological relationship between the sexes was, inevitably, altered. Yet many of the old norms remained as well. With so many changes taking place in women's lives, it is not surprising that some contradictions arose concerning women's role in the family.

Sociologist Mirra Komarovksy recently conducted a study of senior men at an Ivy League college and found that old ideas about traditional relationships were still strong. Although the men supported higher education for both sexes, 30 percent of the sample were reluctant to date women who were their intellectual equals or superiors. Komarovsky quotes one respondent's answer: "I enjoy talking to more intelligent girls, but I have no desire for a deep relationship with them. I guess I still believe that the man should be more intelligent."

About 50 percent of the respondents said they would enjoy female intellectual companionship, but some felt the need for male superiority in other areas. It was all right for a woman to be very intelligent, some students said, if she was homely or emotionally dependent. Even men who sought equals as dates tended to favor tradition-minded women as their future wives.

Of those surveyed, 24 percent wanted their wives to be full-time housewives. The largest number, 48 percent, did not object to their wives' having jobs as long as they gave up working once children were born. Although the men were willing to help with some chores, they rejected others—"not the diapers," "not the laundry." Only 7 percent said they would modify their own roles if that became necessary to further their wives' careers.

The words of one senior summarize many of the contradictory attitudes Komarovsky found: "I believe that it is good for mothers to return to full-time work when the children are grown, provided the work is important and worthwhile. . . . A woman

Many families today are more democratic and less patriarchal than in earlier times. Family fun may involve all members equally.

should want her husband's success more than he should want hers. He should not sacrifice his career to hers. For example, if he is transferred, his wife should follow—and not vice versa."

Few marriages today are truly egalitarian. Women still do most of the housework, even when they are also employed at jobs outside the home. Men are still usually considered more responsible for the family's economic well-being. Couples who challenge this traditional division of labor often depend on social supports outside the family: friends and relatives who give assistance, jobs that provide sufficient income for household help, and adequate child-care facilities.

REVIEW AND APPLICATION

1. How do courtship and marriage customs today differ from those of past centuries?

2. Why does the "dual ritual" of a man first proposing marriage to the woman of his choice and then asking her father's permission represent a "dual value"?

3. Why did feminist Lucy Stone and her husband write their own marriage contract? What was their position on the roles of married men and women in their time?

4. What did Mirra Komarovksy's study of Ivy League college men reveal about the students' contradictory attitudes toward marriage?

CRITICAL THINKING: A survey for married couples contained the following questions: What percentage of the housework do each of you do? How do you divide economic responsibility in your marriage? If either partner were transferred, would the other leave his or her job? How would egalitarian couples most likely answer? Do you consider their responses a norm in our society?

3 Parenthood

Becoming a parent for the first time represents a major change in a person's life cycle. Alice Rossi, a family sociologist, has compared the role of parent with that of spouse or worker and found it to be much more tension-ridden. In fact, she says, the "honeymoon" period of a marriage often ends when the wife becomes pregnant.

Why is learning to be a parent so difficult? First, it is at this time that women in contemporary families experience a radical role change. Few women stop working after marriage, but many do so, at least for a time, after a child is born. Second, young adults receive little preparation for their new role. Parents, especially mothers, are expected automatically to love their infants and to be totally involved in caring for them. Yet childbirth is not preceded by the equivalent of a courtship—a period of growing intimacy in preparation for living together. The birth of an infant is abrupt, suddenly exerting enormous demands on the parents. For most people, being a parent brings a full-time responsibility that is greater than any they have experienced before.

Finally, parenthood is one of the few adult roles from which there is no escape. A marriage that has become intolerable can be ended through divorce. An occupational role that is unsatisfactory can be changed. But the role of parent continues throughout life.

Choosing Parenthood

In most parts of the world, marriage is expected to be followed quickly and automatically by the birth of a child. Failure to have children may elicit community sympathy; it may even be a source of shame. In many traditional societies, it has been one of the few legitimate reasons for divorce.

In highly industrialized countries, the availability of birth control has changed the situation to some degree. Many couples carefully plan the number and spacing of their children. Some couples raise the issue of whether to have children at all.

So far, however, only very small numbers of primarily middle-class couples have deliberately chosen to forgo parenthood. The vast majority of young adults believe that marriage and parenthood are important stages in adult life. No matter what difficulties these new statuses present, most people consider the creation of a family a part of self-realization and fulfillment.

Learning to Be Parents

Who teaches adults to be parents? Most people tend to model their behavior as parents on that of their own parents. Some of their learning comes from others who have recently become parents. Pregnant women and new parents get a lot of advice from friends: "You should nurse the baby for at least six months." "Don't tie yourself down by nursing." "You don't have to sterilize everything." "Heat the baby food." "Don't use baby food." In the past, new parents often had relatives nearby to help train them in their new roles. This is true less often now.

In our complex, mobile society, learning to be a parent, like much other learning, has

While the rewards are great, parenthood is one of life's most demanding roles. Few parents are really prepared for the constant responsibility that comes with the birth of the first child.

Learning to be a parent has become formalized. Parents-to-be may still listen to helpful hints from relatives and friends, but many also attend prenatal classes.

become formalized. Prenatal classes teach prospective parents childbirth techniques and the fundamentals of infant care. "How-to-parent" books offer advice on when to call the doctor, what to do when a baby is teething, and almost everything else an inexperienced mother or father might want to know. Such organizations as La Leche League give classes and offer advice to nursing mothers.

This formalized learning of the parental role is a trend that began in the early twentieth century. Child psychologists and physicians were sure that their research on child care was superior to the abilities of mothers. They no longer assumed that mothers naturally knew what was right for children. Extensive manuals began to dispense "scientific advice."

Some of the advice of the professionals, such as their instructions on sanitation, nutrition, and inoculation, did reduce childhood disease and mortality. But other fashionable theories, such as the emphasis for several decades on bottle feeding rather than nursing, were no more well founded than nonprofessional advice. In any case, today's emphasis on formal training for parents provides a way of introducing new norms. Advocates of prepared childbirth and democratic methods of child raising can present their views more widely and attempt to compete with more traditional advice.

Case Study: A "Natural Mother"

Some parents who have not read the experts on child care and development seem to arrive at many of the same insights and conclusions on their own. (In Chapter 9, you will read in detail about parents' impact on children's early years.) While studies have shown that not all women are "natural mothers," other studies have revealed the excellent psychological knowledge that some parents seem to acquire through love and intuition. For instance, researcher Fred Davis studied fourteen families in which children had been afflicted by polio. In these families, the need for understanding care and special teaching was far greater than normally required.

Six-year-old Laura Paulus was badly crippled. Of the children Davis studied, she

The more "normally" a handicapped child is raised, the more self-accepting and independent that child will become.

was the most severely handicapped. Mrs. Paulus did not attempt to deny her daughter's handicap, but she did do everything in her power to help Laura follow a path of "normalization." She enrolled Laura in her former school and made arrangements for her classmates to help her get on and off the bus. She also encouraged Laura to play with her old friends even though she could not keep up with all their activities.

Mrs. Paulus believed that if Laura did not learn normal roles as a child, she would never be an independent person. She realized that if Laura's daily interactions had been with people who defined her as a victim, crippled and unable to cope, she would have begun to see herself in that light. And she was determined to instill in her daughter a view of herself as a competent person who need not feel inferior.

Therefore, Mrs. Paulus made sure that Laura's contacts and activities with others would maintain her self-image as someone who accepted and who could continue family relationships, friendships, and schooling. She tried to ensure that her daughter's self-concept would reflect the positive images of par-

ents, peers, neighbors, and teachers. Mrs. Paulus acted on the belief that learning is cumulative—that one stage builds on another. And she reinforced the crucial belief that people could be trusted and relied on to lend a helping hand and treat Laura as an equal. (Read pages 196–197 to see how the theories of psychologists Charles Horton Cooley and Erik Erikson coincide with Mrs. Paulus's decisions on how to meet Laura's needs.)

Is becoming a good parent most likely to be based on the treatment by parents one had as a child, one's own basic personality, knowledge of child psychology, or something else? Explain your answer. What might be some limiting factors to becoming a good parent?

Mothers Who Work Outside the Home

A conviction widely held until recently was that children whose mothers worked outside the home suffered from lack of attention. Many studies upheld the belief that the development of infants and small children could be seriously impaired if the mother were absent for long periods of time. For example, the research conducted by René Spitz and his colleagues in the 1940s and 1950s, which was discussed in Chapter 4, demonstrated that children in hospitals and orphanages did not develop as well as other children, despite good care from the hospital staff. Spitz concluded that the children suffered from maternal deprivation and therefore were denied a healthy, normal childhood. Subsequent work on infant attachment by British psychiatrist John Bowlby reinforced the importance of what Bowlby referred to as the "maternal-infant bond."

These and other studies implied that the mother has special biological characteristics that make her the right person to shoulder primary responsibility. Some researchers referred to this bond as maternal instinct. If these researchers had known of Mrs. Paulus, they would probably have explained her care of Laura in this manner.

At the same time, some serious opposition to these theories began to emerge. Some women, it appeared, were not particularly adept at mothering, and they did not seem to enjoy the responsibility. Spitz's findings were challenged on the grounds that his work was done exclusively on hospitalized children, whose lives were much more disrupted than those of other children.

Evidence does indicate that infants require consistent care, stable environments, physical and intellectual stimulation, and love and affection. But some researchers do not believe that the biological mother is the only one who is able to provide such care. And studies indicate that the home may not be the "proper place" for all women. Some women suffer from the isolation of full-time domestic roles, and such women may cause their children to suffer as well. One study quotes a young housewife: "I feel it should be more widely recognized that it is the very nature of a mother's position in our society to avenge her frustrations on a small helpless child, whether this takes the form of tyranny

or of a smothering affection that asks the child to be a substitute for all she has missed."

Recent work by Alice Rossi points out that there may be differences in how easily each sex can learn certain kinds of nurturing behavior. However, since women have always cared for newborn babies, it is not clear how much of their behavior is biologically determined and how much is the result of social and cultural factors. There is still much controversy today among sociologists, parents, and various women's groups about the proper role of motherhood.

? Where do you stand in this controversy? If you are female, do you plan to work after your children are born? Or do you plan not to have children? If you are male, how do you feel about having your wife work after you become parents?

Whether one accepts the traditional view of motherhood or not, economic pressures in today's high-priced society often make the

CHART SKILL *This chart reflects the attitudes of 8–17 year olds on the effect working mothers have on their children. What differences to do you notice in the attitudes of youths whose mothers work and those whose mothers stay at home?*

AMERICAN YOUTH'S PERSPECTIVE ON WORKING MOTHERS

	Total %	Age 8–12 %	Age 13–17 %	Mother works: Full Time %	Mother works: Part Time %	Mother works: Not at All %
Effect on children 12 or under is:						
Good	25	31	19	28	26	19
Bad	39	28	48	35	36	48
No effect	29	31	28	30	33	25
Don't know	7	9	6	7	4	9
Effect on teenagers is:						
Good	26	27	26	29	28	22
Bad	18	20	16	16	20	22
No effect	46	39	53	48	45	47
Don't know	9	14	5	8	8	10

SOURCE: Adapted from Warner-Lambert Company's *The American Chicle Youth Poll*, by The Roper Organization, Inc., 1987.

question purely theoretical. Many women who would prefer to remain full-time home-makers and mothers are forced to go to work to make ends meet. This has brought up a very concrete problem: Who will take care of the children while their parents are away at work?

As the numbers of two-paycheck families and single-parent families have increased, a greater need for child-care facilities has developed. These facilities may vary from care for several children in a neighbor's home to highly organized day-care centers with trained personnel to tend young children throughout the day. Thus, day care in such facilities provides lots of peer-group contact but little individual attention. While most Americans have long recognized the peer group as an important factor in the development of older children and adolescents, they have worried about the effects of day care on young children.

As a result, a number of studies have been made comparing children who have had extensive day-care experience with children raised exclusively at home. In addition, a number of social scientists have analyzed the experience of children in the Soviet Union, Sweden, and Israel, where collective child care is common. Several studies of practices in these countries found that children raised largely in group situations were likely to be more cooperative and less competitive.

Yet research done in American and British day-care centers did not yield the same results. Psychologist Urie Bronfenbrenner analyzed the literature and found that in many cases American and English boys who spend much of their time in day-care centers exhibit more aggressive behavior than those raised at home. The finding is less dramatic for girls. Bronfenbrenner believes that aggressive behavior probably does not result from group care itself. The effects of a peer group on an individual child will vary, depending on the child and on the society in which the group exerts its influence.

A major problem of parents who work outside the home is finding someone to care for the children in their absence. Some parents leave their children with relatives or friends. Others use day-care centers, but such centers are in short supply.

What appears to happen, Bronfenbrenner says, is that peer groups enhance conformity to larger cultural values. Since the Americans and the British tend to emphasize individualism and self-assertiveness, it is not surprising that these values are taught in American and English day-care centers. In the Soviet Union, day-care experience is more likely to lead to conformity. In Israel, there is a different combination of independence and cooperation. Bronfenbrenner reminds us that whatever happens in peer groups never takes place in isolation from the larger society. This would be equally true, of course, in regard to the way a family chooses to raise a child.

REVIEW AND APPLICATION

1. Why is learning to become a parent so difficult?
2. What conclusions about the maternal-infant bond were made by the studies conducted by Spitz and Bowlby?
3. What objections to the Spitz and Bowlby theories have been presented?

CRITICAL THINKING: Urie Bronfenbrenner found that the girls in American day care centers showed less aggressive behavior than the boys. Based on what you have read, what assumption can you make about the larger American society?

4 Divorce

The changes discussed earlier—the decline of family size and the increase in the number of women holding jobs—are concurrent with another change: the present high divorce rate in the United States. According to recent census figures, there is roughly one divorce for every three marriages. But what do these figures actually mean?

The data presented do not say that one out of every three marriages fails. Rather, in a given year, the United States Bureau of the Census recorded one couple getting a divorce for every three couples getting married. Such figures are misleading because they include persons who obtain a divorce for the second, third, or fourth time. And they do not show how many first marriages stay together.

A closer examination of the data shows that people are more likely to divorce in the early years of marriage. The longer a marriage lasts, the more likely it is to continue to last. The number of children in a family is also influential: the more children, the smaller the likelihood of divorce.

Causes of Divorce

Sociologists have offered several explanations for the steady increase in the number of marriages breaking up. Marriages based on romantic love, the norm in the United States, have always been gambles. In earlier times, unhappy couples were kept together by religious rules, state laws, and social pressures. Today, major barriers to ending marriages have been removed. Most churches (the Roman Catholic Church is a notable exception) do not condemn divorce. States have accepted broader and more lenient grounds for dissolving a marriage. Some states have even instituted "no-fault" divorce.

In addition, many working women are financially independent. They don't need husbands to support them, so they feel freer to seek divorces. However, divorced women must sometimes turn to the state to assist them through periods of poverty. Such programs as Aid to Dependent Children have been set up to meet such needs.

Finally, husbands and wives today are less likely to see value in preserving unhappy marriages "for the sake of the children." For all these reasons, divorce has become more common. Indeed, for many people it has become a socially acceptable solution to difficult marital problems.

While divorce rates are rising in all Western industrialized societies, the United States

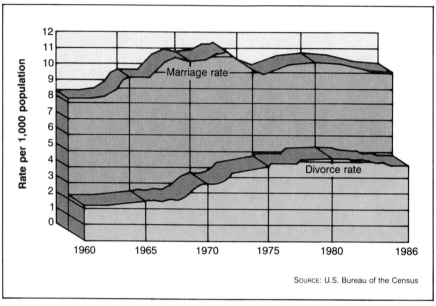

MARRIAGE AND DIVORCE RATES IN THE UNITED STATES 1960–1986

SOURCE: U.S. Bureau of the Census

GRAPH SKILL   Over one million divorces take place each year in the United States. The divorce rate is usually expressed as the number of divorces per 1,000 of the total population. The marriage rate includes remarriages as well as first marriages. How would you describe the trend in the divorce rate since 1980?

now has the highest divorce rate in the world. Perhaps one reason may be the firm cultural commitment of many Americans to freedom of choice. After choosing one partner, a spouse may feel that he or she still has the freedom to replace that choice later.

Effects of Divorce

"Apparently it does not matter how many other people it has happened to—it hurts just as much. Like being hit by an automobile." Dissolving a family may be easier than it once was, but it is still painful, as this quotation shows.

Divorce breaks up an economic and social unit. It disrupts social positions and can lead to severe financial problems. Children especially, and often close relatives as well, may experience great stress.

A man relates his experience: "In the ten years we were married I went from twenty-four to thirty-four and they were a very significant ten years. I started a career, started to succeed, bought my first house, had a child. . . . And then all of a sudden, I'm back to zero! I have no house. I don't have a child. I don't have a wife. I don't even have the same family. . . . All those goals which I had struggled for—every . . . one of them is gone."

Such feelings are common among couples who have separated. In one study, many of those interviewed reported apprehensiveness, anxiety, fear, or panic. When divorcing couples have friends and relatives who provide emotional support, the ill effects are less severe. Those free of economic problems, who can seek counseling if necessary, are better prepared to build a new life.

The increasing divorce rate has, of course, led to a large increase in the number of single-parent families. Since the mother is

SOME CHARACTERISTICS OF "DIVORCE-PRONE" COUPLES

The backgrounds of the two partners are different.

The family of at least one partner has a history of divorce.

The couple was acquainted for only a short time before they were married or had a short engagement period.

The families or friends of the couple disapprove of their marriage.

The couple has always had opposing views on the roles of husband and wife.

The partners have no formal membership in a religious group.

CHART SKILL   *Why some people stay married while others divorce is an extremely complex question. Studies have shown that the rich and the poor have higher divorce rates than those in the middle class. How might educational and cultural differences also contribute to variations in the divorce rate?*

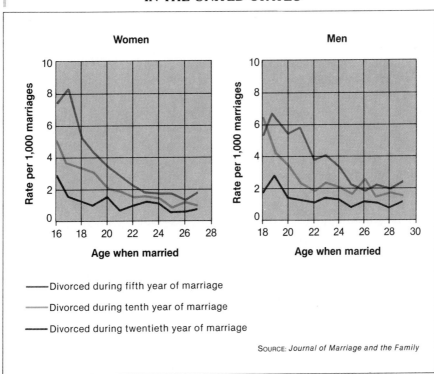

EFFECT OF MARRIAGE AGE ON DIVORCE RATE IN THE UNITED STATES

SOURCE: *Journal of Marriage and the Family*

GRAPH SKILL   *Factors other than those listed above contribute to the probability of divorce. One significant factor, though, is age at marriage. People marrying in their teens are much more likely to be divorced than those marrying in their late twenties. Why do you think this is true?*

The increase in the number of divorces has meant an increase in the number of children being raised in single-parent homes.

women reported that they had to go to work to support themselves and their children. These women earned less than single women of the same age. Only a small number, 4 percent, could afford to hire someone to help with the housework. Perhaps most troubling is the fact that 25 percent of the divorced women said that they feared they might have a "nervous breakdown." Only 8 percent of the divorced men reported having the same fear.

Divorced couples do not seem to lose the desire to be married—to someone. After a period of suffering and readjustment, most eventually remarry. More younger people than older people remarry, and more men than women do so. One study estimates that, eventually, three-fourths of divorced women and five-sixths of divorced men will try again. Women with children are as likely to remarry as those without. Second marriages are more likely to be successful, according to family sociologist Jessie Bernard, if the couple's children, relatives, and friends approve the match.

Remarriages may involve many complex relationships. Sociologists are currently gathering accurate empirical data to explain the sociology of the remade family. They are studying, among other topics, the effects on children of having two sets of parents, more than one home, and, perhaps, new brothers and sisters.

Do the increasing divorce rate and the greater numbers of single-parent families and stepfamilies mean that the family as an institution is in crisis? Most social scientists recognize the great strains placed on family life by rapid changes but argue that the institution of the family is here to stay.

more likely to receive custody of the dependent children than the father, most single-parent families are headed by women. Although divorced persons are more readily accepted than in earlier generations, single parents do not have an easy time of it. They have to make all the decisions and perform all the functions of both mother and father in regard to their children's health, schooling, and discipline.

Economic hardship is particularly common among mothers bringing up children alone, since most women's incomes are lower than those of men. On the other hand, the "weekend parent" (usually the father) has little opportunity to participate in the children's daily lives. Many fathers feel the loss of an intimate relationship with their children.

One study surveyed the attitudes of a random sample of 2,164 adults who were asked to rate how happy they were. The findings showed that divorced women with children face severe problems and are less satisfied with their lives than any other group. Almost three-quarters of the divorced

REVIEW AND APPLICATION

1. At what stage of a marriage is divorce most likely?
2. According to the text, what are the causes of divorce? Do you agree?

CRITICAL THINKING: What do you think divorced people who remarry probably value?

CHAPTER **6** REVIEW

The family is a universal social institution, traditionally sanctioned by authorities and protected by law. The view of the extended family of the past as a center of harmonious relationships may be myth. What is certain is that in the United States the family has changed, becoming smaller in size and less authoritarian.

Marriage, once arranged by parents, is now usually a matter of free choice in Western societies. Husbands are less likely to dominate, perhaps because women are more likely to participate in the labor force. Some studies indicate, however, that many men do not want an equal relationship with a woman, nor are truly egalitarian marriages considered the norm.

Parenthood, too, has changed. Couples are choosing to have fewer children and are more likely to turn to professionals for advice in raising their offspring. However, professional opinion on the effect of maternal deprivation on children is divided.

The responsibilities of parenthood fall especially heavily on parents who bring up children alone. Single-parent households have increased along with the incidence of divorce, which is higher in the United States than anywhere else in the world. Still, the great majority of adults are married, if not always to their original mates.

Key Terms

Define the following:

patrilocal residence
matrilocal residence
neolocal residence
polyandry

polygyny
polygamy
bilateral descent
patrilineal descent

matrilineal descent
extended family
nuclear family

Applying Sociology

1. This chapter discussed how the family's economic function has been reduced. What about its other functions? To what extent does a family today provide protection, recreation, education, and religion for its members? Make a list of the functions your family provides. Then make a list of the functions you expect to provide when you have a family of your own. Explain your reasons. Which list is longer? Or are they the same?

2. On a sheet of paper write four headings: "Husband Only," "Wife Only," "Either or Both," and "Why." Along the left, list the following activities:

preparing meals
cleaning the bathtub
replacing a fuse
writing thank-you letters
sewing on buttons
hanging pictures

buying groceries
renewing auto registration
painting the living room
shoveling snow
arranging flowers
paying bills

Then check off each activity in one of the first three columns, and indicate why you made this choice in the fourth column.

(a) Do you think your parents would divide up chores in this way? Why or why not?

(b) Tabulate the class's answers to see how your peers feel about the roles of husband and wife. You may also wish to see whether there are significant differences between the answers of male and female students.

3. Using a reference book such as an almanac, investigate the various grounds for divorce throughout the United States. Which grounds seem reasonable to you? Are there any that seem to make divorce too easy? Are there any you would add? How else might families resolve their differences?

4. Child abuse and family violence have been related to stress. Survey your community to see what services exist to help families under pressure. Perhaps your teacher can arrange for a therapist or counselor from a family-service organization or mental-health clinic to address the class on the cause and prevention of family violence. Make a list of questions that a parent might want to ask someone skilled in this area.

5. Consider the following problem in family life, a result of divorce, death, or separation. There are about four to five million families in which only a mother is present. There are less than eight hundred thousand with only a father. Until recently, courts tended to award a divorced mother custody of the children; now more fathers are asking for and gaining custody. Do you think a father might face special challenges in this situation? If so, describe what these might be. What are your suggestions to help solve the problems of the single parent? Consider all the possibilities for aid offered by the various social institutions in society.

Extended Readings

Anne McGrath, "Living Alone and Loving It," *U.S News and World Report*, August 3, 1987, pp. 52–57.

1. What changes have influenced family structure in recent years?
2. What effect has living alone had on many women?

Tamara K. Hareven, "Divorce, Chinese Style," *Atlantic Monthly*, April 1987, pp. 70–76.

1. Why have China's divorce laws been unsuccessful?
2. What part do neighborhood committees play in divorce cases?

Claudia Wallis, "The Child-Care Dilemma," *Time*, June 22, 1987, pp. 54–60.

1. How have working mothers coped with the lack of adequate childcare?

2. What concerns do some educators and health care professionals raise about child-care programs?

Drawing inferences about male and female roles Sometimes people mean more than they state directly. When we try to decide what people could be suggesting, we draw inferences. On pages 132 and 133, reread the results of Mirra Komarovsky's study of senior men at an Ivy League college. Draw inferences from the men's statements. Then answer the following questions:

(a) One man in the study said that he had "no desire for a deep relationship" with a woman more intelligent than he. For this man, does enjoyment seem to be his chief reason for dating? From which passage in the text did you infer your answer?

(b) Some men in the study dated equals but planned to marry tradition-minded women. Do these men seem to view dating as preparation for marriage? If one of these men married a woman that he dated, who would the husband ex-pect to change more after the marriage —himself or his wife? Explain your answer.

(c) Forty-eight percent of the men in the study expect their wives to give up working once children are born. Do these men seem to hold child care and housework in high esteem? From which passage in the text did you infer your answer?

Drawing conclusions about male attitudes Which of the following conclusions might you draw about the men in Komarovsky's study? Support each of your choices with passages from the text.

(a) Men who are reluctant to date women more intelligent than themselves feel threatened by intelligent women.

(b) To some men in the study, homely women are inferior.

(c) The last senior quoted plans to treat his wife as an equal.

1. *Identifying Assumptions:* The following statements were made by boys. What assumptions can you identify in each? (a) I enjoy talking with girls who are more intelligent than me, but I have no desire to marry one; (b) My wife could work, but she would have to stop working once we had children; (c) I would help my wife out with household chores, if necessary, but not with cleaning diapers.

2. *Assessing Causal Reasoning:* Look at the chart "Some Characteristics of 'Divorce-Prone Couples'" on page 141. Choose one of the factors (causes) and explain *how* it would lead to divorce (the effect).

Religion and Education

Chapter Preview

- **Before you read,** look up the following key terms in the glossary to become familiar with their definitions:

progressive education   educational traditionalists   mainstreaming

- **As you read,** think about answers to the following questions:

1. What purposes does religion serve in peoples' lives?
2. Why has the influence of religion on many American's lives weakened in recent decades?
3. How has the American system of education changed?
4. What is the relationship between education and economic opportunity in the United States?

Chapter Focus

All social institutions come into being to meet basic human needs. Not only do people require some sort of family life in order to care for, protect, and guide the young, they also need ways of explaining the mysteries of life and death. They need to cope with what some have called the "unknowable," and religion provides a network of norms and social organizations through which they can meet this need.

In many societies, parents and religious leaders have long been the conveyors of wisdom and moral instruction. But they are not the only ones. Professional teachers have also been assigned this task.

This chapter focuses on religion and education, the two institutions that, after the family, have the earliest impact on almost everyone. It examines the social functions of religion and education.

Using Sociologists' Tools

- **Observe** the similarities and differences between "teachers" and "preachers."
- **Describe** some of the specific techniques both "teachers" and "preachers" use to guide people.
- **Analyze** the reward of schooling by examining data on the socioeconomic status of high-school dropouts and college graduates.
- **Predict** what would happen if everyone were afforded an equal opportunity to go to the college of his or her choice.

Attending a house of worship on a regular basis, and sharing in the community of religion, is an important event for millions of Americans.

1 Religion

Religion is found in every known society on the globe. It is practiced in churches and synagogues, in mosques and temples, indoors and out. The sociologist Emile Durkheim defined *religion* as "a unified system of beliefs and practices relating to sacred things, uniting into a single moral community all those who adhere to those beliefs and practices." Like the family and early education, religion molds character traits that can last a lifetime.

The Community of Religion

According to Durkheim's definition, religious beliefs and practices relate to "sacred things." That phrase may make you think of the Jewish Torah, the Christian cross, or the Muslim Koran. But Durkheim wasn't referring just to sacred objects—in fact, there are some religions that have no sacred objects.

Durkheim meant all the objects and ideas that people believe are related to an existence or power beyond the ordinary reality of the senses.

A "unified system of beliefs" is a philosophy about the relationship of human beings to things beyond their immediate understanding. And religion is a philosophy of the *sacred,* concerned with mysterious power not human and yet related to humans. It tries to make sense of human burdens such as poverty, disease, and death. And it offers explanations for things that cannot be understood by reason alone.

Not only does religion give believers an explanation of life, it also offers them a guide for ethical behavior. Many religions have rules for believers to follow that are supposed to prevent troubles and banish sorrow. Some religions promise their followers life after death.

147

Many religions have rituals that believers are to follow, such as eating special foods on certain occasions. You saw in Chapter 2 some of the many ways in which people pray (pages 36–37). And you read in Chapter 3 of one boy's experience with the religious practices accompanying death. Other religious rituals involve making an ordinary act extraordinary; for example, eating and drinking take on symbolic meaning in the Christian rite of communion.

Durkheim's statement that a religion unites believers "into a single moral community" means, first, that all believers follow or try to follow the norms derived from their beliefs about the sacred, such as "Love thy neighbor as thyself," and second, that they have a common bond to the sacred things. All believers are bound both to the object of their worship and to their fellow worshipers. A religion thus unites people into a community, and from that community they derive emotional support.

? What do you think is the basic human need responsible for the near universality of religion? How do unreligious people meet this need?

Religion, Stratification, and Power

The institution of religion is often meshed with a society's economic or political institutions. In many ancient societies, only one religion was allowed by those in power. In some modern societies, this is also true. For many centuries, Roman Catholicism held a key place in Europe, as Islam did and still does in many countries of the Middle East and Southeast Asia. Countries with an official faith have often tolerated other religions, but some have discriminated against their religious minorities. The United States has been a refuge from religious persecution for many Europeans, including the Pilgrims, the French Huguenots, and Eastern European Jews.

Religion and Stratification Sometimes religion can have the effect of reinforcing an existing class structure, as it did in the feudal societies of medieval Europe. You read about the feudal system in Chapter 5. The structured inequality of feudalism was considered part of the natural, or divine—God-given—order, as expressed in this medieval English verse:

> The rich man at his castle
> The poor man at his gate
> God made them high or lowly
> And ordered their estate.

You also read in Chapter 5 about the stratification system in India that was, and to a large extent still is, supported by the caste divisions of the Hindu religion. For centuries, Hindu doctrine has divided its followers into groups from which they can almost never escape. The system grants each person a place in the holy order of things.

Castes had their sacred origin in the body of their Lord. In the words of Manu, the legendary Hindu lawgiver:

For the sake of the prosperity of the worlds, he [the Lord] caused the Brahmana,

Most societies have complex systems of religious practices and beliefs. The Hindu religion of India, the oldest religion still practiced, has many gods and goddesses. Pictured here is Durga, the goddess of destruction.

ESTIMATED MEMBERSHIP OF MAJOR WORLD RELIGIONS

Jewish 17
Taoist 20
Shinto 32
Confucian 151
Buddhist 248
Hindu 464
Muslim 555

Christian:
total 1,062

Eastern Orthodox 59
Protestant 374
Roman Catholic 629

0 100 200 300 400 500 600

Millions of people:

SOURCE: Reprinted with permission from the 1986 *Britannica Book of the Year,* copyright 1986, Encyclopedia Britannica, Inc., Chicago, Ill.

GRAPH SKILL   *Membership statistics for the world's religions are not precise. One problem is that methods of counting vary widely. Many Protestant denominations count only adults as members, while Islam counts all constituents, including infants. Getting reliable statistics is almost impossible in communist nations, where governments are hostile to religion. Which of the world's religions has the largest membership?*

the Kshatriya, the Vaisya, the Sudra to proceed in turn from his mouth, his arms, his thighs, and his feet. . . . But in order to protect this universe, he, the most resplendent one, assigned separate [duties and] occupations to those who sprang from his mouth, arms, thighs, and feet.

To Brahmana he assigned teaching and studying [the Veda], sacrificing for their own benefit and for others, giving and accepting [alms]. The Kshatriya he commanded to protect the people . . . the Vaisya to tend cattle. . . . One occupation

only the Lord prescribed to the Sudra, to serve meekly even these [other] three castes.

Religion and Economics The sociologist and economist Max Weber suggested that a relationship can also exist between a society's economic system and its religion. Weber believed that religious institutions help form economic ones.

In his classic work *The Protestant Ethic and the Spirit of Capitalism,* he was concerned with predestination, a Calvinist

Buddhism is a dominant religion in much of Asia. Buddhists believe that a person's present position in life has been determined by his or her behavior in a previous life. These monks are praying at a Buddhist shrine in Kyoto, Japan.

doctrine. According to this belief, no one can know who is marked for salvation, but outward signs of favor might include the accumulation of earthly goods. In other words, if you are rich, you must be good. Thus, a devout Calvinist might be particularly inclined to take risks and invest capital, which, in Weber's view, help account for the rise of capitalism. Two important virtues of Protestantism—hard work and thrift—also contribute to economic growth.

Throughout history and in the world today, there are many examples of the support religion has provided for established governments. However, other patterns also exist. In some Central and South American countries, the Catholic church actively opposes existing social systems. Priests and bishops have publicly advocated economic and political change. They have encouraged and organized peasants and laborers to work for reforms that might improve their lives. As a result, representatives of this church throughout Latin America have been attacked by governments opposed to their efforts. Priests and nuns have

been not only exiled but also arrested, beaten, and killed.

Religion and Politics Although social scientists have tended to regard economic and political institutions as the basic institutions in a society, it is evident that religious principles and values have great power and the potential for mobilizing millions of people. For example, the last shah of Iran, who came to power in 1941, introduced Western values and culture into many areas of Iranian life. When the shah's autocratic regime was overthrown in 1979, the revolution was led, not by communists or military officers, but by a Muslim religious leader, the Ayatollah Khomeini.

Khomeini mobilized Iranians under the banner of Islam. When the new government came to power, it restored traditional Islamic values, including codes governing dress, eating and drinking, and relations between men and women. Religion is not limited to the mosques, or Muslim temples, but is a vital component throughout Iranian society.

REVIEW AND APPLICATION

1. IDENTIFY: Religion, sacred.
2. What does the *community of religion* mean?
3. What is the role of the Moslem religion in contemporary Iranian society?
4. How does the Hindu religion justify the caste system?

5. Accordint to Max Weber, what role did religion play in the development of capitalism?

CRITICAL THINKING: Compare the political role of the Roman Catholic Church in feudal Europe with its role in present-day Central America. How do they differ? How has the role of the Church changed?

2 Religion in the United States

In the United States, everybody seems to need a "brand name." Most of us define ourselves according to our membership in or affiliation with a particular group. How we treat others often depends on whether we see them as "brothers" or "sisters" or "one of us." In certain situations, some Americans may even discriminate against those who are not members of their religion.

In fact, religious persecutions marred our early history. For example, the Puritans in colonial America did not tolerate religious diversity. Those who disagreed with Puritan norms on religious matters were often banished from the community. Nevertheless, freedom of religion became a cornerstone of the new American nation, and the separation of church and state a central tenet of our Constitution.

By 1900, a flood of immigrants of many different faiths had created a complex and varied society. Religious immigrants often

Society in the seventeenth-century Puritan colony of Massachusetts was dominated by strict and intolerant religious practices. Here Puritans go to church, an important activity in the lives of Puritans of all ages.

had difficulty integrating the mores of their new country into their religious framework. One Orthodox Jew wrote:

> I had only one friend in my loneliness, one whom I met every day in the synagogue and to whom I poured out my heart—the Talmud.
>
> I was alone in the synagogue, sitting at the table and swaying over the open Talmud, chanting in' the old country tone. Loud sounds burst in from the street—the sounds of the new life into which I had been cast. . . . The cries reproached me mockingly: What are you doing among us, you unworldly idler?

American religious institutions tend to have social aspects that this "unworldly" Jewish scholar would have found difficult to understand. And despite the presence of some very strict and orthodox religious groups in American life—fundamentalist Protestants, Jehovah's Witnesses, Hasidic Jews, and others—our society tends to be dominated by a combination of science, technology, economics, and politics. Events in most people's everyday lives are not usually interpreted solely in terms of their religious faith.

The majority of people in American society follow the rites of passage prescribed by their religion. These Roman Catholic girls prepare to celebrate their first Holy Communion.

Organized Religion

Most Americans today identify with an organized religion. Roughly seventy million are Protestants, fifty million are Roman Catholics, and six million are Jews. Religious groups have power in our society. In important moments in people's lives, religion plays a crucial role. Births are marked by baptisms, puberty by confirmations or bar or bas mitzvahs, marriages by wedding ceremonies, and deaths by funeral services.

Moreover, religious institutions continue to have some political functions. Primarily, they defend their rights to carry out their activities. They may also lobby for federal aid to parochial schools or for a tax-free status for church-owned property.

Historically, too, American religious groups have pressed for laws consistent with their beliefs. For example, Quakers and Men-

nonites worked successfully during World War II to convince the government that their members were bona fide pacifists who, for religious reasons, could not serve in the armed forces. More recently, "right-to-life" organizations backed by some fundamentalist Protestants and Catholics have worked for a constitutional amendment outlawing abortion.

Religious leaders continue to play significant roles in the lives of many people. An important event in 1979 was the visit of Pope John Paul II to the United States. Millions of Americans waited for hours for a chance to see him, and many attended huge open-air masses held in several eastern cities. In 1987, the Pope returned. This time millions more saw him as he spent 10 days in the western United States. The Pope reminded Catholics of Church views on many issues.

decline in the Scholastic Aptitude Test scores (SAT).

The report created an expected uproar and a response that it might have exaggerated the problem. Although SAT scores have risen during the last few years, the report inspired direct action on the part of educators. Among the reforms included a curriculum change which would emphasize excellence in written English as the primary educational goal. Other reforms included increasing the years of study of such courses as math, science, social studies, the arts, and language. A number of states have emphasized increasing teacher's salaries in an effort to keep the most qualified educators.

4 Functions of an Educational System

Most modern educational systems like those in our own society have the following major functions:

1. Teaching skills, concepts, and vocational arts
2. Transmitting culture—the values, norms, traditions, and styles of living of a particular society—to youth
3. Training students for future positions by selecting those eligible for further training and preparing them for high-skill, high-prestige positions and assigning others to courses that will prepare them for middle- or low-level jobs
4. Caring for children and keeping them productively occupied until they are legally eligible for the labor market
5. Equipping young people with the proper credentials or certification to make them eligible for certain jobs
6. Teaching the young how to behave toward those who have political authority

None of these functions is easy to accomplish. The level of knowledge in modern technological society is very high, and what is considered merely a basic education is wide-ranging and demanding.

Schools have many functions, one of the most important being the socialization of children to the expectations of society. The preschool pictured here is for Cherokees.

Today relatively unskilled or semiskilled jobs require the ability to read instructions and to become familiar with complicated machinery. Office workers such as secretaries and file clerks must be literate and comfortable in confronting words and numbers. Managers at various levels must have command of technical knowledge and skills to supervise the work of others. Doctors and other professionals go through years of specialized training to master knowledge generated from the practice and research of their teachers.

Schooling and social class are often closely related. This upper-class British boy will receive the education considered appropriate to his status.

As students are socialized and taught useful skills, they are also selected and channeled for various roles in life. Guidance counselors, different courses of study—academic, general, and vocational tracks, for example—and grading systems are all used to separate students into different groups in ways that affect their future working lives.

It is hard to overestimate the importance of schools in making these selections for both individuals and society. In general, the total number of school years completed and the degrees received are major factors in the amount of money one makes in a lifetime. Since children of wealthier and better-educated people tend to receive the best educations, education has the effect of reinforcing our class structure.

The relationship between education and social class is another example of how different social institutions often mesh and overlap to interact with and support one another. Our performance in the economic system is largely based on how we use the educational system. Our performance in school is in turn influenced by our family background and economic position.

Schools and Mobility: Theories

The American sociologist Talcott Parsons believed that success in school—getting good marks—is the measurement by which the school acts as a selection agency for future status. At the start of their school life, he argued, all children are viewed in the same way by their teachers. All are exposed to the same program, but some achieve more than others. As time goes on, teachers begin to reward the achievers and guide them toward more education in the future.

Other researchers question Parsons's interpretation. They maintain that the school is not neutral in its attitude toward its students, simply selecting the highest achievers for advancement. Rather, it favors middle-class students because many teachers themselves hold middle-class values.

For example, Richard Sennett and Jonathan Cobb analyzed the attitudes and behav-

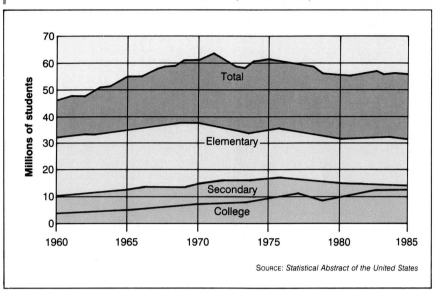

U.S. SCHOOL ENROLLMENT, BY LEVEL, 1960–1985

SOURCE: *Statistical Abstract of the United States*

GRAPH SKILL *A declining birthrate in the United States has meant a reduced number of students attending schools. What is the only school enrollment that rose in the period from 1980 to 1985? About how many students were enrolled in secondary schools in 1980? In 1985?*

ior of some middle-class teachers. They found that these instructors singled out for special recognition those students who were similar to themselves in goals, style of dress, and behavior. They encouraged such students to pursue their studies and expand their range of expectations for future achievement.

But, Sennett and Cobb claim, the teachers acted differently toward working-class students, making them feel that they lacked ability. School for them became a place where they were found wanting. As a result, they stopped trying to gain approval from their teachers and reached out to their peers, who frequently were in groups or gangs that downplayed success in school. When they did this, they confirmed the teachers' views that they were not serious students and would never amount to anything.

The situation was made worse, the report stated, if the parents viewed school as a place for their children to learn in order to get ahead in the world. When these students

were criticized by teachers or did poorly in school, they felt that they had failed their parents as well as their teachers. Ironically, rather than rebelling against the teachers' definition of them, the students would often, in turn, pick on and ridicule their successful classmates.

? Do you agree with Talcott Parsons that scholastic achievement dictates whether teachers will or will not encourage students to further their education? Explain your reasoning. Do you think parents' expectations and emphasis on school success would make students more or less interested in striving for good grades? Explain.

Many sociological studies have been utilized to bolster various opinions about education. Three studies often cited are the Coleman report, the Rosenthal and Jacobson experiment, and the Jencks study. The Coleman study was a massive survey of 4,000 schools that attempted to investigate the impact of different school settings on individual achievement. The results were complex, but

Some sociologists maintain that schools are less influential than homes and families in creating the type of person who will be an academic success.

the educational and sociological professions were surprised by the major finding that the type of school attended was not as important to scholastic achievement as the researchers had anticipated.

This result was particularly true when student experiences in modern, largely white schools were compared with those in older, largely black schools. In both settings, Coleman found that family and neighborhood mattered more in determining achievement than the school environment. Coleman concluded that schools did not wipe out major social differences that students brought with them to the schools.

On the other hand, there is evidence to show that teachers' expectations of students do make a difference. Robert Rosenthal and Lenore Jacobson discovered that when researchers told teachers that a certain group of children had been tested and found to show great promise of growth and high achievement, these children, in fact, later

showed the most growth. Actually, the children had not been pretested at all. They had been chosen randomly to find out whether teacher expectations would influence their growth. One could conclude, therefore, that some children will also perform less well when teachers have low expectations of them.

A subsequent study by Christopher Jencks and his associates appeared to support the findings of Coleman. The study concluded that schools simply tend to reinforce the circumstances of the larger society. Opportunities are affected by social class, neighborhood, and family life. The school alone cannot break the pattern of the environment.

The Coleman and Jencks studies have been the source of great controversy. Both their methods and their conclusions have been challenged. Subsequent studies disagree about the relationship between school and success in life. One—a study of Wisconsin high school graduates—found that a complex combination of family background; cognitive, or intellectual, ability, such as memory, perception, and judgment; educational attainment; type of college attended; rank in class; and certain attitudes toward success all played a part in later achievement. Its authors also criticized the Jencks study for overemphasizing luck in determining future life chances.

Schools and Mobility: Practicalities

The arguments about equality of opportunity continue to be heated. For example, is it right for well-to-do suburban communities to spend a great deal of money on schools while urban ghetto schools suffer the effects of restricted budgets? Should the schools be held accountable for the lower test scores that often plague minority children?

Americans have traditionally placed great faith in formal schooling as a source of preparation for future life and as a way of rising in society. The top graph on the opposite page shows the growing percentages of black and white students graduating from high school in the

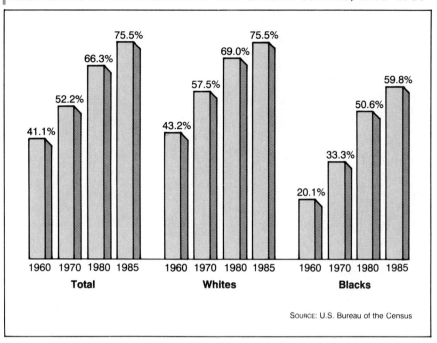

HIGH SCHOOL GRADUATES IN THE UNITED STATES, 1960–1985

SOURCE: U.S. Bureau of the Census

GRAPH SKILL   *The 1980 census was the first to show that in every state a majority of the population had completed four years of high school. Which of the two groups shown made the most notable gains in the 1980s?*

United States during the past two decades. Education as a means to transform one's life, or that of one's children, has been a significant part of the American dream.

A relatively new development has been the expansion of this dream to include the handicapped. There are 3.5 million or more handicapped people—crippled, blind, deaf, speechless, or otherwise impaired—in the United States. In the past, special schools or classes educated those who were able to handle such experience. Generally, handicapped children and adults were kept out of the public eye.

GRAPH SKILL   *Today many students who are academically qualified to attend college are finding it difficult to do so because of rising costs. In 1980, for the first time, more women than men were enrolled in college. What reasons can you give to explain why it is that more women are attending college than ever before?*

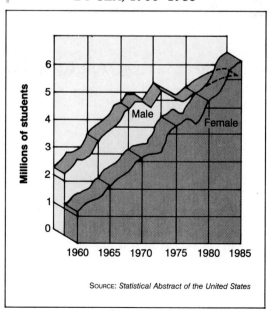

U.S. COLLEGE ENROLLMENT, BY SEX, 1960–1985

SOURCE: *Statistical Abstract of the United States*

In the United States, more blacks are attending college than ever before. Of all undergraduate degrees awarded in 1983, 10.1 percent went to blacks. This figure represents a 111 percent increase since 1970.

A first step toward the elimination of this segregation was taken in 1973 with passage of the Rehabilitation Act. The act stated that an institution or business receiving federal funds or contracts must disregard any disability that does not affect the performance required. Problems of enormous cost loomed since better access to and within buildings— using ramps, for example—was also required. However, many institutions and public places managed to comply.

Then, in 1975, the Education for All Handicapped Children Act carried this philosophy further. The aim of the act was *mainstreaming*—bringing handicapped children into regular classes whenever possible. Each student was to be given an education in the "least restrictive environment" appropriate to his or her disability. Parents and school would cooperate in arranging an individualized instruction program with specific objectives and annual goals. This act clarified the function of public schools with regard to handicapped students: to ensure them access to society in accordance with their capabilities.

Political Socialization

The school is a powerful force in political socialization. That is, it plays a primary role in teaching the young how to behave toward those who have political authority. To take part in a society like our own, citizens must learn about voting, following rules, exercising their rights, and making decisions. They must also understand government processes. Some of this learning takes place at home, but most of it takes place in school during the adolescent years. Courses in government and history, student councils, clubs, and informal friendship groups teach students how to make decisions, exercise power, and think about their rights and political beliefs.

Sociologists are interested in how political socialization takes place. For instance, our society teaches that leaders should be elected peacefully, and that police officers should be obeyed. But individual acceptance of these beliefs doesn't happen all at once. One recent study shows how attitudes toward government develop during adolescence. Researchers asked two groups of students the same question: "What is the purpose of laws?" Compare the responses of the twelve- and thirteen-year-olds to those of the fourteen- and fifteen-year-olds, as shown in the first table on page 163.

The researchers also asked two groups of adolescents for their reactions to the following hypothetical situation: "Imagine that a

POLITICAL SOCIALIZATION: "WHAT IS THE PURPOSE OF LAWS?"

Ages 12–13	Ages 15–16
1. They do it, like in schools, so that people don't get hurt.	1. To ensure safety and enforce the government.
2. If we had no laws, people could go around killing people.	2. To limit what people can do.
3. So people don't steal or kill.	3. They are basically guidelines for the people. I mean, like this is wrong and this is right and to help them understand.

The responses of students to this question demonstrate differences in political thinking between young and older teenagers.

thousand people go to an island in the Pacific to form a new society. They must form a government, devise a legal system, and face the many problems of sharing power and resources. Suppose 20 percent of the people on the island are farmers. The farmers worry that laws contrary to their interests might be passed. What should they do?" The adolescents' responses are summarized in the second table.

From these and many other questions, investigators found that in the early teen years, adolescents grow in their ability to think abstractly about rights, political institutions, and political beliefs. Compared to the older group, the twelve-to-thirteen-year-olds were more authoritarian, less critical, and less able to think out the results of certain plans.

As they mature, adolescents become more realistic and concerned with community welfare, the rights of minorities, and the need to get along peacefully. A few grow very idealistic; even fewer become radical in their beliefs. But adolescents, on the whole, are politically tolerant and unprejudiced. Some studies also show that young people tend to believe strongly in personal freedoms.

Students' responses to a hypothetical situation, stated above in the text, also show the development of political thinking.

POLITICAL SOCIALIZATION: RESPONSES TO A HYPOTHETICAL SITUATION

Ages 12–13	Ages 15–16
1. People wouldn't hurt the farmers.	1. The farmers might form a union or other organization.
2. The farmers should fight.	2. The farmers should appoint representatives and have them petition the legislature.
3. The farmers should move to another part of the island.	3. The farmers should negotiate with other interest groups.

As they grow older, students undergo changes in their political attitudes. Some show their interest in politics by running for school office.

REVIEW AND APPLICATION

1.IDENTIFY: Mainstreaming.

2. What are six major functions of most modern educational systems? Why are these functions difficult to carry out?

3. What did Talcott Parsons conclude about the importance of success in school?

4. How do working-class students respond to their teachers' expectations, according to Sennett and Cobb?

5. What did Coleman find about the importance of the type of school attended?

6. How do the results of the Rosenthal and Jacobson study differ from Coleman's conclusions?

7. What were the results of the Jencks study? Whose findings did the study appear to support?

8. What factors did the study of Wisconsin high school graduates identify as influencing the relationship between school and success in later life?

9. What did the 1973 Rehabilitation Act require? How did the 1975 Education for All Handicapped Children Act carry the philosophy of the Rehabilitation Act further?

10. Clubs and school elections help to socialize people to political participation. Some observers think that many other kinds of social learning go on in the school. Below is a list of ten aspects of school life. How does each of them contribute to personal growth: (a) cliques; (b) pep rally; (c) basketball team; (d) gym class; (e) study hall; (f) student newspaper; (g) class trip; (h) guidance counselors; (i) service organization; (j) debating team?

CRITICAL THINKING: What assumption did Americans make when the handicapped were educated exclusively in special schools or classes?

Recap

Religion and education exert powerful and early influences on the life of almost everyone. Sociologists agree that religion is important to the understanding of any social order. Durkheim stressed the "moral community of believers," while Weber emphasized the linkage of religion to economic institutions.

In many societies, such as those of India and Iran, religion is meshed with the economic and political power of the state. In contrast, the Roman Catholic church in Central and South America has, in some instances, opposed governments in power. In the United States, freedom of religion and separation of church and state are basic values. Although social scientists and others see a trend toward secularization, millions of Americans profess a religious faith and belong to an organized religion.

Educational systems are also based on a society's needs. In the United States, controversy continues over what should be taught, what teaching methods should be used, and how far schools should be expected to go in educating "the whole person." In general, people agree that schools should impart society's norms and prepare children for participation in the world of work. Educational theorists disagree, however, about how the channeling for roles takes place. Some believe it is based on achievement; others feel that social class plays a part.

Upward social mobility is a goal of many students and parents in the United States, and schools can help them achieve it. Recent laws are designed to guarantee equal opportunity for handicapped Americans to achieve their full potential within the educational system. Schools also function as influential forces in political socialization. Through classes and participation, students learn how to make decisions and exercise their political rights as citizens.

Key Terms

Define the following:

religion
sacred
secularization

progressive education
educational
   traditionalists

mainstreaming

Applying Sociology

1. Investigate the beliefs and values of the major religions: Christianity, Judaism, Hinduism, Buddhism, Islam. Write a paper describing any basic ideas they have in common.
2. What aspects of American society, if any, indicate to you a trend toward secularization? How might the trend be halted?

Should it be? Explain. Do you see any indications of a reverse trend?
3. Select a religious minority and do some research on its history and present status. (a) Was it ever attacked? Was it protected effectively by constitutional guarantees? (b) Is its membership growing or declining? Give reasons for change either way.

4. This chapter emphasizes how social institutions mesh. The meshing of social institutions is very evident in developing nations. Do some research on one of the independent African nations to determine its educational policy. *The Ideology of Developing Nations*, edited by Paul E. Sigmund, is one source of such information; consult the *Reader's Guide to Periodical Literature* and the card catalog in your local library for others. Keep in mind the following questions: (a) In what ways does the educational system differ from that in effect when the nation was a colony? (b) What are the nation's goals, and how does its educational policy help achieve them? (c) How does education mesh with the family and religious institutions, and what functions, if any, does it take away from them? (d) What other changes are taking place in society; for instance, how are roles changing?

5. Have a panel debate about some current educational conflict such as dress codes in schools, open classrooms, or some other issue of local interest.

6. Some students in the United States have complained that they were allowed to graduate from high school as "functional illiterates," that is, unable to read well enough to understand the written test for a driver's license or common forms such as job applications. Who is responsible for a student's inability to read? How can functional illiteracy be avoided?

   Prepare a mini-drama in which a failing grade-school student, his or her parents, the teacher, a special educator (such as a tutor), and a school administrator state their opinions about these two questions.

   Conclude this exercise with a paper in which you give your opinion about how the problem should be solved. Consider such points as the following: (a) the importance of reading skills in America today; (b) the idea of "social promotion," or attempting to keep a student in the same grade as his or her age-mates; (c) alternative forms of education; (d) other sources of help.

7. Using your school as a source of data, try to answer the following questions: (a) Does your school socialize students to exercise authority responsibly, and if so, how is this done? (b) What do your fellow students think about their rights and obligations as citizens in the school community? (c) Do seniors' ideas about their rights and responsibilities differ from those of first-year high school students?

8. Some social scientists are most interested in the informal aspects of school life, the student "underworld" of informal cliques and friendship groups. In fact, they think that this second structure, the second society, is more important by far than the one organized by school administrators—certainly to students. One such scientist is Philip A. Cusick, a teacher and author of *Inside High School.*

   Cusick lived with students for six months at a school he called "Horatio Gates." He wrote: "More and more, as I continued in the school, I saw that the students' most active and alive moments, and indeed the great majority of their school time, was spent not with teachers and subject-matter affairs, but in their own small-group interactions which they carried on simultaneously with their class work."

   Comment on Cusick's remark. Do you agree or disagree? Which aspect of school has seemed most important to you? Which will probably have the greatest effect on your future?

Howard S. Becker and Blanche Geer, "The Fate of Idealism in Medical School," American Sociological Review, 23 (February 1958), pp. 50–56.

1. Why are some students disillusioned in their first year of medical school?
2. How do most students manage to keep their idealistic expectations about medicine?

Frederick Edwards, "Students Speak Out Against Textbook Censorship," The Humanist, March/April 1987, pp. 23–34.

Extended Readings

1. What was the students' position on attempts to remove the book from their school?
2. What remedy does one student suggest for those who object to the book?

Dennis A. Williams, "One-on-One Against Illiteracy," Newsweek, July 30, 1984, p. 78.

1. What is being done to help illiterate Americans?
2. What type of problems do illiterate Americans encounter?

Social Studies

Making judgments regarding teachers' philosophy of education Refer to your answer for question 4 on page 157, which lists the points of conflict between traditionalists and progressives in education. Based on this list, write a few multiple choice questions designed to elicit which philosophy someone favors. For each question, note the response that a traditionalist would give and the one a progressive would give. Then ask the questions of teachers at your school. Judge from each teacher's answers whether he or she is a traditionalist or a progressive.

Critical Thinking

Evaluating Samples: The study by Robert Rosenthal and Lenore Jacobson, described on page 160, concluded that teachers' expectations of students are a key to student achievement in school. Write at least two questions you would want to have answered before you decide to accept or reject this conclusion.

Government and Economic Systems

● **Before you read,** look up the following key terms in the glossary to become familiar with their definitions:

traditional authority   rational-legal authority   communism
charismatic authority   capitalism   socialism

● **As you read,** think about answers to the following questions:

1. What is the principal source of power of American Presidents?
2. Why do only a slightly more than a pure majority of eligible voters actually participate in American elections?
3. What is the basic difference between a capitalist and a socialist economy?
4. Why is the American economy not considered a purely free enterprise system?

Sections in this Chapter

1. Political Institutions
2. American Political Institutions
3. Economic Institutions
4. The American Economy

Chapter Focus

Societies can be labeled—capitalist, socialist, communist, democratic, dictatorship—according to the character of their institutions. But one must keep in mind that the network of norms that make up the institutions are meaningless without people. Societies are social units made up of people who relate to one another in particular ways—people who act, react, and interact in groups and associations. Every society has not only a government but also people who participate in political processes—who vote and hold office and whose lives are regulated by laws. Every society has not only an economy, but also people who produce, consume, and distribute goods.

The world of work and people's attitudes toward the economic functions they perform are discussed in Chapter 11. This chapter takes a broader view of the structures and functions of government and the economy. It examines the concepts of power and authority, different economic systems, and some special features of American political and economic institutions.

Using Sociologists' Tools

● **Observe** how local politicians campaign for elective office.

● **Describe** those things that politicians do that seem most effective in influencing voters.

● **Analyze** the results of the most recent national political election in terms of the candidates' campaign techniques.

● **Predict** what the losing party will do to win the next election.

National economic policy is largely determined by laws enacted in Washington, D.C. Here a demonstration seeks to win support for more affordable housing.

1 Political Institutions

You read in the last chapter how religious groups can behave politically and how government is interrelated with the educational system. But you still may not fully realize how pervasive political institutions are in our lives. Our complex legal system affects family behavior, for example, through laws that control marriage, divorce, and inheritance. And political institutions have an immense impact on our economy, since they do everything from providing Social Security for individuals to regulating giant corporations.

The State

Government as we know it today is a relatively new political institution. The nation-state appeared only about four hundred years ago—not a very long period in the span of human history. The ancient Greeks, for example, were organized in independent city-states rather than one Greek nation. Although great empires did exist more than four hundred years ago—such as those of the Romans in Europe and around the Mediterranean, the Incas in South America, and the Mandingos in Africa—they did not unite people as completely as a modern nation-state does.

The history of modern nations shows that a long, hard struggle is necessary before a central power can replace warring lords and petty princes and bring different peoples together in one functioning nation. In Italy and Germany, this kind of unification did not occur until the nineteenth century. It has yet to occur in some African and Asian nations that had colonial governments well into the twentieth century.

Nationalistic feelings are often expressed through holidays that commemorate historic events. When the Statue of Liberty restoration was completed in 1986, thousands of people celebrated in New York.

One of the most compelling forces behind political institutions is *nationalism,* a feeling of loyalty and commitment to one's own nation. Nationalism helps unite those who are organized in a national state, such as Mexicans, Swedes, and Nigerians. And it inspires those without a national state—colonial peoples, for example—to try to form one.

Sovereignty is the supreme power embodied in a modern nation-state. Basically, sovereignty is the state's control over the life and death of its citizens. Through laws, the state regulates what its citizens can and cannot do and punishes those who do not obey. It can even establish instances in which killing is legal.

Control of military and police forces is central to the existence of a nation. And the rise of an armed force outside the control of a national government raises the threat of revolution or civil war. In the United States, it is an accepted norm that North Carolina and South Carolina or Washington and Oregon or Maine and New Hampshire cannot settle disputes by combat between state militias. The national government settles such differences according to decisions made by the Supreme Court.

Where settlement by national power doesn't work, civil war or revolution often results. We Americans learned this lesson in our Civil War, and people in many countries throughout the world have had similar experiences. For example, Pakistan separated from India in 1948 because no national authority could settle differences between Muslims and Hindus. And in recent years, devastating warfare has ravaged much of Southeast Asia as armed political factions struggle for control. Can you think of other examples from history or current events?

Power and Authority

Power is the key to political institutions. The problem of how to distribute power exists in all governing bodies—even small ones such as local city councils or high school student governments. Struggles for power can occur within or totally outside formal organizations. Think, for example, of power struggles that occur among street gangs battling over "turf."

The sociologist and economist Max Weber defined power as the ability to control others, even to the point of being able to make them do something against their own desires or interests. Such power is coercive—that is, it threatens to punish those who disobey. But Weber believed that coercion by itself is the least effective way to control people. He believed that those in power need *legitimacy*. In other words, rulers must be recognized as having the right to control people. That right is authority. As you read in Chapter 5, Weber described three kinds of authority: traditional, charismatic, and rational-legal.

Most societies have found a need for a police force that can exert coercion if people do not follow the laws.

Traditional Authority According to Weber, *traditional authority* is based on the long-held beliefs of a society. For example, the authority of a council of elders might come from the firmly held, unchallenged belief that the elders have wisdom that only the aged possess. Traditional authority is the basis of legitimacy for tribal chiefs, monarchs, and others who inherit their offices. These people do not draw their authority from their personal characteristics or from the offices they hold. Rather, they are persons whom the society normally considers rightful leaders.

Charismatic Authority The second basis of legitimacy, according to Weber, is *charismatic authority*. Individuals who possess to an outstanding degree the personal qualities that are valued or desired in their culture have charisma. *Charisma* in Greek means "favor" or "gift." It comes from another Greek word, *charis*, meaning "grace" in the sacred sense of the word. Charisma, then, is the persuasive force that a particular personality has over the members of society.

In our society, John F. Kennedy and Martin Luther King, Jr., were notable for their charismatic authority. In earlier periods, Thomas Jefferson, Abraham Lincoln, and Sojourner Truth had this quality. History books are filled with charismatic figures: Joan of Arc, Winston Churchill, Charles de Gaulle.

Charismatic authority disappears with the individual who possesses it. Thus any movement or government founded solely on such a leader is bound to have trouble when the leader is gone. For example, the nonviolent movement to unite all Indians faced a doubtful future in 1948 when Mahatma Gandhi, its charismatic leader, died.

Rational-Legal Authority Weber's third basis of legitimacy is *rational-legal authority*. The source of this authority is the position, not the person. As you have read, individuals play a wide range of roles in their daily lives. Some roles are particularly political because they involve the exercise of power and forms of social control. A police officer, a judge, a member of Congress, a Cabinet secretary—

each holds a rational-legal position in the political structure. Rights, privileges, and obligations come with the office. When one individual leaves the office, a successor assumes those same rights and obligations.

While in an office of authority, a person is expected to behave according to its norms. Richard Nixon, who occupied the highest and most privileged office in the United States, was forced to resign under threat of impeachment for wrongdoing. After allegedly violating the rules of behavior required of a person in his position, he lost the powers and privileges that went with it. Upon Nixon's resignation, Vice-President Gerald Ford, next in the line of presidential succession, assumed the presidency along with all its powers and privileges.

In most sectors of American society, the office, not the person, is most important. Traditional authority plays a very small part in our politics, although a few influential families hand power down from one generation to the next. The Rockefellers and the Lodges are examples of families that exercise this kind of political power. And with television as a forum in which to display charisma, charismatic authority may help candidates win elections and govern more effectively once elected. But in the United States, the primary form of authority in our political system is rational-legal authority.

In addition, the methods by which our government exercises control are rational-legal in character. Rules are written in the

Charisma, a special force of personality, can provide a basis for authority. Pope John Paul II is one of the most charismatic and popular pontiffs in modern history. His great personal warmth attracts huge crowds wherever he travels. This popularity, in turn, has reinforced his leadership of Roman Catholics at a time of increased challenges from within the church.

form of ordinances, codes, and laws, and anyone who violates them risks punishment. In a democracy, one of the government's claims to legitimacy is the equality of all citizens before the law.

REVIEW AND APPLICATION

1. *IDENTIFY:* Sovereignty, legitimacy, traditional authority, charismatic authority, charisma, charis, rational-legal authority.
2. How did Weber define power? What did he mean by "legitimacy" in government?
3. Which of Weber's three types of authority is the most important in the United States? Which does the government use to exercise control?

CRITICAL THINKING: Do you think the assassinations of Kennedy, King, Lincoln, and Gandhi were in part the result of their charisma? Why or why not?

Rational-legal authority resides in the position, not in the person. British prime minister Margaret Thatcher, shown here acknowledging her victory, has authority only as long as she holds her office.

2 American Political Institutions

American political life is based on the idea that government derives its authority from the consent of the governed. But how does this really work? How many Americans actually make their wishes known by going to the polls on election day?

Do you have any idea what percentage of eligible Americans voted in the 1980 presidential election? The answer is 53.1 percent—not much more than half. This figure contrasts with much higher average voter turnout in other countries: 85 percent in England and 90 percent in Denmark, Italy, and West Germany.

If these figures surprise you, consider this question: Which Americans are most likely to vote—the old or the young, the wealthy or the poor? Surveys reveal that there is a direct relationship between income and voting. That is, the higher a person's in-

come, the more likely the person is to vote. (See the Appendix for a general discussion of direct relationships.)

Figures also show that a higher percentage of the youngest people eligible to vote do not exercise that right. Many seem to feel their vote won't count. They believe that votes can't influence how decisions are made or that powerful "special interests" really run things. Some have not yet developed a political consciousness.

Political Parties

In European parliamentary systems, political representation is based on overall popular vote. Minor candidates can pick up votes all over the country, and they often win seats for minor parties in national legislatures.

PERCENTAGE OF BLACKS AND WHITES VOTING IN U.S. PRESIDENTIAL ELECTIONS, 1964–1984

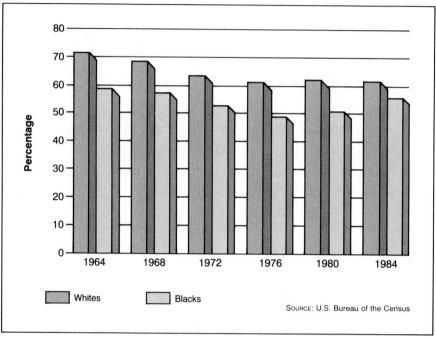

Whites   Blacks

SOURCE: U.S. Bureau of the Census

CHART SKILL   *Studies have shown that age, education, and income influence voting patterns in the United States. People who have attended college, are between forty-five and sixty-four years of age, and are members of the upper or upper middle class are most likely to vote. Whites are more likely to vote than blacks. Why might the numbers voting in 1964 have been larger than in 1984?*

VOTING IN THE 1984 AND 1988 U.S. PRESIDENTIAL ELECTIONS BY EDUCATION AND AGE

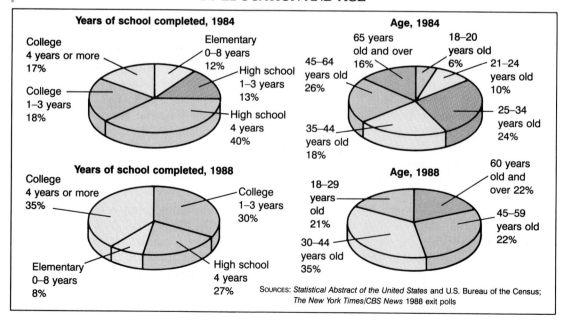

SOURCES: *Statistical Abstract of the United States* and U.S. Bureau of the Census; *The New York Times/CBS News* 1988 exit polls

Many European countries have multiparty systems and must rely on coalitions for government to function successfully.

In the United States, on the other hand, separate elections are held in each congressional district, and the winner is the candidate with the most votes in his or her district. Unless a minor party is particularly powerful in a given district, it has little opportunity to elect members to Congress. One consequence is that two loosely formed parties have almost always dominated American politics.

While party platforms, issued in presidential-election years, indicate some differences between today's Republicans and Democrats, the similarities are more striking. Rather than explicitly identifying with the interests of a particular segment of the population—such as labor, small business, or big industry—each party portrays itself as being ready and able to represent the interests of the American people at large. Definite stands on specific economic or social issues are usually avoided, unless a particular stand seems likely to garner wide support.

In recent years, when either party has become too strongly identified with a particular group or stand, it has often been a substantial loser at the polls. This happened in 1964, when Republican Barry Goldwater was perceived as too conservative and militaristic. It happened again in 1972, when Democrat George McGovern appeared too liberal for many people. Ronald Reagan's election in 1980, based upon promised decreases in government controls, taxes, and inflation, is perhaps one exception.

Because of the two-party system, Americans working for social change have usually operated within a major party rather than through independent organizations. In 1980, John Anderson broke from this tradition and mounted his own campaign for the presidency. Because he was not supported by one of the two major parties, many voters regarded a vote for Anderson as a wasted vote. He received only about 6 percent of the national total.

PERCENTAGE OF MEN AND WOMEN REPORTED VOTING IN U.S. PRESIDENTIAL ELECTIONS, 1964–1984

Year	Women	Men
1964	67.0	71.9
1968	66.0	69.8
1972	62.0	64.1
1976	58.8	59.6
1980	59.4	59.1
1984	60.8	59.0

SOURCE: U.S. Bureau of the Census

CHART SKILL   There are more women than men in every age bracket of the electorate, and since 1964 they have cast more votes than men. However, the 1980 election was the first since World War II in which a larger percentage of women than men went to the polls. Moreover, voting patterns have revealed a "gender gap." Men are more likely to vote Republican, women Democratic. What changes in government policy, if any, might result from the gender gap?

Interest Groups

Many political decisions in America are made as a result of activity by *interest groups,* organizations formed expressly to influence political decisions. Such groups try to win support for their special interests from Cabinet officers, members of Congress, governors, and even presidents by letter writing, advertising, and donating funds to election campaigns. Current newspapers show some of the issues in which interest groups are involved: nuclear power, tariffs, the "right to life." The better organized its efforts, the more supporters a group is likely to gain and the better its chances of achieving its goals.

Some interest groups use the huge amounts of money at their disposal to support the election campaigns of favored candidates and to influence their policies once elected. As a result, the relationships between interest groups and government officials are frequently questioned and investigated. Members of Congress are constantly subject to

The best way for citizens to monitor their government is to participate fully in all its democratic processes. Voting represents both the simplest and most powerful act of an informed citizen.

temptations and pressures to perform favors for a price.

Corruption in government was highlighted in the late 1970s and early 1980s by a large-scale FBI investigation. FBI agents posing as wealthy Arab oil executives approached elected officials at local and national levels seeking favors and promising substantial contributions in return. The responses, recorded on videotape, indicated that in virtually every instance, the public officials were ready and willing to accept bribes to serve wealthy interest groups. Although there were complaints that the FBI was engaging in entrapment—deceiving the officials in order to lure them into misbehavior—the trials and resulting convictions cast a shadow on the ethical standards not only of Congress but also of politicians in general.

Fortunately, government and decision making in America are based on pluralistic principles. Interest groups are recognized as having the right to press their causes. Since the needs and goals of interest groups often compete, not all politicians are under overwhelming pressure to accommodate any one special group. And if politicians fail to meet the ethical standards we demand of our elected representatives, the American political system allows the electorate the opportunity to "throw the rascals out."

REVIEW AND APPLICATION

1. *IDENTIFY:*   Interest groups.
2. What is the relationship between income and voting?
3. How does the American system of electing political representatives differ from the European parlimentary system?
4. What did John Anderson's failed campaign for the presidency illustrate about the two-party system?
5. Why are the relationships between interest groups and government officials frequently investigated?

CRITICAL THINKING: All Democratic and Republican nominees for President of the United States have been white. How might this reality have kept blacks from voting?

3 Economic Institutions

You are probably familiar with the game of Monopoly. Perhaps you have played it with family or friends. Think about the game for a moment. Players are concerned with property, mortgages, bankruptcy, utilities, poor taxes, and luxury taxes—things that are important not only in Monopoly but also in real economic systems.

Economic Activities

Acquiring and controlling property is central in Monopoly, and it is also a major activity of most modern economic systems. As in some societies, the goal of the game is to buy as much as possible. By buying property, a player acquires something scarce, something that can be used, and something that can demand resources—in the form of rent—from another player. Every player knows that acquiring property means acquiring power. Players also know that developing one's property by building on it makes it far more valuable.

Property, of course, means not only homes and hotels but also utilities, such as electric and water companies, and means of transportation, such as railroads. Perhaps the greatest shortcoming of the game is that it doesn't include factories, oil wells, and mines in its catalog of important holdings. After all, controlling natural resources, manufacturing units, and agricultural land is as important as owning other forms of real estate.

CHART SKILL   *In any economic system, people perform a wide variety of tasks. The numbers employed in any given sector, however, can change over time. This table compares the United States work force in 1940, just prior to entering World War II, with the work force of 1986. How many workers were employed in manufacturing in 1940? In 1986?*

CHANGES IN THE AMERICAN WORK FORCE, 1940–1986

	Workers in 1940	Workers in 1986	Percentage of Change
Agriculture	9,540,000	2,740,000	−71.3%
Nonagriculture	32,361,000	100,167,000	223.0
Construction	1,311,000	4,960,000	278.3
Financial[1]	1,485,000	6,305,000	324.6
Government, federal	996,000	2,899,000	191.1
Government, state and local	3,206,000	13,836,000	331.6
Government, total	4,202,000	16,735,000	298.3
Manufacturing	10,985,000	19,186,000	74.7
Mining	925,000	792,000	−14.4
Services[2]	3,665,000	23,072,000	529.5
Trade, wholesale and retail	6,750,000	23,831,000	253.1
Transportation, public utilities	3,038,000	5,286,000	74.0

[1] including insurance and real estate
[2] including personal and business

SOURCE: U.S. Bureau of Labor Statistics

Monopoly also familiarizes us with the concept of taxation as payment for government services, such as schools and welfare, by individuals and businesses. The game teaches us that if we run short of cash, we may have to mortgage property. If worst comes to worst, we may go bankrupt and have to drop out of the game.

In Monopoly, as in real economic systems, people perform various economic tasks. There are bankers and builders, tax collectors and jailers, charity givers and charity receivers, people who run railroads and people who deliver babies. In other words, there is a division of labor. Of course, Monopoly is only a game. Yet it illustrates some important economic activities and institutions.

Economic Systems

To economists, all economic systems have three separate parts, or sectors: (1) the sector that gathers and extracts natural resources through such activities as mining, fishing, and agriculture; (2) the sector that processes raw materials and manufactures goods, such as steel and automobiles; and (3)

the sector that provides services, such as education, health care, and banking. The norms and laws connected with exploiting resources, producing goods, and providing services combine to make up the economic institutions of a society. These institutions can take many different forms, from the relatively simple hunting and gathering activities of a folk society to the complex production and distribution of goods and services in an industrial society like our own.

In all societies, economic institutions are concerned with the nature of property and who owns or controls it. In modern industrial societies, economies are generally classified as either capitalist or socialist. *Capitalism,* or the free-enterprise system, is based on the private ownership of the means of production operated for private profit. Theoretically, the market under capitalism is free, regulated only by competition among buyers and sellers. *Socialism* is based on public ownership of the major sources of wealth. In socialist systems, the market is regulated by central authorities.

There are many varieties of capitalism and socialism. The economy of Canada, a na-

GRAPH SKILL   The dramatic changes in the composition of the American work force that took place between 1940 and 1980 had complex economic and sociological causes. How might the changes in farming shown in the graphs be related to new technology and more money available for investment?

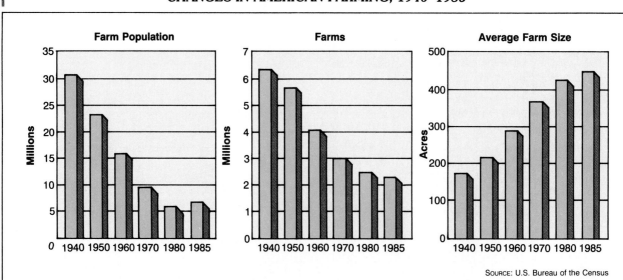

CHANGES IN AMERICAN FARMING, 1940–1985

Source: U.S. Bureau of the Census

All societies have economic institutions, and in many countries they are undergoing change. India, for example, has nuclear power plants, although much labor is still performed by hand. Here, a woman spreads handwoven cotton out to dry.

tion that regards itself as capitalist, has many features of a socialist economy, among them extensive government regulation. Socialist nations range from the heavily industrialized countries of the Soviet system to agricultural societies like Tanzania. Other countries, such as Sweden and Denmark, have a mixture of public and private ownership of the means of production. They characterize themselves as socialist but are frequently described as having *mixed economies*.

Certain socialist societies of Eastern Europe, Asia, and elsewhere are described as communist by people from Western democracies. Actually, *communism* as envisioned by its founder, Karl Marx, does not exist anywhere. It is a utopian condition in which the state has "withered away" because there are no social classes and the society functions without the need for a political apparatus to enforce norms. There is no private property, and all citizens receive the necessities of life according to their needs. Socialist nations such as China and the Soviet Union claim to be striving toward communism, but they are nowhere near this goal. In fact, both societies have been characterized by a dictatorship that Marx saw as an interim stage. They are now undergoing extensive reform in order to modernize their economies.

The word "socialism" has negative connotations for many Americans, since many do not distinguish it from communism and dictatorship. Our norms have long associated free economic enterprise with political freedom. Actually, political institutions vary greatly in socialist nations. The Soviet Union is a one-party state that has dealt ruthlessly with opposition—political dissenters face prison and exile. But Sweden and Denmark have multiparty systems and free elections.

In some democracies, parties advocating capitalist and socialist policies compete openly and often successfully for voter support. France and Great Britain, for example, are democracies, but in 1981 François Mitterrand was elected president of France on a socialist platform. On the other hand, Conservative prime minister Margaret Thatcher of England was elected in 1979 and reelected in 1987 by a public that had previously experienced socialist governments.

REVIEW AND APPLICATION

1. *IDENTIFY:* Capitalism, socialism, mixed economies, communism.
2. How do communism and socialism differ?

CRITICAL THINKING: Although Americans value free enterprise, the United States has many government regulatory agencies. Which country has a similar economy?

4 The American Economy

Monopoly is an American game, based on American values and norms. All players start even. All strive to acquire more. Success is good. All players work for themselves, and each has an equal chance of winning—depending, of course, on the throw of the dice, or luck.

Norms and Values of Capitalism

Real economic systems are guided by societal norms and values which govern the behavior of people in their economic relationships. Important American economic values and norms include competition, individual achievement, lack of government interference, division of labor, and competing economic interests.

Competition Economic life in most cultures is the most competitive of all economic institutions. Americans believe in a system of free enterprise based on competition. Competition serves as the chief regulator of persons and groups engaging in business.

Individual Achievement If we look to the norms and values that legitimize capitalism, we find that most Americans believe that everyone has the opportunity to work hard and improve his or her life situation. Americans do not deny that there are great discrepancies between rich and poor, but they act on the belief that this is an open society where individual achievement can lead to upward mobility. (See page 113 for a complete discussion of "upward/downward mobility.")

Lack of Government Interference Most Americans support capitalism because they feel that it limits the oppressive role of government in daily life. No one is forced to work for the government or to live in government housing. Each person is supposed to have free choice about where to work, when to leave a job, and where to live. Even when faced with serious problems of unemployment or homelessness, most Americans believe their system is preferable to one in which the government controls the economy.

Division of Labor We all know that there are electricians, nurses, bus drivers and thousands of other occupations in our society. We depend on all of these people to contribute some small but significant part in making our economy function. For example, the farmers who grow wheat in the mid-western states need truck drivers to distribute it to every part of the country. There, bakers transform the wheat into wheat flour and the flour into bread and other products, and salespeople sell these products to customers. By this complex division of labor, our society is able to meet the needs of its citizens through production, distribution, and consumption. In the contemporary United States, there are more than 30,000 occupational categories.

Competing Economic Interests People who work in a similar occupational category often have shared interests and needs. They want economic policies that will allow their group to thrive. Farmers want to get good prices for the food they grow. They support agricultural subsidies by the government to ensure that they will earn enough money. Corporate executives running General Motors, Chrysler, or Ford have totally different needs. They are worried about competition from foreign automobile manufacturers that limits their sales both here and abroad.

It is common for these farmers, managers, or workers to organize into economic interest groups to promote their own needs. Individuals cannot normally change policies, but as a group they might have more influence. Not only farmers, managers, and workers form economic interest groups. To promote their interests, doctors organized the American Medical Association; lawyers formed the American Bar Association;

U.S. FEDERAL BUDGET, 1971 AND 1986

Receipts

1971

Corporation income taxes

14.2%

Excise taxes and other

14.2%

Individual income taxes 45.8%

25.8%

Social insurance taxes and contributions

1986

9.1%

9.3%

Individual income taxes 45.5%

36.1%

Outlays

Interest

1971

7.0%

11.3%

Health and education

National defense 36.3%

26.2%

Income security

Other 19.2%

1986

14.6%

9.5%

National defense 27.1%

Other 9.3%

39.5%

SOURCE: *Statistical Abstract of the United States*

GRAPH SKILL   The United States is a capitalist country, the wealthiest nation in the world. Study these graphs of the federal budget to see where the vast sums needed to operate the government come from and where they go. Compare the budgets for 1971 and 1986. From where does the federal government receive most of its money? In which areas does the government spend most of its money?

businessmen often join the Chamber of Commerce; and workers join unions.

In the American economic system, it is legitimate and even desirable to have many competing interest groups. Americans believe that this competition is healthy because it prevents one group from totally dominating the society. In this society, people also believe that as groups strive to achieve their own goals, it will result in the greatest good for the greatest number.

As society changes, new groups are constantly forming. One example in recent years

was the founding of the American Association of Retired Persons (AARP), an organization that lobbies for everything from better health care for the elderly to senior citizen discounts. As the number of elderly citizens has grown, they have realized that they have much in common. They believe they have contributed to the economy by a lifetime of work. They want to be comfortable during their retirement years. They have learned that they must organize in order to compete for scarce economic resources and to avoid discrimination due to their age.

The Military and the Economy

Billions of dollars each year—representing a substantial percentage of the total productive capacity of the economy—are earmarked for the development of defense capabilities, including sophisticated nuclear weaponry. The graphs on page 181 show what percentage of the federal budget went to defense in two recent years.

When he left office in 1961, President Dwight D. Eisenhower—himself a military hero—warned of the continued growth and impact of what he termed the "military-industrial complex."

The conjunction of an immense military establishment and a large arms industry is new in the American experience. The total influence—economic, political, even spiri-tual—is felt in every city, every statehouse, every office of the federal government. We recognize the imperative need for this development, yet we must not fail to comprehend its grave implications.

Many people today still echo Eisenhower's concern about the impact of the military on the economy at large. In recent years, the relationship between the government and certain large corporations has come under attack. Critics have charged that the norms and values central to a free-enterprise economic system are undermined when large corporations obtaining government contracts are allowed to increase the costs of their products to consumers. Assured of income from government contracts, such corporations may lose the incentive to ensure careful management and better productivity.

GRAPH SKILL   The concerns listed in the chart below reflect Americans' worries about their ability to share in the "American dream." Topping off the list of worries are the problems of drug abuse and crime. Why is the diminishing quality of the educational system also a prominent concern?

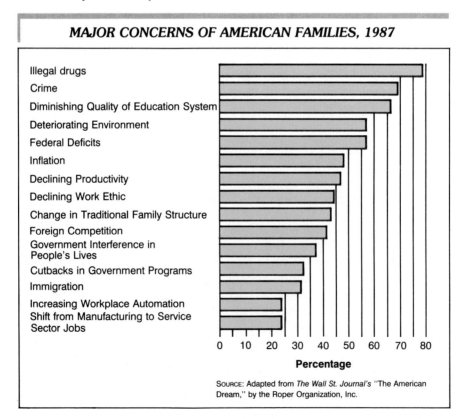

MAJOR CONCERNS OF AMERICAN FAMILIES, 1987

Illegal drugs
Crime
Diminishing Quality of Education System
Deteriorating Environment
Federal Deficits
Inflation
Declining Productivity
Declining Work Ethic
Change in Traditional Family Structure
Foreign Competition
Government Interference in People's Lives
Cutbacks in Government Programs
Immigration
Increasing Workplace Automation
Shift from Manufacturing to Service Sector Jobs

0   10   20   30   40   50   60   70   80

Percentage

Source: Adapted from *The Wall St. Journal's* "The American Dream," by the Roper Organization, Inc.

U.S. CONSUMER PRICE INDEX, 1967–1985

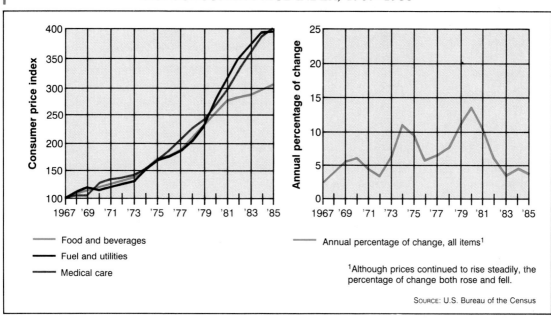

Food and beverages
Fuel and utilities
Medical care

Annual percentage of change, all items[1]

[1]Although prices continued to rise steadily, the percentage of change both rose and fell.

SOURCE: U.S. Bureau of the Census

CHART AND GRAPH SKILL   What has happened to consumer prices since 1970? Why is it important for family income to rise as consumer prices rise?

MEDIAN FAMILY INCOME IN THE UNITED STATES IN CURRENT AND CONSTANT DOLLARS, 1970–1985

Year	Median Income	Median Income in Constant (1985) Dollars
1970	$9,750	$27,336
1971	10,314	27,819
1972	11,152	28,584
1973	11,895	29,172
1974	13,004	28,145
1975	14,156	27,421
1976	15,016	28,267
1977	15,949	28,419
1978	17,318	29,087
1979	18,645	29,029
1980	19,950	27,446
1981	22,388	26,481
1982	23,433	26,116
1983	24,674	26,642
1984	26,433	27,376
1985	27,735	27,735

SOURCE: *Statistical Abstract of the United States*

PERCENTAGE OF TEENAGERS UNEMPLOYED IN SELECTED COUNTRIES

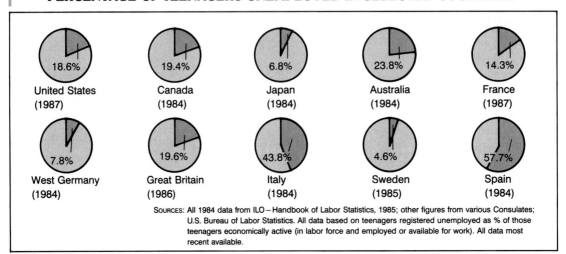

United States (1987) 18.6%
Canada (1984) 19.4%
Japan (1984) 6.8%
Australia (1984) 23.8%
France (1987) 14.3%

West Germany (1984) 7.8%
Great Britain (1986) 19.6%
Italy (1984) 43.8%
Sweden (1985) 4.6%
Spain (1984) 57.7%

SOURCES: All 1984 data from ILO—Handbook of Labor Statistics, 1985; other figures from various Consulates; U.S. Bureau of Labor Statistics. All data based on teenagers registered unemployed as % of those teenagers economically active (in labor force and employed or available for work). All data most recent available.

GRAPH SKILL   Compare the teenage unemployment figures for the United States with other countries. How might the other societies be different? The same?

Today our economy is so complex that the functions of government, business, and labor are meshed. To protect the livelihood of workers, government often directly assists failing private companies with loans. Labor often supports government policies that foster the growth of large corporations in the hope that this will ensure jobs. In times of economic downturn, labor may relax its demands or even accept cuts in order to aid a faltering industry and thus preserve jobs.

The Consumer Movement

In recent years, the consumer movement has urged more effective government regulation of certain economic activities in the United States. Leaders such as Ralph Nader believe consumers often pay high prices for low-quality goods. They argue that the immense power of the giant automobile, food, and chemical industries has prevented adequate regulation of safety hazards in our automobiles and health hazards in our food and our environment.

Consumer groups feel victimized by policies that, in their opinion, benefit private interests while denying public needs. They work for better government regulation of industry and for the passage of public interest laws that provide direct protection to consumers. Government officials as well as corporations are under pressure to respond.

REVIEW AND APPLICATION

1. What are the major norms and values that give legitimacy to the American economic system?
2. What role does competition play in the economic life of society?
3. What are the goals of the consumer movement? What methods do they use to attain these goals?
4. What dangers regarding the military-industrial complex did President Eisenhower warn against in 1960?
5. What American economic norms and values are threatened when corporations fail to meet government contracts at the stipulated cost?
6. How might critics argue that this neglect of basic economic values threatens the defense capability of our nation?

CRITICAL THINKING: In a poll of major concerns, would saving for the future or finding quality medical care rank higher among people in California, where costs are high? Which concern would rank higher among people in West Virginia, where services are scarce?

CHAPTER **8** REVIEW

Recap

Modern political institutions revolve around the state, whose sovereignty is sustained in part by nationalism. According to Max Weber, legitimate political power stems from traditional, charismatic, or rational-legal authority. In the United States, where a relatively small percentage of the electorate votes, political life is characterized by a two-party system. Usually, party platforms avoid taking definite stands on issues. A threat to our democratic system is posed by powerful interest groups whose activities may, at times, encourage corruption. Some social scientists argue that pluralism operates against this threat by providing a balance of interest groups.

Economic institutions can be classified according to whether the production and distribution of scarce resources are primarily controlled by the private sector, as in capitalism, or by the public sector, as in socialism. Mixed economies have some characteristics of each. The United States has a capitalistic economy that stresses competition. However, according to some critics, close government-industry ties, particularly in military production, may be harmful to the traditional free-enterprise system. The consumer movement, which aims at protecting consumers against inferior and unsafe merchandise, encourages further government regulation of industry.

Key Terms

Define the following:

nationalism	charismatic authority	socialism
sovereignty	rational-legal authority	mixed economy
legitimacy	interest group	communism
traditional authority	capitalism	

Applying Sociology

1. Imagine that you are a United States senator sitting on a committee charged with examining a bill requesting more funds needed to fulfill a government contract. At first you are reluctant to vote in favor of the bill. Yet many of your constituents write or call to argue that they will lose their jobs if Congress rejects the bill.

Of course, many of these workers are concerned because they have family responsibilities.

(a) What additional information would you want to know before you voted?

(b) How would you vote? What factors would you take into account when making your decision?

(c) How does this situation show the interrelation of major institutions?

2. List some of the values that underlie our political system. You might use historical documents such as the Declaration of Independence as a starting point. Now list some of the norms that are based upon these values. The Constitution can be of help here. Can you suggest ways in which these norms might be extended further to make the actual functioning of our society closer to the values it holds?

3. A city planning board is discussing the city's need for both a teenage recreation center and a housing project for the elderly. Budget restrictions make it impossible to build both. As a class, list ten sociological conditions—economic, social, or political—that explain the needs of each group. For example, most people over sixty-five exist on Social Security and small pensions that force them to live in very poor housing; or, delinquency rates are high among teenagers, and recreational centers can help keep young people off the streets. Given the conditions on your class list, imagine you are a consultant. Write a recommendation to the planning board explaining the reasons for your conclusions.

4. With the help of an encyclopedia, make a chart comparing capitalist, socialist, and communist systems. Include such headings as "Historical Origins," "Ownership of Means of Production," "Stated Goals," "Relationship Between Political and Economic Structures," "Countries Practicing," and so forth.

Extended Readings

Janet Novack, "The Gold Mine Is Playing Out," *Forbes*, April 6, 1987, p. 146, 150.

1. What technique had the Republican Party relied on to raise most of its operating money?

2. Why does this technique not work as well as it once did?

Mark Jacobson, "The Trouble With Money," *Esquire*, April 1987, pp. 49–50.

1. How did acquiring large sums of money affect the author's friends?

2. How did the author feel about people who were wealthy?

Roger Thurow, "In Romania, Smoking a Kent Cigarette Is Like Burning Money," *Wall Street Journal,* January 3, 1986, p. 1, 5.

1. What are some of the reasons offered for the value of the Kents as currency?
2. What other social message do the Kents carry?

Sequencing key events in modern history

Knowing when important events occurred gives us perspective about history. Down the center of a sheet of paper, draw a vertical line. To the left of the line, list the following events in the order that they occurred. To the right of the line, write the year that corresponds to each event. Refer to Chapter 8 for help.

Dwight D. Eisenhower leaves the presidency.

Mahatma Gandhi dies, and Pakistan separates from India.

Margaret Thatcher is elected Prime Minister of England for the first time.

Francois Mitterand is elected President of France.

Barry Goldwater loses the presidential election because he is considered too conservative.

George McGovern appears too liberal to win the presidential election.

Ronald Reagan is elected president for the first time.

Which three leaders mentioned on the time line most likely met for high level talks?

Critical Thinking

1. *Assessing Cause and Effect:* The graph on page 174 shows that a higher percentage of whites than blacks vote in presidential elections. The chart on page 175, meanwhile, shows that a lower percentage of women vote. Why do you think a lower percentage of blacks vote and what to you think has caused women to vote at a higher rate than men?
2. *Recognizing Values:* Look at the Federal Budget as shown on page 181. What values of our society are shown in the graphs?

187

UNIT APPLICATION

Social Institutions "Out of This World"

Science-fiction movies can be fascinating. If they are well produced, they succeed in transporting us into unfamiliar worlds and making us feel quite comfortable in them. Often, after the initial wonderment at where we are "taken," we settle in to follow the plot much as we would with an old-fashioned "western" or a situation comedy. The unfamiliar quickly becomes commonplace. We begin to believe in the characters, even those who are rather different from us humans.

One reason may be that most science-fiction writers seem bound by earthly concepts of the nature of society. They see it—and portray it—in a rather customary fashion. The social organizations of their new worlds are, like our own, made up of a number of segments, each with a specific set of rules and each related to some central idea. In other words, there are institutions—family, government, economic, religious, and educational—all somehow connected to a common culture.

In fact, without realizing it, the creators of science fiction may be reflecting ideas held by many sociologists: that all societies have to meet certain fundamental needs, and that differences in societies are really only variations on central themes. All living beings have certain basic requirements. And these determine the various ways in which societies are organized.

Now, here is your assignment: write a piece of social-science fiction—in the form of a movie script or "story board" or an outline for a novel—that describes a new society. Where do you begin? First you might give your society a name. Let your imagination come up with something exotic. The name might imply the type of society, or it might be a known word written backwards or scrambled. If you have trouble with the name, it might come to you later, based on the type of society you create.

Now review the different institutions considered in this unit and how each topic was approached. Most topics began with a brief history. Describing the origin of your society may help you crystallize its various functions in your mind. After writing a short description of your society's background—a few core historical traditions will do—answer the questions.

Using and Analyzing Concepts

1. What are the "people" like? How do they look, communicate, and behave toward one another?
2. What is their "family" structure? Who's in charge, if anyone? How do the older creatures treat the younger ones?

3. How do they explain the supernatural or the unknown? What rituals do they use? What symbols? Are there any religious prescriptions or proscriptions?

4. How does your society teach its young? What methods are used? How long does it take to socialize citizens in your world? Remember, you needn't be bound by Earth's time concepts.

5. How is order maintained? What sort of political system regulates conduct—or are the citizens "above" that need?

6. Do they have natural resources to process and production and consumption to organize? Describe how these functions are accomplished. What goods and services make up the economy of your society?

7. Briefly describe how the various social institutions mesh or fail to mesh.

8. Now, returning to Earth, think of a familiar holiday that clearly illustrates the integration and interdependence of social institutions. Christmas is one example. Although primarily a religious holiday, Christmas is also a national holiday, a business season, and a family time.

   (a) Having thought about various holidays, create a holiday in your new society and show how the members of that society celebrate it.

   (b) Compare the society and the holiday you have created with those developed by your classmates. Do you find similarities in their descriptions and your own? If so, why do you think this is the case? If not, why not?

SOCIALIZATION

Unit Focus

What we think, do, and say are reflections of what we have learned from parents, peers, and other members of society. Sociologists refer to this process as *socialization.*

All through life we are constantly having to adapt to new people and new situations. Think, for example, of the transition from childhood to adulthood and of the many things you must learn during this transition. Or think of the challenges you will face in a very short time: the demands set forth by college or the labor market. Socialization to new roles is also important in the lives of older people who are about to retire.

Ceremonies and celebrations such as a confirmation, a graduation, a wedding, a promotion, and retirement are special rites of passage that mark stages in the life cycle. Socialization and the stages in the life cycle are the subjects of this unit.

Applying Sociology

- What rites of passage have you celebrated?
- Why do different cultures have different rites of passage in the work force?
- What new social skills will you need to be successful in college or a job?
- Why is retirement a difficult transition for some people?

The process of socialization may occur in concentrated form on athletic teams such as this, where kids learn to perform collectively.

191

CHAPTER

The Early Years

Chapter Preview

- **Before you read,** look up the following key terms in the glossary to become familiar with their definitions:

socialization   reinforcement   internalizing
looking-glass self   cognitive development   anticipatory
role models   reference groups   socialization

- **As you read,** think about answers to the following questions:

1. What role does the family play in a child's early socialization?
2. What role does television play in American children's social development?
3. How does childhood socialization differ in wealthy suburbs, working-class neighborhoods, and public housing projects?

Sections in this Chapter

1. Socialization in Early Childhood
2. Secondary Groups and Role Models
3. Childhood Socialization in Three Communities

Chapter Focus

Everyone in our culture knows that you eat meat with a fork, not a spoon; put on a sweater or jacket when the weather gets cool; speak in a soft voice in a hospital or church; go to school from the age of five or six to learn reading, writing, and arithmetic; ask doctors for medical care, clergy for religious advice, lawyers for legal help; and bargain, negotiate, compromise, or argue to settle differences.

All people are socialized to face problems in certain ways. The skills we learn, the values we hold, and the norms we live by vary in different societies and in different settings within the same society. In spite of the great variation, socialization takes place in every society. All individuals learn to play many roles—daughter, son, student, friend, parent, worker, citizen. This chapter focuses on the socialization that takes place in childhood.

Using Sociologists' Tools

- **Observe** ways young people try to act like grown-ups.
- **Describe** some specific instances of children trying to copy the behavior of their parents.
- **Analyze** the content of Saturday morning cartoons, paying particular attention to their most common characteristics.
- **Predict** what boys would think of child-rearing if it became commonplace to give dolls to male children.

A father helping his daughter address cards to her friends is an important agent of socialization in her young life.

1 Socialization in Early Childhood

Through *socialization,* people learn to be members of social groups. Social scientists contend that the social environment is the most important factor in determining how people behave and what they believe. Attitudes, values, and rules for behavior are learned, not inherited. The instructors and role models—or *agents of socialization*—are parents, peers, teachers, and other figures with whom a person comes into direct contact. They may also be people who are more distant; for instance, television gives us ample evidence of effective teaching at long range. But the earliest and most important socialization takes place in the family.

The Role of Parents

The cases of Anna and Isabelle, described in Chapter 4, show that the human being depends on others from birth. An infant needs food, warmth, clothing, and some physical contact. The satisfaction of these needs becomes linked with other human beings. Children learn to tell smiles from frowns, approval from disapproval. Although they aren't aware of the process, socialization has begun. Because they need security, warmth, and approval from others, children begin to act in ways that will bring forth these responses. They stop acting in ways that will get them punished.

Socialization could not take place without *significant others,* the people whose attitudes and judgments are important to us. They have the greatest influence over the way we think of ourselves and on our acceptance or rejection of social norms. In infancy, the chief significant others are the parents. They give the food, warmth, clothing, and love that all babies need. Soon brothers, sisters, grandparents, teachers, and friends also become significant others.

193

All babies need love and tender care if they are to develop properly.

Several processes affect socialization in even the youngest children. Significant others set expectations by letting a child know what he or she must do. Through talking, hugging, kissing, spanking, and other means of communicating, these people show the child that certain kinds of behavior are acceptable and others are not. "No, you may not color the living-room wall! Here, use your crayons on this paper." By quickly moving the child away from the wall and providing a piece of paper, the parent teaches certain expectations about proper behavior.

Parents continue to let the child know what they like and what they don't like through *reinforcement,* or strengthening a response. Reinforcement may be either positive or negative. Parents provide positive reinforcement with smiles, words of approval, a cookie, or a new toy. They offer negative reinforcement by removing a restriction in order to reward a behavior. Frowns, scolding, spanking, and other forms of punishment also guide a child's actions.

As a person grows, socialization becomes more complex. The small child learns how to get along in his or her surroundings. Perhaps throwing cereal on Daddy's head results in a scolding. Throwing bread at the dog leads to

Parents socialize children by indicating what behavior is acceptable and what is unacceptable in the home and in society. Rewards and punishment are commonly used to teach mores and norms.

Children learn skills and interests by imitation. In the top picture, a woman shows her daughter how to handle a teacup gracefully. Above, a boy learns the craft of making fine turquoise jewelry from his father. The brother and sister at left are learning to play instruments through formal instruction, but their interest in music may have been sparked by their parents' interest.

a loud "no" and no dessert. Eventually, the child realizes that throwing food anywhere will bring punishment. This process of making a general rule from specific instances is called *generalizing*.

The next step occurs when the child makes the decision beforehand that throwing food is wrong. Threats are no longer necessary to make the child refrain from the forbidden behavior. In fact, the child will probably be disgusted if a younger brother or sister begins throwing food on the floor.

Acquiring personal standards for behaving in socially acceptable ways is a crucial part of development. No one can be watched all day long. Ultimately, the social system depends on people's coming to regard certain behavior as "natural." At this point, the individual takes an important step by *internalizing* values, adopting the values of society as his or her own.

Imitating is a part of the socialization process that takes place without any specific teaching. Because parents are so important, it is natural for children to imitate much parental behavior. Look at the pictures on page 195 and see how children copy their parents' actions.

? What skills are the children learning in the photos? How will these skills make the child a more acceptable family member? Are the skills being taught or imitated? List the

According to psychologist Erik Erikson, children who are encouraged and praised as they develop skills gain self-confidence and avoid feelings of inferiority.

cultural values that parents are transmitting to their children in their interactions with them.

Development of the Self

The ability to imitate and learn does not by itself explain why the process of childhood socialization works in every society. Socialization also depends on a complex process within each child: the development of self.

One of the first sociological theories about the self—the concept of the *looking-glass self*—was developed by Charles Horton Cooley. According to Cooley, we gain a definition of our self in three steps:

1. We form beliefs about how we appear to others.
2. We then form beliefs about their judgments of how we appear to them.
3. In response to the imagined judgment, we develop pride, shame, improved self-esteem, slightly damaged self-esteem, and other attributes of the self.

Cooley says, in other words, that we see ourselves as *we think* others see us. As in the example of table manners mentioned earlier, children develop a sense of what others find acceptable as they are taught and become socialized.

Another important theorist, Erik Erikson, described a set of stages, beginning with infancy and early childhood, through which each person passes in the life cycle. Those stages are illustrated in the figure. According to Erikson, each stage is marked by conflict, and the manner in which each conflict is resolved strongly affects an individual's personality development.

Erikson maintains that learning occurs in each of the stages throughout life. What occurs in one stage can be undone or enhanced by what happens in the next stage. For example, children who learn to trust others because their parents have met their needs as infants may become less trusting if they encounter other adults who do not live up to their word. Conversely, children who have not learned trust at home can develop this capacity by interacting with a thoughtful and caring teacher.

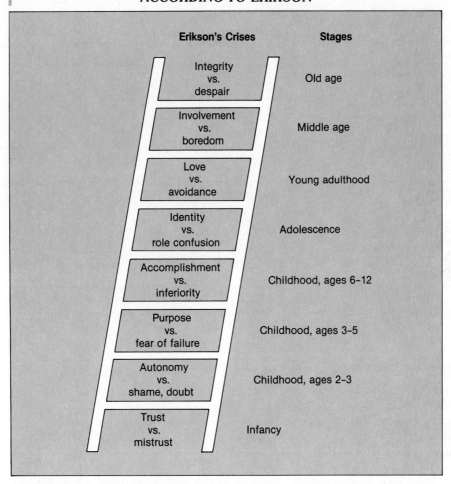

HUMAN DEVELOPMENT: CRISES AND STAGES ACCORDING TO ERIKSON

Erikson's Crises	Stages
Integrity vs. despair	Old age
Involvement vs. boredom	Middle age
Love vs. avoidance	Young adulthood
Identity vs. role confusion	Adolescence
Accomplishment vs. inferiority	Childhood, ages 6–12
Purpose vs. fear of failure	Childhood, ages 3–5
Autonomy vs. shame, doubt	Childhood, ages 2–3
Trust vs. mistrust	Infancy

CHART SKILL   Erik Erikson views life as a series of "crises" that must be resolved if a person is to develop satisfactorily. The ladder shows positive and negative aspects of the struggles typical at each stage of life. What are infants struggling to do? What is the major concern of adolescents? What must the elderly struggle to avoid?

Developmental psychologists have also studied *cognitive development,* or the ability to think, reason, and solve problems. An influential developmental theorist, Jean Piaget, made thousands of observations of children. He concluded that all children develop their thinking abilities by the same step-by-step processes.

Piaget also noted, however, that the content of what children think and believe is in-fluenced by their culture. Thus, all children need social learning and experiences to move from one stage of development to a more advanced one. For example, for an infant to learn to speak requires biological development, but without appropriate social stimulation, the acquisition of language won't take place. Again, remember Anna and Isabelle.

According to Piaget, children at first cannot separate themselves from the rest of their

Children are socialized by their peers as well as their parents. If baseball is a popular neighborhood game, a child may want to join the team. At a certain stage of development, children enjoy making up their own games with their own sets of rules.

environment. They have no sense that there is a world they cannot see. If a teddy bear is taken away from an infant, he or she thinks it no longer exists. Even after children learn to talk, their thinking process is still very concrete. That is, the child may be able to think of the particular teddy bear as a permanently existing toy, but yet be unable to generalize about it, to realize that it is part of an abstract category called "stuffed animals" or "toys."

As children mature, Piaget observed, they develop cognitive skills and the ability to participate in more complex social situations. They can play "house" or "school," games that require role playing in imaginary situations. Gradually, they develop the capacity to think abstractly and to pursue activities that require abstract reasoning, such as telling time or dealing with numbers.

? How is the process of socialization related to the development of the self? Would it be possible to have one without the other? Explain.

The Role of Peers

Parents don't have total control over a child's life. They don't produce little robots who act on adult wishes at the press of a button. Children are also socialized by their *peers,* those of their own age group with whom they share experiences. In their peer group, children learn to play, compete, and fight. They practice grown-up roles, exchange secrets, interact with others, and explore their world.

The following reading captures some of the quality of childhood in the United States and the distance that exists between the child's world and the world of adults:

It never occurred to us that there was anything wrong in doing nothing, so long as we kept out of the way of grown-ups. These days, you see a kid lying on his back and looking blank and you begin to wonder what's wrong with him. There's nothing wrong with him, except he's thinking. He's trying to find out whether he breathes differently when he's thinking about it than when he's just breathing. He's seeing how long he can sit there without blinking. He is considering whether his father is meaner than Carl's father, he is wondering who he would be if his father hadn't married his mother, whether there is somewhere in the world somebody who is exactly like him in every detail up to and including the fact that the other one is sitting there thinking whether there is someone who is exactly like him in every detail. He is trying to arrive at some conclusion about his thumb.

But when we were kids, we had the sense to keep these things to ourselves. We didn't go around asking grown-ups about them. They obviously didn't know. We asked other kids. They knew. I think we were right about grown-ups being the natural enemies of kids, because we knew that what they wanted us to do was to be like them. And that was for the birds. "Pop, look at this. It's a pollywog, look at it." "Um," said your father. Another kid said, "Jeez, where'd you get it? Are there any more? What'll you take for it?"

Perhaps if you think back over your childhood and the various friends you had, you can recall having similar feelings. Most children in our society have a relatively large amount of time free from adult supervision, when they can be themselves. In some cultures, however, the peer group can play a still larger role.

Let's look, for example, at children who grow up in an Israeli kibbutz. A kibbutz—kibbutzim in the plural—is a communal settlement, often a farm, where families share work and earnings. Children in a kibbutz learn from infancy that their peers are very important people in their lives.

In some kibbutzim, children go to an infant house when they are only four days old. Parents may visit only a few hours a day. Children spend all their school-age years with their peers, first in an infant house, then in a children's house, and so on.

The parents love their children and see them often, but they cannot meet all their needs. Help has to come from the peer group or from the kibbutz itself. If, for example, a child runs to the parents' house in the middle of the night out of fear of sleeping alone, the parents take him or her back to the children's house. Even in a kibbutz where the children sleep in their parents' house, they spend the entire day in the children's house.

Children spend busy days caring for their group's own animals and exploring the kibbutz, as well as attending school. They do all these things together, with much less supervision than other children generally have. A counselor looks after six or eight youngsters. With this many boys and girls to care for, the counselor cannot spend much time feeding, coaxing, and pampering each child. Even by the age of two, children learn to help each other with such basic tasks as eating, dressing, and learning to go to the bathroom.

In an Israeli kibbutz, where children live with peers, the peer group exerts a greater influence than in societies where children live with their parents.

Kibbutz children are self-reliant. Because they do not have to fit into an adult world, their lives are relatively free of no's and don'ts. Their immediate surroundings are designed to be safe, with few fragile objects for children to break. Because everyone has the same things to share, there is little jealousy of what another child owns.

[?] Would you like to have been brought up in a kibbutz? Why or why not?

REVIEW AND APPLICATION

1. IDENTIFY: Socialization, agents of socialization, significant others, reinforcement, generalizing, internalizing, looking-glass self, cognitive development, peers.

2. How does the process of generalizing take place?
3. What aspects of development are discussed by, respectively, Cooley, Erikson, and Piaget?
4. Describe life for children raised in a kibbutz.

CRITICAL THINKING: Compare living in an Israeli kibbutz with living in the United States. How does life in a kibbutz differ from your life? What do you think are the advantages of being relatively free from adult supervision in a kibbutz? What do you think are the disadvantages? Which way of life do you think your parents would prefer for you? Why? Which way of life would you prefer? Explain your answer.

2 Secondary Groups and Role Models

Parents, brothers and sisters, and playmates all belong to a child's primary groups. They all contribute greatly to socialization and the development of the self. Then, in industrial societies like ours, sometime during the first six years children are introduced to their first major secondary group: the school.

Schools

Whether it is a day-care center, a nursery school, a kindergarten, or the first grade; whether it is a public or a private school; whether it is traditional, progressive, or experimental—school places major demands on a child to learn new roles and rules.

In school, children are taught to play special roles that help them achieve immediate goals and prepare them for the future. Slowly, through the years, children learn to play the role of student. At first, it means learning how to share the attention of the teacher with a group of classmates. It requires being at a particular place at a particular time and leaving when the school session is over. There are definite things to do and rules to learn. New norms are introduced as students receive grades and other evalua-

tions of their achievements and punishments if they don't conform.

Schools also fulfill an important custodial function in caring for children during the school day. In addition, they track, or group, students in ways that help determine future job and social possibilities. Success in adapting to school regulations and teachers' expectations plays a central part in influencing what happens later in life.

At home and among friends, children learn to accept the individual differences of others in their groups and to expect others to do the same for them. In school, there is a more rigid set of rules. Their stated purpose is to allow the school to accomplish the education of the student in the most effective way. The school is thus an early model of the secondary groups that a person will belong to as an adult in our industrial society.

Reference Groups

As they grow older, children observe people whom they don't know personally but admire very much from a distance. They begin to imitate their behavior as well. Children might try to throw a ball like a famous player,

Schools exert a strong socializing influence on children, teaching society's norms and expectations.

or they might dress or talk like a well-known movie star. They sometimes imitate the activities of certain groups, such as quiet scholars or tough-talking business people. These people thus become *role models,* and their groups often become what sociologists call *reference groups,* groups children hope to join someday or against which they measure themselves.

Young children often practice the grown-up behavior of adults through role play. Children dress up and pretend they are mothers, fathers, teenagers, astronauts, and firefighters in anticipation of future work and play roles. Sociologists refer to this process, by which we try out certain roles in advance, as *anticipatory socialization.*

For example, in describing how he first thought of his future career, the New York policeman Frank Serpico recalled how impressed he was as a child when the police walked through his neighborhood. Everyone respected them for their badges, the guns they carried, and the authority they commanded. Serpico recalled how he played at being a police officer and dreamed that someday he could join the force.

Young children often model themselves after people whose roles they admire. This girl enjoys imagining herself as a courageous firefighter.

Television is an important socializing agent in American society. Whether its influence is helpful or harmful has been the subject of many studies and much debate.

? Were there any specific people in public life who had a strong influence on your interests or tastes as a child? If so, did their influence last, or were these people replaced by others? Is any one person outside your own groups influencing your goals now?

Television

In our society, other agents of socialization also teach the young. These agents add to, or sometimes contradict, the teachings of families, schools, and peer groups. In the next chapter, you will read about the influence that children's books can have on social learning, especially regarding sex roles. Another major factor is advertising, which is discussed in Chapter 13. Even more important is television.

Studies have shown that television has a significant socializing effect on children who watch it several hours a week. It provides

child viewers with factual information about our society and other societies. It gives them additional information on norms they have already learned and others new to them. It also increases their vocabularies.

Children may watch educational programs such as "Sesame Street," which are designed to teach them; programs aimed at entertaining them; or programs geared primarily for adults. In any case, television offers the widest view of the world that a child can obtain. A child watching a quiz program sees contestants scream with excitement when they win a car, a major appliance, or a trip to Hawaii. The child can hardly fail to sense that both material things and winning are desirable.

A child watching a program about a team of detectives is fairly certain to see a lot of action—chases on foot or by car, shoot-outs, and fistfights. Several values are also being displayed, however: courage in the face of danger, dedication to the job, loyalty to the team, and the virtue of upholding the law. However, a child who regularly watches television probably learns a number of values and norms parents may not agree with.

In particular, violence on television and its possible effects on children have been subjects of scientific study and of much debate. A report of the Surgeon General's Scientific Advisory Committee on Television and Social Behavior found a slight tendency of children who constantly watch violent programs to show more aggressive attitudes than other children. Another study in England came to the same cautious conclusion. In addition, it pointed out that the relationship between television watching and aggressive attitudes existed among children regardless of social class, age, or race.

Later studies indicate that the impact of television on children is a complicated phenomenon about which much is yet to be learned. Its influence appears to be strongest when it reinforces the attitudes, expectations, and definitions that the child has already learned through socialization or experience. But it can also have an impact if no other sources have provided information.

Research indicates, for example, that white children from rural or suburban backgrounds are more likely to accept suggestions from TV programs on how to relate to blacks than are children brought up in cities with substantial black populations. In this case, urban children tend to base their attitudes more on their personal experience.

Before television was common, experience and socialization by parents and groups were the only teachers for the young. Children who could not read, for example, had to rely much more on their parents for information. This required adult time and attention. Even after they learned to read, children in past generations had access to only limited information. Books and magazines for young children were generally written, as they are now, with children's limited skills and special interests in mind. Television, however, provides an immense variety of subjects and treatments.

Fortunately, it has been found that, beyond turning off the program, parents can still exercise a great influence by the comments they make while children are viewing. For example, a study of "Sesame Street" revealed that children watching it in the presence of their parents learned more than those who viewed it alone. Children's attitudes toward violence on television were also influenced by the comments of their parents. If the comments were critical, children were far less likely to imitate the behavior shown.

What these findings indicate is that parents and other adults have an important role to play, not only in deciding which programs can be watched, but also in helping children interpret what they view. Parents can help the young child draw the line between fact and fantasy. By their remarks to older children, they can counteract effects of advertising they disapprove of and initiate discussion of important issues, values, or views.

Parents who are happy that their children sit quietly before the screen and keep out of trouble often have only a partial idea of what's happening in front of the tube. Television is clearly much more than a babysitter. Research indicates that interaction

SOURCE: Drawing by Robert Day; © 1970 The New Yorker Magazine, Inc.

"Don't you understand? This is life, this is what is happening. We can't switch to another channel."

between adults and children, even during the watching of a TV program, is a significant, even necessary, socialization experience.

? Do you think that violent scenes on television help people get rid of any hostile feelings they may have? Or do you think that watching violence is more inclined to make them violent? Might such scenes have any other effects? No effects? Explain.

REVIEW AND APPLICATION

1. *IDENTIFY:* Role models, reference groups, anticipatory socialization.

2. What are some aims of school socialization?
3. How can parents help assure the best results from children's television viewing?

CRITICAL THINKING: Cite an excerpt from the text that explains the connection between the events in each of the following cause-and-effect relationships: a) As a first grader, Clare was placed in the top math group and remained there through high school. As an adult, she became an award-winning engineer. b) As a little boy, Dan admired the grace of the figure skaters whom he often watched practice at the local ice rink. At age 18, Dan qualified for the Olympic speed skating competition.

3 Childhood Socialization in Three Communities

Child-raising practices differ greatly from one society to another. They also differ from place to place within the same society. The child-raising practices in a big city, for example, often differ markedly from those in a small town. They also differ from one social class to another.

Social class, as you read in Chapter 5, means many things, including the amount of money people have and the style of life this permits them to lead. Wealthy people usually bring up their children differently from middle-income people. The poor often have still other ideas about socializing their children.

For example, some parents socialize their children to follow all the rules, earn good grades, and work hard to "get ahead." These parents firmly believe their children can succeed. Other parents who are struggling just to pay the rent may come to think that failure and bad luck are their lot in life. In short, the attitudes most people transmit to their children depend on their own experience.

In the pages that follow, you will read about modern family life in three communities. They differ from each other in terms of social class—the income level and life styles of the residents. One is a wealthy suburb,

one is a working-class urban neighborhood, the third is a public-housing project. As you read, see if you can identify the agents of socialization and the processes being used.

Case Study: An Affluent Suburb

Crestwood Heights, a suburb of a Canadian city, has many of the features of the "American dream." It has the kinds of houses, yards, and parks pictured in a magazine like *Better Homes and Gardens*. This wealthy suburb measures a person's standing in the community by where one went to college, the kind of home one lives in, and the things one owns. Proper possessions include good furniture, art objects, and books. Many families living there originally came from less well-to-do homes and worked hard to get where they are. Parents try hard to prepare their children for a life like their own.

In the 1950s, a group of researchers spent five years studying this community and its child-raising practices. They found that couples planned when to have children and how many to have. During pregnancy, the mother carefully followed the advice of her doctor. At birth, children were taken from their mothers in the hospital, and the mother saw her baby only on a regulated feeding schedule.

When the new baby came home from the hospital, a hired nurse often helped the mother for the first week or two. Later, babysitters would take over so that the parents could go out. Families were very concerned about their children and did many things together. Children quickly learned that life was well ordered and proceeded according to rules and schedules.

Crestwood Heights families valued their material belongings. There were many objects in the home that children were not permitted to touch and rooms where they couldn't play. Instead of total freedom in the house, children received costly toys, often educational in design. Very early, then, children learned that property is valuable.

At an early age, the child's life began to center around organized activities. At three, children went to nursery school. Here they would be away from their families for several hours a day. Since there were many children, they had to learn to share the teacher and act independently. Teachers expected the children to get along with others without fighting, to share toys, and to explore their environment freely. The school tried to help children overcome "angry impulses" and learn proper attitudes and skills.

The parents deliberately turned over part of the socialization of their children to the nursery school. Parents regarded the teachers as trained experts. Learning in school was reinforced in the home as parents stressed how important school was.

Nursery school, of course, was followed by grade school and a series of after-school activities ranging from ballet lessons to judo. Children were taught to try hard to do well in their activities and to take on more and more responsibility as they matured.

For children five to twelve years old, the values of responsibility and punctuality were stressed in many ways. Children learned that they were expected to be on time for such after-school activities as Scouts, music lessons, and religious education. Each activity

Most middle-class parents place a great deal of emphasis on intellectual skills and education. They introduce their children to books at a very young age.

was designed to help the child develop a sense of responsibility. As the child grew older, the obligations were stressed more and more. Parents taught their children to be responsible for such things as doing their homework, helping with household chores, and learning how to spend an allowance.

Talks with children in the junior high school showed how they had internalized the values of their parents. Here are the notes from a discussion of allowances:

A girl expressed the idea that an allowance should be considered from the viewpoint of training for later life; the student will learn the value of money through management of an allowance; if all the allowance is not spent, that part should be saved. . . .

One boy felt an allowance helped develop a sense of responsibility; boys could save if they had a purpose in mind, such as a gift for Mother's Day.

[?] What values did the parents of Crestwood Heights seem to hold regarding family, education, and success? How did parents teach these values to their children? Which additional significant others were involved in the socialization process? What experiences outside the family had an impact on Crestwood Heights children?

CASE STUDY: A
Working-Class Community

Sociologist Herbert Gans decided to study a community in the West End section of Boston that officials had declared a "slum" and made plans to tear down. He wanted to find out whether the residents thought of their community as a slum that should be replaced with new, high-rise apartment buildings. Gans moved into an apartment in the West End. In the process of finding the answers to his principal question, Gans also learned a great deal about the way urban working-class people raise their children.

Although the West End included other ethnic groups, Gans focused on the Italian Americans, who made up 40 percent of the neighborhood. In general, their income was low, and less than a third had finished high school or gone to college. The men were factory workers or low-paid service workers. Most were born in the United States, although a number of the older people had come from Italy in the early 1900s.

The West End had narrow, winding streets. There were some vacant stores and garbage-strewn alleys. The housing looked run-down, but Gans's first impression changed as he found many inexpensive apartments in good condition. In addition, he soon saw that the residents liked their seemingly crowded living conditions. They en-

Many residents of working-class neighborhoods enjoy living close to people of similar economic backgrounds and values.

joyed having friends and family nearby and did not approve of the isolated privacy of suburbs or farms.

Among the West Enders, the nuclear family did not do many things alone. Families shared their problems and pleasures with neighbors and relatives. Adults of the same age and sex met often to talk about daily events and the good old days or to comfort those facing unemployment, illness, or death.

West End families were large, although somewhat smaller than a generation earlier. There was little planned parenthood. A birth was usually regarded as God's will. How did parents treat their children? In the West End, parents wanted their children to succeed and to live a good life, but the children were not the center of the parents' lives. Parents were very concerned that their children not become "bums," that they be able to meet their obligations to their peers. But they didn't stress education or moving to a higher social position. It was much more important to parents that their children should not disgrace their families.

Boys and girls learned behavior considered appropriate to their sex. For example, boys were taunted and called sissies if they did anything that seemed unmasculine, such as playing the piano. Again, getting along with peers was stressed.

Parents didn't think that they should sacrifice themselves for their children. Unlike parents in Crestwood Heights, they rarely involved themselves in the schools. Many children went to church schools because the parents valued the discipline and religious training offered there. Parents would visit the school, whether church or public, only if the child was in trouble. Children needed to know enough to be able to get a job. Beyond that, education was not highly valued.

Parents spoke to their children as if they were adults and expected them to behave like little adults. Girls of seven or eight were expected to help their mothers with housework and the care of younger children. Boys were fairly free to roam the streets. Mothers tried to teach their children rules of good behavior, which often contradicted the street rules learned from peer groups. But by the time they were teenagers, boys and, to a lesser extent, girls spent little time at home. When they were at home or school, they were often withdrawn and quiet. On the street, they acted much more freely.

If, after the age of ten or twelve, a boy got into trouble with the police or the priest, the parents rarely felt responsible. They would blame their son for being a "bad kid" or having bad friends. Similarly, parents didn't worry too much about whether they were being too strict or too easy. They rarely thought about whether their methods of child raising might have a psychological impact. They told the child what they expected in the direct way they would speak to an adult.

What did the children learn from this kind of socialization? They quickly saw that the family expected a certain kind of behavior. But they also saw that much that was important in their lives went on in their peer groups. These groups of friends were of the same age and sex, and they shared standards of behavior. For example, doing well in school was scorned as behavior for boys. As a result, the studious boy had to find new friends or, more likely, play down his academic interests to stay in the group.

? What values did West End parents seem to hold regarding the family, education, and success? How did parents teach these values to their children? For most boys and girls growing up in the West End, who were the significant others? Who were the important role models? How was reinforcement used to encourage values and behavior?

CASE STUDY: *An Urban Housing Project*

In some places, the dangers and difficulties of living are so great that children must be socialized quickly to protect them from the hazards of their environment. Such was the case in a large urban housing project studied by sociologist William Moore, Jr., and reported in his book *The Vertical Ghetto*.

Moore's study was of life among poor people in a high-rise slum in an urban ghetto in St. Louis. He wanted to look at the effects this environment had on the children who grew up there. He hoped his research would increase public awareness of the problems faced by the urban poor and lead to new laws to benefit this group.

Moore found that parents had much less control over the socialization of their children than parents in Crestwood Heights or the West End. Many wanted to protect their young from violence or crime but were unable to do so. People outside the home became important agents in teaching children to survive in this tough environment, often by fighting and stealing.

Moore recorded that the housing project was overcrowded and dirty. Many of its play areas, laundry rooms, and elevators needed repair. Its halls and stairwells were the scene of gambling, thefts, and occasional murders. Families lived in small, cramped apartments.

In urban housing projects such as this, parents often have little control over the socialization of their children.

Sleeping space was hard to come by, the bathroom was in constant use, and rarely was there a quiet place to study or to be alone. The noise level throughout the building was high. Children played in the halls, and music blared from radios and record players. Outside there was heavy truck traffic, which added to the noise.

When another sociologist, Lee Rainwater, asked the tenants of the same project to cite the biggest problems at the project, they made these comments:

There's too much broken glass and trash around outside.

The elevators are dangerous.

The elevators don't stop on every floor, so many people have to walk up or down to get to their apartments.

There are mice and cockroaches in the buildings.

People use the elevators and halls to go to the bathroom.

Bottles and other dangerous things are thrown out of windows and hurt people.

People who don't live in the project come in and make a lot of trouble with fights, stealing, drinking, and the like.

People don't keep the area around the incinerator clean.

The laundry rooms aren't safe: clothes get stolen, and people are attacked.

The children run wild and cause all kinds of damage.

People use the stairwells and laundry rooms for drinking and things like that.

A woman isn't safe in the halls, stairways, or elevators.

Rainwater also provided tenants with a list of behaviors and asked them to pick the ones that took place often in the project. Over half the people he talked to felt that the following were frequent occurrences there:

Holding somebody up and robbing them.
Being an alcoholic.
Stealing from somebody.
Teenagers yelling curse words at adults.
Breaking windows.
Drinking a lot and fooling around on the streets.
Teenagers getting in fights.

In his study, Moore observed that many of the fathers had no jobs. Many did not live with their families. Encouraged by welfare rules that give aid to families only if there is no father in the home, they left home despairing of ever being able to support their families.

These disruptive conditions in the home had a serious impact on the children. Boys lacked the chance to learn from and identify with their fathers and to use them as role models. Girls were luckier in being able to identify with their mothers, but they also faced some serious problems. Many of the mothers worked away from home all day, so girls often had to care for the smaller children.

Children had to grow up quickly. Even preschoolers knew how to cross busy streets and buy the family groceries. With little chance for parental supervision, children learned to take care of themselves.

Playing in the playground and on the streets was rough, and fights often broke out. Children discovered at an early age that they had to learn how to defend themselves. In contrast, children from richer communities, such as Crestwood Heights, are constantly told that fighting is bad. They are urged to "get along" with other children. This type of socialization is right for Crestwood Heights, but such children would get along poorly in the rough-and-tumble world of the housing project in St. Louis.

Parents in the housing project hoped for better futures for their children, but most could not provide an environment or pass on skills that would make such success possible. Moore believes that growing up in a "vertical ghetto" teaches children attitudes and skills that are essential to survival there but that can rarely be used to succeed in a less hostile environment.

Moore notes how many times the project children saw their parents treated harshly by housing authorities, social workers, or police. The children knew that their parents felt insulted but could not force others to treat them with respect. The children got similar treatment in neighborhood stores. The store owner would watch them closely as they moved about the aisles or would search them as they left the store.

The children of the project, according to Moore, did not learn to respect themselves, nor did they put much stock in their chances for the future. They knew that few people had made it out of the vertical ghetto via education and a career. More often they saw examples of failure. Their upbringing did not teach them that they could change their lives for themselves, their brothers and sisters, or their peers.

? What values did parents in the project seem to have regarding family, education, and success? In what ways did the poverty of the parents shape their attitudes and what they taught their children? Who seemed to be the children's role models? What kinds of behavior did they imitate?

REVIEW AND APPLICATION

1. What are some of the things that determine differences in child-raising?
CRITICAL THINKING: Of the three case studies, which community's children probably assumed that getting ahead was both possible and desirable? Explain. Why do you think the other children did not share this assumption?

CHAPTER **9** REVIEW

Recap

Socialization is the lifelong process by which people learn the values, norms, and role expectations of their social environment. Most important is the teaching by significant others, such as parents, from which children learn to generalize and to internalize values. Becoming socialized, according to Cooley, involves acquiring a looking-glass self—a judgment of ourselves based on how we think we appear to others. Erikson's theory concerns a process of personality development through the resolution of conflicts. Piaget's theory describes stages of cognitive growth and the part that social experiences play in this growth. Peers, especially close friends, are instrumental in child development and socialization.

Among the most important influences on older children is school. Schools help individuals prepare for adult roles in society. At school age, children adopt new role models and reference groups. Television may exert a powerful influence, but there is controversy concerning what it actually does. Studies reveal that active parental participation with children in television viewing can make the experience a positive one.

Child-raising practices differ greatly among the varied subcultures in America. Of major importance is a family's social class, but other differences arise from the ethnic background of the parents, the physical conditions in the family's home, and many other complex factors.

Key Terms

Define the following:

socialization
agents of socialization
significant other
reinforcement
generalizing

internalizing
looking-glass self
cognitive development
peer
role model

reference group
anticipatory socialization

Applying Sociology

1. American children are generally taught what is considered proper behavior about such things as (a) table manners; (b) personal grooming; (c) respect for property; (d) care of younger brothers and sisters; (e) household chores; (f) courtesy toward adults; and (g) citizenship obligations. Drawing on your own experience, what are some specific "do's" and "don'ts" that you have learned about each of these topics? Where and from whom did you learn them?

2. Compare the upbringing of two friends whose families enjoy different styles of life, that is, different racial, class, ethnic, or educational backgrounds.

3. Try to observe one or more play groups or small children who are not being closely watched by adults. Report what the children do and what skills, values, and roles might be taught by their activities.

4. Describe the socialization process of a child, age six to twelve, whom you have been able to observe.

(a) Who have been some of the child's significant others?

(b) What kinds of positive and negative reinforcement did the child receive?

(c) Were you able to note any of the stages described by Erikson or Piaget?

(d) What values has this child internalized?

(e) Who are some of the child's role models? How can you tell?

(f) Cite an example of anticipatory socialization by this child.

5. Watch a popular children's cartoon program. Write down all the actions that might affect a young child's ideas about right and wrong behavior. Compare this with what an educational program, such as "Sesame Street," teaches. What values and skills are being stressed in the educational program?

Extended Readings

Lilian G. Katz, "Punishment and Preschoolers," *Parents,* May 1987, p. 205.

1. According to the author, what is the best way to discipline a preschooler?
2. What does the author mean by compliance and internalization?

Paul Chance, "The Making of Whiz Kids," *Psychology Today,* April 1987, pp. 72–74.

1. What characteristic makes child prodigies different from regular children?

2. What factors must combine to ensure the development of a prodigy?

Claudia Wallis, "Is Day Care Bad for Babies?," *Time,* June 22, 1987, p. 63.

1. How have views on day care changed over the past four decades? What explanations can you give for these changing views?
2. On what points do researchers of child care tend to agree?

Social Studies Skills

Perceiving cause-and-effect relationships within children's socialization patterns.
Detecting the cause-and-effect relationships in human behavior is sometimes tricky. In the chapter, find the probable effects of the following causes:

(a) Children need security, warmth, and approval. (See page 193.)
(b) Everyone in a kibbutz shares certain things. (See page 200.)
(c) Children watch television several hours a week. (See page 202.)

Critical Thinking

1. *Analyzing Comparisons:* Evaluate this claim: "Children from poor families don't work as hard as children from middle class families and thus remain poor."
2. *Recognizing Values:* What values are conveyed in the following television pro-

grams? (a) The good guys kill some of the bad guys and capture the rest, thereby saving North America from destruction; (b) Adults work with children to solve problems through cooperation and compromise.

10

Adolescence

Chapter Preview

- **Before you read,** look up the following key terms in the glossary to become familiar with their definitions:

adolescence   puberty   stereotype

- **As you read,** think about answers to the following questions:

1. Why does adolescence last longer for younger Americans than for teenagers in many other societies?
2. Why do adolescents assert their independence from adults?
3. What does the fact that sex stereotypes differ from one culture to another tell us about the source of people's attitudes concerning what is appropriate behavior for women and men?
4. What are two sources of sex-role discrimination in the U.S.?

Chapter Focus

In the last chapter, you read how class differences cause American children to be socialized differently. Although a great deal of basic personality development occurs in childhood and many cultural attitudes form during that period, social learning is a lifelong process. Many important changes occur through socialization during adolescence.

In modern American society, adolescence is a special stage of development. Most young people no longer leave school at 15 or 16 to work in factories or as apprentices to tradespeople to begin their adult work lives. Rarely do they marry and take on major family responsibilities in their teens, as often happened just a few generations ago.

This chapter looks at the challenges facing teenagers and explores how they think about the future. It also discusses sex roles, an area in which socialization becomes especially important for teenagers.

Using Sociologists' Tools

- **Observe** the ways students in your school tend to form into groups.
- **Describe** the differences you observed in "gender-preference" among first-year high schoolers and seniors.
- **Analyze** what it is that characterizes a particular peer group.
- **Predict** how your friends might react to you if they were average students and you were at the top of your class academically.

Learning to get along with parents and friends, and to resolve the conflicts that arise, makes adolescence an exciting time of self-discovery.

1 The Meaning of Adolescence

While the biological differences that distinguish infancy, puberty, and adulthood are universal, the meaning of these distinct developmental states is cultural. In some societies, there is no *adolescence,* or period of gradual transition from childhood to adulthood. As soon as children can take care of themselves, they are treated as small adults. For example, in French society before the eighteenth century, children older than seven were dressed like adults, were allowed at gambling tables, and were witness to all adult activities. It took centuries for our special ideas about childhood to develop.

The anthropologist Ruth Benedict showed how some small, traditional, agricultural societies were able to smooth the transition from childhood to adulthood without a special period of adolescence. Among the Cheyenne, for example, little boys were given tiny bows and taught to hunt as they would in adulthood. Among the Papago, young children of both sexes were given responsibilities that were miniature versions of adult tasks.

Even in societies where the behavior of children and adults is expected to differ, there may be specific time periods and specific processes that formally mark the step to more grown-up behavior. In these *age-graded societies,* everyone of the same age "graduates" from childhood to adulthood at the same time. Participating with one's age-mates in such a rite of passage eases the transition from one group to another.

Although in our society adulthood is considerably delayed, some ceremonies resembling rites of passage survive. For example, Jewish boys and girls at thirteen undergo the bar mitzvah or bas mitzvah, by which they symbolically become full-fledged members of

213

The bar mitzvah is a rite of passage in Judaism. By performing certain rituals at a bar mitzvah, a boy of thirteen becomes a member of the adult religious community.

The period between childhood and adulthood now called adolescence did not exist as such in the nineteenth and early twentieth centuries. Until child-labor laws were passed, many people began their working lives as children employed in mills and factories.

the religious community. Confirmation in many Christian denominations is a similar event.

Although there are few clear-cut *secular,* or nonreligious, ceremonies to signal the passage to adulthood, certain experiences take on the character of a rite of passage: the first day of high school, graduation, the first date, obtaining a driver's license, among other occasions.

☐? What events have taken place in your life that can qualify as rites of passage? Did you feel any different after they occurred? Explain.

Psychologists studying adolescence have often viewed it as a period of "storm and stress." G. Stanley Hall described adolescence as a time of "lack of emotional steadiness, violent impulses, unreasonable conduct . . . the previous selfhood is broken up . . . and a new individual is in process of being born."

Later social scientists have challenged some of Hall's theories. Ruth Benedict, for example, argued that adolescent storm and stress results from the way a culture handles the transition between childhood and adulthood. Adolescence, as such, doesn't exist in many traditional age-graded societies. Instead, there is preparation for adulthood followed immediately by adulthood.

Other social scientists hold that the long American adolescence is related to our historical development. As the need for unskilled labor decreased early in the twentieth century, trade unions, political groups, and reformers supported an organized effort to prohibit child labor. Advocates argued that children and teenagers needed more education and protection from labor abuse. For society and for the young workers, it became advantageous to keep adolescents out of the labor market. Reformers also supported and obtained special treatment for young people who broke the law: holding trials in juvenile courts; placing those convicted in reformatories rather than prisons; and showing more compassion, particularly toward first offenders.

Only recently have people recognized some negative aspects of these reforms. In establishing special legal proceedings for adolescents, the authorities, in effect, created a special legal category—such as "youthful offender"—in which the normal due process of the law was often limited. In recent years, some adolescents have demanded the same protections and procedures that are granted to adults and are considered basic constitutional rights. A concurring demand, based on different reasons, has come from adults in urban areas with high rates of violent juvenile crime. They, too, have argued that teenagers should be tried and penalized as adults.

REVIEW AND APPLICATION

1. *IDENTIFY:* Adolescence, secular, age-graded societies.
2. How did G. Stanley Hall and Ruth Benedict interpret adolescence? In what ways were their views different?

CRITICAL THINKING: Originally, laws restricting child labor were passed to protect children. Do you think these laws may cause hardships for adolescents today? Would relaxing these laws be dangerous? How?

2 Characteristics of Adolescence

Researchers on adolescence in the United States have been interested in discovering whether this period is as difficult and stormy as is customarily believed. Their investigations have covered several areas in which psychological disturbance might be found. These areas include the degree of self-consciousness adolescents experience; the stability of their self-image in relation to others; the degree of their self-esteem; and their "perceived self," or the way they think others view them.

In one recent study, researchers interviewed 1,917 students, ranging from the third to the twelfth grade, from twenty-five schools in Baltimore. Findings showed that the greatest degree of unhappiness with self occurred in the twelve-to-fourteen age group. In later years, the disturbance, although still present, became less.

What accounts for this? The researchers believe that the biological changes of *puberty,* or sexual maturation, combine with the challenges of junior high school to create a crisis in self-confidence. In their words, a youth

moves from a protected elementary school, where he usually has one teacher and one set of classmates, to a much larger, more impersonal junior high school where his teachers, classmates, and even his rooms are constantly shifting. He moves from a

setting where the teacher is a parent-surrogate[1] to a more impersonal environment. Here he is expected to behave more independently and more responsibly, and he must make his first career decision—whether to take an academic, commercial, or vocational course.

These findings agree with Erik Erikson's emphasis on adolescence as a time of identity crisis. Erikson's theory is summarized in the figure on page 197. The findings also pinpoint the age and social circumstances in which this crisis occurs—the time of biological maturation.

Biological Maturation

What is happening to young teenagers physically that can cause them such stress? During this time, many changes are taking place in the body: rapid growth, sprouting hair, changing shape. Along with them may come feelings of self-consciousness, awkwardness, and fear. To cope with all these changes, young people take on new roles, or alter the nature of old roles so they are more comfortable with them. A playmate becomes a dating partner, a friend, or a fellow gang or club member. The sex role takes on more importance in the building of an identity.

[1]substitute

For many young teenagers, puberty brings on feelings of self-consciousness and anxiety.

In American society, biological maturation occurs earlier today than it did half a century ago. For girls, the average onset of puberty has dropped from seventeen to twelve and a half. Boys usually begin puberty at about thirteen. Nevertheless, the feelings accompanying these changes remain pretty much the same as they were in the past. Consider the following statement, which expresses an attitude that is common during adolescence:

Self-consciousness about my body and appearance were overwhelming for several years. I did not put it into words, or even think about it, but there was always the possibility that my body, like some not quite predictable tyrant . . . would betray me, that something else would bulge or sweat or all at once sprout hair and so depart from the firm, predictable body of childhood.

Male athletic activities applied further pressures:

We used to play basketball a lot, and the obvious way to tell the teams apart was by one team taking off their shirts. It was known as the skins against the shirts. "All right, your team's the skins . . . get those shirts and sweaters and underwear off."

Why was it so embarrassing, this exposure of skin and the display of our chests and backs? Some of us had acne and that was humiliating, but I think that more than anything, it was that physically we simply were not up to the ideal stature and the ideal posture, size, and strength. The idea was evidently present in all our minds.

? Now that you are older, can you think of any way adolescents can avoid or lessen such "growing pains"?

Conflicts

Adolescence is the time when individuals learn new role behavior in anticipation of adulthood. At the same time, they are not really free from childhood role expectations. Parents are anxious for their children to get good grades and to plan careers. Adolescents, however, are still financially dependent. They live with their parents and are subject to parental authority just as they were in childhood. Thus, they remain dependent while training to be independent.

Tension between dependence and independence occurs outside the family, too. Young people are often openly critical of much around them, especially of their schools. At the same time, many are aware that their performance in high school and college will have a crucial effect on their future work possibilities. In the following reading, a student is outspoken about what she feels to be a stumbling block in preparing for the future:

I began to think of what I was going to be when I was older. I realized I had no real plans for the future—college, maybe, and after that was a dark space in my mind. In talking and listening to other girls, I found that they had either the same blank spot in their minds or were planning on marriage. If not that, they figured on taking a job of some sort *until* they got married.

The boys that I knew all had at least some slight idea in their minds of what career or job they were preparing for. Some prepared for careers in science and math by going to a specialized school. Others prepared for their later jobs as mechanics, electricians, and other tradesmen in vocational schools. . . . It seemed to me that I should fill in the blank spot in my mind as the boys were able to do, and I decided to study science . . . much more intensively. It was then that I encountered one of the many blocks which stand in the woman student's way: discrimination against women in the specialized science and math high schools in the city.

[?] Do you think that attitudes and conditions in specialized schools in the 1980s are different from those mentioned here? If so, how? Do you think that schools are mainly responsible for a person's career decisions? If not, who is responsible?

Peer-Group Influence

Adolescents are peer group oriented. As young people mature, they begin to rely less on their families and other adults. For some, it is a time to turn to friends for values, norms, and styles. Teenagers often join cliques, gangs, and other kinds of friendship groups. These groups give them a chance to talk, share new experiences, exchange ideas, and show loyalty, anger, and love.

In this youth culture, adolescents act out their independence from adult authority. The high school youth culture has several different subcultures from which teenagers can choose, identifying with the group that most closely expresses their own feelings and interests. In some groups, peers emphasize the importance of dating, parties, and dances. Other peer groups may be more interested in academic pursuits. Members emphasize getting good grades and involvement in school activities, such as the newspaper, debating club, or clubs that are directed toward subject matter taught in class.

Still other groups may be engaged in activities that break the law. These groups include gangs of young people who most actively reject the values of the larger society. Some gangs engage in criminal activity, such as robbery and car theft. Others are more

Peer groups are extremely important to adolescents, from a small group of close friends in a car to larger groups of teens joined by common interests of dance and camping.

involved in defending the neighborhoods they claim as their own—their turf—and battling with rival gangs. Still other gangs retreat from the goals of their conformist peers and find escape or "kicks" through the use of drugs.

Among these various groups, different styles of dress and possessions usually prevail, often serving as badges of belonging. The following reading shows one girl's attempt to "hold out" against peer pressure.

> For the first time in my life, I had to think about my weight; I wasn't getting enough exercise. I also had to think about my socks. I'd never thought about my socks before; they were just something that covered my feet. But in this sophisticated world, socks were a social signal. If you wore the wrong socks (anklets) instead of the right ones (thick bobbysox) or wore the right socks the wrong way (folded down instead of straight up), you were out of it. That is, the boys wouldn't like you,

and the "right" girls—the ones who were popular with the boys—wouldn't like you either or, worse, would look down on you. I held out on the socks for three mulish miserable months, finally seizing on the cold weather as an excuse to give way. It is not fun to be in the out group.

Although pressures to conform to the image of the favored group can distress teenagers, these pressures often create markets worth millions of dollars to adults. Advertising and mass communications media glorify youth culture and the world of the young. Promoters of clothing, cosmetics, phonograph records, posters, motorcycles, stereos, magazines, movies, video games, and books make special appeals to the youth market. Even adults copy the symbols of youth—the hairstyles, clothes, music, and dances—because no one wants to get old in our society. Thus teenagers may find themselves at the same time imitated and scorned.

? What "cultural items" and "culture traits" comparable to those identified on page 28 are representative of the groups to which you belong? Did you resist or resent conforming to any of the groups' requirements? Explain.

While involved in their own groups, teenagers are also thinking ahead to their place in the adult world. Family, friends, television, books, and school experiences give rise to thoughts about the future and the kinds of roles that will be played. Youths often feel pressured to make decisions about their futures. Will they go to college? What will they study to be?

Most young people see themselves seeking typical family and work roles—husband and father, wife and mother, worker. To prepare for these roles, teenagers begin choosing the skills and attitudes most likely to be of use to them in the years ahead. For some, this may mean taking a business math course instead of woodworking or spending less time studying academic subjects and more time learning auto repair.

The influence of earlier socialization is apparent in the ways young people plan for the future. Teenagers already have some no-

Young people's interests have created million-dollar industries. In the 1980s, video games and arcades became a source of controversy as many adults objected to a fad that was expensive, kept players indoors, and replaced activities that seemed more worthwhile.

Social class is influential in determining how far a teenager will go in life. Wealthy parents often send their children to boarding schools for college preparation.

tions about how far they can go in life. They have ideas about the types of activities they like and in which they can expect to succeed. These attitudes show up in the voices of two adolescents in the case studies that follow. The two boys live only two blocks apart in a large American city.

CASE STUDY: *Juan Gonzales, an Underprivileged Teenager*

Juan Gonzales is poor, and he is a member of a minority group.

I think about what I should do when I get out of school, and I just don't know. The people in my neighborhood . . . they're all doing it wrong. And if one tries to get out, the rest laughs. Like they say that they tried and couldn't do it, so you're not going to do it either. And this guy feels, "Well, maybe I can't do it," and he comes back into the slum. You figure, you know,

they failed, man, I might as well give up. . . .

I don't know any boys from those big houses. As long as I'm living here, all the boys over there have been going to private schools and they're very snotty. They think they're way superior. They can't show it by a fight because they lose. . . . A boy like that has a lot of protection from his parents and then, when he is away from them, he doesn't know how to handle himself. I usually go all the time away from my parents and I do pretty well.

The way I see it, right now, I think I have it better than the other one. But when I was small, then he had it, and when I get *older*, he will have it still better. He will have a better education. He will have a better atmosphere.

Like I wouldn't be able to go to a rich nightclub, or hire a nightclub singer, or have a good career. He might turn out to be a lawyer or a doctor or something, whereas I could only be maybe a mechanic or a machinist. I might make money, but I won't make the same kind of money he makes.

CASE STUDY: *Peter Quinn, an Affluent Teenager*

Peter Quinn is well off. His dreams, worries, and plans are evidence of his socialization by family and peers in his social class.

The one thing I'd like is to be finished with college and have all that worry behind me—all the difficulty of whether I'm going to get in, how my marks are going to be and all that over with. I'd like to be settled down in a good job with enough money to buy all the necessities and some luxuries. The thing I'd like is a lot of clothes, an awful lot of clothes. I love buying clothes. Then I'd buy a car if I were old enough and a house of my own and, of course, a dog. I see myself in a life with a lot of friends around me and a good family. . . .

I see myself with two or three children whom I can take care of financially, physically, and in every way. And the kind of girl I'd want to marry would be well-mannered, respectable, and good-looking, with a good personality.

? Have you made any definite plans for your future, or are you still investigating different fields and possibilities? If you have definite goals, who or what do you feel was instrumental in helping you form them?

REVIEW AND APPLICATION

1. *IDENTIFY:* Puberty.
2. According to one recent study conducted in Baltimore, people of what ages show the greatest unhappiness with self? Why is this true?
3. What are some psychological changes that often accompany puberty?
4. What are some of the conflicts many adolescents face?
5. How do peer groups generally affect adolescents?

CRITICAL THINKING: "I began to think of what I was going to be when I was older . . . . I decided to study science . . . it was then that I encountered one of the many blocks which stand in the woman student's way: discrimination against women in the specialized science and math high schools in the city." Based on this excerpt, what assumption do you think the administrators of the specialized science and math high school probably made about girls?

3 Socialization to Sex Roles

As adolescents go through the biological and emotional transition to adulthood, they must face certain questions. What kind of role behavior is acceptable or unacceptable for young men concerned about their developing masculinity? What does it mean to be feminine? Are there special expectations for each of these roles?

In Other Cultures

Every society divides tasks into those appropriate for males and those appropriate for females. But there is a great deal of variation in which tasks are assigned to which group. The anthropologist Margaret Mead discovered several New Guinea tribes that displayed sex roles quite unlike ours. One, in fact, had roles the direct opposite of ours.

The importance of Mead's discovery didn't lie simply in the fact that different tasks and activities were assigned to men and women. Rather, it was in the revelation of how widely the mental and emotional traits displayed by men and women in different cultures could vary. Among the Mundugumor people, for example, both men and women exaggerated what our society considers male characteristics: aggressiveness and competitiveness. Among the Arapesh, both men and women displayed what are considered female traits in our society: gentleness and submissiveness to the needs of others. And among the Tchambuli, the women were aggressive, authoritative figures, and the men were dependent, "flighty" creatures—the opposite of what our own society would expect.

Socialization has such a profound effect on people that they cling to beliefs and values even when confronted by strong contrary evidence. In reading about the New Guinea cultures just described, you may have been struck by feelings of uneasiness. Probably you felt that something was wrong with the patterns of traits displayed, particularly those of the Tchambuli. Even if you are sympathetic to feminist principles and claims, you may find it hard to accept a society in which men are considered vain, helpless creatures.

The notion of flighty, passive men may be unpleasant to you if you are male because people tend to internalize their culture's beliefs and values into their self-images. Yet the analysis by Mead demonstrates that social and cultural influences are crucial in establishing how males and females act, think, and feel.

? In your studies of history or in literature you've read, were there any examples of societies in which sex-role behavior was radically different from our own? If so, describe them. As an alternative, describe any society existing today where such differences are displayed.

In the Early Years

Most of our early learning of sex roles comes from watching, imitating, and talking with the significant others in our lives. The

Fathers often serve as role models for their sons in both simple and complicated ways. The youth below has learned a typical male behavior.

*Some parents today try to avoid sex stereotyping by encouraging free choice of toys.
Parents may select nursery schools like this one, where boys and girls alike can
"cook" and play with planes and trucks if they wish.*

first and most important "others" are our parents. But relatives and friends can also act as models. Even the media can influence attitudes toward sex roles.

Socialization by Parents The norms in our society say that blue is a color for baby boys and that pink is for girls. Boys receive chemistry sets as gifts; girls get dolls. A boy who likes to cook or work with children may be told not to be a sissy, that is, too feminine. A girl who likes to tinker with machinery or play with cars and trucks may be told not to be a tomboy, that is, too masculine.

Socialization into sex roles begins so early in life that as young adults, or even as children, people usually lose the memory of how it was accomplished. As far back as they can remember, they were pretty much like the finished product—a boy or a girl.

In fact, by the time children are two years old, most parents have instilled in them some idea of what is expected of their sex in their particular culture. Some studies have shown that, even from birth, the treatment of girls and boys is different. Researchers have observed that mothers of six-month-old girls touch their babies much more than mothers of boys the same age. Sociologist Lenore Weitzman maintains that this early interaction causes little girls to seek more maternal contact later on. In contrast, little boys internalize the expectation that they will be independent.

Not everyone in our culture develops the attitude that women should be dependent, however. One study found that children of working mothers had less traditional ideas about sex roles. Similarly, girls whose fathers encourage high achievement more often seek roles that are not typically female.

Parents transfer their sex-role expectations, whatever they are, to their children in many ways, sometimes quite unconsciously. By the time children leave their teens, the process of parental socialization is complete.

The self-image teenagers have developed affects all their decisions about their future lives.

Socialization by Media Parents are not the only powerful influence in establishing sex roles. Television programs, as you read in Chapter 9, and books are other agents that socialize children. The illustrations on page 224 are from traditional books designed for children in the elementary grades. As you look at them, consider these questions: Based on these pictures, what kinds of activities are men supposed to carry out? What about women? What ideas might a female reader develop about her future role in society? What might a male reader expect?

"Feminine" and "masculine" images are what social scientists call sex stereotypes. A *stereotype* is a set of oversimplified, exaggerated ideas about a group of people. It is often unfavorable, and it implies that all members of that group are exactly alike. A stereotype doesn't take into account individual differences. Those who think in sex stereotypes, for example, assume that all men like sports and adventure and that all women prefer cooking and homemaking.

The following excerpt, from *The Lady's Almanac* (1875), is an example of sex stereotyping:

> The education of a girl as a housekeeper should be begun by the mother early and continued until the marriage of the daughter. No other duty of the mother and no other study of the daughter should interfere with it. This and the school education should go on simultaneously. If anything is to be postponed let it be music and drawing and philosophy, which, as experience shows, are usually unattended to and unpracticed after "the happy event."

Young men were also told what they were to be—educated, energetic, and competitive. One popular book, *The Student Manual*, written by the Reverend John Todd in about the same period, described the will and energy boys needed to develop so that their vigor and vital powers could be used to improve civilization. Women should not be too educated since that might interfere with their preparation for motherhood. But men needed a "course of suitable discipline" in addition to the useful "rivalry" and the "pressure" of frightening competition.

In 1972, the National Organization for Women (NOW) conducted a study of sex stereotyping in children's readers. Reviewers looked at 145 elementary school readers from fourteen publishers. Among the items they looked for were the number of stories with a boy as the central character and the number with a girl, the number featuring adult males and adult females, the number of biographies of men and of women, and the jobs shown for men and for women.

The study showed that boy-centered stories outnumbered girl-centered stories five to two. There were three times as many adult males as females and six times as many male biographies as female. Men in the stories had 147 different kinds of jobs; women had 26. Men worked as architects, astronauts, bankers, computer operators, and television newscasters. Women held positions as cashiers, cooks, librarians, secretaries, and teachers.

Later research confirmed the survey done by NOW. One study of children's books revealed that boys were shown as persons who express themselves. Girls were there to please others. In a group of leading picture books, there were five times as many males as females. Famous books by such authors as Dr. Seuss and Maurice Sendak featured mostly males. Favorite animal characters, such as Babar and Curious George, are male, too.

Big differences also appeared in the kinds of activities shown. Girls seldom rode bicycles, and women rarely drove cars. Women were nurses and teachers, but the doctor and the school principal were always male. Of course, to some extent this reflected realities of employment. One well-known children's book showed thirteen male animals doing such active things as digging, building, breaking, pushing, and pulling. The two female characters sat and watched.

Until relatively recently, children's books showed women mainly in traditional, passive, or homemaking roles. Illustrations like these reflected only part of the reality.

What happens in female socialization when women are stereotyped as passive people whose main concerns are love, clothes, and marriage? Do girls come to connect school, athletics, and job success with loss of femininity? What happens to male socialization if boys are always presented as active and aggressive? Do boys begin to associate expressing affection or caring for children as symbols of lost masculinity?

We do not fully know whether the greater aggressiveness of boys is something they are born with or learn or both. Tests have shown most girls to have greater verbal ability, while boys usually excel in math and science. Yet no one can state for sure what effect a different socialization process would have on such results.

? Did any particular book influence your career ambitions? Do you feel you were encouraged or discouraged in your plans by the roles portrayed by fictional characters? Explain.

Sex Stereotyping in Adolescence

According to several research projects, schools present another source of sex-role discrimination. Many of the older history books used in grammar school and high school showed a past created by men. To be sure, this omission of women partly reflected their exclusion from active participation in politics, war, business, and the arts, but they were not as absent as these history books suggested. Think of the textbooks that you have recently read. How are male and female characteristics presented? Have sex-role stereotypes changed in recent years?

At the high school level, guidance counselors and the tracking system reinforce the socialization accomplished in earlier grades. Boys and girls of equal intelligence and similar interests are frequently channeled into different programs preparing them for different occupations. Suppose a female student wants to become an engineer, a physicist, a mathematician, a doctor, or a professional in some other occupation that is almost exclu-

sively male. Unless her parents, teachers, and counselors accept her ambitions, she may face a great deal of resistance. Until the feminist movement became a major cultural force, many young women succumbed to this resistance. Today fewer do. In fact, today some young women who would prefer full-time homemaking and motherhood feel pressured to seek careers.

Exposure to sex-role stereotyping is bound to have an effect on young adults, perhaps in unknown ways. Matina Horner, a psychologist and the president of Radcliffe College, hypothesized that young women who were capable of career success were more fearful of it than comparably talented men. To test her theory, she asked male students at a leading university to tell a story based on the sentence "After first-term finals John finds himself at the top of the medical school class." Over 90 percent of the male students wrote with delight about John's success. They forecast a great future for him.

Female students were asked to write a story based on the same sentence, but the name was changed from John to Anne.

Most schools now offer the same courses to male and female students. The photograph shows a typesetting-shop class in Newville, Pennsylvania.

About two-thirds of the young women wrote stories that indicated they were worried about professional success. For example:

> Anne is an acne-faced bookworm. She runs to the bulletin board and finds she's at the top. As usual she smarts off. A chorus of groans is the rest of the class's reply. . . . She studies twelve hours a day and lives at home to save money. "Well it certainly paid off. All the Friday and Saturday nights without dates—fun. I'll be the best woman doctor alive!" And yet a twinge of sadness comes through—she wonders what she really has.

> Anne feels guilty. . . . She will finally have a nervous breakdown and quit medical school and marry a successful young doctor.

> Anne is talking to her counselor. Counselor says she will make a fine nurse.

Horner's study used other questions and activities, all of which showed that young women are affected by the notion that achievement is a masculine trait. They felt that even very bright women should play down their skills and knowledge to fit society's definition of feminine. Horner found, for example, that many female students scored higher than males on tests when men and women were tested in separate rooms. When women were given a similar test in competition with males, the women's scores fell. For the men the opposite was true: over two-thirds raised their scores in a competitive situation. Horner saw some hope for the future in the women students who did not fear success. Said one:

GRAPH SKILL   Though changes are taking place in the workplace, the division of labor has remained the same in the United States for decades. How would you describe the "division of labor"?

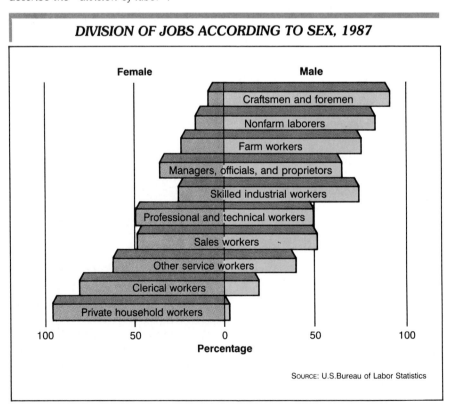

DIVISION OF JOBS ACCORDING TO SEX, 1987

Female — Male

- Craftsmen and foremen
- Nonfarm laborers
- Farm workers
- Managers, officials, and proprietors
- Skilled industrial workers
- Professional and technical workers
- Sales workers
- Other service workers
- Clerical workers
- Private household workers

100   50   0   50   100
Percentage

SOURCE: U.S. Bureau of Labor Statistics

TOP TEN OCCUPATIONS HELD BY WOMEN, 1987

Occupation	Women (millions)	Percentage Held by Women
1. Clerical and other administrative support	6.1	74.6%
2. Secretaries, including typists and stenographers	4.9	98%
3. Salesclerks and related workers	4.1	68.5%
4. Food service workers	3.2	61.5%
5. Bookkeepers and computer operators	2.8	84.8%
6. Health service workers, including practical nurses, aides, orderlies, and dental assistants	2.6	86.2%
7. Noncollege teachers	2.6	73.5%
8. Registered nurses, dieticians, and therapists	2.0	67.3%
9. Personal service workers, including hairdressers and beauticians	1.8	82.7%
10. Private household workers	0.9	96.8%

SOURCE: U.S. Bureau of Labor Statistics, 1987.

CHART SKILL *Although more and more women are assuming managerial positions, certain clerical, service, and professional occupations have always been viewed as "female" in orientation. What social factors would serve to perpetuate that expectation?*

[Anne] is liked and admired by her fellow students—quite a trick in a man-dominated field. She is brilliant but also a woman.

Horner followed up her study of college students by giving the same tests to students in high schools. The responses demonstrated that young men and women had different learning patterns about what is appropriate for their sex and that many capable young women who might have succeeded had been taught to fear success. (See the Appendix for an explanation of the research process.)

Horner's research has generated a number of follow-up studies. These findings show the complexity of the issues facing young women who desire professional careers. For example, one study found that women did not fear success itself. Rather, they feared appearing unfeminine if they were too successful.

Men also seem to fear success but for different reasons. Many men wonder whether success is worth the extraordinary effort they have to invest in order to reap the rewards. Finally, and very importantly, one study followed up the Horner's sample of female subjects to see what had become of them. Despite their fears of success, most of the women had completed their advanced degrees.

One indication that women are respected leaders is their appointment or election to public office. Sandra Day O'Connor, top left, is the first woman Supreme Court Justice. Pat Schroeder, top right, is a member of the House of Representatives from Colorado. Lottie Shackelford, bottom left, is mayor of Little Rock, Arkansas, and Nancy Kassebaum, bottom right, is a Senator from Kansas.

REVIEW AND APPLICATION

1. *IDENTIFY:* Stereotype.
2. What were the sex roles displayed by the Mundugumor, the Arapesh, and the Tchambuli tribes in New Guinea? As revealed by Margaret Mead?
3. How do parents socialize children to sex roles?
4. In what ways does the media promote stereotyping?

5. What were the results of Horner's study of sex-role stereotyping?

CRITICAL THINKING: Review the stories on page 226 that indicate how female students at a leading university feel about success. Which of the following do you think the author of the first story values: fun, success, hard work, thrift, popularity?

CHAPTER **10** REVIEW

Although the foundations of socialization are laid in childhood, crucial developments take place in adolescence, too. The "storm and stress" associated in our society with adolescence—and especially with physical maturation—is not present in all societies. In many, the socialization process differs greatly from ours.

Adolescent years in the United States are a time of preparation for future roles in work and family life. Teenagers move toward independence but, at the same time, are kept under the authority of family and school. In their search for identity, young people choose from among many different groups within the youth culture, both in and out of school. Social class is an important determinant in these choices and has a powerful impact on the young, influencing their chances, hopes, and plans for the future.

Throughout their socialization, young people also learn what it means to be male and female. Sex-role stereotypes, instilled from birth by parents, are reinforced by the media and by schools and teachers. In the past, such socialization tended to undermine the confidence of girls and to limit their aspirations.

Key Terms

Define the following:

adolescence	secular	stereotype
age-graded society	puberty	

Applying Sociology

1. List the following factors in order of their importance in influencing adolescents' plans for the future, beginning with the most important:

   (a) ability
   (b) aptitude
   (c) luck
   (d) economic resources
   (e) parents' wishes
   (f) type of school attended
   (g) friends choices

   Explain your reasoning.

2. In your own experience, what norms have you learned about proper and improper behavior for young women and men as they plan their current studies and future work lives? Did you learn these norms from friends, parents, or others? What rewards or punishments reinforce these norms?

3. Conduct your own study of males and females in school readers. Ask a younger sister or brother or a friend if you may borrow their school books. Or ask the local librarian for two or three books most popular with youngsters. Make a table like the one on page 230 and check or fill in the boxes to record the data you collect. Counting male and female animals as

boys and girls, make lists of male and female occupations, and determine how many males are portrayed compared to females. After everyone has completed a data sheet, the totals can be computed. How do the results correspond to the study done by NOW? Review page 223 as a basis for your comparison.

ANALYSIS OF SEX ROLES IN CHILDREN'S BOOKS

| | Story | | | | | | | | |
	1	2	3	4	5	6	7	8	Total
Featuring boys									
Featuring girls	✓								
Featuring adult males	✓								
Featuring adult females	✓								
Featuring males and females equally	✓								
Male biography									
Female biography									
Occupations shown for men	*editor*								
Occupations shown for women	*judge*								

See question 3, page 229.

James M. Dubik, "An Officer and a Feminist," *Newsweek*, April 27, 1987, pp. 8–9.

1. What experiences changed the author's mind about the roles of women?
2. Why didn't the author view women as equals earlier in his life?

Joshua Fischman, "The Ups and Downs of Teenage Life," *Psychology Today*, May 1987, pp. 56–57.

1. According to the study, how do most teenagers spend their time?

2. What have the researchers concluded about teenagers' problems?

Lawrence Steinberg, "Bound to Bicker," *Psychology Today*, September 1987, pp. 36–39.

1. How do nonindustrialized societies deal with parent-adolescent conflict?
2. What effect did industrialization have on contacts between parents and children?

Formulating steps to achieve a personal goal

Achieving any kind of goal requires a plan. Rearrange on a separate sheet the following steps in Juan's plan to get an education:

1. Ask the university that offers a pre-law program what credits it accepts from junior colleges.
2. Do you have enough money for junior college?
3. Work at a fast-food franchise to save money.
4. Apply to the university.
5. Do you have enough money for the university?
6. Obtain a grant or loan.
7. At a low-cost junior college, accumulate credits that the university will accept.

1. ***Identifying Assumptions:*** Read the case study of Juan Gonzales and Peter Quinn again. What assumptions do these two teenagers make about life and society? To what extent are their assumptions similar and different?
2. ***Recognizing Values:*** What values are expressed in each of the three pictures on page 217?

The Adult Years

Chapter Preview

- **Before you read,** look up the following key terms in the glossary to become familiar with their definitions:

blue–collar work   white–collar work   pink–collar work
affirmmative action   role loss
  programs

- **As you read,** think about answers to the following questions:

1. In what ways is adulthood as challenging as adolescence?
2. What are the origins of the term "blue–collar worker"?
3. What are the origins of the term "white–collar worker"?
4. What is the rationale behind affirmative action programs?

Sections in this Chapter

1. Challenges of Adulthood
2. Blue Collar Work
3. White Collar Work
4. The Professions
5. Women in the Workforce
6. Growing Old

Chapter Focus

Children and teenagers look forward to the day when they will be on their own and will truly be adults. They think of adulthood as a time of independence, of choosing the kinds of jobs they want and making all sorts of decisions that affect their lives. Once they are established in the state of adulthood, though, they sometimes wish they could have remained children forever.

Between the idealized state of adulthood and the reality of life as a spouse, parent, and breadwinner there is often quite a difference. Adults quickly learn that there is still much to learn.

For most adults, the processes of socialization are related to marriage, parenthood, working, retirement, and old age. This chapter concentrates on the world of work.

Using Sociologists' Tools

- **Observe** the behavior of juniors and seniors as they make decisions about the future course of their lives.
- **Describe** the future plans of 15 members of your junior or senior class selected at random.
- **Analyze** their career choices in terms of how and where they grew up.
- **Predict** the things that will be most and least satisfying to you once you enter the workforce.

Work supplies a large part of the definition of who we are and provides a number of satisfactions, including a sense of kinship with fellow workers.

1 Challenges of Adulthood

Teenagers crossing the threshold into legal adulthood may feel that they have left the world of "identity crisis" and constant adjustments far behind them. Perhaps they view the adult years as a time of steady growth, free from personal confusion and the demands of others. But, as you learned in Chapter 6, the "must-do's" increase, and are harder to accomplish, once you have matured.

Marriage and Parenthood

Almost every discussion of marriage these days stresses changes and problems: the rising divorce rate, proper roles for wives and husbands, and confusion over the division of family responsibilities. What factors contribute to the choice of a partner and to the stability of those families which endure? What socialization processes are involved in marriage and parenthood?

Most young people have been socialized throughout childhood and adolescence to prefer members of the opposite sex who have the same background and are in other ways similar to themselves. Partners tend to have similar educational levels, to be fairly close in age, and to belong to the same religious, racial, or ethnic groups. When it looks as if a couple is "getting serious," many families will exert various pressures to influence their children to marry within their own social group.

The choice of a partner may be influenced as much by proximity as it is by parents. You may fall in love with the girl or boy down the block or in the apartment on the

233

fourth floor because you feel comfortable with someone whose way of life is similar to your own. Your neighborhood crowd and classmates—your peers—as well as your parents will help form your vision of the ideal mate you hope to marry.

Once married, a couple finds that marriage is in itself a constant process of socialization. Each partner must learn to appreciate, or at least to adapt to, the interests, tastes, and habits—and the relatives—of the other. Since change is never easy, you can see that having much in common with your spouse would provide the best basis for a successful union. (See the list on page 141, which notes some characteristics that may lead to a shaky marriage.)

Even with near-perfect adaptation to one another, a couple faces a whole new set of prescriptions with the birth of the first child. Socialization to parenthood is perhaps the most difficult process of all. The demands of parenthood are incessant and ever-changing. Most people rely on parents, peers, and professionals for aid. But the many theories of experts, as well as opinions unsubstantiated by research, may confuse new parents seeking rules on parenting. Some parents may fall back upon their own intuitive reac-

tions, or they may just repeat the methods used in their own upbringing. Parents brought up differently may strongly disagree. How children are socialized was discussed in Chapter 9.

Of course, for most adults, striving for success in love, marriage, and parenthood takes up only part of their time and energy. Psychoanalyst Sigmund Freud, when asked what were the human experiences in which competence was most necessary for a fulfilled life, replied, "love and work." These two aspects of living are interwoven in the modern world. For most people, work provides the wherewithal for meeting the family's many needs.

The World of Work

Work plays a central role in the life cycle of almost everyone. And almost everyone is socialized to important new roles "on the job." To a large extent, success on the job decides style of life, self-image, prestige, and influence in the community. The way in which we earn a living also deeply affects our family life.

As young adults prepare to enter the job market, they ask what kinds of jobs are open to them, what type of preparation they need, and what their co-workers and surroundings will be like. They are curious, too, about how much money they will earn. Will other people respect them for the work they do? How much control will they have over their working lives?

In twentieth-century American society, work has become increasingly centered in large bureaucratic organizations, which offer many different work roles. Even in the same firm, there is little resemblance between the job of custodian and that of manager. Yet there are similarities as well as differences. All workers must learn to deal with pressures toward conformity. All must be able to play the role the organization requires.

Since job restrictions frequently create discontent, people learn to *legitimize* their

Accepting the role of parent means assuming full-time responsibility for another person's physical and mental well-being.

Many employees of corporations share large, impersonal offices with others doing the same kind of work.

work—to give it meaning so that they can put up with its undesirable aspects. Sometimes legitimacy comes from the task itself, as when a person performs an important public service. In other situations, people learn to live with boring or difficult work because they believe they have no better alternatives.

The variety of occupations in an industrial society is tremendous. Although classification systems vary, most occupations can be placed into a few categories by asking the following questions: (1) How complex is the work—that is, how much talent or training is needed to acquire the necessary skills? (2) Where are the skills acquired and how long does it take to acquire them? (3) Where is the work performed—in a factory, in an office, in a store, on a farm, or elsewhere? (4) What are the financial rewards and prestige that go with the job?

REVIEW AND APPLICATION

1. *IDENTIFY:* Legitimize.
2. What socializing agents influence a person's choice of a mate?
3. In what way is marriage a constant process of socialization?
4. In what ways does one's choice of work influence one's life?
5. What are some similarities shared by all jobs?
6. How do people legitimize their jobs?
7. What questions might one ask when categorizing various occupations?

CRITICAL THINKING: Compare the jobs of custodian and partner at an accounting firm by asking the following questions about each: How much skill is required? Where are the skills obtained? What rewards go with the job?

2 Blue-Collar Work

Blue-collar work includes unskilled, semiskilled, and skilled labor. Farm work and service occupations, which are sometimes considered separate categories, overlap with blue-collar work because they require varying degrees of skill. Most blue-collar jobs involve manual labor. Instead of wearing business suits, these workers tend to wear uniforms or work shirts—hence the term "blue-collar."

Unskilled Work

Several million American men and women perform unskilled work. These jobs require little formal education and only a few basic abilities. Dishwashing, operating an elevator,

Like this worker, millions of people perform unskilled labor, which requires little training or education.

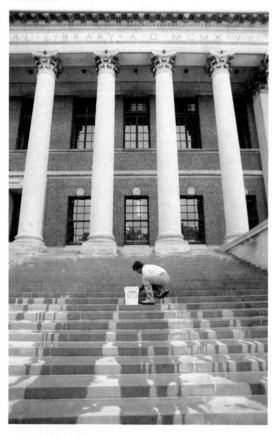

carrying bricks, and cleaning a building can be learned on the job in a brief time, ranging from a few minutes to a few hours. The pay for these jobs is low, and so is the social prestige attached to them.

To study unskilled workers, sociologist Elliot Liebow became a participant observer of black male workers in Washington, D.C. He lived among the workers and their families for about eighteen months in the early 1960s, becoming intimate enough with them to learn of their joys and troubles, their dreams and frustrations. Most of the men did hard physical labor for low pay. The jobs held out no hope of future advancement, and the men constantly shifted from one job to another. They were never able to make enough money to provide for their families adequately, to get satisfaction from their work, or to develop much self-respect.

From the employer's viewpoint, these men should have been socialized to be cooperative, reliable, and respectful of the boss. They were supposed to be pleasant, to learn quickly, and to assert no independence in doing their work. Some unskilled laborers were like this, but most were influenced by other attitudes.

Liebow found that most of the men had little interest in specific details of a job. All they cared about was the size of the paycheck. In doing the menial work of the society, Liebow points out, there is little difference between "pushing a mop and pulling trash in an apartment house, a restaurant, or an office building." A laborer doesn't care "whether he's pushing a wheelbarrow, mixing mortar, or digging a hole." Given the choices in the unskilled labor market, they felt that "a job is a job." Unemployed and underemployed unskilled workers like those Liebow described reflect one of the most serious problems of industrialized society: not everyone shares in the good life offered by new technology.

Although most unskilled labor is boring and unsatisfying, some unskilled jobs are different. They may provide not only steady work but other rewards as well. David Sudnow studied jobs in a large county hospital. He learned some interesting things about John, the morgue attendant. John's major tasks were to move dead bodies from the wards to the morgue and to help the pathologist do autopsies. A pathologist studies the causes and progress of disease, partly through dissection and examination of bodies. The work was not hard, but the attendant had to learn a great deal about proper role behavior.

Most people, whether staff, patients, or visitors, feel uneasy around dead bodies. John learned a number of ways of putting others at ease. When getting on an elevator, for example, he called out to passengers that he was about to wheel in a body. People could decide whether to ride with him or wait for the next elevator.

As John walked through the halls with a body, he learned to lower his head and to avoid eye contact with others. This way his friends didn't have to greet him or make conversation. John was dating one of the nurse's aides, but he was uneasy about meeting her while on the job. He told her that chatting or joking in the presence of a body was not the thing to do.

In the course of this socialization, John learned to set his work role apart from other aspects of his life at the hospital. Unlike other staff members, he changed clothes when he went to the lunchroom. He never discussed his work on a coffee break or at a meal, although others on the staff often talked about what they did.

These efforts succeeded to some extent, but most of the staff knew what John's work was. This, he felt, raised a subtle barrier between him and others. So the hardest part of his job was not the work itself but loneliness on the job.

Yet the work had many rewards. John's pay was better than that of other unskilled workers. The doctors in the morgue treated him well. One doctor jokingly but admiringly told others that John knew more about pathology than he did. John did learn many of the details of human anatomy. Although he had not finished high school, he was able to study surgical texts and even attend operations.

⁇ What rewards did John get from his job? How did he learn to deal with the problems connected with his work? Do you think he handled them effectively? Have you had any experience as an unskilled worker in a summer or after-school job? How did you learn what you were or weren't supposed to do in your on-the-job relationships?

Semiskilled Work

An essential feature of an industrial society is the assembly line, where semiskilled workers make complicated products, such as automobiles, electronic equipment, and washing machines. A semiskilled worker who operates a machine is sometimes known as an operative. Usually each worker performs a single operation on the product as it passes by on a mechanical conveyor. By organizing the tasks systematically and by breaking them into simple steps, the assembly line makes it possible to turn out large numbers of the product every day. Each worker is assigned to do one simple task quickly over and over and over. Unlike a skilled tailor who makes an entire suit, a semiskilled operator learns only how to sew sleeves or make buttonholes.

Most factory jobs require some training. Operating a machine differs from pushing a mop or washing dishes. The worker needs to know what the machine can do, how to use it, and what to beware of. Mastering these skills may take only a few days, but it must be done if the worker is to turn out an acceptable product safely.

The assembly line in an auto plant is perhaps the most typical. Learning the job is not hard, but doing it day after day and week after week is. Auto workers must learn to deal with the tension and pressure of being "on the line," as assembly-line work is called. Their pay tends to be good. Their union has bargained successfully to ensure seniority rights, good pensions, and cost-of-living raises. But workers often show the strain of eight or more hours a day at a hard and boring task.

The assembly line, a feature of industrialized society, requires semiskilled workers who have been trained for particular tasks.

The wife of one worker said: "I don't know much about what he does in the plant, but it does something to him. Of course, I shouldn't complain. He gets good pay. We've been able to buy . . . a lot of things we wouldn't have had otherwise. But sometimes I wonder whether these are more important to us than having Joe get all nervous and tensed up."

In his study of auto workers in Detroit, sociologist Ely Chinoy found that the hardest thing they had too learn was keeping up with the ever-moving assembly line. Newcomers learned to do their joking and talking when the line broke down and to focus on the work once it started. They couldn't leave the line until a scheduled relief worker took over. Even going to the washroom could be a problem.

The high noise level, the separation from other workers, and the rapid pace made teamwork and sociability on the line impossible. As a result, workers often felt tired, lonely, and bored. "I've been here over a year," said one worker, "and I hardly know the first names of the men in the section where I work."

The work had practically no meaning for the individual. There was little in the social- ization process that related a factory worker's one task to the finished project. "I'm just a cog in the machine" is how one worker saw his job. Workers tended to feel that their jobs were dead ends. Those who had been around for a while had little hope for promotion, more interesting work, or a more promising career.

Many sociologists view this loss of worker autonomy, or control, as a problem for both worker and industry. Workers, they feel, need to have a relationship to the final product and to participate in decisions about it. Reducing tasks to minute operations does more than make work boring. It excludes workers from any responsibility or under- standing of the process and often robs them of their skills. Indifference and apathy can then lead to poor workmanship and inferior products.

Several modern observers believe that new methods have the potential for giving more meaning to assembly-line work. Swe- den and Germany have experimented with assigning a variety of tasks to each person. For example, an entire Saab car is built by a team of five or six workers gathered in one area, who divide the tasks among them- selves.

The idea of workers making decisions about the work process and having some control over technology is only in its infancy in the United States. However, the Ford Motor Company has tried giving workers greater motivation by allowing them to test-drive the cars they build. Their unions also work closely with management to achieve quality control.

Other cultures use different methods of socializing workers to appropriate norms and values. You will recall the Matsushita Electrical Company, discussed in Chapter 4. There Japanese workers sing this song each morning:

For the building of a New Japan,
Let's put our strength and mind together.
Doing our best to promote production,
Sending our goods to the people of the world,
Endlessly and continuously,
Like water gushing from a fountain.
Grow, industry, grow, grow, grow!
Harmony and sincerity!

? What might a worker mean if he or she said, "In assembly-line work, the rewards are off the job"? What suggestions can you make that might improve the lot of the semiskilled laborer? Would techniques used in other countries work here? Which ones? Why?

Skilled Work

Skilled labor, as the name implies, requires training. Plumbers, electricians, carpenters, ironworkers, and craftspersons are all skilled workers. They must go through an apprenticeship, a training period during which they learn their trade. Often they are restricted to certain kinds of work until they have been licensed as master workers. Unions of skilled workers also regulate work and protect their members in a number of ways.

In contrast to work "on the line," skilled work often requires that people cooperate closely with each other. John Haas did a participant-observer study of ironworkers, focusing on the way they socialized apprentices to become trustworthy members of their work

In recent years, many industries have replaced production lines with teams of workers. Having more control gives workers a greater sense of responsibility and pride in their products. These people are assembling a helicopter.

Skilled work often involves an apprenticeship period.

group. Apprentices usually had to be sponsored by a relative or friend who was already an ironworker. Once chosen, the apprentice had to "punk" for the experienced worker. This included going up on the steel beams and doing such chores as moving tools and getting coffee. Newcomers had to learn that to be accepted they had to walk across beams without showing fear.

A key part of the learning process was called "binging." This meant that experienced workers teased the apprentice to see if he could "keep his cool" when the going got rough. If not, they shut him out of the group and refused to work with him on dangerous jobs. Only when he was accepted by the group could the apprentice "bing" back, showing that he was acting as a group member.

In his study, Haas recorded a conversation that he had with an older worker and an apprentice:

"You know, it's interesting. I see you guys kidding each other a lot. When a new fellow comes, it seems like the kidding is all one way. That is, you older men who have completed their apprenticeships give it real hard to a new fellow coming in, but after he begins to become more like one of you, then he starts kidding back. Is there anything to this?"

Dave says, "That makes me laugh. I mean I've never thought of it that way. I don't want to call it an initiation, but it's something like that. If you're going to work with a guy, you want to know whether he can take it or not, and just what kind of guy he is."

Dick, the newer apprentice, says, "Yeah, you're always a punk and they rib you pretty hard, but you've got to show them you can take it. Now sometimes they give me that and I'll just tell them, 'Hey, you know, back off, I'm not your slave.' Then they begin to appreciate you a little more and understand that you're a human being. I mean you can't get angry at them, because then they get on you worse. You've got to show that you can take it, but then you've also got to show that you can dish it out."

Ironworkers form values that stress skill on the job, coolness in danger, and loyalty to fellow workers both on and off the job. Apprentices take on these values as a part of their new work role. Being successful as an ironworker means meeting certain expectations of co-workers. Loyalty to the group, for instance, requires that ironworkers lend money to a fellow worker who needs help, that they spend time drinking together in

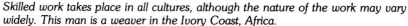

Skilled work takes place in all cultures, although the nature of the work may vary widely. This man is a weaver in the Ivory Coast, Africa.

bars, and that they pass along information on how to deal with certain contractors.

Ironworkers often also agree about non-work issues such as government policy, welfare programs, and minority groups. Sharing values and attitudes draws the group together. Ironworkers, Haas found, need each other on the job and enjoy each other's company after work.

Robert M. Cook, a sociologist who had been an engineer and Marine Corps captain, became an ironworker in 1969. His observations support Haas's findings and emphasize the importance of cooperation, teamwork, and control over working conditions:

> When a crew has been together for awhile, when there are no clashes of personalities and they have gotten to know each other's ways, the work can proceed without orders or even conversation. Each man knows what "moves" to make and how his actions mesh with the others. A rhythm and flow develops, an unsung harmony exists. There is little waste motion. Choreographers[1] and coaches would marvel at the coordination of mental and physical effort. Productivity is unbelievable. You leave the job exhilarated and almost (but not quite) sorry that the day is over. Sometimes when we're working in miserable weather or extremely difficult conditions we joke, "Time flies when you're having fun." It sure does. . . .
>
> We're often called prejudiced, bigoted, or worse. Those who say that miss the point. When your life depends on every move the other guy makes, you've got to know what to expect from him. Given a choice, you're going to work with a skilled friend, relative, or neighbor over someone you don't know or trust. In theory, the apprenticeship program and on-the-job training should ensure that all those who carry a journeyman ironworker's card are relatively competent in most phases of the work. In practice, skill and experience and ease of entry into the trade vary so widely that you can't assume anything about a new hand.

[1] arrangers of dance patterns

Being an ironworker requires steady nerves as well as skill.

REVIEW AND APPLICATION

1. *IDENTIFY:* Blue-collar work.
2. What is a major problem of semiskilled assembly-line workers? How have some societies attempted to make semiskilled work more meaningful?

CRITICAL THINKING: Name the ironworkers' values Robert M. Cook stresses in the following excerpt: "When a crew has been together for awhile, when there are no clashes of personalities and they have gotten to know each other's ways, the work can proceed without orders or even conversation. Each man knows what "moves" to make and how his actions mesh with the others . . . . Choreographers and coaches would marvel at the coordination of mental and physical effort."

3 White-Collar Work

As our industrial technology has grown in the last century, so has the number of our business organizations. A business may have a small office with a handful of employees and one boss, or it may have several branches around the world, employing thousands of office workers. Most of the jobs in these offices are considered *white-collar work*. These jobs revolve around "paperwork"—producing, recording, classifying, and storing information. Today the term also includes the use of computers, which employ magnetic or electrical impulses rather than paper to convey information.

White-collar workers now make up the largest percentage of the work force in our society. Positions range from low-paid file clerk to executive secretary, computer programmer, office manager, and salesperson. The tasks range from the routine and tedious, such as filing invoices, to the responsible and interesting, such as maintaining confidential records or dealing with clients and visitors.

We have seen that semiskilled workers on an assembly line have little control over their work. Many office workers are similarly regulated, if not quite as closely supervised. For example, secretaries, file clerks, and bookkeepers are often responsible for a certain output per day or per week. Employees who protest about the work situation may well be fired. Like semiskilled factory workers, most white-collar workers can be quickly replaced.

Office workers learn that certain attitudes are an important part of their work roles. They must accept norms about dress, manner, and attitude toward work, and they must learn the skills of stenography, typing, bookkeeping, or office management. Although there is great variation from office to office, most white-collar workers expect cleaner and pleasanter surroundings, more varied tasks, and more prestige than factory workers. At the same time, they learn that they can make few or no decisions in the office.

White-collar workers have rarely had strong unions to protect their interests in such matters as working conditions, salaries, health and pension plans, and other fringe benefits. In the last twenty years, however, growing numbers of them have joined unions. One sociologist made the following observation:

> Many white-collar workers who in the past considered trade union tactics beneath them are today finding unionization more and more attractive. While the proportion of the U.S. labor force that is unionized actually declined about 1 percent (from 23.6 to 22.6 percent) between 1960 and 1970, the proportion of unionized white-collar workers among all American unionists increased from 12 percent in 1960 to 16 percent by 1970. Moreover, white-collar unions are growing at a faster rate than blue-collar unions, and the gains are impressive: in the last decade the American Federation of Government Employees gained 362 percent and the American Federation of State, County, and Municipal Employees, 111 percent.

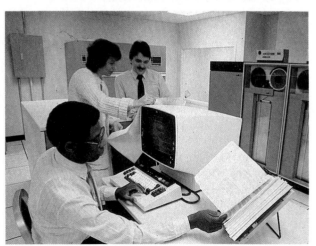

White-collar work today often involves the use of computers, an innovation that tends to blur the distinction between technicians and clerical workers.

These rates slowed in the late 1970s, but white-collar unionization continues. Why have these changes occurred? Anthony Giddens, a British sociologist, has summarized a number of factors:

1. Clerical workers now often make substantially less than skilled laborers.
2. With the advent of highly technical equipment, clerical employees now do less "pencil-pushing" and more work with office machines.
3. Most white-collar workers are now employed in jobs with little possibility of advancement.
4. White-collar workers are now more apt than ever to be working with hundreds, even thousands, like themselves in a single locale.

Frequent contacts with fellow white-collar workers in large-scale industries may make white-collar personnel more conscious of salaries and working conditions. If these workers believe that they will probably remain at the same level in the future, they may be more likely to organize for better working conditions in the present.

Clerical Work

Depending on the temperament, values, and norms of the worker and the conditions on the job, white-collar work can be rewarding or frustrating or both. For example, a secretary to two physicians in England described her hectic schedule and overcrowded conditions at work. Although she was unhappy about the tiring pace and the variety of tasks she had to do, she was satisifed with her job: "The reason, quite briefly, is that I feel I am doing a necessary job. But even that wouldn't be sufficient if I weren't lucky enough to be working for two such good doctors."

To succeed at this job, the secretary had to learn to keep track of appointments, answer phone calls, and make children in the waiting room happy. She also had to handle correspondence, keep in contact with the hospital, and file records. Mastering the job skills and learning to get along with the many people in the clinic made her feel good about herself:

One of the chief attractions of the job for me is the feeling of being in charge, feeling that I matter. Patients often comment that without me the surgery[1] would be in chaos. . . . I'd find it difficult to be just a small part of some large organization. In the four years I have worked at the surgery I have never been late, although in previous jobs I was never on time.

Clearly, this woman found recognition and satisfaction in her job. Where these rewards do not exist in white-collar jobs, tension and frustrations can rise.

In a study of the clerical work force in a large bank and several of its branches, sociologist Robert Jackall found attitudes similar to those of assembly-line workers. To increase speed and efficiency, the banks had reduced many jobs to limited, repetitious tasks. The clerks were soon bored and dissatisfied. In addition, they had little control over their time. The inability to pace their work meant not only that they were overburdened at certain periods but also that they often had too little to do. Nevertheless, the clerks quickly learned that they always had to appear busy:

We get off at five o'clock and it was four o'clock. It had really been a quiet day—nothing had come in. I had finished everything I had to do that day and all the girls in my section had, too. . . . [The manager] comes over and asks if I don't have anything to do. I say that I don't, which is the worst thing I could have said, and he goes into the storeroom and comes back with two big boxes of rubber bands and two boxes of paper clips. Then he dumps it all on my desk and mixes them up and tells me to sort it and says, "*That* ought to keep you busy." After that, I always make sure to keep something around to work on.

[1]clinic

MEDIAN EARNINGS OF MALE AND FEMALE WORKERS, 1965–1985

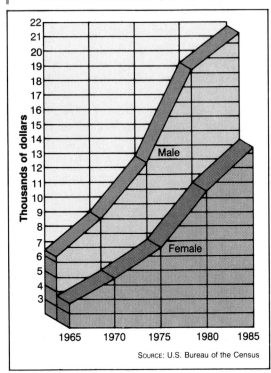

Thousands of dollars

Male

Female

1965   1970   1975   1980   1985

SOURCE: U.S. Bureau of the Census

GRAPH SKILL   According to the graph, who earns a higher median income, men or women? What was the median income for men in 1985? For women? How would you explain the gap between median earnings of men·and women?

Jackall found that despite the drawbacks of the job, the bank clerks, 90 percent of whom were women, found ways to legitimize their work. They appreciated the money they earned and the independence that working gave them. Young adults could be independent from their parents. Older people could remain self-reliant and not be dependent on their children. Mothers who worked outside the home felt that earning money helped them achieve greater status at home. One woman explained, "The job has made me more independent. It's shifted responsibility at home. I'm contributing income which is a real *symbol* of something."

[?]   Do you think the bank clerk in Jackall's study who was forced to sort the rubber bands might have done something to provoke the manager into his spiteful behavior? How might white-collar workers improve their working conditions and status on the job?

Managerial Work

Almost all large organizations have managers and administrators. These are the people who hire and fire, who recommend raises and promotions for those in their charge. Managers go to the meetings where major business policies are made. They are responsible for the success or failure of the branch of work they manage.

Managers work in business firms, government agencies, school systems, and nonprofit organizations. Although working conditions vary, most management positions involve a high degree of responsibility, a good salary, and a great deal of training, either in school or on the job.

Training   Who are managers? Studies show that top managers in large companies tend to be college graduates with degrees in accounting, business, or engineering. Some have advanced degrees from business schools. New managers usually go through a training program run by the company that hires them. This program teaches technical skills and offers such courses as personnel management, human relations, and public relations to help trainees manage events and people.

During training programs, employers make key decisions about the future of the trainees. Will employees be given routine work or will they be pegged for an executive spot? What kind of learning makes one a successful manager?

This account by sociologist William H. Whyte describes an elaborate training program at one of the largest firms in the United States:

As in all training programs, the bulk of the instruction is on specifics. Unlike most, however, there is considerable study in subjects that cut across every kind of job. Trainees study personnel philosophy, labor relations, law, and most important, the managerial viewpoint.

Only a minority of the trainees will ever become managers. . . . Most of the thousands of young men trained during this time will never get further than middle management. Nevertheless, it is the future executive slots that the company is thinking of, and it makes its concern plain to the trainee. On the report card form for trainees, there is a space for evaluation as to whether the trainee is suited "for individual contribution" or whether, instead, he is suited "to manage the work of others.". . .

To get ahead, of course, one must compete—but not too much, and certainly not too obviously. . . . The trainee is, first of all, a member of a group, and the group is entrusted to a surprising degree with the resolution of his future. That is, the group makes many important decisions about the trainee's future. How well, the com-

pany wants to know, does he fit in? His fellow trainees provide the answer, and in group discussions the eager beaver or the one who violates essential norms is quickly exposed. And brought to heel. Trainees speak frequently of the way the close fraternity-life atmosphere helps in ironing out some trainees' abnormal tendencies. It may be tough on him, they concede, but better now than later. In a few years the trainee will be released from this close association . . . ; he will be moving from one company branch to another, and he must be able to fit into the same kind of integrated social system.

Rewards and Drawbacks The rewards are many. Executive jobs pay well, bring high status in the community, and promise an exciting future. But there are many drawbacks. The individual must put the company first. He or she must consider the interests of stockholders, employees, customers, and the public. At times, managers may have to carry out projects that conflict with their personal

Few people reach the rank of top management. Most top managers have been trained within the company for their jobs, and they tend to have degrees in business administration, accounting, or engineering. The photograph shows an executive conference at a food-processing plant.

ethical standards—for instance, promoting products they don't believe in.

Only a few managers make it to the top. In looking up the corporate ladder, the young managers quickly learn that success means total commitment to their work. Family and fun must often take second place. One study found that superiors preferred those who worked a sixty-hour week and then took more material home for study.

Consider the kind of role model this utility company president makes for young managers in his firm:

In the middle of a rate or wage fight, I lie awake nights wondering what . . . I'll say next. Sometimes I get up from one wage-bargaining session, go home, lie awake thinking until it gets light, and then go back to the bargaining table with maybe only an hour's sleep. I've got an ulcer that acts up on me in times like that. It goes to sleep again when the bargaining is all over

and I can start eating decent meals again. I turn in at the hospital every once in a long while just to get some time off to think quietly. Is it overwork? Well . . . I grew up in this business. I like it. There's always something happening.

In the 1970s, sociologist Rosabeth Kanter studied a large multinational corporation. She focused on how the structure of people's jobs affects their behavior at work. Her report stated:

Managers had to look the part. They were not exactly cut out of the same mold like paper dolls, but the similarities in appearance were striking. Even this relatively trivial matter revealed the extent of conformity pressures on managers. . . . The norms were unmistakable, after a visitor saw enough managers, invariably white and male, with a certain shiny, clean-cut look.

CHART SKILL *Industrial societies offer a great variety of jobs, but the demand for certain kinds of workers changes over time. Sociological factors such as race have influenced job opportunities in the past. In what ways does the 1987 labor force differ from that of 1970?*

OCCUPATIONS OF EMPLOYED WORKERS, BY RACE
1970, 1980, 1987

Occupation	White			Black and Other		
	1970 (%)	1980 (%)	1987 (%)	1970 (%)	1980 (%)	1987 (%)
White-collar workers	51.6	53.5	57.8	27.9	39.2	43.6
Professional, technical	15.5	16.5	16.6	9.1	12.7	11.1
Managerial	11.4	11.6	12.2	3.5	5.2	6.2
Sales	6.7	6.8	12.6	2.1	2.9	7.3
Clerical	18.0	18.6	16.4	13.2	18.4	19.0
Blue-collar workers	34.2	30.5	27.1	34.5	31.5	31.7
Precision production, craft, and repair	17.2	17.0	12.6	10.8	12.1	8.8
Operatives	17.0	13.5	14.5	23.7	19.4	22.9
Service workers	10.7	12.1	12.4	26.0	23.1	23.0
Farm workers	4.0	2.9	2.7	3.9	1.8	1.6

SOURCE: U.S. Bureau of Labor Statistics

? Kanter's study was made in the 1970s. Do you think the same comments could be made about the corporate image of managers today? What changes have taken place in some companies' requirements for managerial positions?

Where there is much similarity among managers, on what might corporate pressure for such conformity be based? Managerial work in a large corporation emphasizes communication with other divisions and central headquarters. Evaluating individual productivity is difficult, and managers have to rely heavily on their own discretion and judgment. Managers feel comfortable if they can place their trust in people who are like them.

It was this factor, Rosabeth Kanter found, that made most managers wary about admitting women into their ranks. Many had never dealt with women in roles other than wife or secretary. "You never knew where you stood" was one manager's comment. Another said, "I never know what to call them or how to treat them." Introducing women to fellow employees caused tension. Similarly, most managers felt most comfortable with those of their own race and religion, making it difficult for minority-group members to earn top positions.

Managers can derive satisfaction from the power of decision-making roles and the rewards that come from being highly placed in organizations. But, at the same time, many live with considerable anxiety. Kanter found that managers were constantly looking for clues as to how they were doing. Most felt that reliability and skill with people were main criteria for their promotion. Above all, they felt that visible loyalty to the company—including a willingness to work long hours and to subordinate their personal life—was a basic requirement for the job.

REVIEW AND APPLICATION

1. *IDENTIFY:* White-collar work.
2. Is the percentage of white-collar workers increasing or decreasing in our society?
3. Do white-collar workers have more autonomy than blue-collar workers? Explain similarities and differences in the controls they face.
4. Why, according to Giddens, have some white-collar workers joined unions?
5. What are some of the drawbacks to a managerial position?

CRITICAL THINKING: What aspects of their white-collar jobs resulted in the most satisfaction for the secretary and clerks discussed on pages 243 and 244? What aspects caused the most frustration?

4 The Professions

For many centuries only the sons of wealthy families became doctors, lawyers, and clergymen. Today these professionals include both men and women from all levels of society. There are also many more professional jobs than there used to be, from architects and chemists to physicists and veterinarians. Although professionals are sometimes classified as white-collar workers, as in the table on page 246, they must have a more extensive or more specialized education than most white-collar workers.

Learning a profession is not easy. Professionals are highly trained specialists, and most have spent many years in school. Normally this education takes place in professional schools with limited enrollments. Not all the students who apply get in. Those who do realize that they are a select group.

Trainees learn not only technical skills but also proper professional behavior: the norms of their profession. People entering a profession are taught such things as appropriate places to work and proper working

Professionals are highly educated people who are usually accorded great respect in their communities. Even when their income is lower than that of other professionals, teachers rank nearly as high as bankers on the occupational prestige scale (See page 104). This woman is a math teacher.

plete nature of medical knowledge and their own inability, despite their best efforts, to master all that is known.

Professional organizations work to assure that careful licensing procedures are set up and that these procedures are followed and enforced by members of the profession. This is how professionals try to keep nonprofessionals from practicing or from influencing legally licensed practitioners.

Professionals hold a special place in modern society because of their advanced training. Most people agree that professionals should earn a good income, but professionals are not supposed to be overly influenced by the profit motive. Scientists, for example, ideally work to contribute to knowledge. Physicians are expected, above all, to be concerned with the health of their patients. Professional norms call for competent and service-oriented behavior.

conditions. They also learn that the responsibility for decision making on the job must be theirs. They are taught that laypeople, who have not gone through the years of specialized education, should not regulate professional work.

Student doctors, for example, are taught that nonphysicians—whether government officials, hospital administrators, or patients—cannot be allowed to dictate proper medical procedures. This, the medical profession argues, would hamper doctors from providing good medical care. It would also reduce the respect the profession is given by the larger community. New physicians are also taught to deal with uncertainty—with the incom-

REVIEW AND APPLICATION

1. What are the purposes of professional organizations such as the American Medical Association and the American Bar Association?

CRITICAL THINKING: What value is demonstrated by the professional in each of the following situations: a) Dr. Blair examined the bleeding child even though the child's mother had informed her that the family had no medical insurance. b) James Kain postponed his family's vacation so that he could complete tests on sewage treatment equipment that his engineering firm had recommended for the city.

5 Women in the Work Force

You have read how, throughout much of American history, girls were socialized for the roles of wife, mother, and housekeeper. In rural America, a mother and her daughters had outdoor duties, including tending the garden, feeding the chickens, gathering

eggs, and perhaps milking the cows. Rarely did girls have any other career goal.

At the same time, many poor women performed difficult, heavy labor. Slave women often toiled long hours under backbreaking conditions, and immigrant women often

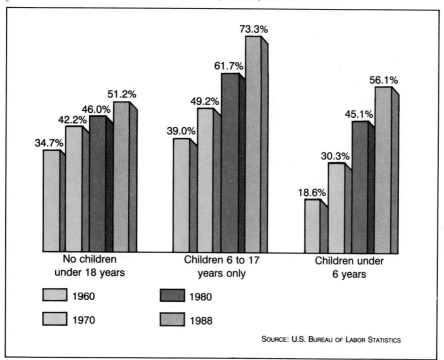

MARRIED WOMEN IN THE WORK FORCE, 1960, 1970, 1980, 1988

No children under 18 years

1960	1970	1980	1988
34.7%	42.2%	46.0%	51.2%

Children 6 to 17 years only

1960	1970	1980	1988
39.0%	49.2%	61.7%	73.3%

Children under 6 years

1960	1970	1980	1988
18.6%	30.3%	45.1%	56.1%

■ 1960   ■ 1980
■ 1970   ■ 1988

SOURCE: U.S. BUREAU OF LABOR STATISTICS

GRAPH SKILL   The number of women in the workforce in all categories—both single and married, with children of all ages—has continued to rise steadily. On the average, women in professional and managerial positions have fewer children than other women. In 1981, their birthrate was 37.2 births per thousand as compared to 70.9 for women in general. Many complex factors combine to influence birthrates, inluding economic and political conditions and social attitudes. What reasons could you give for the increase in women with young children who work outside the home?

worked twelve-hour shifts in sweatshops. Reformers in the nineteenth century strongly protested such inhumane work conditions. Feminists then, like those today, sought autonomy, independence, and equality. While some became the first women to enter higher education and the professions, others organized support for the rights of working-class women.

In the twentieth century, the number of women in the work force began to rise. Because of a manpower shortage during World

COMPOSITION OF THE FEMALE WORK FORCE, 1987

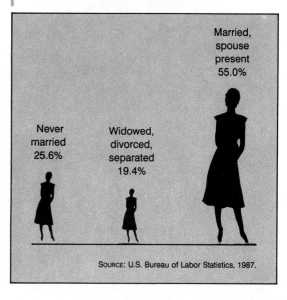

Married, spouse present 55.0%

Never married 25.6%

Widowed, divorced, separated 19.4%

SOURCE: U.S. Bureau of Labor Statistics, 1987.

War II, women were permitted to enter many fields formerly closed to them, including blue-collar work. Some served with distinction in the military.

After the war, however, the men returned to claim their jobs. A "feminine mystique," as a leading feminist, Betty Friedan, called it, emerged to socialize women to go back to the home. More and more middle-class women moved to the suburbs and became full-time homemakers and consumers. This situation began to reverse itself in the 1960s, when the number of women in the labor force again began a steady increase. Rising prices made two paychecks a necessity for many families.

However, as women began to reenter the job market, they generally found that the jobs open to them were in low-status occupations. Many went to work at office jobs, such as clerk, receptionist, and typist, and service jobs, such as waitress and hairdresser. These occupations have been referred to as *pink-collar work* because the majority of workers are women. Pink-collar workers have little prestige and are poorly paid.

Of course, every generation has had social norms about the kinds of jobs suitable for women, and social class has always played a part in the formation of these norms. It has been thought that rich women should not do the same kind of work poor women do. The norms about certain jobs have changed as the need for women in special fields has risen or fallen. Thus, in the 1880s many men thought women should not do office work. In the 1900s, as the demand for office workers exceeded the supply of men, women became clerks and secretaries.

Today job opportunities for women are expanding, although slowly. In the past few years, awareness of job discrimination against women has grown. Such groups as the National Organization for Women (NOW) have campaigned for job equality. Laws forbid employers from limiting jobs to members of one

Women as well as men find running their own small businesses appealing. This woman makes and sells pottery.

SOURCE: Drawing by Weber; © 1982 The New Yorker Magazine, Inc.

"Mommy will see you later. Mommy has to go to law school now."

sex. The government requires businesses, universities, and other large employers to follow *affirmative-action programs*—hiring policies designed to bring more women and minority-group members into positions formerly closed to them.

What happens to those women who reach the upper levels in their career fields? Almost all research indicates that female scientists and other women with doctoral degrees advance more slowly in their careers than their male colleagues, despite equal productivity, measured, for example, by the amount of their published research.

Several observers have noted that women lack access to sponsorship, special encouragement by a senior person in the field. Such a person informally teaches a young professional the trade secrets and helps determine whether the newcomer is invited to conferences, given a good hearing, and offered helpful suggestions on papers. Many women have reported that subtle forms of discrimination tend to keep professional women "out of the club."

REVIEW AND APPLICATION

1. *IDENTIFY:* Pink-collar work, affirmative action programs.
2. What factors seem to have an effect on the number of women in the job market and the kind of work they do?
3. What was the influence of World War II on women in the work force?
4. What does research indicate happens to women today who reach the upper levels in their fields?

CRITICAL THINKING: Determine whether the graphics on page 249 can be used to answer each of the following questions: a) How many millions of women were part of the work force in 1988? b) Did the work force include more married than unmarried women in 1987? c) In 1987 what percentage of working women depended solely on their income?

6 Growing Old

Work occupies the longest span of years in most people's lives. What happens when the job is done and the employee is "put out to pasture"? Today more and more people are living to advanced ages. What role will they play in society?

You have studied how, as people move through the life cycle, they go from one status to another—from child to adolescent to adult, from single person to spouse to parent, from student to worker. For each status, they have been socialized to play new roles and interact within new groups.

What happens when the roles a person has played for a long time suddenly end and are not fully replaced by new ones? At such a time, the individual must cope with *role loss*, the reduction or ending of a role that contributed to his or her self-image. Role loss

As part of socialization to old age, people must learn to cope with role loss. Some older people, such as these dancers, seem to handle the transition well.

GRAPH SKILL   What has happened to the percentage of people in the United States who are 65 years and over, from 1960 to 1985?

DISTRIBUTION OF POPULATION, BY AGE, 1960, 1970, 1980, 1985

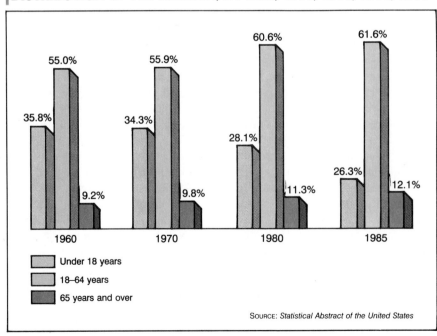

	1960	1970	1980	1985
Under 18 years	35.8%	34.3%	28.1%	26.3%
18–64 years	55.0%	55.9%	60.6%	61.6%
65 years and over	9.2%	9.8%	11.3%	12.1%

SOURCE: *Statistical Abstract of the United States*

can be a problem for older people in modern industrial societies and for many of the unemployed.

As children grow up, leave home, and form their own families, the role of parent is substantially reduced. At retirement, whether voluntary or required, the role of worker is diminished or ends. Work and family roles are central to an adult's sense of self. The loss of these roles marks a great change in the life cycle.

Many older people experience not only role loss but also a decline in the prestige and social rewards that went with their former roles. Since people in our society are frequently judged by their occupations, retirement can create a feeling of uselessness. Pensions, Social Security payments, and personal savings must substitute for salaries or wages. A large portion of the population cannot maintain the standard of living they had before retirement.

In some other societies, old people are honored for their experience and their knowledge of tradition. But in a society such as ours—which values youth, change, and progress—the elderly tend to be held in less esteem. In recent years, old people have begun to protest ageism, or discrimination against the elderly, in our society. In 1970, an organization called the Gray Panthers was formed to work for equal rights for old people. Other groups of the elderly have organized for specific goals, such as the formation of senior citizens' centers.

Roles in Retirement Years

Socialization to old age differs from socialization to other statuses since it involves a decrease, rather than an increase, in abilities. How do older adults learn to deal with this situation and to play new roles? What norms are established? What are the socializing agents?

One recent book contends that the process is especially difficult because norms are not clearly defined. Individuals have to face new roles without guidance about how they

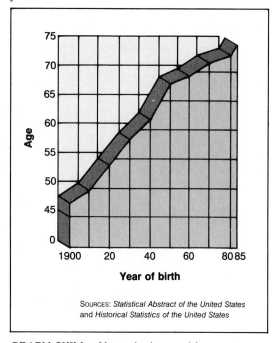

CHANGES IN LIFE EXPECTANCY, 1900–1985

SOURCES: *Statistical Abstract of the United States* and *Historical Statistics of the United States*

GRAPH SKILL   *Using the human life expectancy graph above, what was the life expectancy of Americans in 1900? In 1940? In 1985? How does the data confirm the information presented in the graph on page 252?*

Many cultures reward old age with community respect and positions of authority. One satisfaction common to most cultures is pleasure in the role of grandparent.

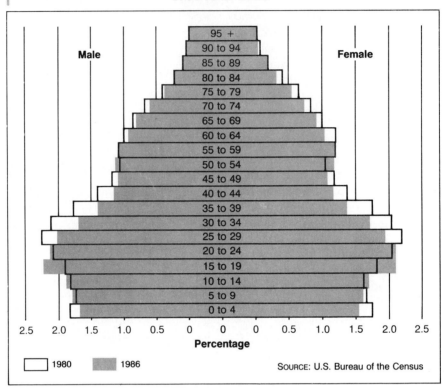

DISTRIBUTION OF POPULATION, BY AGE AND SEX
1980 AND 1986

Male   Female

95 +
90 to 94
85 to 89
80 to 84
75 to 79
70 to 74
65 to 69
60 to 64
55 to 59
50 to 54
45 to 49
40 to 44
35 to 39
30 to 34
25 to 29
20 to 24
15 to 19
10 to 14
5 to 9
0 to 4

2.5 2.0 1.5 1.0 0.5 0   0   0 0.5 1.0 1.5 2.0 2.5
Percentage

☐ 1980   ▨ 1986   SOURCE: U.S. Bureau of the Census

GRAPH SKILL   The phenomenon sometimes referred to as "the graying of America"—meaning that Americans are living longer and longer—is reflected in this graph. Who lives longer in the 80 to 84 age bracket? The 90 to 94 bracket? How would you compare the life span of men to women?

should behave. Anticipatory socialization prepares us to assume most roles in our lives, but no one likes to rehearse for getting old, becoming sick, being widowed, or becoming unemployed. Journalist Kenneth Woodward describes some of the fears experienced by many of the old:

What bothers the aged most, after fear of crime, is poor health, not having enough money to live on, and loneliness. The elderly are afraid of dying and at the same time afraid of outliving their capacity to cope with sickness. The worst nightmare is that of a long-term illness which wipes out their financial resources and leaves them hanging—indefinitely—between life and death. . . .

For many Americans, however, retirement itself—whether by force or choice—can be the most traumatic experience of growing old. The shock of suddenly having nothing to do, the feeling of being put on a shelf, can bring on profound physical and emotional crises, especially among people who derive their self-esteem from work. When Max Joseph was forced to retire last year at the age of sixty-four, the hard-driving production chief for a New England garment firm immediately sought other employment. But wherever he applied, he was told that he was overqualified—and too old—for the job. "I felt beaten by life," the tall, white-haired Bostonian recalls. "I was ready for a psychiatrist. I am too intelligent to get up in the morning and wonder what I am going to do." Last fall, Max signed on as a volunteer in the state consumer-protection office. "This volunteer business is a beautiful thing," he says, "but I'm still resentful at giving my ability for nothing."

Should older people be allowed to work as long as they want and are able to do so? Why or why not? How might the skills of older people be put to good use?

CASE STUDY: *Housing the Elderly*

Perhaps our society's failure to value older members such as Max Joseph is the main reason for the immense growth of "leisure villages" in the last generation. The elderly band together for mutual support. Sharing the same problems, they serve as a reference group for each other—that is, the group by whose standards they are judged. Of course, these communities are available only to those who can afford them. People must have savings or pensions large enough to pay the cost of surroundings that provide a real "home" rather than a bleak and depressing atmosphere. Sometimes agencies help. In the reading that follows, journalist

Judith Wax describes Weinfeld, a sectarian retirement home that seems to have solved many of the problems of institutional life:

"To be exact and to be truthful to the fact, my nerves are a little out of commission," she sighs, putting down the silverware she's been dispensing. She's wearing white tights, like a little girl going to a party—but the black oxfords are orthopedic, and she is eighty-three.

"So you'll sit and I'll set," says a fork arranger in green house slippers. There are twelve places at the big dining-room table. Still another white-haired woman grasps the table's edge as she lays napkins in the fork lady's wake.

Soon eleven women—their average age eighty-two—have seated themselves beneath a reproduction of Chagall's painting *The Praying Jew*. On a blackboard hung nearby, a wavering hand has written, "Sarah, remember you should take yr. medcine." As one man straggles in last, the green-slippered woman calls, "Over here, Abe boy."

"You'll try this soup, your nerves will commission themselves," white tights is advised. "Also your appetite."

Homes for the aged are a type of controlled environment, where people are resocialized to new routines. The challenge is making such environments stimulating.

"At my age, what is appetite? A spasm!" Nevertheless, her appetite turns out to be impressive. But Bessie, eighty-six, only looks at her food. She just arrived today, and the large brown eyes are watchful, wary. "I'm a greenhorn again," she sighs softly. "A greenie!". . .

Later, some diners clear plates, others load the dishwasher. Two women linger on in hot debate over teaspoon etiquette; finally they phone Marshall Field's silver department for a ruling to settle the matter. "We fight every day," one assures me. "It's absolutely wonderful." Newcomer Bessie looks doubtful.

The dozen diners are geriatric[1] communalists, among the first in America. Most have been at the Weinfeld Group Living Residence—an experiment in "congregate housing" for the elderly—since it opened nearly four years ago in a renovated townhouse complex here in Evanston, one block from the northern boundary of Chicago. Before Weinfeld, they had lived alone or with relatives, in nursing homes or even in psychiatric hospitals. Like the 1.1 million older Americans the Urban Institute estimates could manage living outside institutions if they had an alternative, the Weinfeld twelve couldn't quite make it on their own in public or private housing. Now, pooling what strengths age permits, they give each other emotional and physical sustenance in an environment that feels and smells more or less the way home once did.

. . . The aim is to encourage each resident's independence by maintaining community and family ties while providing only as much help—counseling, homemaking, health care—as is needed, no more, no less. That demands careful staffing: a cook and "careworker" on-site daily, a part-time activities therapist, a domestic who comes twice a week, a nurse who comes when she is needed, and a nutritionist who visits to plan menus and special diets.

[1]of an advanced age

LIVING ARRANGEMENTS OF PERSONS SIXTY-FIVE YEARS AND OVER, 1985

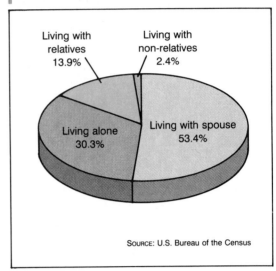

Living with relatives 13.9%

Living with non-relatives 2.4%

Living alone 30.3%

Living with spouse 53.4%

SOURCE: U.S. Bureau of the Census

GRAPH SKILL *Loneliness is a major fear of the elderly. According to the above graph, what percentage of people sixty-five years or older end up living alone? How many live with a spouse? With relatives?*

"Our baby sitter," a college student, sleeps in each night; council workers are on call, and a psychiatrist helps screen candidates for the traits that will make them compatible members of the Weinfeld group. . . .

"Weinfeld costs half what would be spent by the taxpayers if these same people were institutionalized," says Ronald Weismehl, the council's executive director. "But when government is unable to meet needs, sectarian agencies have to do it as innovators."

The U-shaped complex of townhouses, located on a quiet, middle-class street and convenient to shopping, cultural, and religious centers, makes an ideal setting for the experiment. After its purchase in 1971, the one-story complex was remodeled into one big home; dividing walls were torn down so that residents can stroll to each other's living rooms and the communal dining and recreation rooms at the center.

You can't be a recluse at Weinfeld, but privacy is easy; each of the six units, shared by two residents, has two bedrooms, a bathroom, a spacious living room, and a door to the outside that may be used at will. Nobody needs to ask permission to be part of the world. Most prized: the small private kitchens, for snacks, treats, and breakfast at any hour one chooses.

Colors and fabrics are different in each unit, and though the basics are provided, residents are encouraged to add on— plants, photographs, old treasures and new handicrafts. Hung over the entrance to one woman's bedroom, a cherished stole keeps perpetual vigil; long retired from active duty, it is a permanent decor.

[?] What human needs and special problems of being old seem to be handled successfully at Weinfeld?

Unfortunately, there are relatively few communities like Weinfeld. Although reli-gious and various social organizations sponsor many satisfactory facilities for the aged, newspaper, television, and government investigations have uncovered other types of homes where scandalous conditions exist. Chronic neglect and fire hazards are but two of the horrors faced by the elderly in substandard nursing homes.

Social Class

Outside private, sectarian, and public institutions, many other old people are forced by poverty to live in "geriatric ghettos." In New York City, for example, over one-third of the over-sixty population live in the city's twenty-six poorest neighborhoods. There they are often victimized by crime and subjected to unhealthful conditions, isolation, and role loss.

Among the less well-off elderly, the best adjustment to the retirement years is often made by blue-collar workers. Studies show

Social class can have a strong influence on how and where a person spends the last years of life. Those who have maintained good health and can afford the cost may choose to live in a retirement village, as do these residents of Sun City.

For many people, the retirement years are filled with exciting challenges and great personal satisfaction.

that they are more likely to remain in an intact, functioning family unit. The working-class parent is more likely to see at least one of his or her children every day and to be currently living with a spouse. Moreover, former blue-collar workers often experience relief at being released from a lifetime of boring or physically demanding jobs. On the other hand, economic problems may cancel this benefit, as financial resources run out.

Sociological research indicates that well-educated middle-class people have often developed personal interests and social skills that serve them well in retirement. For some, individual resources can make up for their loss of status. Many old people, though, whether rich or poor, don't find satisfying relationships. They endure lives of loneliness, occasionally relieved by visits from children and grandchildren. This is especially true of women, who usually outlive their husbands. Many face a decade or more of widowhood, alone, with declining abilities and health.

Yet most of us know at least one old person who is full of vitality and love of life. Such a person is usually involved with younger people and has earned their respect. And in spite of our society's attitude toward the elderly and differences among the genera-

tions, many children continue to feel love and loyalty to their elderly parents.

Nevertheless, the bleak picture of the problems of aging in our society describes reality. Those with financial independence, strong family ties, and good health are less burdened than the poor, the sick, and the isolated. Even in the best of cases, this society does not fully meet the needs of our growing population of older citizens. Those who live long enough must eventually come to terms with the fact that they are increasingly dependent on others and increasingly isolated from many social roles and institutions.

REVIEW AND APPLICATION

1. IDENTIFY: Role loss.
2. Why doesn't anticipatory socialization usually play a part in growing old?
CRITICAL THINKING: What are some advantages of retirement villages and retirement homes? What are some disadvantages? Design what you consider the ideal place for an elderly person to live—building plans, room layouts, and so on. As an alternative, describe the type of life you would like to live at the age of eighty.

Socialization continues through adult life as people assume various roles in marriage, parenthood, and the world of work. The role models provided by significant others and the expectations of family and culture influence one's choice of spouse. Marriage involves a continuous process of adaptation to the wants and needs of another. Even more demanding is parenthood, a role for which advice is freely given and often contradictory.

Much of an adult's self-concept is derived from his or her occupation. Many blue-collar workers work on assembly lines, and the monotony of their jobs may result in poor attitudes and defective products. Experiments in increasing worker motivation have had some good results. In certain jobs involving both skill and danger, such as that of ironworker, workers undergo intense socialization, both on and off the job.

Like most blue-collar workers, white-collar clerical employees are subject to a large degree of control. Especially in large organizations, they are expected to look right and appear busy but to make no decisions on their own. Managers are the decision makers and coordinators. They are expected to put the company first, even in matters that may affect their personal lives. Professionals have achieved a special position because of their presumed level of knowledge, careful training, and high level of ethical conduct.

Women's work outside the home has long been confined largely to such areas as clerical and service jobs, and the majority of women still hold this type of employment. Women's salaries remain lower than those of men, and women's possibilities for advancement tend to be fewer.

Because productivity is so highly valued in our society, retirement presents a painful problem for most people. Loss of job status, diminished responsibility and contacts, and failing health often characterize old age. However, old people who retain interests and find dignified places to live improve their chances for experiencing these as "golden years."

Key Terms

Define the following:

legitimize
blue-collar work
white-collar work

pink-collar work
affirmative-action
 program

role loss

Applying Sociology

1. Do you know anyone who makes a living as a skilled worker—for example, a plumber, electrician, tailor, or carpenter —or as a service worker in an occupation that requires specific preparation—for example, a hairdresser, barber, or cook? If so, ask these questions of one or more of these people:

   (a) What kind of training did you have to prepare you for your job?
   (b) What do you like best about the job?
   (c) What would you tell a young person coming on the job? How does one get into such a field? Is it a good trade for a young person?

2. Compare the rewards of assembly-line, clerical, and professional work in terms of (a) security; (b) satisfaction; (c) control over the work; (d) pay and prestige; (e) responsibility; (f) ability to pursue family leisure activities.

3. Interview a person in one of the professions to find out what it means to work as a professional. For suggestions on interviewing and preparing your own interview survey, see the Appendix. These are questions that you may wish to include:

   (a) What is the name of your professional organization?
   (b) When did you first decide to enter this field?
   (c) Who were the important people in helping you make the decision about your career?
   (d) How important were each of the following in attracting you to your profession: the nature of the work, the income, the prestige in the community, the influence in the community, and the opportunity to help other people? What were the other attractions?
   (e) Describe the training needed to achieve your professional degree.
   (f) What is it about the work that you now find most enjoyable?
   (g) What is least enjoyable?
   (h) About how many hours a week do you work?
   (i) Does your work schedule allow you sufficient time to spend with your family, friends, community activities, and hobbies?
   (j) Is your work as personally satisfying as you expected when you decided on your profession?
   (k) Do you think your work is appreciated by those you are trying to help?
   (l) Do you think that members of your profession earn an income that is fair?
   (m) Do you think that your profession commands sufficient respect or prestige in the community?
   (n) Would you recommend that capable young men and women go into your profession?
   (o) Does your profession have a code of ethics?
   (p) If so, who is in charge of enforcing this code?
   (q) Do you know of any case in which a fellow professional has violated some tenet of this code? If so, what happened?

4. Make a list of the problems frequently associated with old age. Now list any solution you can think of for each of these problems. With your lists in mind, compose a brief article, "How to Prevent Unhappiness in Old Age."

Susan B. Garland, "The Graying of America Spawns a New Crisis," *Business Week*, August 17, 1987, pp. 60–62.

1. Why is the problem of caring for the elderly a pressing concern for Americans?
2. What kinds of programs exist to provide care for senior citizens?

Ann M. Morrison, Randall P. White, and Ellen Van Velsor, "Executive Women: Substance Plus Style," *Psychology Today*, August 1987, pp. 18–26.

1. What kinds of contradictory behavior do female executives display in order to win approval from their male employers?
2. What "male" behaviors are women executives encouraged to use?

Anne Rosenfeld and Elizabeth Stark, "The Prime of Our Lives," *Psychology Today*, May 1987, pp. 62–72.

1. Do researchers agree on a single timetable of adult life stages?
2. What factors influence the life changes made by adults?

Interviewing people in various occupations
Nearly any employed adult will admit that there are both satisfying and frustrating aspects to their job. Interview someone who is either a teacher, a factory worker, a doctor, or a computer operator. Ask that person to explain his or her various responsibilities. Make a list of those tasks that the person you interviewed finds satisfying and those that are more frustrating. Then decide—would you enjoy this job?

Job Description
Satisfying Tasks   Frustrating Tasks
Conclusion

Obtaining information from reference books
Sometimes graphics raise questions as well as answer them. For example, look at the graph on page 254. If the word *phenomenon* in the caption is unfamiliar to you, in what source book can you find its pronunciation and meaning? If you want to know what percentage of Americans were 65 or older about one hundred years ago, where can you look? Check your answers by finding the information in the sources you have suggested.

1. *Analyzing Comparisons:* How strong is this comparison argument? "Older people in Japan are honored for their experience and wisdom. Americans, meanwhile, value youth, not old age. As a result, the elderly in Japan lead more fulfilling lives than do the elderly in the United States."

2. *Identifying Assumptions:* What assumption is this person making? "Men should be given preference over women for jobs since men have to support families."

UNIT APPLICATION

Famous Physician and War Hero Dead at Seventy-three

Dr. Francis X. Walker, world-renowned specialist in surgery, died today after a brief illness. At the time of his death he was a patient at University Hospital, where he had worked for forty-two years.

Dr. Walker was born in Monroe, Massachusetts, the youngest son of Dr. Thomas F. Walker, a general practitioner, and Sarah (Smith) Walker. He attended local parochial schools, St. Michael's Academy, and Massachusetts State College, where he majored in premedical studies, played varsity basketball, and sang in the Newman Choir. After graduation from State in 1932, he attended New York Medical College, receiving his M.D. in 1936. That same year he was married to Margaret Ann Ryan, a nurse at the Sisters of Mercy Hospital for Crippled Children, where Dr. Walker had studied for several months. It was there that he first became interested in crippling diseases and the effects of traumatic injuries.

Dr. Walker spent a year as an intern at University Hospital in Boston and began a residency in general surgery. He planned to enter practice upon completion of this training. The war intervened. On September 6, 1942, he entered the army as a first lieutenant in the Medical Corps. He was given three months of special training in military protocol and procedure and sent to the Pacific theater.

With his unit he moved from island to island, setting up emergency facilities just behind the lines. Three months before he was to be rotated back to the States, he himself was severely wounded. He lost the use of both legs and was never to walk again.

During his lengthy convalescence, Dr. Walker, then a lieutenant colonel, was interviewed by the military newspaper *Stars and Stripes*. He spoke candidly of his life:

"Growing up in a doctor's house I guess I always wanted to be a doctor like him. The nuns at school knew it and encouraged me. So did my scoutmaster, Tom Warner. My father was sympathetic—and very pleased—but he kept telling me it would involve a good deal of hard studying and unglamorous hard work. I was to learn what he meant. As a medical student I felt myself changing from a starry-eyed young man who dreamed of being a great healer into a tough-minded physician. . . .

"Medical school was only my first major transformation. No sooner had I become a physician than they took this doctor and made him into a soldier. And, after three years of soldiering, they are now trying to make this cripple into a man again."

Dr. Walker became a man again, a man of great stature. Recipient of the Medal of Honor, the nation's highest award, he returned to Boston, completed the last year of his surgical residency and joined the staff of the University Hospital and of the Medical School. In time he became Chief of Service and Marvin S. Gordon Professor of Orthopedic Surgery. He was co-author of two major surgical texts and contributed to many professional journals.

Three years ago Dr. Francis Walker reached mandatory-retirement age and gave up his positions at the hospital and in the medical profession. At a banquet in his honor, Dr. Walker said that he had always been an active man, ready to face anything; but, he confided, he was not certain he was ready to face retirement.

He spent the last years of his life traveling and visiting with his children and grandchildren.

Dr. Walker is survived by his wife; his daughter, Suzanne (Walker) Brown, a senior editor at the publisher Prentice-Hall, Inc.; his son, Sean, a free-lance artist; and five grandchildren.

Using and Analyzing Concepts

1. Reread the article about the life and death of Francis X. Walker, M.D., and see if you can pick out phases in his life cycle.

   (a) What individuals and agencies were influential in his early socialization?
   (b) What were his interests during his youth and while he was a student? Did they prepare him in any way for later life?
   (c) What statuses did Dr. Walker occupy and what roles did he play?
   (d) When Dr. Walker was about to retire, he said he wasn't really ready. Do you think he meant he was too young or something else?
   (e) How might Dr. Walker have been better prepared for retirement?

2. Dr. Walker's obituary tells his life story. Life stories are fascinating because they present material for understanding changes in the life cycle.

   (a) Interview two men and two women in their sixties or seventies. Ask them to think back over their lives. What stages do they remember as being particularly important? Ask them to specify individuals, groups, or events that influenced them.
   (b) From their responses, pick out any aspects of their lives that seemed out of the ordinary and that forced them to reconsider their previous way of living—perhaps the loss of a job, a military experience, or some serious illness. Which people were particularly important in helping them cope with the necessary changes in moving from one stage of life to another?
   (c) Compare your findings with those of the other members of the class. How closely do the data reflect the principles of socialization that you studied in Unit Four?

CONTINUITY AND CHANGE

Communities and Change   CHAPTER 12
Social Movements and Collective Behavior   CHAPTER 13

Unit Focus

Change is a constant feature of modern life. In this century, American society has undergone numerous dramatic changes. The influx of millions of immigrants whose cultural patterns have differed markedly from those of the population already here has changed American society in fundamental ways. So have two world wars, the labor movement, the anti-war and civil rights movements of the 1960s, and the women's movement.

In the United States and throughout the world, the latest phase in the industrial revolution has brought both unimagined opportunities and unexpected problems. Sometimes technology has outpaced society's ability to cope with the problems caused by technological change. This unit addresses a wide range of issues raised by technological and other social changes and discusses how people attempt to maintain a sense of community in a changing world.

Applying Sociology

- What changes have taken place in your community?
- What opportunities and problems do you face?
- How have technological changes affected your education?

Cities reflect, often dramatically, the forces of change that run through an entire society. Here a group of new skyscrapers looms above an older, smaller office building.

12

Communities and Change

Chapter Preview

- **Before you read,** look up the following key terms in the glossary to become familiar with their definitions:

  cultural diffusion
  metropolitan-area
    model

  urban ecology
  multiple-nuclei
    model

  concentric-zone
    model
  sector model

- **As you read,** think about answers to the following questions:

  1. What aspects of community life most concern sociologists?
  2. Why do communities undergo change?
  3. What causes cities to develop differently?
  4. What distinguishes a city from a town?

Sections in this Chapter

1. Characteristics of Community
2. How and Why Communities Change
3. Urbanization in America
4. City Life

Chapter Focus

When you think of home, what do you think of? Three things may come to mind. Home is a place—perhaps a street, a neighborhood, a small town, a village, or a city. Home is people—the friends, relatives, and neighbors with whom a person shares many basic values and beliefs. Above all, home is a sense of belonging.

Social analysts have long debated the value of people's sense of community, or "consciousness of kind." To some analysts, the emotional bonds that people feel toward their own groups are limiting, and restrictive to progress. Other analysts believe these basic ties produce feelings of loyalty, patriotism, and pride.

This chapter examines the meaning and characteristics of community. It discusses the loss of community and several causes of community change, and it explores growth and change in cities.

Using Sociologists' Tools

- **Observe** what residents do to foster pride in your community.

- **Describe** the principal geographic, economic, and social characteristics of your community.

- **Analyze** the results of some recent proposal for change that divided the community, indicating what each side sought to achieve.

- **Predict** how residents would react if a natural disaster hit your town.

Nestled amid the Green Mountains, this village has a meaning for its residents which may not be obvious to the casual visitor.

1 Characteristics of Community

The word *community* stems from the Latin *communis,* meaning "in common" or "sharing." Because "community" denotes sharing, people use the term in a number of ways. We speak of "the community of scholars" and "the community of nations." But, in this chapter, "community" refers to organized human settlements and the people who share a life in such places. What, then, are the features of a community when the term is used in this way?

The Geographical Aspect

When people think of home, they think of a specific place. That place usually has a name, such as Middletown, East Hampton, Westport, Kalgoorie, or East Los Angeles. The name alone often gives rise to a special feeling of "my town" or "my neighborhood."

In a story on East Los Angeles, the largest Mexican American community in the United States, a reporter described this feeling about place:

Three major freeways lead east from downtown Los Angeles, bisecting a series of hills covered with little houses painted in pastel shades of yellow, white, lavender, and pink. In between the houses fig, cypress, and cedar trees reach through the smog. This, together with a scattering of old cars, is all you can see from the freeway.

But a turn onto a side street reveals a city apart from the homogenous sprawl of Los Angeles. Suddenly the signs change from just English to Spanish and English. "Villa Real Drugs Botica, Yerbas de

267

To sociologists, "community" means both a place and a feeling of belonging.

Mexico": a drugstore featuring herbs from Mexico for every ailment. "Tortilleria. Tortillas. Wholesale and Retail." "Montezuma Café": a Mexican restaurant featuring carne asada, tacos, and tamales.

And there is a religious-articles store: "Articulos Religiosos," with the added attraction of "Also Beauty Supplies." At the movies Charles Bronson is playing in *Breakout* but with Spanish subtitles. Signs proclaim "Naturalization Papers Prepared," "Chicano Power!" and "Go, Dodgers, Go!"

On the streets there are people everywhere, walking, talking, buying avocados and oranges from produce stands, reading Spanish-language newspapers and romantic magazines at corner newsstands. Old women in black mantillas and floral dresses walk with their grandchildren. Chicano teenagers in white T-shirts and baggy chinos shine their Chevies. "Hey, man," says one. "Welcome to East Los."

East Los is . . . a collection of little homes and yards that wanders all over the brown hills and arroyos of the area. . . .

The little wooden bungalows and stucco houses may be inadequate, but almost every yard bursts forth with vegetables, flowers, bushes, and trees. Although the walls of many of the stores and houses are graffiti-covered with names of gangs like Rock Maravilla, Arizona, and Lil Valley, the walls of other buildings are decorated with splendidly colorful murals, also painted by the gangs.

The ties of the family in East Los are still powerful. Families are large and divorce is frowned upon. Even the few young people who go to college aren't likely to move too far away from their parents. Everyone seems to know everyone else in East Los.

"Here I have a sense of belonging, a sense of community," says Maria Elena Yepes, a teacher of Chicano studies at California State University at Los Angeles who lives in East Los. "I lived for many years in Mexico and then returned here. When I came back to East Los it didn't seem as if I had left Mexico. Every face was a Mexican face. Everyone was friendly."

There are thousands and thousands of communities like "East Los" all over the world. In these places people share that special sense of community. They know one another. They know where they stand in relation to others who live within as well as beyond the borders of their community.

Communities, therefore, are places with people. Communities can be found on a map:

Aztec, New Mexico. Pop. 5,512. 40 miles south of the Colorado border and 120 miles from the Arizona line in northwestern New Mexico.

Mason City, Iowa. Pop. 30,379. At the intersection of Highways 18 and 65, 135 miles south of Minneapolis, 125 miles north of Des Moines.

Hudson Street, Greenwich Village, New York. A street area in lower Manhattan set off by certain landmarks: St. Luke's School to the south, St. Veronica's to the west, and Public School 41 on the east.

These places are permanent settlements. Some nomadic communities are harder to locate because the people move about from season to season to pick crops, to hunt, or to graze livestock. However, even these people often have a village or campsite where they stay for part of the year.

The Psychological Aspect

Hundreds of other places that can be found on a map are not true communities. The people of a true community share a common set of norms. Because so much of what a community "means" is in the minds of the people who belong to it, we can call this second trait a psychological one.

Springdale, a small village in upstate New York, is the sort of place one thinks of as the typical "Main Street, U.S.A." Here is a picture of Springdale as sociologists Arthur Vidich and Joseph Bensman saw it.

When one becomes . . . acquainted with the people of Springdale, . . . one finds that they like to think of themselves as "just plain folks." The editor of the paper, in urging people to attend public meetings or in reporting a social event, says "all folks with an interest" should attend or "the folks who came certainly had a good time." Almost any chairman of a public gathering addresses his audience as folks—"all right, folks, the meeting will get under way"—and the interviewer in his work frequently encounters the same expressions—"the folks in this community," "the townfolk," "the country folk," "good folks," and "bad folks." Depending on context, the term carries with it a number of quite different connotations.[1]

First and foremost, the term serves to distinguish Springdalers from urban dwellers, who are called "city people," an expression which by the tone in which it is used implies the less fortunate, those who are denied the wholesome virtues of

[1]meanings

Most communities are permanent settlements whose members share norms.

rural life. City people are separated from nature and soil, from field and stream, and are caught up in [a] . . . web of impersonality and loneliness, of which the public statement in Springdale is: "How can people stand to live in cities?" . . .

The [term] "folk" includes everyone in the community. . . . It excludes neither the rich nor the poor. . . . To be one of the folks requires neither money, status, family background, learning, nor refined manners. . . .

The term also includes a whole set of moral values: honesty, fair play, trustworthiness, good-neighborliness, helpfulness, sobriety, and clean living. To the Springdaler it suggests a wholesome family life, a man whose spoken word is as good as a written contract, a community of religious-minded people, and a place where "everybody knows everybody" and "where you can say hello to anybody."

Communities are special places to the people who live in them, places where each person feels at home.

Moving from one community to another can be hard. Being uprooted is not only physically exhausting but also psychologically upsetting. One leaves familiar haunts and old friends and enters a new and unknown environment. It is in moving, perhaps more than at any other time, that one becomes aware of the psychological aspect of community.

The Organizational Aspect

Communities also have an organizational aspect. This aspect includes the way a community is set up and the networks by which people are tied to one another. A community has all sorts of rules for members. It has roles for people to play, and it has defined relationships between people and between groups. Those who are members are supposed to

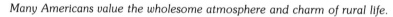

Many Americans value the wholesome atmosphere and charm of rural life.

know how they are to behave and how far they can depart from a set of norms without upsetting others. Members are expected to perform certain tasks, to "pull their weight." Members also have to know more subtle things, such as where they stand in relation to others in the social "pecking order," or rank. And members must know how to adjust their personal wants to the needs of the community.

In Springdale, both rich and poor were "just plain folks." Yet, despite this image of equality, the researchers found proof of differences in status. Certain "folks" had high status, and others had low status. Certain people were pretty sure to move up the social ladder, while others learned to content them-

selves with less power, money, or prestige. It took a while, but Vidich and Bensman were able to find out who was who and where each stood in relation to others.

REVIEW AND APPLICATION

1. IDENTIFY: Community, *communis.*
CRITICAL THINKING: Compare the Springdalers' idea of city people on page 270 with the description of people in East Los on pages 267–268. Does the Springdalers' idea apply to East Los? Why or why not? How are Springdale and East Los similar? Support your answer with excerpts from the text.

2 How and Why Communities Change

Any of the three characteristics of a community may change. When communities change geographically, the most common pattern is to spread out. Sometimes one community merges with another. A community may shrink, and even become a ghost town, if its main source of income is lost. A community may be uprooted and forced to resettle at a new site.

The psychological character of a community is also subject to change. The feeling of community, "community spirit," may grow or decline. Sometimes a shared threat—a flood, storm, fire, or enemy—brings the people of a community closer together. In other cases, a group of people who thought they had a common outlook face an issue that splits them into opposing camps. At times, a part of the community, often the younger people, finds the life styles of outsiders more and more attractive and tries to change community norms. If these "rebels" become too unhappy, some may leave in search of another community.

Organizational changes also take place over time. Springdale and many towns like it have been able to remain communities over

the years by accepting some of the changes taking place in the larger society. The little red schoolhouse gives way to consolidated schools and regional high schools. Shopping malls replace the stores on Main Street.

Change is rarely an isolated thing. A new idea, a new invention, or a new set of values can produce change in one area that, in turn, changes other aspects of the social system. Because social change is so far-reaching and so complex, it will be useful to break down the causes of change into several major types.

Changes in the Natural Environment

The way of life of any society is bound to be affected by that society's natural habitat. This includes soil, water supply, climate, natural resources, landforms such as mountains or plains, and other geographical features. The natural habitat has a great effect on a society's economic institutions—on how people make a living. The following examples demonstrate what happens when the environment undergoes a swift, major change.

A small Mexican village had as its economic base the farming of corn. Most of the people lived the simple life of peasants. Then a nearby, long-dormant volcano suddenly erupted and made the villagers' land useless for farming. The spectacle of the erupting volcano soon brought tourists, and former peasants became tour guides. They learned some English, earned some cash, and adopted a new style of clothing. Their new way of life went on for a few years until the volcano burned out. Then the tourists stopped coming, but the land remained unfit for farming. Young people left the village. Old-timers picked up any work they could

Natural disasters can cause severe social dislocation when people are uprooted from their homes and lose touch with friends and neighbors. The eruption of Mount St. Helens in Washington did great damage to the area. Sometimes, however, a disaster may bring people closer as they work together at restoration.

find. The villagers were forced to adjust to a new and crushing poverty.

Similar dramatic social change took place in 1972 when the community of Buffalo Creek, West Virginia, was hit by disaster. Buffalo Creek was a coal-mining town of some five thousand people, who shared a strong sense of community. They had lived through the years of struggle to form labor unions and, despite the automation of mining, now had well-paid jobs. Most of the people knew each other and felt comfortable visiting each other's houses. Many later said that they never worried about getting help in times of trouble. A neighbor was always there if someone was sick or needed to talk about a problem. They looked on each other as members of the same family. This was especially important to these miners and their families, who were descendants of the original settlers in Appalachia. Living off the land—whether by hunting, farming, or mining—was hard. Having good neighbors provided a special feeling of security.

That feeling came to an end on February 26, 1972. For years, the coal companies had been storing the waste material from mining operations in a large, deep lake just above Buffalo Creek. Heavy rains had raised the water level to the danger point. Although company inspectors had tried to monitor the situation, the roaring, black, muddy waters suddenly crashed down on the unsuspecting families. Houses, trailers, cars, and people were washed away in a few terrifying moments. What people had built over many years was lost.

The survivors were moved to new quarters by the National Guard and by an agency of the federal government. While these men, women, and children had been spared the fate of those who perished in the muddy flood, they had lost something precious. Their new homes were not far from the old ones, but even a short distance made a great difference. Their neighbors were no longer people they had lived next to for years. Old relationships were gone; new ones would take years to build. The special feeling of community had been destroyed.

Sociologist Kai T. Erikson spent many days talking to the survivors. Here are the words of one:

> We did lose a community, and I mean it was a good community. Everybody was close, everybody knowed everybody. But now everybody is alone. They act like they're lost. They've lost their homes and their way of life, the one they liked, the one they was used to. All the houses are gone, every one of them. The people are gone, scattered. You don't know who your neighbor is going to be. You can't go next door and talk. You can't do that no more, there's no next door. You can't laugh with friends. You can't do that no more, because there's no friends around to laugh with. That don't happen no more. There's nobody around to even holler at and say "Hi," and you can't help but miss that. You haven't got nobody to talk to. The people that is there are so busy trying to put back what they have lost.

? Explain how the words of this survivor reveal the three dimensions of community.

Change may be equally dramatic in a more positive way if people find a new natural resource. A rich mining strike or the discovery of oil or natural gas has often had startling effects on the organization of an area. For example, think of the changes taking place in the oil-rich nations of the Middle East and North Africa.

Change in the natural environment may also occur slowly and still have far-reaching effects. Land may be torn up by strip mining. Erosion may slowly wash away once-rich farming land. Water and air pollution may create a need for new norms and laws governing how producers and consumers get rid of waste. Such legislation has been dramatically seen in recent years, as government regulations have required cleaning up hazardous waste sites throughout the country.

Conquest and War

Like changes in the environment, conquest and war can cause both short-range and long-range social change. For example,

Throughout history, war has been a major cause of social change. This is a street scene in London after an air raid by the Germans in World War II.

the age of discovery and exploration beginning around 1450 started a long period of domination of non-Europeans by Portugal, Spain, Holland, England, and France and later by Germany, Italy, and the United States. The Western nations brought economic, social, and political changes to the subject peoples.

In some places, the native peoples were enslaved or driven from the land to make way for European settlers, who destroyed or greatly weakened ancient cultures. In a later wave of conquest beginning around 1850, Europeans showed less interest in settlement than in trade and political control. This control of weaker nations by stronger ones was known as *imperialism*. Typically, the imperialists set up new governments to rule the colonies, introduced new legal systems, and brought Western ideas and technology to people with little technical know-how. Most often the skilled jobs and their administration were kept in the hands of the imperialist nation. Natives generally were not taught how to run the new industries, and they remained at the bottom of the social and economic scales.

The colonial powers introduced many planned changes, particularly to promote the extraction of minerals, petroleum, rubber, sugar, and other raw materials. which were shipped to the mother nation for production and manufacturing. But sometimes they did not foresee the changes that would result from their activities. The introduction of modern medicine, for example, led to rapid population growth and pressure. In some cases, native armies that were trained to support a colonial regime later led the fight for independence. Western ideas of *self-determination,* or self-rule, made inroads into people's thinking. Even after colonies won independence, many of the changes introduced by the imperialist powers remained part of the social patterns in the new nations.

War is another source of change. Defeated people sometimes have to leave their homes to become exiles in a foreign land or refugees in hastily constructed camps. War often stimulates the creation of inventions: weapons, transport equipment, and synthetic products to replace raw materials needed for the war effort. War always means some changing of budget priorities as governments put off civilian projects to pay military expenses.

War can gravely affect family life. Some marriages are postponed; others are hastened. If many young men are killed in battle, marriage rates in the postwar period may change. Widows and orphans have to adjust to new roles. A "baby boom" may follow the return of men to their civilian lives.

In World War II, the normal work roles in the United States changed greatly. As men went to war, women took jobs that had been thought impossible or inappropriate for women. "Rosie the Riveter" became a national symbol. After the war, traditional roles returned, but some changes became permanent.

War can also create major changes in political systems. Governments have fallen because of battlefront defeats. The Russian czar was overthrown during World War I. War nearly always results in some loss of liberty at home. And legislative bodies often grant the executive branch special powers during war.

? Recall or look at current or old newspaper and news-magazine articles that show how war brings about social change. What specific changes were talked about?

Technological Change

Some sociologists consider technology the biggest source of social change. (Chapter 13 discusses this theory further.) Around the middle of the eighteenth century, technological progress began to speed up at such a rate that the changes were called an industrial revolution. As this industrial revolution spread through Western Europe and the United States, the number of people working on farms dropped, and the number working in factories rose. Thus, economic institutions underwent major changes.

Because most factories were located in cities, thousands of people moved from rural to urban areas in search of work. City life presented different housing arrangements, different forms of entertainment, and different problems. Families left their relatives behind and took on a new style of life. Parents often worked long hours in the factory, bringing changes to traditional roles and relationships in the family.

The products of modern technology include mechanized farms, crowded cities with tall skyscrapers, irrigated desert land, superhighways, and nuclear power. Each of these spurs changes in values, roles, and institutions. But technological changes can have both negative and positive effects. The car and the airplane can produce pollution, accidents, and energy shortages. But because of them, we can visit family and friends who live far away, send a letter in a matter of days, have food and other products flown in

Modern technology has brought a revolution in the way many things are done. Yet people often resist changes that threaten to change their way of life. Sometimes the old and the new are combined. The little figure participating in the Japanese tea ceremony is a robot.

from all over the globe, and travel in foreign lands. As a nation, we now have worldwide economic ties.

Technology has given us greater independence and freedom of choice. And each advance has also brought alterations in community behavior. For instance, shopping centers and drive-in movies are only two of the many changes that have come about as a result of the automobile.

CASE STUDY: *The Yir Yiront*

In studying technological change, sociologists are most interested in understanding its effects on people's relationships with each other. They are mainly concerned with changes in values, norms, roles, and institutions. In a society that is much less complex than that of the United States, a single invention can have widespread, even devastating, sociological effects. Try to pick out such changes as you read about an example of technological change in one primitive culture.

Some industrial methods have been responsible for negative effects. Strip mining, opposed by environmentalists as damaging to the land, creates a barren landscape through the use of giant stripping shovels to extract coal from the earth.

The Yir Yiront were a primitive Australian tribe who supported themselves through hunting and fishing. Since the Yir Yiront had no knowledge of metal, the stone axe played an important part in their daily life. Women used it to cut wood for the ever-burning campfire. Men, women, and children used the axe to make other tools, build homes, and gather food.

The stone needed by the Yir Yiront men to make the axeheads was not found in the area where the tribe lived but came from quarries four hundred miles to the south. It reached Yir Yiront men through a complex system of trade with other tribes. Each older adult male had regular trading partners both to the north and to the south. In exchange for one stone axehead from a trading partner to the south, a Yir Yiront male would give twelve spears, some of which came from other trading partners. An orderly pattern of social relationships had developed to ensure that everyone got what was needed.

The adult males were the only ones allowed to trade with other tribes for the axes. They were also the only ones allowed to make and own the axes. When women and children needed to use an axe, they had to borrow it from one of the older men.

The borrowing also followed strictly defined rules. A woman could expect to use her husband's axe unless the couple weren't on good terms. If a woman was single or her husband was away, she would go to her older brother or her father to borrow an axe. Only under extreme conditions would a woman ask her mother's brother or other male kin for his axe. Children would borrow an axe from a father or older brother but never from a mother's brother.

The stone axe was a key symbol of male domination in Yir Yiront society. It helped to define sex roles and social relationships among tribe members. The pattern of axe ownership also stressed the superiority of age over youth.

When white missionaries came, all that was changed. The missionaries, in an effort to raise the standard of living of the tribe, freely gave steel axes to younger men, women, and children as well as to the older males. However, the older males, because of their distrust of the missionaries, usually stayed away from the mission festivals where the axes were given away. Thus, they were least likely to get the steel axes.

The steel axe changed many aspects of the social relationships among the Yir Yiront. Women and children, who now

Societies undergoing technological change develop unevenly, with some people continuing to live as they always have. Both photographs are of modern Kenya. The first shows a Masai village; the other is the airport in Nairobi.

owned their own axes, became less dependent on the older males. Thus, the men suffered a loss of influence and power. Trading relationships among the many tribes to the north and south were upset. Trading partnerships weakened, and tribal gatherings that brought many tribes together to trade axes and spears lost much of their importance.

Over time, many of the norms, customs, and values of Yir Yiront culture lost their meaning. The steel axe gave women and children new freedom but left them uncertain about how to behave and what to think. Ownership of the axes became less clear, so people gradually began to steal. The old festivals died out, and the Yir Yiront began to forget rites and rules which had been part of their culture for centuries.

? Can you think of a similar change occurring in American society? What about the increased availability of telephones, cars, and computers?

The Power of New Ideas

People with new ideas about how to make work easier and life more comfortable bring about technological change. But other kinds of ideas are powerful, too. Throughout the ages prophets, philosophers, natural scientists, and social scientists have introduced ideas that have had profound effects on values and behavior.

Sigmund Freud's[1] ideas about the development of personality influenced the treatment of people with emotional problems. His ideas changed certain child-raising and educational practices as well. His reports on the healing effect of bringing hidden thoughts out into the open led to new attitudes and values concerning sexual behavior.

Charles Darwin's[2] investigations of how animal species adapt to changes in the environment led to new ideas on the origin of life.

[1]Sigmund Freud (1856–1939), a Viennese physician, developed the theory and technique of psychoanalysis.

[2]Charles Darwin (1809–1882), a British naturalist, outlined his theory of evolution in *The Origin of Species*.

The idea of passive resistance to authority, advanced by charismatic leader Mahatma Gandhi, was instrumental in freeing India from British rule. Here Gandhi approaches the viceroy's lodge in New Delhi in 1946.

His theories influenced the development of the science of biology. But his ideas clashed with the ideas of creation that are part of many people's religious faith.

A new religion or a new way of looking at an old faith can have a great social impact. The teachings of Jesus, Mohammed, and Gautama Buddha have led millions of people to live a special kind of life and to follow certain rituals and rules as believers in particular faiths. The challenge of Martin Luther and other reformers to certain Roman Catholic beliefs and practices led to great social change in the sixteenth century. Pope John XXIII stirred the world in the 1960s with his ideas for change in the Catholic Church and his efforts to reunite the diverse Christian churches.

Social scientists may be responsible for certain changes by suggesting new ideas that challenge old values. For example, ideas from social science played a part in the 1954 school-desegregation decision *Brown* v. *Board of Education of Topeka, Kansas.* The findings of psychologists and sociologists on the effects of racial segregation on self-concept and learning were presented in the United States Supreme Court and were cited by Chief Justice Earl Warren in his opinion on the case.

As you read in Chapter 8, the idea of nationalism has had a profound effect in modern history. Other significant changes have been based on the idea of modernization. For example, the idea that technological advances bring economic progress has reached the most remote villages of the world.

The spread of ideas from one culture to another is known as *cultural diffusion.* It is a process that has gone on throughout hu-

Cultural diffusion, or the spread of ideas from one culture to another, is now a rapid process. Today the idea that technology is the key to economic growth is accepted in all societies. This is a photographer in Kenya.

GRAPH SKILL   The reasons for immigration are varied and complex. In the past, many immigrants came to the United States to escape hunger, as some still do today. Other immigrants are political refugees from totalitarianism. Many of today's immigrants are well educated and skilled. According to the graph below, when did European immigration reach its peak? Where are most immigrants coming from in the 1980s? What has been the trend in Asian immigration since 1979?

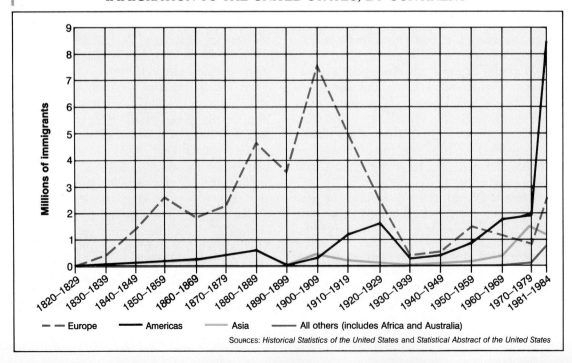

IMMIGRATION TO THE UNITED STATES, BY CONTINENT

- - - Europe   —— Americas   —— Asia   —— All others (includes Africa and Australia)

SOURCES: *Historical Statistics of the United States* and *Statistical Abstract of the United States*

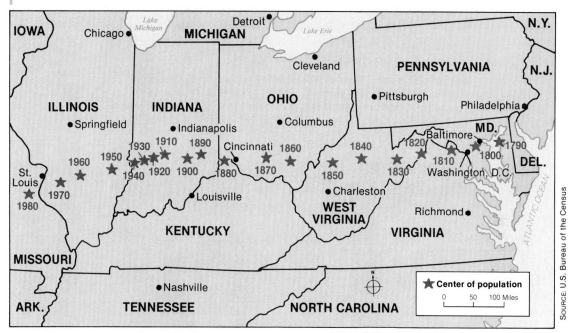

CHANGES IN THE CENTER OF POPULATION OF THE UNITED STATES

SOURCE: U.S. Bureau of the Census

MAP SKILL The center of population is the point at which an imaginary, flat, weightless, and rigid map of the United States would balance if weights of identical value were placed on it to represent the location of each person. In what direction has the center of population moved since the first United States Census in 1790? Why has the movement occurred?

Population Growth and Movement

Major changes in the population of a society are likely to cause other kinds of changes. Consider population size, which is discussed in Chapter 17 as one of the problems of mass society. The population of any region or nation rises or falls depending on the birthrate, death rate, and movement in or out of the area. Slow rises or drops in populations have little impact on social institutions. Rapid population increase puts new demands on a society's economic and political institutions. More of everything is needed—food, clothing, housing, schools, and hospitals.

In recent years, the growth of world population has been called an explosion. The alarming population rise in certain nations results largely from a sharp drop in the number of people who die during infancy or childhood. Population growth in peasant societies where people depend on food grown on small plots of land creates great pressure for change. Families need to grow more food in order to feed the larger number of surviving children. Some peasants turn to technology—machinery, fertilizers, insecticides—to increase the yield from the crowded land. Others make new contacts with regional cities and towns for jobs or for markets to sell their surplus produce.

If this process of change succeeds, population growth can help raise the standard of living for a time. However, to provide housing, schools, and health services for a growing population, the labor force often has to be

(Continued from man history. In recent years, cultural diffusion has been speeded up by modern methods of communication.)

reorganized. Capital, which is hard to come by, is needed to pay for these new services. In some areas, such as parts of India, good land, trained workers, and other productive resources are so strained that a rapidly rising population can cause a drop in the standard of living for many people. Population growth also increases wastes and can destroy open space.

As minority populations of cities have increased, more minority-group members have been elected as public officials. Henry Cisneros of San Antonio, shown at bottom left, was the first Mexican American mayor in the United States. Continuing clockwise, Senator Daniel Inouye of Hawaii, Mayor Wilson Goode of Philadelphia, and Mayor Andrew Young of Atlanta are among the many minority group members who have risen to important offices in recent years.

If resources become very scarce and people are forced to compete for food, land, or jobs, conflicts can become serious. Pressure for additional land or raw materials to supply a growing population has often led to wars among nations. Poverty or an inadequate food supply may lead families to migrate, either to major cities or, at times, to other countries where they hope to find work.

Immigration was a great boon to America's economic development. Blacks from Africa and the West Indies were unwilling immigrants, but they, along with farmers from Europe, provided much of the labor for American agriculture. Most of the laborers on the first railroad that spanned the nation were Chinese and Irish immigrants. Other immigrants mined the coal and ran the factory machinery in developing America.

Poor living conditions often cause people to move, and the migrations themselves typically cause further social change. The westward movement, the farm-to-city movement, and other internal migrations have had great effects on American society. Two migration patterns have had an especially strong impact on social change in recent years: southern blacks in large numbers have moved into northern cities, and many whites have moved to the suburbs.

These twin movements, in turn, have led to many other changes in American life. For example, urban blacks took the lead in the civil-rights revolution of the 1960s. Black mayors won elections in many big cities. Further changes resulting from population growth and migration patterns are discussed in Chapter 17.

? Name some other recent social changes that have come about partly from population movement, growth, or decline.

REVIEW AND APPLICATION

1. *IDENTIFY:* Imperialism, self-determination, cultural diffusion.
2. In what ways can a conquest cause social change?
3. In what ways does technology cause social change? What effect did technology have on the social relationships of the Yir Yiront?
4. Which migration patterns have had an especially strong impact on social change in the United States?

CRITICAL THINKING: "The car and the airplane can produce pollution, accidents, and energy shortages. But because of them, we can . . . send a letter in a matter of days, have food and other products from all over the globe, and travel in foreign lands." According to this passage, what do Americans value more than safety and the environment?

3 Urbanization in America

The study of the social structure of cities is one of American sociology's oldest subfields. It came out of the University of Chicago in the 1920s and is called *urban ecology. Ecology* is the study of the relationship of living things to their environments; urban ecology looks at the relationship of a population to the urban setting.

To the Chicago sociologists, led by Robert E. Park, the city was more than just the people who lived in it. They saw the city as a living organism that is born, grows, and changes. These sociologists also considered the three aspects of community mentioned earlier—geographical, psychological, and organizational—and their relationship to the city. For example, they found that geography affects city location and growth. Community, or "neighboring," is influenced by natural and artificial borders, such as rivers, lakes, roads, and railroad tracks.

Searching for common themes and patterns in the history of urban development, the Chicago sociologists noted that cities are

Sociologists view the city as an organism that changes as new groups move in and older groups leave for other areas.

often market villages grown up. The villages that became cities were often found at a bend in a river, on the edge of a natural harbor, by an oasis, or at a major crossroads. With the coming of the railroad, some cities grew up at railroad junctions.

Three Models of City Growth

In the United States, cities grew quickly. People built homes in the lowlands and the ports. Commercial buildings, warehouses, banks, and buildings to house entertainment followed in short order. Moreover, housing was first built near the center of activity. Often the houses of the rich and the poor were in separate sectors. The rich built upriver, the poor downriver, below them.

As more people came to the cities, the richer people left the downtown area. Their large homes were often turned into offices or apartments. Some workers, as they made more money, also began to move out. They formed a new residential zone of one- and two-family dwellings. Those who were better off, or who were moving faster, often "leap-frogged" the second and third zones. These people set up a still better residential area far from the center but still dependent on it. In many cities, still another zone was made up of those who were to become real commuters. That zone is what we now call "suburbia."

This pattern is one of three models of city growth. The Chicago sociologists called it the *concentric-zone model.* At the center is the downtown business area. Then comes a "transition zone" of rooming houses, pawnshops, warehouses, parking lots, and so on. Next come circles or semicircles of housing. The farther the circle from the center, the less dense the housing. Chicago is a good example of this model.

A second model, the *sector model,* suggests that some cities grow not in ever-widening circles but in parts, or sectors. Often the growth pattern follows the topography, or surface features, of the land. A river cutting through the city may create an industrial sector that stretches for miles right through the middle of town. In another city, three hills at different points may be the sites for better residential neighborhoods, while working-class homes fill in the valleys between them. Providence, St. Louis, and San Francisco are examples of cities that have grown according to this pattern.

The *multiple-nuclei model* describes cities that have grown by taking in outlying towns and villages. In this model, there is a main downtown business area with wholesalers, light industry, and housing nearby. But there are also the scattered business districts of the former villages and towns. One or two of the annexed places may have been industrial towns, and they remain in the city as industrial districts. Other places may have been chiefly residential suburbs, and they stay on as residential districts. Los Angeles is a good example of this third model. Its downtown business-and-shopping district is small for a city of its size. But there are sizable business districts in other sections: Brentwood, Hollywood, Westwood, Watts, and others.

TYPES OF CITY GROWTH

The Concentric-Zone Model

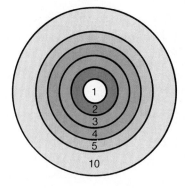

The Sector Model

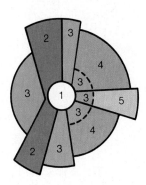

The Multiple-Nuclei Model

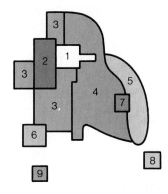

1 Central business district	6 Heavy manufacturing
2 Wholesale, light manufacturing	7 Outlying business district
3 Lower-class residential	8 Residential suburb
4 Middle-class residential	9 Industrial suburb
5 Upper-class residential	10 Commuter zone

SOURCE: C. D. Harris and E. L. Ullman, "The Nature of Cities," *Annals of the American Academy of Political and Social Science*

CHART SKILL   Cities can expand outward, as shown by the concentric-zone model, which describes Chicago in the 1920s. They can also develop in sectors, which often adapt to geographic features, as in the sector model. Or they can grow by absorbing outlying towns and villages, as in the multiple-nuclei model. Why are the residential areas located near the central business districts?

When moving out of the city becomes impossible, people may join their neighbors in improving the area where they live. Here former President Jimmy Carter and his wife Roslyn lend a hand at renovating a building in New York.

Urban succession is the movement of groups within cities according to certain patterns. As people get better jobs, their social mobility is often reflected in greater physical mobility, and they become commuters.

Mobility and Urban Succession

In Chapter 5, you learned that social mobility is the movement of people up or down the ladder of social class. Moving "from rags to riches" is an example, though a rare one. Moving from a blue-collar job to a white-collar one, thereby changing one's style of life, is more common. Physical mobility is actual movement from one place to another. Moving into the city from the countryside is an example. So is moving from one neighborhood to another.

In urban areas the world over, a good deal of both social and physical mobility takes place, and the two are often related. As people get better jobs or more money, they often move to "better" neighborhoods. When they are laid off or earn less, they may face downward mobility. Sometimes they have to move back to the old neighborhood or to one that is poorer and has less prestige.

Sometimes entire groups move out, and their places are quickly taken by others. Sociologists refer to such a process as *urban succession*. This process has taken place especially in northern and eastern American cities. In many such cities, families that had settled near the center decided to build newer homes farther out. Their places were taken by newcomers. In time the newcomers, such as the Germans and the Irish, moved on themselves. Their places were taken by Eastern European Jews and Italians. They, in turn, moved on. The movers left their old neighborhoods to new arrivals, such as southern blacks and Puerto Ricans.

Proof of these succession patterns may be found in the streets and buildings of many cities. Clues are supplied by the names of streets and shops that remain as reminders of earlier groups. One also finds proof in the buildings that began as churches, became synagogues, and were later changed into churches once again. It is also seen in the changing patterns of names of pupils who went to neighborhood schools. If you were to look at the class lists of an old inner-city school for each decade from 1880 to 1990, you would notice how the names of one ethnic group replace those of another on the class rosters.

The Move Outward

People moving out of the inner city often skipped nearby zones to move to the city's edge and beyond. When horse-drawn vehicles gave way to trolleys and cars, people no longer had to live so near their jobs. Some chose a single-family house and yard beyond the city limits.

The automobile spurred the movement outward. No longer did people have to think

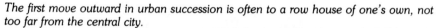

The first move outward in urban succession is often to a row house of one's own, not too far from the central city.

about being near the trolley line, which so often stopped at the city's edge. In the 1920s, auto ownership in the United States grew rapidly. Towns and villages near the city took on new life. People could live there and still work in the city. New housing developments sprang up.

Suburban movement slowed during the depression of the 1930s. Then the scarcities of World War II put limits on building materials, and gas rationing reduced the use of private cars. But after the war ended in 1945, a suburban boom got under way. It was sparked by lack of housing in the central cities, low-cost housing loans, road building, and a rising birthrate.

While the houses were going up in suburbia, so were shopping centers. They drew customers from both the suburbs and the center city. And many corporations chose building sites outside the central city for new plants and offices.

The economic ties between the central city and its suburbs remained strong even though they belonged to different local government units. Many suburbanites had jobs in the city. Some city dwellers worked in the suburbs. Many of the stores in the shopping

CHART SKILL How many satellite cities are included in the model below?

THE METROPOLITAN-AREA MODEL

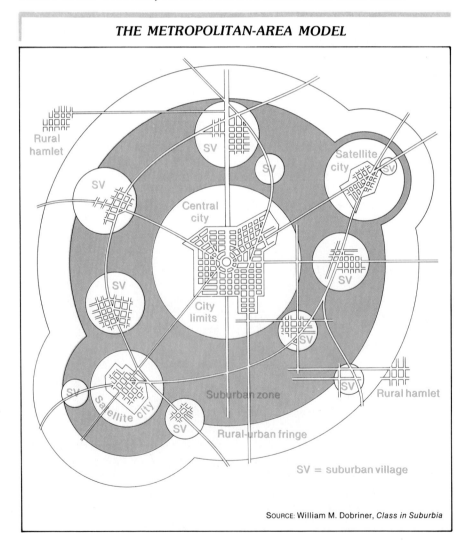

SV = suburban village

SOURCE: William M. Dobriner, *Class in Suburbia*

MAJOR STRIP CITIES IN THE UNITED STATES

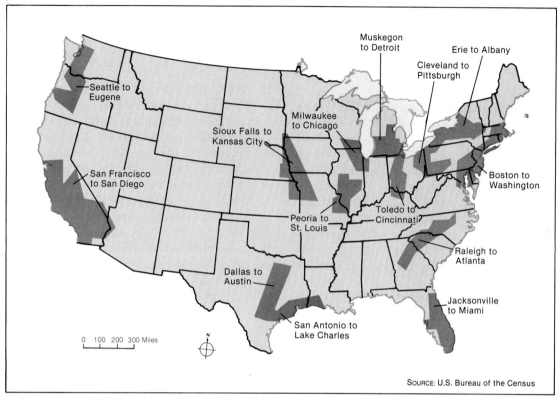

Muskegon to Detroit

Erie to Albany

Cleveland to Pittsburgh

Seattle to Eugene

Milwaukee to Chicago

Sioux Falls to Kansas City

San Francisco to San Diego

Boston to Washington

Peoria to St. Louis

Toledo to Cincinnati

Raleigh to Atlanta

Dallas to Austin

Jacksonville to Miami

San Antonio to Lake Charles

0 100 200 300 Miles

N

SOURCE: U.S. Bureau of the Census

MAP SKILL   In the United States, many highly populated areas run together into what are sometimes called strip cities. *Where are most of these areas located?*

centers were branches of downtown stores. Radio and TV stations and the daily newspapers of the central city sent out their messages to the city and surrounding areas.

Thus, a new pattern of urban growth began. The *metropolitan-area model* fits this extended city that has burst its borders. The illustration shows a central city with a smaller city on its edge. Farther away are two other satellite cities. Around the central and satellite cities are suburban villages. Farther out is a rural-urban fringe, the outskirts. Here are mainly rural villages and farms. But some of the people in the rural fringe are part-time farmers who work in the city. Others are city workers or retirees who choose to, live in the country. Networks of roads tie the various places in the area together.

No metropolitan area fits this diagram exactly, but the various elements are real. A few metropolitan areas have two or more central cities next to each other. Examples are Minneapolis–St. Paul, Gary–Hammond–East Chicago, and Kansas City in Missouri and Kansas.

In the past, a metropolis was defined as the chief city of a nation, state, or region or as a center of trade and activity. Today, however, the term usually refers to a major city and its satellite suburbs. We often set it apart from the core city by using the adjective "greater." Thus we speak of "Greater Boston," "Greater Atlanta," and "Greater New York."

These great, or extended, cities are so important in the American economy and in social-science research that it is useful to gather census data about them. This is complicated because a metropolitan area does not have precise boundaries like those of a central city. If a metropolitan area is a large city and its urbanized fringe, where does the edge of one urbanized fringe end and another begin?

To get around this question, the Census Bureau came up with a practical definition. It defined a *Standard Metropolitan Statistical Area* (SMSA) as either (1) a county or group of contiguous counties (except in New England, which has towns) containing at least one central city of 50,000 inhabitants or more, or (2) a city with at least 25,000 inhabitants that has contiguous areas making a combined total of 50,000, providing that the city and its areas are a single economic and social community.

In 1982, there were 323 SMSAs in the United States. The seven largest were New York, Los Angeles–Long Beach, Chicago, Philadelphia, Detroit, San Francisco–Oak-

land, and Washington, D.C. Some of the problems of living in such areas of mass society are discussed in Unit Six.

REVIEW AND APPLICATION

1. *IDENTIFY:* Urban ecology, exology, concentric zone model, sector model, multiple-nuclei model, urban succession, metropolitan-area model, Standard Metropolitan Statistical Area (SMSA).
2. When and where did the study of urban ecology begin?
3. What geographical factors have influenced city location and growth?
4. What are the regions in the concentric-zone model of city growth?
5. Describe the pattern Los Angeles followed as it expanded.

CRITICAL THINKING: Suppose that your city does not fit any of the patterns of city growth described on page 283. Create and describe a new model.

4 City Life

What is responsible for the remarkable growth of cities? Why have people throughout history tended to leave their farms and small towns and move to the city? What is its special appeal? In *The Culture of Cities,* Lewis Mumford noted that the city has always been the center of power and culture, "the seat of the temple, the market, the hall of justice, the academy of learning." The city is where, working and playing together, individuals and groups create new ideas, new products, and new forms of social life.

Of course, the presence within a rather small area of many people who hold differing views and have different styles of life is not always good. Mumford also wrote that "when the city ceases to be a symbol of art and order it acts in a negative fashion. . . . In the close quarters of the city, . . . evils spread more quickly." The negative aspects of the city are considered in Chapter 17.

What makes a city? At what point does a place acquire the population and character-

istics sufficient to earn it the label "city"? Although "SMSA" has been precisely defined, experts don't agree on the number of people needed to make a town a city. Figures given range from 10,000 to 100,000 persons. Most urban sociologists don't use a fixed number. Instead, they say that a city has many more people than can easily know one another.

This does not mean that nobody knows anybody, however. Bonds of kinship and neighborliness exist in the city. Within its borders are many separate communities where people differ from those around them in what they are, what they think, and what they do. Recall the reading on page 267 describing East Los Angeles.

To the outsider, perhaps the most obvious form of diversity in American cities is racial and ethnic. Our cities, and many others throughout the world, are checkerboards of different peoples. The seaboard cities and the new towns growing up along the transportation lines were natural stopping places

POPULATION SHIFTS IN THE UNITED STATES, 1880–1985

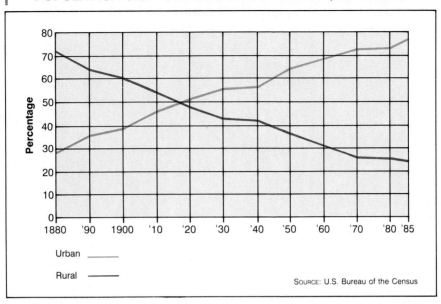

Urban _____

Rural ———

SOURCE: U.S. Bureau of the Census

GRAPH SKILL   According to the graph, what percentage of Americans lived in rural areas in 1880? In 1985? What percentage of Americans lived in urban areas in 1880? In 1985? How would you describe the overall trend in urban-rural population patterns from 1880 to 1985?

for the people from many lands who came to America. In place after place, one finds the remains of segregated living patterns between blacks and whites. One also sees ethnic neighborhoods with names like "Little Italy" and "Chinatown."

In his classic study *The Ghetto,* Louis Wirth looked at a Jewish neighborhood in Chicago. It was a neighborhood much like the villages that Eastern European Jews had left behind when they came to the United States. Chicago's bustling Maxwell and Halsted streets had the language, the folklore, the religious beliefs, the family structure, the humor, and the sadness of the villages left behind in Europe.

CASE SYUDY: An Urban Village

Herbert Gans coined the term "urban village" to describe ethnic communities in the city. Gans studied one such place, an Italian American neighborhood in the West End of Boston. You read about this study in some detail in Chapter 9. Here is an excerpt from Gans's account:

Everyday life in the West End was not much different from that in other neighborhoods, urban or suburban. The men went to work in the morning, and, for most of the day, the area was occupied largely by women and children—just as in the suburbs. . . . In the afternoon, younger women could be seen pushing baby carriages. Children of all ages played on the street, and teenagers would "hang" on the corner, or play ball in the schoolyard. . . . Many women went shopping every day, partly to meet neighbors and to catch up on area news in the small grocery stores, and partly to buy foods that could not be obtained in the weekly excursion to the

Many people enjoy the excitement and cultural variety of city life. While large cities may at times be places of isolation and loneliness, feelings of community can be developed through neighborhood associations. In the scene above, neighborhood children perform for a block party. At the street festival below, neighbors raise funds for improvements by selling food and articles they have made.

supermarket. On Sunday mornings, the streets were filled with people who were visiting with neighbors and friends before and after church. . . . A few people have moved into the area to hide from the world. . . . Generally speaking, however, neighbors were friendly and quick to say hello to each other, although more intense social contact was limited to relatives and friends. . . .

The sharing of values was also encouraged by the residential stability of much of the population. Many West Enders had known each other for years, if only as acquaintances who greeted each other on the street. Everyone might not know everyone else; but, as they did know something about everyone, the net effect was the same, especially within each ethnic group. Between [ethnic] groups, common residence and sharing of facilities—as well as the constant struggle against absentee landlords—created enough solidarity to maintain a friendly spirit. Moreover, for many families, problems were never far away. Illnesses, job layoffs, and school or discipline problems among the children occurred regularly. Alcoholism, mental illness, desertion, the death of a loved one, serious financial difficulties, and even violence were familiar to everyone. If they did not take place in one's immediate family, they had happened at some time to a relative or a neighbor. Thus, when emergencies occurred, neighbors helped each other readily; other problems were solved within each ethnic group.

For most West Enders, then, life in the area resembled that found in the village or small town, even in the suburb. Indeed, if differences of age and economic level among the residents were eliminated, many similarities between the life of the urban neighborhood and the suburb would become visible.

Gans thinks that, despite all the problems of trying to make a living, poor education, and other hardships, the West End was "by and large a good place to live."

? What kinds of racial and ethnic neighborhoods are there in the large city that you know best? Can special foods, crafts, religious services, or other attractions native to the various peoples be found there? Name a few.

Cities offer not only ethnic diversity but also a wide range of events for every taste. Think of the kinds of activity found in the larger urban centers. Do you like yoga, soccer, team tennis, coin collecting, old movies? Come to the city.

CASE STUDY: *Hudson Street*

All told, the city is a busy place with many people, crowded together, who differ from each other in all sorts of ways. They often compete and clash. But, amazingly perhaps, they often get along and learn to enjoy the benefits of size, density, and diversity. Urbanologist Jane Jacobs's account of Hudson Street in the Greenwich Village section of New York City shows her joy in city life:

The stretch of Hudson where I live is each day the scene of an intricate sidewalk ballet. I make my own first entrance into it a little after eight when I put out the garbage can, as the droves of junior high school students walk by the center of the stage dropping candy wrappers.

In some parts of the country, whole new planned towns have been built to create an ideal environment that will encompass the best of city and suburb. On a smaller scale, planned communities, such as Roosevelt Island in New York City's East River, pictured here, combine proximity to work with recreational space—private vegetable gardens and sports fields, for example.

While I sweep up the wrappers I watch the other rituals of morning: Mr. Halpert unlocking the laundry's handcart from its mooring to a cellar door, Joe Cornacchia's son-in-law stacking out the empty crates from the delicatessen, the barber bringing out his sidewalk folding chair, Mr. Goldstein arranging the coils of wire which proclaim that the hardware store is open. . . .

Now the primary children, heading for St. Luke's, dribble through to the south; the children for St. Veronica's cross, heading to the west, and the children for P.S. 41, heading toward the east.

Two new entrances are being made from the wings: well-dressed and even elegant women and men with briefcases emerge from doorways and side streets. Most of these are heading for the bus and subways, but some hover on the curbs, stopping taxis which have miraculously appeared at the right moment, for the taxis are part of a wider morning ritual: having dropped passengers from midtown in the downtown financial district, they are now bringing downtowners up to the midtown.

Simultaneously, numbers of women in housedresses have emerged, and as they crisscross with one another they pause for quick conversations that sound with either laughter or joint indignation, never, it seems, anything in between. It is time for me to hurry to work too, and I exchange my ritual farewell with Mr. Lofaro, the short, thick-bodied, white-aproned fruit man who stands outside his doorway a little up the street, his arms folded, his feet planted, looking solid as earth itself. We nod; we each glance quickly up and down the street, then look back to each other and smile. We have done this many a morning for more than ten years, and we both know what it means: all is well.

On Hudson Street, the same as in the North End of Boston or in other animated neighborhoods of great cities, . . . we are the lucky possessors of [an] order that makes it relatively simple to keep the peace because there are plenty of eyes on the street. But there is nothing simple about that order itself, or the bewildering number of components that go into it. Most of those components are specialized in one way or another. They unite in their joint effect upon the sidewalk [the community itself], which is not specialized in the least. That is its strength.

REVIEW AND APPLICATION

1. Look at the newspaper ads below. (a) What interest groups do they appeal to? (b) Which groups are more likely to be found in a city than in a small town?

TIME FOR NEW DIRECTIONS. High-impact creative workshop in assertiveness training for men and women. Exciting FREE intro session. Call 232-4155.

ANTIQUE & FLEA MARKET. Free adm. Indoors. 80 dealers. Open Fri. 5–10 P.M., Sat. 11–9, Sun. 11–7.

FIND NEW PARTNERS, places to play tennis, squash, bridge, chess . . . any game. SPORTS-MATCH. (444) 342-9077.

SMALL-GROUP WORKSHOP FOR DIETERS. New approach. 456-3201 (after 1 P.M.).

TATTOOS, Missi Wilkie & Co. Custom work. 535-4809.

CRITICAL THINKING: On page 291 what assumption does Herbert Gans make about the differences between West Enders and suburbanites? Cite the passage that supports your answer.

CHAPTER 12 REVIEW

Recap

A community is made up of people living in a settlement who share a strong sense of belonging. Often their feelings are based on a common religion or national origin. A community may change and remain a community, but sometimes change can destroy the bonds among its members. Changes in values, norms, roles, and institutions have followed geographical change, war, technological developments, and population growth and migration. Scientific discoveries, advances in thought, and new religious ideas may cause people to alter their systems of belief and role expectations. Sometimes change can have unexpected or even negative effects.

Urban ecologists have noted that the growth of cities follows a pattern of change that they call urban succession, the replacement of one's distinct population group by another. Within the city, there may be many distinct areas that have the characteristics of community. Many people move outward to escape the crowding of the city, but others remain to enjoy its cultural richness and diversity.

Key Terms

Define the following:

community
imperialism
self-determination
cultural diffusion
urban ecology

ecology
concentric-zone model
sector model
multiple-nuclei model
urban succession

metropolitan-area
  model
Standard Metropolitan
  Statistical Area
  (SMSA)

Applying Sociology

1. Take part in a team study of a nearby neighborhood or village that seems to have some sense of community. (a) Get as much background information as you can from the library, city hall, or county courthouse, including settlement history and population changes. (b) Spend a day in the place you have chosen, noting common names on the storefronts, in cemeteries, and in the newspaper. Speak to several storekeepers, public officials, and householders. Ask them to tell you about the character of the town or neighborhood. Ask, for example, "Is this a good place to live? Follow up with, "Why do you feel that way?"

2. Has the area where you live ever been hit by a natural disaster? Find out if your parents or grandparents have had such an experience. What social changes took place? What kinds of changes were short-term adjustments? What changes were longer-lasting? Interview friends and relatives to locate someone who has seen such an event and record his or her descriptions.

3. What social changes, particularly long-term changes, might be brought about by (a) a major earthquake or typhoon resulting in a state of emergency in a particular reigon; (b) drought in a crop-growing area? If either of these events has occurred lately anywhere in the world, collect news items describing the results for the bulletin board.

4. At present rates of growth, some countries will double in size in about twenty-two years. What are some likely effects if such growth continues? Assume that the leaders in these countries foresee the problems. What social changes might leaders try to bring about to avoid the problems? Pretend you are the head of such a government and draw up a plan.

5. For fifteen to twenty years after World War II, the American population grew rapidly. Then there was a slowdown in growth. Name some social changes that resulted, in part, from the rise and then the drop in birthrates.

6. Draw a rough map of a metropolitan area near you and compare it to the diagram on page 286. Consult a road or subway map for help. How well does it fit the model?

7. If you don't live in a city now, do you plan to move to one someday? Why or why not? Write a paragraph that sums up your thoughts about city living.

8. On a special ethnic holiday, such as the Chinese New Year or a saint's day, visit a local area where such a celebration takes place. Note whether people who are not members of the racial or ethnic group have come to enjoy the events. Do you or your friends usually attend? Why? Give a report on your observations and experiences.

Extended Readings

Kate Skorpen, "Soda Fountain Philosophy," *Salt*, August 1987, pp. 38–51.

1. Describe the attitude of the people toward their town.
2. What changes have taken place in the town?

Kurt Anderson, "Spiffing Up the Urban Heritage," *Time*, November 23, 1987, pp. 72–83.

1. What were some early measures taken to preserve old buildings in American cities?
2. What has restoring old buildings taught many planners and architects?

Rafael M. Salas, "Urban Population Growth: Blessing or Burden?," *USA Today*, July 1987, pp. 74–77.

1, What changes in world population do futurists see for the 21st century?
2. Does the article view the coming changes positively or negatively?

Social Studies Skills

Extracting the facts from people's opinions
The statements below are opinions expressed in interviews from Chapter 12. From each statement, eliminate those words which reflect the speaker's opinion. Then rewrite each statement so that it is purely factual.

(a) "When I came back to East Los it didn't seem as if I had left Mexico. Every face was a Mexican face. Everyone was friendly."

(b) "Gans thinks that, despite all the problems of trying to make a living, poor education, and other hardships, the West End was 'by and large a good place to live.'"

(c) "We are the lucky possessors of [an] order that makes it relatively simple to keep the peace because there are plenty of eyes on the street."

Detecting the stereotypes
Reread the passage about Springdale, New York on pages 269 and 270. How are the people of this town stereotyped in the passage? According to this stereotype, how are the members of the group alike?

Critical Thinking

1. **Evaluating Cause and Effect:** What factors caused the population shifts described in the line graph at the top of page 289?
2. **Evaluating Samples:** Suppose, based on the study *The Ghetto* of a Jewish neighborhood in Chicago (described on page 289), someone made this statement: "Immigrant neighborhoods in America were very much like the villages these people left in the old country." How valid is this statement?

13

Social Movements and Collective Behavior

Chapter Preview

- **Before you read,** look up the following key terms in the glossary to become familiar with their definitions:

evolutionary theory	functionalist theory	conflict theory
pluralist movement	assimilationist	revolutionary
secessionist movement	movement	movement

- **As you read,** think about answers to the following questions:

1. What causes social change?
2. What characteristics do all social movements have in common?
3. What is propaganda?
4. Why is the behavior of large groups sometimes unpredictable?

Sections in this Chapter

1. Theories of Change
2. The Importance of Social Movements
3. Characteristics of Social Movements
4. Classification by Goals
5. Communication and Change
6. Collective Behavior

Chapter Focus

Change is a by-product of many things. Discoveries such as fire, and inventions, from the wheel to the computer chip, are obviously important in altering customs and behavior. Even more important are ideas themselves, new conceptions of how to cope with traditional problems —problems of explanation, order, and economic exchange. Throughout the centuries, religion, politics, and economics have been affected by challenges to the existing order.

This chapter examines social change from several perspectives. First, it considers some of the theories put forth by social scientists to explain what fosters or inhibits change. Then it looks at social movements that seek to bring about alternative social patterns.

Using Sociologists' Tools

- **Observe** how local politicians mobilize people for a campaign or cause.
- **Describe** the methods used to attract support by those wanting to put forth a particular idea or political candidate.
- **Analyze** the effectiveness of methods used by a national movement, such as the campaign for equal rights for women, to attract support.
- **Predict** whether a campaign for year-round schooling would succeed in your community. Who would favor it? Who would oppose it? Why?

People united by a common cause, such as these farmworkers demonstrating for better working conditions, may struggle for decades to achieve their aims.

1 Theories of Change

In the last chapter, you read how change can result both from accidents and catastrophes and from planned human behavior. It can range from the temporary and superficial to the permanent and profound. Sociologists who study social change seek to explain complex *systemic changes,* changes that affect entire social systems. They have developed several major theories of general social change. Each of the following theories of change was put forth in the expectation that it would help people to predict future events.

Evolutionary Theory

Auguste Comte, Herbert Spencer, and Lewis Henry Morgan are associated with an *evolutionary theory* of social change. Evolu-tionary theorists, whose views prevailed in the late nineteenth century, believe that all societies progress from the simple to the complex, with increasing social and cultural specialization. For example, because of the need for oil in the contemporary industrialized world, Saudi Arabia, a simple society of Bedouin tribes, is being transformed into a complex modern state. Evolutionary theorists would assert that as societies evolve, new technology transforms and weakens traditional social relations. They would agree that this is occurring in the oil-producing states.

Other evolutionary social scientists, among them Leslie White, emphasize the development of culture and the greater mastery of the environment that results. For example, the oil-rich countries, now expanding culturally, are also in a better position to control

As technology transforms a society, people may find themselves straddling two worlds, the traditional and the modern. This Egyptian camel driver is leaning against a saddle in his courtyard.

their national and international environments. This type of change often produces severe social and political tensions, as happened in Iran in the 1970s, where intensive modernization was followed by revolution.

All evolutionary theorists, however, view problems of development, even severe disruptions such as those in Iran, as side effects in an inevitable process by which societies move toward another stage of progress. Critics of the evolutionary approach argue that many societies today are not progressing. If progress is measured by the adoption of democratic processes instead of authoritarian rule, some societies are actually moving backwards.

Conflict Theory

The basic ideas of *conflict theory* are that social change and social conflict are everywhere, that every element in a society helps break down and change society, and that every society is based on the rule of some of its members by others. Most conflict theorists agree with economist Karl Marx on the central place of the class struggle, or conflict between economic classes, in social change. Others see changes as derived from other forms of conflict. Ralf Dahrendorf, for example, focused on the struggles of certain groups to achieve positions of authority. For example, he and some other conflict theorists would regard the desegregation struggle as the attempt of an underdog group to achieve more power.

Other conflict theorists emphasize race rather than economic position as the prime source of conflict. Blacks of different social classes, they would say, have all experienced racial discrimination. In any case, whether class or race is seen as the most important factor, all conflict theorists would agree that the primary source of change is the conflict between what Dahrendorf calls the rulers and the ruled.

Critics of the conflict approach argue that societies are also characterized by agreement on values and goals. Such agreement is crucial if people are to cooperate and work together. Social life, they maintain, is more than just conflict and tension.

Functionalist Theory

According to *functionalist theory,* each society has ways of creating consensus, or agreement in norms, which serves to restore and maintain order. Thus, although conflict and tension exist, society continually strives to meet the needs of various role players. Common values develop to govern relationships and allow for the resolution of disputes.

According to Talcott Parsons, who was the leading functionalist, every society is a relatively stable and well-integrated structure. Every element in a society helps to keep it operating as a system, because social structures are based on a consensus of values among members. Changes occur within a social system so that it can adapt to challenges and maintain its overall pattern. For example, functionalists would view the struggle over desegregation as an effort by American society as a whole to meet the needs of its black members. They would note that order did not collapse when blacks went to white schools and were elected to public office.

Critics of this theoretical approach argue that it does not always succeed or always apply. For example, it has never been adequate to explain major upheavals and revolutions. Nor has any consensus in norms arisen to prevent racial clashes and the continued resistance of many whites to black bids for social equality.

All three schools of social-change theory try to explain not only what happens but why. Given the complexity of social change, both in its causes and in its effects, which explanation, if any, seems to be the best?

REVIEW AND APPLICATION

1. IDENTIFY: Systemic changes, evolutionary theory, conflict theory, functionalist theory.

CRITICAL THINKING: The critics of evolutionary theory believe that progress is measured by the adoption of democratic processes. What other aspects of progress might the evolutionary theorists take into account so that their theory would encompass countries that have moved away from democracy?

---

2 The Importance of Social Movements

Many students of social change—including evolutionary, conflict, and functionalist theorists—emphasize the power of *social movements.* A social movement is a continuing, collective effort to promote or to resist change, to press the view that some aspects of social or political life are unfair or wrong and need to be altered. A reading of the daily newspaper reveals how much a part of our social scene social movements have become. The following are some examples of issues that are now or were once at the base of social movements. As an introduction to the variety and appeals of social movements, imagine that you belong to the time and place of each situation below. You are part of the scene, and you are the same age as you are now.

It is December 5, 1955, in Montgomery, Alabama. You are walking down the street and notice that every bus is almost empty. As you approach the bus stop, a young black woman hands you a leaflet with this message:

DON'T RIDE THE

BUS

to town, to school, or anywhere on

MONDAY, DECEMBER 5.

Mass Meeting, Monday at 7 P.M.
Hott St. Baptist Church

It is 1968. A number of students at the state university are wearing these buttons:

Bumper stickers and posters carry these messages:

Suppose they gave a war and nobody came?

WAR

is unhealthy for

CHILDREN

and other

LIVING THINGS

It is the spring of 1973. In January, the United States Supreme Court decided that state criminal laws against abortion during early pregnancy are unconstitutional. Now "right-to-life" organizations are springing up, and foes of legalized abortion are marching, picketing, and carrying signs.

It is a bright summer day in 1990, and you are walking on a beach in southern New Hampshire. You come upon a group of people who are chanting and carrying banners opposing a nearby nuclear plant. They say they are part of the Anti-Seabrook Coalition and try to persuade you and your friends to support their movement to close down plants producing nuclear energy. They hand you leaflets and buttons and ask you to start an anti-nuclear movement in our school.

As a senior in high school, you are making plans for next year. On one of your visits to prospective colleges, you see a plaza marked "Speakers' Area," where representatives from different groups are talking to small clusters of students. Each speaker is surrounded by several supporters, many of whom wear buttons and armbands. You listen to a speech by a member of the Campus Crusade, a religious group. Soon afterwards, a young woman comes up to you and gives you a brochure. She asks whether you know the Lord.

A friend of yours is disgusted with the slow pace of nuclear-disarmament negotiations. Believing you share his feelings, he takes you to a secret meeting of the "Patriots for Peace," where you listen to serious discussions about the idea of planning attacks on several Armed Services Recruiting Offices. You are opposed to terrorism, but the leaders try to persuade you that the only way to stop the arms race is by popular attacks on the institution that supplies the personnel for war.

⁉ How do you think you would have reacted to each of the appeals cited above? How effective do you think each approach is for bringing about social change? Might some of these tactics have effects that were not intended by the members of the social movements that practice them? Explain.

You can see from the examples above that there can be great variety among different social movements. Yet each movement is a continuing, collective effort to promote or to resist social change. The way in which social movements grow, however, may also vary considerably.

Social movements range from loosely organized to tightly knit groups. At the core of some are formal organizations, such as the National Association for the Advancement of Colored People (NAACP), and the Socialist Workers party. But even these often have supporters who may not be official members of the organization. Indeed, many leaders of social movements rely very heavily on sympathetic and often helpful outsiders. For example, in the 1930s, those alleged to have agreed with many of the positions of the Communist party were referred to as "fellow travelers."

Although some social movements grow out of formal organizations with members deeply dedicated to a cause, usually the process is reversed: organizations spring from social movements. Leaders of social movements first achieve positions of influence by daring deeds and charismatic appeal. Basing their arguments on underlying frustrations in the sociopolitical order, they offer visions of economic, social, political, or religious salvation. Then, once they have a following, they give their cause a label, set up chains of command, and begin to recruit followers in some systematic way.

As a social movement becomes a permanent fixture on the social landscape—as it becomes *institutionalized*—its leaders frequently abandon the tactics that brought the movement into prominence, such as sit-ins, demonstrations, and other forms of protest and disruption. The movement becomes respectable. The development of religious denominations from sects is an example of this type of transition, as are the histories of many political parties worldwide.

Each of the imagined incidents described on pages 299–300 portrays groups of people organized to bring about a change. As you read more about these movements in the pages that follow, note their similarities and differences.

The Civil-Rights Movement

In 1955, many black people in Montgomery, Alabama, decided to boycott buses until the city bus company ended its policy of forc-

ing blacks to ride in the back of the bus. Black demonstrators chose this tactic to publicize the fact that they would no longer accept segregated seating and the inferior status it denoted.

Victory in Montgomery, after more than a year, was one major event in the continuing development of the civil-rights movement. It made one of the chief organizers of the boycott, Martin Luther King, Jr., a national leader. He advocated the use of nonviolent civil disobedience to bring about social change. The media publicized his efforts, exposing people throughout the country to his ideas, his goals, and his ability to inspire support against tough odds.

The Peace Movement

The peace movement cited in the second vignette opposed American involvement in the Vietnam War. Hundreds of thousands of American citizens wore buttons and displayed bumper stickers like those shown on

Dr. Martin Luther King, a leader in the civil-rights movement, won the Nobel Peace Prize for his advocacy of nonviolent demonstrations as a form of political action. Below, an address in Washington, D.C., in 1963.

page 300. Many marched repeatedly in Washington and other cities, signed newspaper ads calling for troop withdrawal, and urged members of Congress to vote against war appropriations and to draft antiwar legislation. A smaller and more militant group took more controversial steps: sitting in at military bases or draft boards, burning draft cards or American flags, ransacking draftboard offices, even fleeing the country.

The "Pro-Choice" and "Right-to-Life" Movements

A third powerful issue, one that has spawned two opposing movements, is abortion. The 1973 Supreme Court decision declaring that state anti-abortion laws were an abridgment of personal liberty was regarded as the culmination of a social movement to make abortion legal. The Court decision spurred a countermovement, however, the "right-to-life" movement, which continued to grow in influence into the 1980s. Its supporters hold that abortion is murder and should be permitted only if the life of the mother is endangered. They believe that life begins at conception and that the unborn fetus should therefore have the same protection as a newborn baby and all other human beings.

"Pro-choice" advocates feel that the decision to have a child or not should be the responsibility of the mother. To this end, their goal is to prevent an amendment to the Constitution or any change in the interpretation of the Ninth and Fourteenth Amendments on which the right to abortion is based.

Three Other Movements

The three other movements illustrated also reflect concerns emerging out of heartfelt issues. The nuclear-energy protest, for example, followed a long-smoldering debate that was activated in the late 1970s when several accidents at nuclear power plants brought national attention to the issue. Many who had long felt uneasy about the hazards of nuclear plants joined with long-term opponents and formed groups such as the Clamshell Alliance.

During that same period, perhaps in reaction to what many saw as the unrestrained permissiveness of the 1960s and to the social evils accompanying a rapidly changing world, many people began turning "back to basics." It happened in politics with a resurgence of conservatism, in education with a renewed emphasis on "the three Rs," and in religion with the fervent move toward a more "fundamental" interpretation of sacred texts. The Campus Crusade was only one of a number of religious movements that began sweeping the campuses.

Some social movements include terrorist factions. The hypothetical "Patriots for Peace" mentioned in the last vignette, although extreme, represent such a movement. Various social movements in Europe, the Middle East, and Latin America have also spawned terrorist factions. In this country as in others, terrorists aim to strike at the very core of the social system, which, they insist, cannot be altered in any other way.

REVIEW AND APPLICATION

1. *IDENTIFY:* Social movements, institutionalized.
2. What is the usual process by which a social movement grows? How do leaders of these movements often achieve influence?
3. How did Martin Luther King, Jr. advocate bringing about social change?
4. What were some of the actions undertaken by people opposing the Vietnam War?
5. What are some of the social movements that grew out of the wish to go "back to basics"?

CRITICAL THINKING: What values did the followers of Martin Luther King, Jr., and many members of the peace movement share? Support your answer with passages from the text.

3 Characteristics of Social Movements

As you read about various American social movements, you were asked to reflect upon similarities among them. The following are some of the characteristics that you may have noted. They are characteristics that all social movements share:

1. They have a distinct purpose or ideology and are directed toward a definite set of goals.
2. They have some form of leadership.
3. Their members show a strong sense of solidarity.
4. Unlike social fads, they are long-lasting.
5. They use specific tactics to achieve their ends.

Using a current movement, the Moral Majority, as an illustration, let's look at some of these characteristics more closely.

The Reverend Jerry Falwell is a leader of the Moral Majority, a social movement opposing trends in American society that members view as morally objectionable and harmful to country and individuals alike.

Ideology

The main function of an *ideology* is to state the reason for the movement and to justify its existence. The ideology asserts the movement's views of the current situation, how that situation came about, and how change can be attained. It gives members a purpose or direction and serves as a source of inspiration and hope. Members also use ideology to defend the movement's goals to those who oppose it.

The Moral Majority grew into a major social force in the late 1970s and early 1980s. Its prime movers were religious figures such as the Reverend Jerry Falwell of the Thomas Road Baptist Church in Lynchburg, Virginia. The religious basis of the Moral Majority's appeal is a Christian philosophy that stresses a strict interpretation of the Bible. Adhering closely to biblical tenets as a means to personal salvation is an important tenet of their faith.

This perspective also stresses that religious belief and practices can rid the country of what members and others see as its major problems: family breakdown, unwanted teenage pregnancy, drug abuse, abortion, and homosexuality. The ideology opposes any proposed or existing legislation considered threatening to the nation's moral fiber. In this category, the Moral Majority includes those laws which would guarantee civil rights for homosexuals or, through funding day-care centers, provide government aid to women who wish to enter the job market.

Members of the Moral Majority also believe that educational curricula should be changed to reflect the religious view of the origins of life on earth. Rejecting the Darwinian theory of evolution, they argue that schools should also teach "creationism," the biblical explanation of the beginning of life as set forth in the book of Genesis.

Leadership

Decisions have to be made. Day-to-day work must be given out to workers and carried through. Speeches and articles must be written to explain the movement to others. Fund raising, building public support, and recruiting members are key aims of many social movements. Those who speak for the group, help guide its efforts, and serve as inspiring role models to the rank and file are the movement's leaders.

Leadership styles vary. Some leaders, such as Jerry Falwell of the Moral Majority, have *charisma*. This means that, in the eyes of their followers, they are unique. They are believed to possess unusual qualities, including a special understanding of historical conditions and of the present situation. The charismatic leader offers an inspiring vision of the future and how it can be achieved. Central to this is the conviction among followers that the leader can be trusted to help the members achieve their goals. Charismatic religious leaders are able to develop huge followings and much influence as they reach into homes through their television ministries.

Some social movements favor a shared or rotating leadership in which no one person holds a great deal of power or responsibility. Some of these leaders might have an exceptional ability to analyze and describe the movement's ideology or goals—that is, to provide intellectual leadership. Other leaders may excel in administrative ability.

A social movement needs various kinds of leaders if it is to gain members, followers, and sympathizers and if it is to survive and work toward its goals over a period of time. Leaders must develop an ideology that can be communicated in everyday language. They must organize the long-term efforts needed to bring about changes in values, roles, and institutions.

Goals

Although its ideology may make broad statements about such ideals as justice, equality, morality, decency, or peace, a social movement must set specific goals that its leaders and members can easily understand and strive for on a day-to-day basis. A movement's goals are the specific changes it hopes to bring about.

In keeping with its ideology, the Moral Majority lobbies for the passage of bills and even constitutional amendments that would restrict the intrusion of government in everyday life and permit the introduction of prayer in public institutions. In the presidential campaign of 1984, many members of the Moral Majority took an active part in promoting the candidacy of conservative candidates. When Ronald Reagan was re-elected by overwhelming numbers, members of the movement urged the president and many members of Congress to honor campaign promises to pass legislation in keeping with the Moral Majority's religious and political stands.

Tactics

Just as goals must be defined, so must tactics be devised. Specific tactics serve as means of achieving a movement's goals. Types of tactics include educational tactics, political tactics, and direct action.

Educational Tactics Most movements include some form of public education as part of their tactics. Supporters may issue leaflets, make speeches, or, like the Moral Majority, sponsor television and radio programs to spread their message to the public. Giving away buttons, bumper stickers, and posters with slogans describing the cause can be another part of the educational process. By these methods, supporters hope to win support for their movement and decrease the strength of any opposition. Many of the smaller, less influential religious groups use educational tactics to further their goals. The leaflets handed out by members of the Jehovah's Witnesses, the Hare Krishna movement, and the Temple of Islam are all meant to educate readers to the meaning of the believers' faith.

Political Tactics Movement leaders often feel that education alone is not enough. In such cases, they seek to enforce their views through the political system. In addition to lobbying and voting for candidates sympathetic to the cause, they may hold mass meetings in Washington, deliver petitions to public officials, and organize letter-writing campaigns.

You have probably noticed that as an election approaches, the amount of mail urging you or your parents to vote a particular way or to write to local representatives, members of Congress, or the president increases rather sharply. Similarly, special appeals are made on particular controversial issues. In 1982, for example, a battle raged concerning the use of federal lands. Secretary of the Interior James Watt and others wanted to allow more federal land to be used for energy exploration and development. Environmental groups, such as the Sierra Club, opposed this policy and sought to influence public opinion by the use of strongly worded brochures about the harm that might result from ecological imbalance.

Direct Action   The most forceful tactic is direct action, which usually means going beyond the normal activities of educational or political campaigns; it may involve taking the law into one's own hands. Members of the movement decide who is "the enemy," or the main obstacle to their cause, and take action against them. Strikes such as the famous Montgomery bus boycott referred to earlier, or those of Poland's Solidarity union before the establishment of martial law in December 1981, are good examples of nonviolent direct action.

Sometimes direct action has a potential for violence, as when a group of neo-Nazis sought to march through the streets of Skokie, Illinois, a community with many Jewish people who had survived the Holocaust, Hitler's genocidal attempt to rid Germany and the rest of Europe of all Jews. After considerable pressure, the march there was canceled.

Hundreds of thousands of Americans have marched in support of nuclear disarmament, as shown here in New York City in 1982. Similar anti-nuclear-weapon demonstrations have taken place in Italy, Germany, and other European nations.

Terrorism has increased worldwide as extremists in various social movements use violence in trying to achieve their aims. Here luggage is strewn across a runway in the wake of a terrorist assault in Pakistan.

Direct action is often resorted to when leaders of social movements feel that other tactics are not succeeding in making changes as rapidly as they desire. Members may then take to the streets to protest and to show their power, or they may go underground to work in a more clandestine fashion. Underground activities characterize those groups who often call themselves "freedom fighters" but who are widely regarded as *terrorists* by others. Advocates of and participants in criminal direct action, such as armed robbery, kidnapping, airplane hijackings, and assassination, are found in a number of contemporary social movements: the Italian Red Brigades, the Popular Front for the Liberation of Palestine, the Irish Republican Army, the Basque separatists of Spain, and the Muslim opponents to the established rulers of the Philippines, among other terrorist groups.

REVIEW AND APPLICATION

1. *IDENTIFY:* Ideology, charisma, terrorist.
2. What characteristics do all social movements share? How does the Moral Majority reflect these characteristics?
3. What are three tactics that may be employed by those seeking to bring about social change?

CRITICAL THINKING: You have read in this chapter that the Moral Majority grew into a major social force in the late 1970s and early 1980s. What do you think caused the rise of the movement at that time?

4 Classification by Goals

Social movements vary considerably in aims and methods, as you have seen. One way to make the complexity of social movements easier to understand is to classify them according to their goals, as pluralist, assimilationist, reformist, and secessionist movements.

Pluralist Movements

Pluralist movements are organized to obtain recognition of the needs of a segment of the society and to have those needs satisfied. Members want to carry on their own traditions and live a style of life they find acceptable. They do not necessarily seek to convert others to their beliefs and values. The Mennonites and Hutterites, both religious minorities seeking toleration, are two pluralist movements from earlier in our history. Another example of a pluralist movement is an ethnic group organized to pressure schools to recognize its language as the primary language of its members' children. Other such movements emerge among groups that have been ridiculed, shunned, or harassed, such as homosexuals.

Assimilationist Movements

Many movements strive for inclusion within society rather than just acceptance of their right to be different. History has many examples of people who banded together in *assimilationist movements* to demand access to power and privilege being denied them. Thousands of people in the civil-rights movement and the women's movement

Native Americans were active in the struggle for civil rights and equal opportunity that took place in the 1960s. Besides demanding access to American society, Native Americans demonstrated for the return of land that they felt was rightfully theirs. Here Sioux Indians protest at Mount Rushmore in South Dakota, and demonstrators in Washington, D.C., attend a national rally.

organized to gain access to good jobs, equal pay, and better education. Mexican Americans and Native Americans have also struggled for the chance to play the more highly rewarded roles in American society. The labor movement, too, embraced assimilationist goals: not to destroy or to change society but rather to receive a bigger share of the pie.

Reformist Movements

Many social movements, known as *reformist movements,* are set up to change some specific aspect of social life. The prohibition, conservation, prison reform, and abolition movements focused on changing specific values, roles, or institutional norms. Reformist movements do not want sweeping changes in the social system. They tend to believe that certain problems can be solved by educating the public and pressuring the government to respond.

In the 1970s and early 1980s, for example, concern increased about mental hospitals. Reformers were upset by what happened to many people who ended up under inferior, custodial care, and they made efforts to reduce the number of people confined in government-supported mental hospitals. The government agencies in charge of these hospitals were petitioned by reformers who argued that smaller facilities closer to patients' homes would be more effective. Breaking down the large, impersonal, and bureaucratic organization was the goal.

During the same period, groups of lawyers led another reform movement that set out to establish that mental patients had rights that psychiatrists and hospital administrations had to respect. The emphasis here was that every American was legally protected against involuntary confinement. Yet most people didn't know their rights under the law. To publicize these rights, books

Reformist movements can succeed by making a grievance public. Five government officers were jailed after these Argentine mothers marched in the early 1980s to protest the unexplained disappearance of some 9,000 of their children.

The number of homeless people on city streets represents a growing problem in the United States. Among these homeless are "shopping-bag people," men and women who carry all their possessions with them everywhere in bags. This woman searches through a trash bin for food.

were published, meetings held, and lawyers urged to defend patients against illegal hospitalization.

Revolutionary Movements

Many societies contain political groups that believe they must overthrow the existing government to achieve their aims. The goal of these *revolutionary movements* is the complete change of the social system, usually by sudden and often by violent means. For a revolutionary movement to develop, people must feel not only that their political institu-

tions are failing to bring about necessary changes but also that they can defeat the government in power.

Once revolutionaries are in power, they frequently continue to use force to bring about changes they desire, even if there is strong resistance among some groups in the population. The new government then exercises control over the values people hold, the roles they play, and the structure of their social institutions. The workplace, the family, the school, and the church are among the institutions affected.

Alex Inkeles, a sociologist who studied the Russian Revolution, described the radical changes in the Russian countryside under Joseph Stalin's program of collectivization. Economic relations were changed. Peasant families no longer cultivated small plots of land for their landlords; instead, they worked on collective farms. A new, state-run political and economic administration was set up that regulated the workday, decided what the rate of production should be, and controlled education and the mass media.

Some 25 million farm families, constituting more than 100 million souls, were forced in the span of a few short years radically to change the whole pattern of their lives. Five million of these people, those in the families designated as "kulaks," [wealthy peasants] were dispossessed outright of their land and property, and a large proportion forcibly transplanted to other parts of the country. The Russian countryside glowed red, the sky with flames of burning peasant huts and government buildings, the ground with the blood of cattle slaughtered by the peasants and peasants slaughtered by the militia and by the flying squads of Communist workers and the agitated peasant "Committees of the Poor." Between 1928 and 1933, the cattle population fell from 70 to 38 million, sheep and goats from 147 to 50 million, and pigs from 26 to 12 million. . . . Once again famine stalked the land.

The Russian Revolution made radical changes in almost every aspect of life for millions of people living in the Russian countryside. Privately owned land was taken from its owners and "collectivized"—made into vast farms owned and run by the state. Above, a potato harvest in the Byelorussian region of the USSR.

Secessionist Movements

Some social movements are formed not to transform a society but to make that society, or a segment of it, independent. One of the best examples of a *secessionist movement* is the movement that led to the American Revolution, which you have studied in your history classes. From the time the first settlers founded Jamestown, Virginia, the first colony in the New World, in 1607, the English colonists remained loyal British subjects for more than 150 years. The colonial governments were tied to the king and Parliament, and economic policies were influenced by English needs. Whether they came for religious or economic reasons, citizens considered themselves loyal subjects of the British monarch.

Yet, in the course of time, a distinctive way of life emerged. British subjects had conquered a new wilderness, establishing a society well fitted to the new environment and quite different from that of their fellow English citizens in Europe. Tensions between colonial governments and the London government were not uncommon, but in 1763, they took a turn for the worse. A heavy taxation policy, designed to benefit England, fell very hard on the colonists. For more than a decade, they tried to improve their situation with Parliament legally, but the effort failed.

Finally, in response to English repression, the colonists formed political groups to plan together for their goals. They developed acts of resistance, worked out their ideology, and organized an army to support their position. Many people in the colonies who opposed the British decrees did not want to think about independence. Yet, by the mid-1770s, the leaders—George Washington, Thomas Jefferson, James Madison, Patrick

Henry, John Adams—believed this was necessary. The statement of their intention to separate, or secede, is that famous document you know:

> We hold these truths to be self-evident, that all men are created equal; that they are endowed by their Creator with certain unalienable rights; that among these are life, liberty, and the pursuit of happiness. That to secure these rights, governments are instituted among men. . . . That whenever any form of government becomes destructive of these ends, it is the right of the people to alter or to abolish it, and to institute a new government. . . .

About one-third of those living in America did not believe the colonies should secede. They remained loyal to the Crown and were known as Tories. Some fled to Canada.

The War of Independence, or the American Revolution, took the ideas of secession expressed in the Declaration of Independence and made them a reality. In recent history, similar secessionist movements have arisen all over the world. Independence movements throughout European colonies in Asia and Africa have succeeded in ousting the colonial power.

REVIEW AND APPLICATION

1. *IDENTIFY:* Pluralist movement, assimilationist movement, reformist movement, revolutionary movement, secessionist movement.
2. How do assimilationist movements differ from pluralist movements?
3. Explain recent reforms in mental health.
4. How do revolutionary movements maintain their power once they have overthrown a government?

CRITICAL THINKING: The leaders of the American Revolution believed . . . "that all men are created equal; that they are endowed with certain unalienable rights; that among these are life, liberty, and the pursuit of happiness." Compare this philosophy with Stalin's. With what part of the passage might Stalin have agreed? With what part of the passage might he have disagreed? Explain your response.

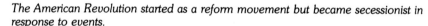

The American Revolution started as a reform movement but became secessionist in response to events.

5 Communication and Propaganda

Our study of social movements has focused on efforts to bring about change in which large numbers of people band together, ally themselves to a common ideology and a set of goals, and follow the guidance of recognized leaders. The success of such efforts is strongly influenced by the ability of the movement to get its message across through the media and to influence public opinion in its favor.

In nation-states, ideologies often are intertwined with various theories of change, which are reflected in attempts to influence public opinion. For example, evolutionary theorists may stress the idea of progress. Functionalists may emphasize harmony and compromise on social issues. Conflict-oriented politicians may tend to play up differences between social classes and to stress the advantages of a worker-dominated society.

In democratic societies like the United States, candidates for political office are constantly attempting to gauge public opinion. Indeed, much of the effort to win public office now focuses on getting across the message, via the media, that a candidate has the characteristics that people say they want in a leader. Effectiveness and reliability are among the traits that turn up as important in most elections, but the emphasis frequently shifts from election to election. Successful politicians are skillful in gauging these shifts. In a similar way, the marketing of new products or maintaining the market for an established product are both influenced by understanding and shaping public tastes. Once again, the media are an essential vehicle in this process.

Propaganda

When a television commercial attempts to sell a product or push a particular political candidate, it is easy to note that particular themes are stressed. In both types of efforts, the advertisers attempt to appeal to the values of the watchers and to show how well these values fit the product or candidate. Sociologists Alfred McClung Lee and Elizabeth Bryant Lee have identified some themes to watch for. They note that, mild though these techniques may be, they are all part of a propaganda campaign, a concerted effort to put forth particular ideas, principles, or doctrines.

First, the propagandist may use *glittering generalities*. In political contests, the emphasis is usually on the candidate's espousal of "freedom," "democracy," and some sort of a new beginning. In recent years, the emphasis has been on recapturing America's greatness by rejecting those with insufficient faith who would bring us down. Thus, there is a stress on the positive and a contrast with the negative. The message is that one candidate has all the virtues while the opponents have none.

Second, to emphasize the distinction between candidates, *name-calling* is often employed. Advertisements may stress that one candidate is in favor of "the family" or "a strong America" and that the opposition is far weaker in or is actually antagonistic to these positions. The effort is to place a negative label on the opposition in the hope that voters will always connect the label with that candidate.

Third, whether selling toothpaste or a candidate, advocates try to effect a *transfer*. Toothpaste, for example, may be shown with an attractive teenager. The candidate is shown with family members or helping in some community activity. The goal, of course, is to identify the product or candidate with other people or with efforts that the public already supports or finds appealing.

Fourth, a *testimonial* technique draws on the good will garnered by famous personalities, usually people in the entertainment or sports world. Their testimonials are a favored method to push products or candidates. Many Americans can recall popular faces now associated with a particular soft drink, automobile, or charitable cause. Similarly, political candidates often employ the campaigning skills of well-known Hollywood stars who speak on television or at fund-raising dinners.

Fifth, propagandists often employ a homespun approach—a *plain-folks technique*. People who could be your neighbors or friends are interviewed for their evaluation of a particular product or candidate. The argument is that these people, very much like you, the audience, have similar tastes and would not lead you astray.

All these techniques are used by interested parties—those who have much to gain or lose—to influence an audience. The concept of "public opinion" is primarily important in a political and economic system such as ours where candidates compete for voters and producers vie for consumers. In a totalitarian political system where there are no elections, or in an economic system that cannot produce enough for a mass market, such advertising efforts are not likely to occur. In the United States, the attempt to measure public opinion has become a prime importance in recent years.

⟨?⟩ Think back to your last session of television viewing. Which of the propaganda techniques just identified did you notice?

In a democracy, surveys help office seekers gauge public opinion. Here a poll taker conducts an interview.

Public-Opinion Polls

Public-opinion polls strive to determine attitudes on such questions as how the president of the United States is performing at any given time and whether people support a given social issue. Polling techniques have actually predicted the outcomes of national elections by drawing careful samples from as few as three thousand householders. Such efforts can be of great assistance to candidates as they plan their campaigns or as they evaluate how their "message" is coming across.

Pollsters have a much more difficult time, however, in isolating the factors that lead people to assume certain positions. Attitude formation may be based on people's personal experience or on their position in the larger society. For example, political appeals to reduce taxes usually strike a responsive chord with those who feel burdened by heavy local, state, and federal taxes. Religious leaders often exert great influence on people's attitudes when the issues involve personal morality. Labor leaders are in a position to create opinion on economic issues affecting workers' welfare. Family and friends help form people's tastes in films, books, or theater. Although polls can discover where the public stands on a given issue at a given time and can show comparisons with former times, they are much less effective in tracing these various sources of opinion.

An analysis of public-opinion polling also reveals a significant problem: frequently polls do more than measure attitudes. Their results, once announced, can actually influence the course of a political campaign. The side that is in the lead will stress the results, for example, and encourage those who are still undecided to join the "bandwagon," or the side of a winner. Or the supporters of the side that is behind may lose their enthusiasm. Thus, public opinion may be influenced by the very process of attempting to measure it.

1. *IDENTIFY:* Glittering generalities, name calling, transfer, testimonial, plain-folks technique.

2. Why is measuring public opinion so important in a country like the United States?
3. Why is polling ineffective in tracing sources of people's opinions?
4. What is one significant problem resulting from public-opinion polling?

CRITICAL THINKING: A candidate appears in a campaign commercial with his wife, children, and dog. What value of the viewers is he trying to appeal to?

6 Collective Behavior

In your everyday life, you have become accustomed to playing certain roles in a predictable manner. You also expect others to do their parts, whether it's your parent who prepares breakfast, your school-bus driver who stops at the assigned locations, or your friends who meet every Saturday night for pizza and a movie. Yet even a casual look at the daily newspaper or a glimpse of the evening television reports reveals that all is not predictable. A plane crash in a populated area, riots by settlers in disputed territory, resistance by a populace against military rule, and a huge gathering to hear a singing group are all examples of situations in which behavior is difficult to predict and hard to explain in retrospect.

In this chapter, you have studied many situations where people banded together in movements to change others' attitudes and values or to reorganize a given society. But there are times when behavior is more spontaneous and less goal-directed. This does not mean, however, that it cannot be analyzed, or that those engaged in the behavior do not have an ideology, goals, and, at times, even leaders.

Crowd and Mass

John Lofland has attempted to analyze spontaneous social events by first distinguishing between a *crowd* and a *mass*. A crowd is "a relatively large number of persons who are in one another's immediate face-to-face presence." For example, a crowd is any group of people involved in a riot; they can see each other and are influenced by each other's actions. Such events have occurred around racial issues in inner-city areas. They have also occurred at rock concerts where ticket holders literally crushed each other to gain entrance to an arena.

A mass is a "set of people who attend to a shared object of attention but who are not in one another's immediate physical vicinity." The concept of mass was illustrated clearly by the reactions of millions of Americans to the taking of American hostages in Iran in 1979. This mass reaction turned into group formation when people gathered together in communities to light candles, to pray, or to behave in other ways that showed support for their compatriots held hostage thousands of miles away.

Lofland's analysis also stresses that the emotions of the participants are a major factor in the outcome of the event. These emotions include fear, hostility, and joy.

Can you think of examples that characterize crowd fear? Think, for instance, of the panic that occurred in Cincinnati's Riverfront Coliseum on December 31, 1979. Thousands of young people were there to hear a rock concert by the Who. The tickets were mostly for unreserved, general-admission seats, and as the crowd grew to several thousand still outside the auditorium, the Who began to test their instruments inside. The sound of the music led to pushing from the rear of the crowd as latecomers surged forward to the entrances. In the ensuing press of bodies, many people fell, stumbled to their feet, and tried to beat off those who pushed against them. By the time the crowd had forced its way into the Coliseum, eleven people had died. Some of the survivors to this day remain traumatized by the events.

Other types of crowd events are based not on fear but on hostility. Examples are the race riots that have occurred in the United States, England, and elsewhere. Pent-up frustrations and anger often find their expression after a police action against a local resident. This can spark many hours of violence in which property, police officers, and individuals of other races become targets.

Of course, not all crowd reactions are characterized by fear and hostility. There are many instances of crowd joy when thousands of people come together to celebrate and re-commit themselves to some fundamental beliefs. This may occur at a religious gathering, where a charismatic leader leads the crowd in an outpouring of faith and love. It can occur at a musical event, where the sharing of sound leads to the sharing of space, food, and drink.

According to Lofland's analysis, the emotion of fear is also involved in mass reactions. There is no better example of a mass-fear response to *rumors*, or unconfirmed reports, than the incident that occurred on the evening of October 30, 1938. A weekly radio program presented a dramatic portrayal of H. G. Wells's classic story *The War of the Worlds*. Many of the listeners tuned in late and did not realize that the realistic broadcast was not the report of an authentic invasion from Mars. It has been estimated that as many as one million of the six million listeners were genuinely frightened. Many left their homes and fled the areas where the invasion was said to be occurring. In panic, thousands of others called police stations and military installations for a report on the danger.

Sports events are frequently emotional. The crowd at left enacts "The Wave" during a baseball game in Detroit's Tiger Stadium. At right, soccer fans in Belgium riot prior to a World Cup qualifying match in 1985. Thirty-nine people died and 200 were injured when a wall collapsed.

Why was there such a reaction of mass fear? The program was broadcast at a time in history when there had been many reports of the possibilities of war in Europe and of German invasions of neighboring states. The broadcast was presented in the form of a news program, with actors playing the parts of scientists and military experts commenting on what was occurring. Finally, the radio was regarded by the public as an authentic vehicle of communication. Many people felt its reports had to be taken seriously.

Two actual events serve as examples of long-lasting bases for mass hostility. The Japanese bombing of Pearl Harbor on December 7, 1941, led to nationwide outpouring of anti-Japanese feelings in this country. Thousands of Japanese, many of them United States citizens, were interned and forced to leave their homes on the West Coast.

As this cartoon shows, fads can be based on new technology. Listening to portable stereos through headphones has become so popular in the United States that some towns have felt it necessary to legislate against the use of headsets while driving or walking in traffic.

SOURCE: Drawing by Sempé; © 1981 The New Yorker Magazine, Inc.

Similar feelings were directed against the Iranian government during the 444-day period between 1979 and 1981 when fifty-two American hostages were held. Many Iranian students studying in this country were the targets of verbal and physical abuse by angry Americans. Iranians were also deported if their visas were not in order.

Both these events thus provoked mass hostility. Reactions turned into actions against people living in the United States.

Mass emotions, like crowd emotions, are not limited to fear or hostility. Mass joy can also sweep a city or a nation in the form of a musical fad, a popular fashion, or a celebration. The Beatle mania of the 1960s provides a prime example, when millions of young people gave vocal and enthusiastic support to a visiting group and its recordings. Again, the triumph of the American ice hockey team against the Russians in the Winter Olympics of 1980 created national joy and celebration.
🄿 Have you had an experience with either crowd or mass emotion? If so, write a brief description of the event.

Fashions and Fads

In small, isolated societies, entire populations may at times share the same emotions, as they similarly share the same habits and behavior, types of housing and clothing, year after year. Modern industrial societies, however, are characterized by heterogeneity and by ongoing changes in styles of clothing, housing, automobiles, even jewelry. People who follow such fashions wish to emphasize the new, the chic, and the different. Fashion helps those who want to show that they are distinctive, are of higher status, or have greater income than their neighbors.

For this reason, some governments, such as the People's Republic of China, may discourage differences in style to emphasize that social class and even sex distinctions are scorned. Thus, for a time the Chinese dressed alike, in drab uniformlike outfits. This is currently changing, however.

Fashion changes also result from the continual need of a highly productive society to find new markets for the products of its industries. Where industry lags, as in contemporary Cuba, many goods are rationed, and each person is allowed only two or three outfits of colorful though simple clothes. In complex, industrialized societies, however, wide variety exists, and demand and taste are often created by concentrated sales campaigns.

CASE STUDY: The Demand for Diamonds

An example of how fashions are set occurred in the diamond industry. Most people believe that diamonds are rare and valuable. Actually, their numbers on the market are controlled by an international cartel based in South Africa. The value of diamonds is determined by people's willingness to define diamonds as precious and to attach such sentimental importance to them that they are seldom resold. If large numbers of owners ever decided to cash in their diamonds, the market would be quickly flooded, and the price would plummet.

How did the desire for diamonds grow in the first place? According to a recent study by Edward Jay Epstein, the sale of diamonds had declined substantially in the 1930s. The South African diamond cartel hired a New York advertising agency, which developed a plan to associate diamonds with elite status and with romance. The larger the diamond worn or given, the higher the social position represented or the feeling of affection expressed. The campaign used the newly developing motion picture industry to show off diamonds on the fingers or around the necks of glamorous movie stars. Glossy photos were also placed in magazines.

Then, just after the end of World War II, diamond executives decided to enlarge sales further by concentrating on a mass market. Now, the advertising emphasized, diamonds were not just for the wealthy but for all people, especially those who were to be engaged. The romantic bond could not be concluded, so the ads suggested, until the young man had placed a diamond on the finger of his future bride. Obviously, the larger the diamond, the greater the expression of love. "A diamond is forever" became the slogan of the industry.

In the mid-1960s, the effort was extended beyond the United States, when a major advertising campaign fostered the Western fashion of diamonds in Japan. For fifteen hundred years, Japanese couples had been betrothed by drinking rice wine from the same wooden bowl. Now the giving of a diamond was to be the symbol of future devotion.

How was this accomplished? The advertisers associated diamonds with modernity, with a break from oriental tradition. They appealed to young people who desired change and who wanted to feel part of the international community. The results have been impressive. In 1967 barely 5 percent of Japanese women received a diamond engagement ring. By 1981, 60 percent of Japanese brides wore such rings. That change represents a massive shift from traditional behavior.

? Is there a fad in dress or behavior in your school at the present time? Make some observations about who seems to be following it and who seems to be ignoring it. Can you determine who started the fad? Keep an eye on it from now on to see if it is on the upswing or the decline.

A Theory of Collective Behavior

Sociologists have attempted to systematize their observations of such phenomena as public opinion and social fads into general theories that explain collective behavior. A useful theory was presented by Neil J. Smelser, who identified six conditions that are necessary for collective behavior to occur. If one of these conditions is missing, the event is less likely to happen. If all are present, it is almost certain that some collective action will take place.

Structural Conduciveness This condition relates to the surrounding environment. For example, Americans reacted to the taking of the hostages by Iranian militants because the hostages were government employees, and the government was responsible for their well-being. Without such governmental institutions, the hostages would have had no direct relationship to the American public. As it was, they had clear-cut roles and relationships to American institutions.

Structural Strain As the days passed, it became clear that the Iranian militants were intent on holding the hostages until some major concessions were made by the American government. A tense standoff occurred. The tension increased, and it became clear that a long period of uncertainty was likely. This uncertainty raised the feeling of frustration in many sectors of American society.

Generalized Belief Beyond structural conduciveness and structural strain, collective action also requires a generalized belief about what is happening. In the hostage situation, the daily television, radio, and newspaper reports fueled the public's feeling that the holding of hostages was illegal, that the hostages were in constant danger, and that the Iranian militants were making unreasonable demands. As a result, there was a general belief that some action had to be taken to save the hostages and to salvage American honor.

Precipitating Factors All these conditions may not be enough to cause action unless some particular event occurs to set off collective behavior. During the hostage situation, violent action was occasionally taken against Iranian students living in the United States when the Iranians attempted to march in support of their government. For some Americans, this act was a direct provocation.

Mobilization for Action A fifth ingredient, according to Smelser, is the ability of people to organize to express their feelings about a situation. Most of the action taken against Iranian students in this country occurred because their marches were publicized in advance, by both their own groups and the media. In addition, American students were available on nearby campuses to stage counterdemonstrations. At times, these were peaceful; occasionally they led to direct confrontation.

Mechanisms of Social Control Whether the collective behavior occurs and what form and direction it takes are influenced by the degree of social control exercised by the authorities. Where the police are alert and in sufficient force, confrontations can be limited or avoided. In the Iranian case, this was often the case as demonstrators and counterdemonstrators were kept blocks apart.

? Review Smelser's six conditions. Now try to apply them to some of the situations cited in this section, such as the panic at the Cincinnati Who concert, the fashionableness of diamonds, the rumored invasion from Mars, and race riots.

REVIEW AND APPLICATION

1. *IDENTIFY:* Crowd, mass, rumor.
2. According to Lofland, what are some emotions that cause reactions in both crowd and mass behavior?
3. Cite some reasons for fashion changes.
4. What really determines the value of diamonds? How have diamond executives encouraged the sale of diamonds?
5. According to Smelser, what are the six conditions that are necessary for collective behavior to occur? How can Smelser's six conditions be applied to the taking of hostages by Iranian militants in 1979?

CRITICAL THINKING: Compare the conditions leading up to the American Revolution with those in the Iran hostage situation. Does the American Revolution follow Smelser's theory as well as the hostage situation does? Cite examples from pages 310–311 that fit the descriptions of the six conditions that are necessary for collective behavior to occur.

Recap

Theorists of social change try to explain not only what has happened but why. Proponents of the evolutionary theory emphasize the inevitability of progress, with societies advancing from the simple to the complex. Conflict theorists view change as a result of struggle, whether for power or status. Functionalists argue that change maintains a society's equilibrium.

A key to social change lies in the tensions in any given social order caused by differences in values or by unmet needs. When groups of people come to believe that they have no chance within the existing order to fulfill their desires, they may organize social movements to achieve change. Whatever the basic issue, each social movement has an ideology, leaders, goals, and tactics.

According to sociologists, social movements may be classified as pluralist, assimilationist, revolutionary, or secessionist. Reform movements constitute a fifth category. Pluralist and assimilationist movements strive to gain better acceptance for themselves within the existing society; reform movements want improvements; secessionist and revolutionary movements aim at overthrowing the existing order.

The success of any given movement depends on its ability to influence public opinion in its favor. Five propaganda techniques that are often used are glittering generalities, name-calling, transfer, testimonials, and the "plain-folks" technique. Polls, in addition to measuring public attitudes, can influence events as people "join the bandwagon" or lose enthusiasm in response to poll results.

John Lofland has analyzed less goal-directed collective behavior, such as that of a crowd or a mass. The behavior of masses can often be manipulated by those who wish to create fashions and fads for economic profit. Neil Smelser devised a theory that identifies the social conditions that substantially determine whether collective behavior will occur and what form it will take.

Key Terms

Define the following:

systemic change	terrorist	glittering generalities
evolutionary theory	pluralist movement	name-calling
conflict theory	assimilationist	transfer
functionalist theory	movement	testimonial
social movement	reformist movement	plain-folks technique
institutionalized	revolutionary	crowd
ideology	movement	mass
charisma	secessionist movement	rumor

Applying Sociology

1. A social movement is often composed of a number of groups that share some ideological points and goals but may differ in others. Choose one social movement to investigate in depth and write a paper about its history, including its origins, the organizations that presently comprise its membership, and the splinter groups that have emerged.

2. Does the social movement you selected in Application 1 seem to reflect evolutionary, conflict, or functionalist theory? Does it seem to combine these theories in any way? Give examples to justify your answer.

3. Movements must have local as well as national leaders. Seek out a movement in your community and find out who the leaders are. Are these people mentioned in the local newspaper? Do they give public talks, chair meetings, write articles? What other roles do they play as leaders of a movement?

4. Find a parent, friend, or acquaintance who has been involved at some time in a social movement. Ask them such questions as these: Why did you join? How active a member were or are you? What are, or were, the goals of the movement? What tactics were used? What changes, if any, did the movement help bring about? What goals were not met?

5. Look through newspapers or news magazines for reports on a social movement. What kinds of activities is it engaged in? Who are the leaders, and what are they like? What does the movement want to achieve—that is, what are its goals? Who are the movement's opponents?

6. You are in charge of a television talk show well known for its controversial guests. To prepare for a series of shows on current social movements, your staff agrees to the following plan:

   (a) You will look into some social movements that have recently been given TV and newspaper coverage. Your research will focus on identifying the leaders of the movement.

   (b) Several leaders from different types of social movements will be invited to appear on your show on consecutive nights.

   (c) You will prepare a series of questions for the leaders that will focus on the movement's ideology, goals, and tactics.

   Now do the research suggested by the plan and report to the staff, actually the entire class, about the people you want to invite and the questions you want to ask.

7. As a bulletin-board activity, collect articles and pictures that illustrate any protracted campaign to convince the public about some product or, if an election is coming up, some political candidate.

Extended Readings

Ellen Hawkes, "Willie Nelson's Harvest of Hope," *Ladies' Home Journal*, September 1987, p. 88, 90.

1. What motivated Willie Nelson?
2. What has his organization done to help farmers?

Anastasia Toufexis, "Silver Bullets for the Needy," *Time*, March 16, 1987, pp. 72–3.

1. How does the current volunteer movement differ from one that affected campuses in the 1960s?
2. How have colleges rewarded volunteers?

Wendy White, "Putting the Brakes on Drunk Driving," *Teen*, March 1987, pp. 22–27, p. 82.

1. What purpose or set of goals is the group called SADD striving toward?
2. Describe a tactic used by the organization to achieve these ends.

Social Studies Skills

Seeing Others' Point of View In the United States, people wear a wide variety of clothing. How would a government official of the People's Republic of China probably view this diversity? Base your answer on what you have read in Chapter 13 about the Chinese.

Recognizing propaganda techniques
Propaganda is used liberally in political campaigns. Imagine you are running for president of your class. Make up five campaign slogans, using each of the following propaganda techniques explained on page 312.

(a) glittering generalities
(b) name-calling
(c) transfer
(d) testimonial
(e) plain folks

Detecting propaganda in advertising
Advertising is sometimes referred to as the art of persuasion, and propaganda techniques are used freely to get across the advertiser's message. Reread "Case Study: The Demand for Diamonds" on page 317. Identify the propaganda techniques that advertisers used to increase the desire for diamonds.

(a) in the United States during the 1930s,
(b) in the United States after World War II, and
(c) in Japan during the 1960s.

Explain your answers.

Critical Thinking

1. *Recognizing Values:* One aspect of social movements discussed in this chapter is terrorism. Terrorists are found in a number of social movements, and the number of terrorist actions has increased dramatically in the past decade. What values are shown in the actions of terrorists? How do their beliefs differ from your beliefs?

2. *Evaluating Samples:* Public opinion polls are explained on page 313. Suppose an opinion poll were put in the *New York Times* newspaper surveying the television viewing habits of Americans. Readers would fill in the survey and send it in a postage paid envelope. How strong would this survey be?

UNIT APPLICATION

Breaking Social Barriers

In 1946, Brooklyn Dodgers president Branch Rickey secretly decided to hire the first black player for major league baseball in the 20th century. Since the 1890s, professional baseball had been totally segregated. The major leagues accepted only white players. Blacks played in all-black leagues, travelling from town to town performing stunts and comedy in local parades in an attempt to drum up paying customers to watch an evening game.

For his attempt to break the color bar, Rickey chose Jackie Robinson, an outstanding athlete who had earned varsity letters at UCLA in football, basketball, track, and baseball. Robinson was a competitive player who had fought discrimination in school and in the Army.

After a great deal of preliminary research, Rickey finally met with Robinson. In a three hour discussion, Rickey warned Robinson about the special responsibility that the first black major league player would have. "He portrayed the hostile teammate, the abusive opponent, the insulting fan, the obstinate hotel clerk. Rickey challenged the black man with racial epithets . . . Robinson finally responded, 'Mr. Rickey, do you want a ballplayer who's afraid to fight back?' He (Rickey) had awaited this moment. 'I want a player with guts enough not to fight back,' he roared." (Tygiel, p. 66)

Jackie Robinson joined the Dodgers in 1947 and quickly became a great star. Initially, the graceful infielder had to withstand insults of all kinds. Many times opposing players tried to spike him at second base, attempting to gash his leg. He always played down these incidents to the press. Robinson's influence went well beyond sports. He was a national hero to blacks and to many whites. Within a few years many baseball teams were filled with outstanding black players. Today, blacks make up about 20% of all major league players. Some of Robinson's impact is reflected in the observation of Red Barber, the Dodgers' well-known Southern announcer who had opposed Mr. Rickey's "experiment." "I know that if I have achieved any understanding and tolerance in my life . . . if I have been able to follow a little better the great second commandment, which is to love thy neighbor, it all stems from this . . . I thank Jackie Robinson. He did far more for me than I did for him."[1]

[1]The material in this unit application is taken from Jules Tygiel, *Jackie Robinson and his Legacy*, New York: Vintage Books, 1983.

Using and Analyzing Concepts

1) Was Branch Rickey's method of integrating baseball the only way it could have been done? What might have happened if he had signed two or three players at the same time so that all the pressure would not be on one person? Why do you think Rickey chose the route he did?

2) Many observers feel that professional sports still bears signs of inequality. Despite the presence of outstanding black baseball stars throughout the major leagues, only one has been appointed manager and virtually no one has made it into the teams' upper management ranks. As of 1987, blacks held just 17 of 879 top administrative jobs in baseball.

Several explanations are offered for this dismal statistic. Some baseball executives contend that blacks qualified to fill management slots tend to be lured away from the sport by the chance to make more money in other fields. Some executives claim that black managerial candidates are often deficient in minor league managing experience. Unfortunately, others side with the view of Al Campanis, a former vice president for player personnel at Robinson's old team, the Dodgers. In an interview in 1987 Campanis remarked that the reason why there are so few black baseball executives and managers is that blacks fall short on natural ability when it comes to the challenge of management. Many people were upset by the racist tone of Campanis' comments, causing him to be fired from the Dodgers' organization.

Suppose Branch Rickey approached you to design a plan to integrate blacks and other minorities into these positions in the next few years. What kind of plan would you propose? Whom would you consult for advice and assistance? Compare the plan you devise with others in the class. Are there alternative ideas about paths to integration?

3) Interview someone old enough to remember when Jackie Robinson entered baseball. What kinds of events do they remember? Did they regard Robinson as a hero and an agent of change? If not, how did they define his role? To whom would they compare him today?

Examine the interview materials collected by the class. Based on this evidence, would you classify Jackie Robinson as an important figure in history?

SOCIAL PROBLEMS

Unit Focus

What causes "social problems"? People do. And, according to sociologists, the actions that produce social problems are rooted in the very nature of society.

To understand social problems, it is necessary to look at the social, political, and economic conditions that produce and perpetuate racial and ethnic tensions, poverty, crime, and other social ills. It is important to consider not only the people who commit deviant acts but also the social contexts in which these people live. Many theories have been offered to explain why societies malfunction and why groups and individuals can fail to fit into society. This unit examines some of these theories.

Unit Six also discusses several of the larger social problems that have arisen with technological progress. Some of these problems, such as overpopulation and pollution, are worldwide. They have the potential to affect the entire earth and all of its inhabitants.

Applying Sociology

- What causes social problems?
- What social problems exist in your community?
- Compare the social problems in your community with social problems for the nation as a whole.
- What social problems affect all nations?

This garbage dump near Manhattan, New York, like many others in the country, is full to capacity. What to do about the nation's waste is a pressing issue.

Minorities and Discrimination

Chapter Preview

● **Before you read,** look up the following key terms in the glossary to become familiar with their definitions:

intergroup conflict	dominant group	minority group
ethnocentrism	scapegoat theory	amalgamation
assimilation	pluralism	accommodation

● **As you read,** think about answers to the following questions:

1. What distinguishes minority groups from dominant groups?
2. What causes prejudice?
3. What forms does discrimination take?
4. How do minority groups react to discrimination?

Sections in this Chapter

1. Dominant and Minority Groups
2. Prejudice and Its Causes
3. Patterns of Discrimination
4. Reactions to Discrimination

Chapter Focus

A striking feature of almost every modern nation is its mixture of peoples. It would be hard to find any country in the world whose people all share one culture.

Many people think that a mixed society is better. An ideal society, they argue, is made up of people of different races, national origins, and religions living in peace. Such a society can provide an enriching variety of choices, from exotic foods to interesting ideas. But there are problems, too. All too often there is conflict instead of harmony. A look at newspaper headlines over even a short period of time indicates that racial, religious, and ethnic conflict is widespread.

This chapter considers the roles of dominant and minority groups in society. It examines the nature and kinds of prejudice and discrimination that many minority groups face.

Using Sociologists' Tools

● **Observe** evidence of racial harmony and tension in your community.

● **Describe** the sources of tension between different social groups.

● **Analyze** the effects on the attitudes of those in the "dominant" group when school assemblies or local festivals celebrate ethnic diversity.

● **Predict** what your community would be like if everyone had the same racial, religious, or ethnic background.

Members of a black fraternity at the University of Illinois share good times and bad.

1 Dominant and Minority Groups

A common situation in many countries, including our own, is *intergroup conflict*. Such conflict frequently occurs between groups or social categories that differ in certain traits, such as skin color, religion, language, national origin, social class, and ideology.

In most cases of intergroup conflict, one group is dominant. The *dominant group* is in a position of power. Usually it has some sort of control over the opposing group or groups, which gives it a chance to enjoy certain privileges. It may have the better schools, jobs, neighborhoods, and so on. Tensions arise, in most cases, over the dominant group's power and privileges. The lower, or subordinate, groups—the *minority groups*—see themselves as victims of *discrimination*.

Discrimination may be defined as unfair treatment of people, usually because of their race, nationality, sex, or religion. Discrimi-

nation is usually caused by *prejudice*, which will be examined more closely later in this chapter. Prejudice is an unfair or false belief about a person or group of people, usually that the group has inferior or undesirable traits. When such beliefs are put into action, the result is discrimination.

Often the dominant group defends its power and privilege by claiming that it is superior in one area or another. The white- or black- or yellow-skinned group claims that it is on top because it has superior traits. A religious group may claim that it has the only "right" system of beliefs. A tribe or other cultural group may claim that its value system and lifeways are best.

Minorities reject the dominant group's claims of superiority. Some minorities say that *they* should be on top. For example, a group may say, "Our people were here first.

329

Newspapers reflect the many conflicts raging among the world's peoples. In each of these headlines, which type of conflict is in evidence—racial, religious, or ethnic?

We have a right to be in control." Other minorities simply seek some sort of equality—political, economic, religious, or other.

Sociological Minorities

To sociologists, the term "minority" means mainly that a group is in a lower position in the society even though it may be much larger in sheer numbers than the dominant group. This is the case of blacks in South Africa, who are a numerical majority but a sociological minority. They receive unequal treatment. Blacks outnumber whites in some parts of the United States, as do Native Americans and Mexican Americans in some

other areas. But if they are kept in a lower position in these places, they, too, are sociological minorities.

An individual may be a member of a minority in one society and a member of the dominant group in another. Jews in Israel are dominant; in the Soviet Union, they are clearly members of a minority group. In Singapore, the Chinese are the most powerful element and others, such as Malays and East Indians, are subordinate. But in Los Angeles, San Francisco, New York, and Boston, the Chinese or descendants of Chinese immigrants are part of a distinct minority group.

According to Louis Wirth, minority groups generally share the following characteristics:

A minority must be distinguishable from the dominant group by physical or cultural marks. In the absence of such identifying characteristics it blends into the rest of the population in the course of time.

Minorities objectively occupy a disadvantageous position in the society. As contrasted with the dominant group they are debarred from certain opportunities—economic, social, and political.

The members of minority groups are held in lower esteem and may even be objects of contempt, hatred, ridicule, and violence.

They are generally socially isolated and frequently spatially separated.

They suffer from more than the ordinary amount of social and economic insecurity.

And, Wirth wrote, because of these attributes "minorities tend to develop a set of attitudes, forms of behavior, and other subjective characteristics which tend further to set them apart."

In a given society, however, a minority group may occupy strong positions in certain localities. For example, although American blacks are collectively a minority, in some cities they are not only a numerical majority but also the dominant political force. In sociology, we limit the term "minority group" to subgroups that suffer disadvantages because of prejudice and discrimination. Children are a subordinate group in most cultures, but we don't call them a minority group. In sociology, "minority" refers mainly to racial, religious, and nationality groups. Let's look at each of these categories.

Racial Groups If one wants to divide humans into statistical categories, it makes sense to group them by general similarities. From ancient times to the present, the Western world has tended to separate the human species into *races*. Skin color—black, white, red, yellow—has served as the principal divider. Other outward features, such as head form, shape of nose, height, and the color, texture, and amount of body hair, have also been used as guides for grouping.

The problem is that too often appearances are assumed to be related to culture traits, intelligence, and morality. Physical traits have nothing to do with these things, although many who use the term "race" seem to believe that there is a relationship. Since "race" is such a loaded word, some modern anthropologists have decided not to use it. Those who continue to use it define a race as a category of persons who share a certain combination of inherited physical traits.

When most people in the United States and in many other places speak of racial groups, they use these combinations of physical features as social labels. To most social scientists, what is popularly called a "racial group" is actually more of a social category than a purely biological one. Thus, a race, in the sociological sense, is any group that is socially defined, treated differently, or given a different status because of physical features.

If American society made no value judgment about racial ancestry, it would matter little what one was called or into which

Ours is a multiethnic society, composed of different races and subcultures and offering possibilities both for cultural enrichment and for conflict. This street scene in New York City demonstrates this ethnic diversity.

pigeonhole one was placed. But in a race-conscious society like the United States, those who are "colored," as opposed to "white," have too often been placed in inferior positions and treated accordingly. Thus, "racial" differences have often served as a means for labeling and placing people according to how they look.

In fact physical appearance doesn't tell us that one person's way of life is better than another person's. It does, however, have much to do with the way a person acts and is treated. As one young black American put it, "It is not the fact that I am black but the meaning of being black that gives me my special character."

Again, one must be careful not to confuse race with culture. White and black southerners in the United States share more culture traits with one another than the white southerners do with their English forebears. Black southerners share more culture traits with white southerners than with their African forebears.

Religious Groups Compared to race, religion is quite easy to define. Religions are, after all, organized bodies whose members have certain beliefs and practice certain rituals. Catholicism, Judaism, Protestantism, Islam, and Buddhism are all religions. Those who belong are known as Catholics, Jews, Protestants, Muslims, and so forth.

You read in Chapter 7 about nations with one official religion. Sometimes toleration is the rule in such states, but in other cases, the members of religious minorities suffer persecution. Many Europeans who settled in America sought refuge here from religious hatred. In the United States, luckily, attempts to use religion as a basis for ranking people have rarely worked. Here the idea of freedom of religion has been widely accepted, far more so than that of racial equality. Such is not the case in many other countries today.

Nationality Groups Nationality, like race and religion, divides people and often causes conflict among them. Where you come from, the language you speak, the customs you

In the United States, freedom to follow the customs of one's religion is guaranteed by the Constitution and is widely accepted as a basic value. The skullcaps, called yarmulkes, worn by Jewish males are evidence of American religious diversity.

share, often the names you are given, all merge to form a sense of nationality. Sometimes the term refers to a particular cultural group within a nation. The Basques in Spain, for example, have a unique language and culture. They think of themselves as a nation. Belgium is really made up of two nationalities: the French-speaking Walloons and the Dutch-speaking Flemish. Yugoslavia is made up of several nationalities: Serbs, Croats, Slovenes, Bosnians, Macedonians, and others. The Soviet Union recognizes the existence of a large number of separate nationalities living under its flag; the Russians are simply the dominant group.

Sometimes political boundaries separate the members of a "nationality." The Lapps live in northern Norway, Sweden, and Finland. The borders of Greece, Bulgaria, and Yugoslavia divide the Macedonians.

All the nonindependent peoples just cited occupy homelands that are parts of one or more larger nations. Each people's attachment to the homeland goes back hundreds, and sometimes even thousands, of years. Other national groups are relatively recent settlers in a new land. Besides the Malays, the Republic of Malaysia has large numbers of Chinese and East Indians. Sometimes the word "ethnic" is used to refer to these "outsiders." Thus, throughout Southeast Asia, one hears the expression "ethnic Chinese."

The United States is a mixture of nationality groups. A few of the many nationalities that make up the population of the United States are indicated in the accompanying table from the alumni magazine of the University of Pittsburgh. The names of 7,500

CHART SKILL   *What does this sample of names from a university student directory indicate about the national backgrounds of Americans?*

WHAT'S IN A NAME?

Nationality	Total	Samples of Names
Chinese	48	Chang, Lee, Lim, Oh, Pong, Wong, Wu, Yee
Czechoslovak	139	Bilohlavek, Buchko, Droby, Janasek, Kacmar
English	796	Allen, Barker, Clark, Cook, Hall, Hill, Miller, Taylor
French	96	Beaumont, Belle, Bourgue, Carabin, Delong, Faux
German	1,115	Ackermann, Brittenbaugh, Dietrich, Eichenlaub, Froehlich
Greek	28	Antinopoulos, Apostolakis, Karnavas, Kladitis, Pallas
Hispanic	450	Benitez, Flores, Garcia, Gonzalez, Guerrero, Herrera, Salgado, Sanchez
Irish	646	Ahearn, Brannigan, Callahan, Gleason, Hurley, Maloney, O'Neill
Italian	812	Adonizio, Bascelli, DeAngelis, Francellini, Gentile, Nardo
Lithuanian	18	Abramitis, Dudemas, Kaleida, Miskihis, Shukis, Toaras
Norwegian	13	Berg, Hansen, Larsen, Slomberg, Slota, Strandberg, Strom
Polish	316	Bajkowski, Bednarek, Chybrzynski, Matuszak, Sapolsky
Russian	158	Aleseief, Ekimoff, Fetcanko, Ivanoff, Krushin, Tabachnik
Scottish	410	Andrews, Baird, Beatty, Lang, McFeaters, Scott, Stewart
Swedish	70	Anderson, Freeberg, Holmquist, Persson, Peterson, Uhlmann
Yugoslav	196	Bosiljevac, Bradjic, Gluscic, Javonovich, Pavlovich

students in the *Pitt Student Directory* were examined to identify those which seemed to indicate a national origin. Only a small sample is included here.

More thorough research would be required to determine how many of these names had been "Anglicized"—that is, changed from a foreign-sounding name to a more familiar English or American one. Thus, Peters might originally have been Petropoulos, Mansfield might have been Feldmann, and Davis might have been Davidowich. The names of many immigrants to the United States were changed, either by the immigrants themselves or with the flick of a pen by immigration officials at Ellis Island, where thousands of hopeful new Americans were admitted.

Ethnic Groups The word "ethnic" is often popularly used to refer to nationality. But in the field of sociology, it has come to have a broader meaning, sometimes referring to racial, sometimes to religious, and sometimes to nationality groups—often to a combination of all three. Chinese Malaysians, Italian Australians, Irish Americans, and Polish Americans are considered ethnic divisions. So, too, are certain groups of blacks, Jews, and some of the others discussed earlier under racial or religious labels. Groups whose members share a unique social and cultural heritage passed on from one generation to the next are known as *ethnic groups*.

Ethnic groups are often identified by their patterns of family life, language, recreation, religion, and other customs. Ethnic groups often live—by force or by choice—in their own sectors or neighborhoods. Above all else, members of ethnic groups feel a closeness with those who share their traditions and their status in society. They may feel a sense of pride in the distinctive patterns of their culture.

A Mexican American, a Polish American, or an "old-stock" American learns who "we" (the insiders) are and who "they" (the outsiders) are from parents, friends, and teachers. This knowledge gives members of the ethnic group both a self-image and images of others. If the socialization process works, these people take on the cultural norms and values of their group.

[?] Do you think of yourself as a member of a particular ethnic group? Why? If you do, what is this group and how would you describe it?

Ethnic pride is not limited to minority groups. Members of dominant groups may also feel pride in their ancestry and the achievements of their people. Note how one American worker expressed this feeling of pride: "I'm an American. White. Protestant. American. My ancestors settled this country and I'm proud of them. They brought civilization to this continent. They built it. I get excited when I go to Deerfield and see the old tavern or to Williamsburg. I love the fife and drum corps on the Fourth of July. I enjoy the meetings of the D.A.R. After all, those are my people. No nonsense. Proud. Good American stock."

Members of ethnic groups often see their ways of life as better than those of others. This attitude was given the name *ethnocen-*

GRAPH SKILL The United States grew as a nation of immigrants, although the percentage of the population born in foreign countries has declined through the years. When did the percentage of foreign-born begin to decline? When did this percentage reach its lowest point? What factors account for the foreign-born rise in 1980?

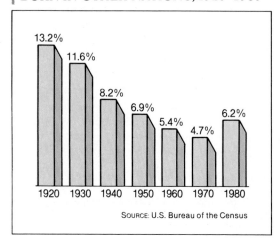

PERCENTAGE OF U.S. POPULATION BORN IN OTHER NATIONS, 1920–1980

13.2% 11.6% 8.2% 6.9% 5.4% 4.7% 6.2%

1920 1930 1940 1950 1960 1970 1980

Source: U.S. Bureau of the Census

W Miller

"Forgive me, dear, for asking, but were you as ethnic when we were first married?"

trism by sociologist William Graham Sumner, who used it to describe a people's sense of superiority and use of its own cultural standards to judge others. As he put it, ethnocentrism is the tendency by members of a group "to exaggerate and intensify everything in their own folkways which differentiates them from others." Ethnocentrism is a key factor in prejudice. The following example from our country's history illustrates the results of narrow, ethnocentric thinking:

In the summer of 1901 I proposed to bring my family from Los Angeles to San Francisco. I tried many times to find a suitable house outside of Chinatown so that my children might be properly brought up in the ways of the Americans, that in the years to come they may perform the duties of American citizenship.

I found a good flat with five rooms and bath, and the rent was within my ability to pay. The landlady was willing also to rent the house to me after having heard the explanation I made regarding myself. The rent was paid and preparation was made

for moving in, but after two days the landlady came to my office and returned the money to me and explained the situation: the whole neighborhood had risen in arms against the idea of having a Chinese family in their midst, and since the landlady would not give up the house to me it was out of the question to move in, so my first attempt to find a home outside of the district where my own people live was a flat failure.

A few weeks later I again tried my luck, and in the course of an afternoon, I found two houses which I thought would be suitable to me, since they were not far from Chinatown and the rent was not exorbitant.[1] The agents kindly made arrangements to rent the premises to me but when the landlords [learned] of the nationality of their prospective tenants all arrangements were annulled.

After all these failures, I was not yet dismayed. I resolved to try again and hoped for better results. Accordingly, one

[1]unreasonably expensive

Feelings of ethnic identity and pride are expressed through ethnic and religious observances. Shown here, clockwise from top, are the Nisei Festival, celebrated by second-generation Japanese Americans; the Chinese New Year, celebrated by Chinese Americans; and a gathering of Scottish and Irish Americans.

ideal afternoon, after having gone through the rush of business, I sallied forth putting aside the memory of all previous defeats from my mind. I found a flat on Mason Street near Sacramento, which I thought was the ideal place for a home. The landlord was a good-natured Frenchman. He had no race prejudice in his mind and what he had there was only dollars and cents. So he agreed to rent the place to me provided his other tenants would not object and that he would let me know one way or the other in two days.

At the end of the two days I called at his house and he told me that it was out of the question to rent me the house since the other tenants objected strenuously to renting the flat to a Chinese family. I was greatly disappointed but not the least surprised. I had the temerity[1] to ask him what family objected to my living there, and he replied that it was a family of negroes. That was the last straw that broke the back of my buoyancy of hope. I then repeated again and again to myself saying, if negroes even object to my getting a house outside of Chinatown, how can I ever succeed in getting a place where no one objects. From that time on I never made another move. The proverbial Chinese perseverance seemed to have left me for good.

This Vietnamese father and son wait patiently at an immigration processing center in New York.

? What does this account tell us about how people may view each other? Who are the "we's" and who are the "they's"?

The type of discrimination the Chinese American apartment hunter encountered is not the only way in which a people may be set apart. Sometimes their own *ethnicity* sets them apart. Ethnicity is the degree to which ethnic identity is held to be important by individuals, groups, or societies. A person's ethnicity reflects the extent to which he or she feels, or is made to feel, part of some ethnic group. Here is how one Polish American worker describes himself:

My family has been here for four generations; that's a lot. My great-grandfather came over here, from near Cracow. I've never been to Poland. I'll never go there. Why should I? It's in your blood. It's in your background. But I live *here*. My wife is the same, Polish. We're just like other people in this country, but we have memories, Polish memories, that's what my grandfather used to say: "John, don't let your kids forget that once upon a time the family was in Poland!" How *could* I forget? My wife won't let me. She says you have to stay with your own people. We don't have only Polish people living near us, but there are a lot. Mostly we see my family and my wife's family on the weekends, so there's no time to spend doing anything else. . . .

I don't know who's *really* an American. There are guys I work with, they're Italian

[1]boldness

and Irish. They're different from me, even though we're all Catholics. You see what I mean? We're buddies on the job. We do the same work. We drink our coffee together and sit there eating lunch. But you leave and you go home and you're back with your own people. I don't just mean my family, no. It's more than your wife and kids; it's everything in your life.

? Do you have feelings of ethnic identity? Explain them. Does a society tend to benefit or to lose when its citizens retain a sense of ethnic identity? Under what conditions might the opposite be true?

Minorities in Conflict

Tensions exist not only between dominant groups and minorities but also between minorities, particularly when they are competing for limited resources and jobs. For example, economic rivalry caused conflict between Irish and blacks in Civil War days and betweeen the Irish and Chinese immigrants who worked on the railroads in the late nineteenth century. More recently it has caused tension between blacks and Puerto Ricans in northern cities, between blacks and Cuban exiles in Florida, and between Chicanos and Native Americans in the Southwest.

Sometimes an inability to live peaceably with the ways of life of others, or culture conflict, is a cause of disagreement. For example, in one Chicago neighborhood, immigrants from Middle Eastern countries amplified the Muslim call to prayer that the Koran requires five times a day. Other residents objected. It was not the exercise of Islam they objected to, they said. Rather, they were bothered by the noise, which disturbed the peace.

Sometimes minority tensions are complicated by an uneasy association, such as has occasionally occurred between some Jewish Americans and blacks. Both groups have a long history of suffering. Partly from a sense of shared experience with blacks, Jews were strong supporters of the black struggle for civil rights. In fact, Martin Luther King, Jr., said, "it would be impossible to record the contribution that Jewish people have made

toward the Negro's struggle for freedom—it has been so great."

When tension appears between blacks and Jews, some sociologists claim that it is based on the circumstances of the inner city. There white merchants and landlords, many of whom are Jewish, sometimes represent white economic power to the black residents. Other social scientists see economic causes as less important than certain political issues. For example, Jews who support Israel may find themselves in conflict with certain black supporters of the Palestinian Liberation Movement. These blacks see the Palestinians as fellow sufferers, while Jews see them as a threat to the existence of Israel. Despite these difficulties, there is considerable opinion that the ties that have long bound the two minorities together are basically strong and that the old alliance should be maintained for the good of both.

A relationship between peoples cannot always be maintained by voluntary cooperation, however. Sometimes an institutionalized system of ethnic stratification exists among ethnic groups. Minority conflict is held in check by a rigid system that prevents all social mobility. In the United States, fortunately, the idea of equality of opportunity for all and the constitutional guarantees in the Bill of Rights tend to minimize stratification and to leave open the avenues by which people can rise.

In some other countries, however, stratification is enforced by laws. For example, in South Africa, the Afrikaners, or descendants of the first Dutch settlers, and the English are the dominant groups. Then come the Asians, mainly from India, and the Cape Coloured, who are of mixed racial ancestry, usually European combined with Hottentot or Bushman. At the bottom are the Africans. Each group enjoys less power and social prestige than the one above. The regulations that govern the economic, social, political, and housing arrangements of each group are called *apartheid*.

On pages 343-344 is an account of one man's experiences in South Africa. The various institutions of that society—schools, industry, government—systematically deny equal opportunity to certain groups. When this occurs, the society is practicing *institutional racism*.

REVIEW AND APPLICATION

1. *IDENTIFY:* Intergroup conflict, dominant group, minority group, discrimination, prejudice, race, ethnic group, ethnocentrism, ethnicity, apartheid, institutional racism.

2. How does prejudice differ from discrimination?
3. What are some basic divisions between people other than race that become sources of conflict?

CRITICAL THINKING: Prejudice against minority groups takes many forms. Race, religion, nationality, ethnicity, and gender are all sources of prejudicial attitudes. When prejudice leads to unfair treatment of a minority group, sociologists say discrimination is being practiced. What is the difference between prejudice and discrimination? Explain your response.

2 Prejudice and Its Causes

As you read earlier, prejudice refers to beliefs and feelings, whereas discrimination refers to harmful actions. Thus, although prejudice and discrimination are related, they are not the same thing. The difference between prejudice as an attitude and discrimination as behavior was summed up by an English judge in talking to nine youths convicted of race rioting in London: "Everyone irrespective of the color of his skin is entitled to walk through our streets with head held erect and free from fear. . . . These courts will uphold [these rights]. . . . Think what you like . . . but once you translate your dark thoughts into savage acts, the law will punish you and protect your victim."

The Roots of Prejudice

It is easy to document cases of institutional racism. It is more difficult to account for the attitudes that cause it. Why do real or imagined differences in physical or cultural characteristics lead people to develop negative and hostile feelings about others? Why do members of certain groups believe that members of other groups are inferior?

Social scientists who have studied prejudice disagree about its cause. Some emphasize psychological factors. Others blame cultural training, whereby the views of the dominant group in society are accepted as guiding principles. Still others suggest that

the structure of society itself is responsible. Finally, some see prejudice as the result of a combination of forces.

The Psychological Dimension Social scientists who emphasize the psychological causes of prejudice have developed the so-called *scapegoat theory:* when people are unable to achieve their goals but cannot directly attack the cause of their failures, they vent their anger on a weaker person or group, the scapegoat. For instance, a woman frustrated in her office work might shout at her child instead of confronting her boss.

Scapegoating on a national scale occurred in Nazi Germany. In the 1920s, after Germany's defeat in World War I, Adolf Hitler found an especially receptive audience among the middle and working classes, which had suffered the most severe economic dislocations. Blaming the Jews for the nation's economic and social disorders gave people the satisfaction of having someone lower on the social scale than themselves.

Another psychological theory about prejudice connects a certain type of personality with antidemocratic ideas. Some social scientists hypothesized that a person with what they called an *authoritarian personality* was prone to prejudice. In attempting to prove their hypothesis, researchers gathered background information on hundreds of students and adults. They then asked their subjects to

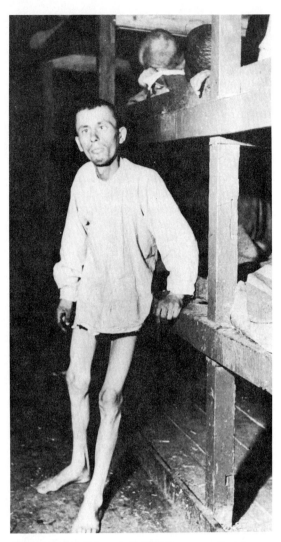

The most horrifying example of scapegoating occurred in Nazi Germany, where millions of Jews were blamed for the nation's ills and sent to die in concentration camps. This photo was taken in the concentration camp at Buchenwald, Germany, when it was liberated by the Allied forces in 1945.

Those classified as antidemocratic were found to be extremely conservative, highly conventional, and intolerant of unconventional behavior, values, and beliefs. They were also judged to have the following attitudes or personality characteristics: (1) a tendency to glorify power; (2) a tendency to view people as good or bad and things as black or white; (3) deep concern with status and toughness; (4) a view of the world as a jungle; (5) cynicism about human nature; and (6) a tendency to blame others rather than themselves for misdeeds and trouble. They often viewed outsiders with hostility.

Critics attacked this theory of the authoritarian personality almost from the time the results of the study were first published. Sociologists and political scientists suggested that the conclusions resulted from slanting the questions to elicit particular responses. Subsequent research with more neutral questions has demonstrated that authoritarians are found on both the extreme right and the extreme left.

Critics have also found fault with the researchers' follow-up choices. By interviewing and assessing in depth only the extremely "prodemocratic" and "antidemocratic" respondents, they ignored a very significant group—those in the middle, called by one sociologist "the gentle people of prejudice." Such "gentle people" are not likely to be excessively rigid or intolerant. Instead, they are apt to be extremely well socialized to whatever prejudicial norms exist in their society.

The Cultural Dimension   During the process of socialization, an individual learning the beliefs, norms, and values of a culture is also likely to learn its prejudices. Sociologists who link prejudice to cultural factors argue that, although prejudice is harmful to many, it is a normal rather than an abnormal phenomenon in a number of societies. Of course, extremists do exist, and fanatics can aggravate certain potentially tense situations. But, say these theorists, the character of a culture is as much to blame for prejudice as are the psychological needs and behavior patterns of individual members.

agree or disagree with a number of statements designed to reveal feelings of ethnocentrism, anti-Semitism, political-economic conservativism, and leanings toward fascism. Next, the investigators chose those with the most extreme "prodemocratic" and "antidemocratic" scores for further examination through psychological tests and clinical interviews.

Prejudices are often learned from stereotypes—generalized, unverified images of racial, ethnic, religious, or other groups. The following are examples of stereotypes: "The Irish are all heavy drinkers." "Blacks have natural rhythm." "Chicanos are lazy." The resentment of each group at such "typecasting" shows that such stereotypes can have a deep social impact.

Stereotypes not only reinforce prejudice but also affect our perceptions. For example, if Native Americans suffer from a high rate of alcoholism, others may view this as a racially inherited weakness rather than as an escape, a response to the poverty and hopelessness of life on a reservation.

Culturally based prejudice can place a minority group in a vicious circle. That is, society first discriminates against the minority to keep it in a low stratum. Then it justifies its prejudice against the minority by observing that its members are obviously in a low social position.

The Structural Dimension   Many societies have incorporated discrimination into their social structures and institutions. Social theorists disagree about how to view these patterns. Conflict theorists believe that consistently placing groups in positions of inferiority is neither necessary nor universal and that it is likely to result in rebellion. Functionalists, by contrast, contend that no society can exist without hierarchies. However they believe that the ranking in hierarchies should be based not on racial or ethnic criteria but on performance and production.

Whatever the theorists argue, there is little question that some people always profit from exploitative relationships. Most often they are members of dominant groups who, according to social psychologist John Dollard, reap both material and psychological benefits. They make money through the labor of others, and, by having others to look down on, they enjoy their feelings of superiority.

Groups, organizations, corporations, and even nations can benefit from economic advantages. Being in a dominant position may also be a cause of group pride, company

pride, and nationalism. Such facts of social life help explain why systems like slavery, imperialism, and fascism emerge and persist.

[?]   Which theory explaining the causes of prejudice seems most accurate to you? From what you have read about functionalists and conflict theorists, to which group do you think you belong? Explain your reasoning.

Variations in Attitudes and Behavior

The prejudiced person may not actually discriminate against others. Conversely, many individuals behave in a discriminating way without feeling hostile toward the groups they are acting against. Sometimes people may even behave toward others in a manner quite the opposite of the way they truly feel. This happens because the behavior seems "appropriate" for the situation. For example, in times past many northern antisegregationists went along with practices of segregation when vacationing in the South.

Robert K. Merton analyzed prejudice and discrimination in the United States and distinguished four types of Americans that he felt were basic to our society. One, the unprejudiced nondiscriminator, is deeply committed to American egalitarian values. Such a person, however, may not try to eliminate discrimination. "Since his own spiritual house is in order," writes Merton, "he is not motivated by guilt or shame to work on a collective problem." The second type, the unprejudiced discriminator, discriminates when it seems practical. For example, a white suburban homeowner might refuse to sell to a black family because he or she is told that the sale would lower property values.

Merton's third type, the prejudiced nondiscriminator, is a "timid bigot" who feels but does not show hostility toward a minority group. The fourth type is the prejudiced discriminator. This "active bigot" does not believe in equality and does not even pretend to.

Although Merton's distinctions help to classify prejudicial attitudes and behavior, in reality one seldom finds a single individual who is all saint or all sinner. Moreover, although many people prejudiced against one minority also dislike others, prejudice toward one minority does not necessarily mean prejudice toward all. An anti-Hispanic midwesterner is not necessarily anti-Jewish. And, of course, minority-group members may themselves be prejudiced against other minorities. Furthermore, many racial, religious, and ethnic minorities harbor prejudicial feelings toward all members of the dominant group.

REVIEW AND APPLICATION

1. IDENTIFY: Scapegoat theory, authoritarian personality.

2. What have researchers identified as the six personality characteristics and attitudes of the authoritarian personality? How, according to critics, might those studying the authoritarian personality have come to inaccurate conclusions?
3. Explain how culturally based prejudice can create a vicious circle for a minority group.
4. What are the four variations in prejudicial attitudes described by Robert K. Merton basic to our society?

CRITICAL THINKING: On what basis did Robert Merton divide the population into distinct groups of bigots and non-bigots?

3 Patterns of Discrimination

Discrimination includes any outward expression of prejudice that affects others. The children's chant "Sticks and stones may break my bones, but names will never hurt me" is simply not true. Name-calling hurts a great deal. It is also a clear example of discriminatory behavior. So are expressions containing racial slurs and ethnic jokes. Other forms of discrimination range from simple avoidance to violence, and even mass violence.

Avoidance

One common way in which people discriminate against minority groups is by avoidance, staying away from them. Whole groups may move out of a neighborhood to get away from others who they feel threaten life, property, or status. Avoidance is also seen in the establishment of exclusive clubs, fraternities, and other private organizations whose bylaws require membership in the "proper" group. Sometimes communities have tried to maintain restrictive rules to prevent "undesirables" from buying property or moving in. Avoidance behavior accounts in

part for the move to the suburbs by middle-class whites after World War II. As non-whites and ethnic minorities migrated to the urban centers in search of jobs, middle-class whites left the cities behind.

Two sociologists of the early twentieth century, Robert Park and Ernest Burgess, studied the population distribution in urban areas and found that ethnic groups tended to form cultural islands, or *ethnic enclaves*. These groups were often reluctant to let others into what they considered to be "their" neighborhoods. However, as the ethnic groups became wealthier and their children grew up, they, too, moved outward. You studied this movement in detail in Chapter 12.

Segregation

To be exclusive usually means to deny others access to certain organizations, places, forms of wealth, goals, or activities. Forbidding contact between certain groups by custom or law is called *segregation*. In a segregated society, access to the place and positions of the dominant group is limited to a select few. Barriers are set up to keep all members of a minority group "in their place." Residential segregation, school segregation, and occupational segregation are three obvious examples.

Patterns of residential segregation vary. *De facto segregation* occurs without legal authority when minority groups gather in racial or ethnic enclaves. When segregation is actually written into the laws of a city, county, state, or nation, the result is *de jure segregation*.

One of the most complete systems of de jure segregation is the South African pattern referred to earlier, which has the goal of apartheid, "apartness." In reading the following account by an American social scientist of his experiences in doing research in South Africa, note how involved Pierre van den Berghe felt in the apartheid policies enforced by the white-dominated government.

I quickly became aware that, try as I may, there was no escape from the color bar, and that I must, however reluctantly, comply with segregation much of the time. Inviting arrest for violation of apartheid

Shown in the photograph below is a segregated bus in South Africa, one of the few countries in the world where a racial minority—the whites—control the government. The South African government divides and regulates people into four racial classifications: White, Black, Asian, and Colored, a mixture of the first three. Whites make up only 16 percent of the population while Blacks comprise 71 percent. Under apartheid the races are kept segregated as much as possible.

regulations would have defeated the purpose of my stay, and besides, jails are also segregated, so that even in prison I should have enjoyed against my will countless special privileges.

Probably to save my self-respect and allay my feelings of guilt, I decided that I would engage in some symbolic protest actions, that I would refuse "customary" white privileges. . . . For example, I refused to be served before nonwhite customers in shops or in government offices; similarly, I filled in the item labeled "race" on official questionnaires with the term "human" or "American," often to see it changed . . . surreptitiously[1] to "white" by a state official who must have wondered at the stupidity of foreigners who do not even know that they belong to the master race. When I invited Africans to my house, I offered them alcoholic beverages, a criminal offense until 1962, and when in the company of nonwhites, I always tried to avoid using segregated facilities, or, when I did, I used the nonwhite ones.

In addition, I [ignored] regulations not so much on grounds of principle, but because compliance with them would have jeopardized[2] my research more than their evasion. For example, whites are required to carry special permits to enter most African "locations" and "reserves." I entered such places countless times without ever asking for a permit. . . .

[Whenever I was caught in a violation], my skin color . . . protected me . . . and I always got away with a warning. Most of the time I pretended to have lost my way, and the police gave me elaborate road directions, while commenting on the danger of traveling unarmed in "Native areas." Had I had a black skin, of course, I would have been repeatedly arrested and convicted for "pass" offenses. Even in my defiance of the law, I was given preferential[3]

[1]underhandedly, sneakily
[2]risked
[3]preferred

and often deferential[4] treatment, simply because of my [color].

How effective do you think van den Berghe was in trying to avoid discriminating against those labeled nonwhite? List the aspects of social life that were regulated by law and that discriminated against nonwhites. How were the laws enforced?

Some aspects of de jure segregation existed even in areas of the United States until 1954. Although the Supreme Court decision in *Brown* v. *Board of Education* that year forbade de jure segregation, it has continued to exist de facto for over a quarter of a century. Segregated residential patterns create school segregation; for if the neighborhoods are segregated, neighborhood schools will be, too.

Violence

The most extreme form of discrimination is physical aggression directed at individuals of minority groups. It ranges from harassment to property damage to bombing and lynching. Sometimes violence is spontaneous, as when angry members of one group take out their frustrations on members of another group. Often, however, violence has been premeditated, as in the case of planned attacks by the Ku Klux Klan.

Sometimes social systems have gone even further and carried out *genocide*, the mass murder of entire groups. Two examples are the annihilation of thousands of Armenians by Turks early in this century and the more recent slaughter of an estimated several million by the Pol Pot regime in Cambodia. Millions more starved to death in Cambodia when the succeeding government refused to allow relief supplies to reach the remnants of the former government's forces.

History recounts many acts of heroism performed by those resisting persecution. Martyrs have figured in many movements for civil rights and freedom from discrimination. But apart from those capable of heroism, there are millions of people throughout the

[4]highly respectful

The Ku Klux Klan uses terror to oppose all forms of racial and religious integration.

world suffering from the effects of prejudice and exploitation. These people, too, must develop ways of reacting.

REVIEW AND APPLICATION

1. IDENTIFY: Ethnic enclave, segregation, de facto segregation, de jure segregation, genocide.

2. Why can avoidance be considered a form of discrimination?
3. What is apartheid?

CRITICAL THINKING: Reread the account of Pierre van den Berghe's experiences in South Africa on pages 343–344. List at least three things he valued. Cite examples to support your answers.

4 Reactions to Discrimination

Many societies have a pattern of ethnic stratification. Rarely, however, are minority groups content to accept this situation with any degree of happiness. The black poet Langston Hughes sums up what happens when a society doesn't give an ethnic group a real chance to fulfill its dream.

What happens to a dream deferred?
Does it dry up
like a raisin in the sun?

Or fester like a sore—
And then run?
Does it stink like rotten meat?
Or crust and sugar over—
like a syrupy sweet?
Maybe it just sags
like a heavy load.
Or does it explode?

For many black Americans, the "dream deferred" is the "American dream" of freedom, equality, and unrestricted opportunities for achievement. Hughes's poem has a broader application, however, for it touches on several of the most fundamental reactions to discrimination.

Sociologists have made many attempts to describe the responses of minority-group members to their social situation. Within most minorities in the United States are those who "want in" and are willing to do almost anything to be accepted. These are also those who simply want to be left alone and those who want what they feel they deserve by right. Sociologists George Simpson and Milton Yinger suggested that most minority responses belong in one of these three categories: those who favor "acceptance," those who seek "accommodation," and those who are "aggressive." Those in this last category may be aggressively for reform, to get them-

selves in; or they may be aggressively for separatism, to get themselves out or to form an entirely new society.

Other sociologists believe that reactions to minority status are best explained by asking: (1) Does the minority-group member have the lowly self-image imposed on the minority by the majority or does he or she reject it? (2) Is the minority-group member willing to play a humble role as expected by those in power? Answers to these questions reveal at least four types of reactions: submission, withdrawal, imitation, and agitation. These reactions, in some ways, represent points on a continuum through which some individuals may pass at various stages in their lives. In any specific case, all of these patterns are possible, and a given individual may manifest two or more of them at different times or in different circumstances.

GRAPH SKILL   Asians are a minority group in the United States and have been subjected to discrimination. Their response to their minority status, however, seems to reflect a pursuit of the American dream of achievement. What do the graphs below show about Asian achievement? How do Asians and whites compare in their level of education? In median family income?

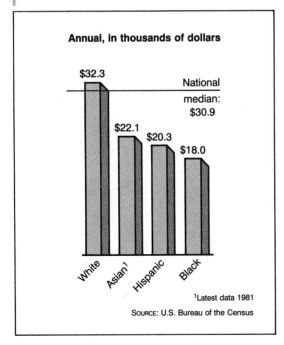

MEDIAN FAMILY INCOME IN THE UNITED STATES, 1987

Annual, in thousands of dollars

$32.3 White
National median: $30.9
$22.1 Asian[1]
$20.3 Hispanic
$18.0 Black

[1]Latest data 1981

SOURCE: U.S. Bureau of the Census

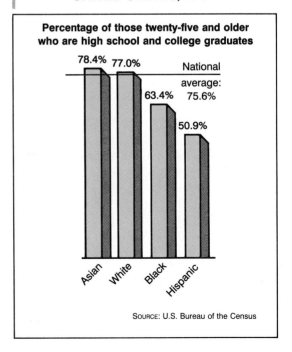

LEVEL OF EDUCATION IN THE UNITED STATES, 1987

Percentage of those twenty-five and older who are high school and college graduates

78.4% Asian
77.0% White
National average: 75.6%
63.4% Black
50.9% Hispanic

SOURCE: U.S. Bureau of the Census

Submission

In the words of Langston Hughes, some minority-group members "dry up"—that is, abandon hope and submit without complaint to unfair treatment. Malcolm X once said that the worst crime the white man committed was to teach blacks to hate themselves. When minority-group members come to see themselves as inferior, they are most often internalizing the views of others. These are the people labeled "Uncle Toms," "Tio Tacos," or "Uncle Tomahawks." They play the roles called for by members of the majority group.

Withdrawal

Other members of minorities "fester"; their resentment against the majority is turned inward, and they seethe with rage. Some of them try to deny their minority-group membership. They may change their names—from Cohen to Cane, for example. They may have their eyes or noses "fixed" to look more like the "ideal" dominant type. They may straighten their hair or try to lighten their skin. Some who make these changes attempt to "pass" in the wider society where, they hope, they will finally find acceptance. More often than not, however, they find themselves trapped between the ethnic world from which they want to escape and the wider one in which they never feel quite at home.

Some minority-group members go farther still—literally. They leave the country, seeking refuge in places that are less hostile. Recorded history is filled with the stories of such refugees. Some American blacks moved to Europe, especially to Paris, in the early part of this century. Thousands of Jews fled from Germany and Austria in the 1930s to seek asylum in safe havens. Many Hungarians, Czechs, and Poles have come to the United States in flight from communism. Since Saigon fell to the communists in 1975, more than 550,000 Indochinese have immigrated to safety in this country.

American novelist and essayist James Baldwin lived in France for much of his life.

Imitation

Langston Hughes suggests that some minority people respond to discrimination by crusting and sugaring over "like a syrupy sweet." Instead of knuckling under or fleeing, many members of ethnic groups imitate the dominant group in what might be called "ethnic one-upmanship." They set up schools, businesses, clubs, and so on that parallel those of the dominant society. A number of years ago, most campus fraternities did not permit non-Christians to join. Jewish students therefore set up their own Greek-letter societies. Black newspapers used to be filled with stories of elegant balls and parties that were clearly mirrors of those held by and for white people.

Some sociologists feel that such attempts at mimicking the dominant group are self-deluding. They lead people to live in worlds of make-believe. Others believe that although fraternities and formal social affairs offer little relief from the pressures of minority status, they do provide a means of showing success. Such things are important for many people.

Agitation

Over the years, many members of minority groups have grown tired of trying to accept their status in the dominant society. They want to lift the "heavy load" of discrimination off their backs. These people have reacted in a number of ways, expressing their dissatisfaction in many different forms and in many different places. The recent history of black Americans indicates the forms this agitation may take. In some cases, as Langston Hughes foresaw, there have been explosions, explosions of pent-up frustration.

The Civil-Rights Movement Black agitation in America has challenged our democratic system to live up to its own ideals. The civil-rights movement, which was also discussed in Chapter 13, has included many different activities and organizations. Among the better-known groups are the National Association for the Advancement of Colored People (NAACP), founded in 1909; the Urban League; the Congress of Racial Equality (CORE); and the Southern Christian Leadership Conference (SCLC), which was led by Martin Luther King, Jr.

Over the years, these groups sought their objectives by various activities—court challenges, boycotts, voter-registration drives, sit-ins, mass marches. All used forms of nonviolent direct action. Whites and blacks often marched together. The goal was *desegregation,* the removal of all legal and informal barriers to full integration and equality. The civil-rights movement reached its peak in the early-to-middle 1960s.

Black Pride Another focus of black agitation has been a challenge to black Americans to take pride in their blackness. Followers of Booker T. Washington, who founded a school for blacks at Tuskegee, Alabama, in the 1880s; Marcus Garvey, who led a "black nation" and a "back-to-Africa" movement in the 1920s; and the Black Muslims of more recent

In recent years many minority groups have developed a strong sense of identity and pride in the achievements of their culture. Here a parade in Santa Ana, California, celebrates black history.

times all took this approach. Rather than attacking the system directly, they urged black people to take pride in and improve themselves—in their words, to be "revitalized."

Black Power Both the civil-rights movement and the movement for black pride made some gains for blacks. The civil-rights movement was responsible for weakening segregation and broadening the voting and public accommodation rights of black citizens. The black-pride movement raised the ethnic consciousness of many blacks, but somehow for a long time, protest and pride were not joined.

In the mid-1960s, continued white resistance to desegregation turned many blacks away from the civil-rights movement. They began to mobilize the power that a tightly confined and segregated population could wield both in city halls and in the streets. Seeing integration as an unrealistic goal, some black leaders began to stress blacks' uniqueness and to reject all association with whites. They sought control of their own

BLACK ELECTED OFFICIALS, 1970–1985

Year	Federal Officials	State Officials	Municipal Officials
1970	10	169	623
1973	16	240	1,053
1976	18	281	1,889
1979	17	313	2,224
1982	18	336	2,477
1985	20	396	2,898

CHART SKILL   *Many American blacks have made integration into society their goal. One indicator of the increase in power of blacks is the number elected to political offices. What generalizations about black political power can you make from this table?*

communities and of the institutions that served them.

These challenges were most obvious on the campuses, where there were repeated demands for courses and programs in black studies, for black cultural centers, even for separate living facilities. Many administrators and faculty members accepted and implemented these demands. But many were confused by the attack on the principles of integration and by the new emphasis on group, rather than individual, achievement.

[?] Sum up in a few words four different ways of reacting to discrimination. What other responses can you think of that are not discussed above?

The Situation in the 1980s

Among some poor and working-class whites, especially those called "white ethnics," there was growing resentment of what seemed to be unfair treatment of them, a form of racism in reverse. Some sought to challenge such laws as those requiring compulsory school busing and the active recruitment, in education and employment, of minorities and women. The result was heightened conflict in some parts of the country.

On balance, however, sociologists saw many positive gains for minorities resulting from the attitudes of pride engendered by movements such as the black-power movement. Many who participated in these groups emerged better able to face others on the basis of true equality. These psychological gains were often paralleled by political gains. For example, in the American South, the "black vote" became an increasingly important factor with which politicians had to reckon.

Socioeconomic gains were often harder to achieve. Those who benefited from the opportunities afforded by affirmative-action programs, who were generally working- or middle-class to begin with, often did well. But those living in the depths of the inner city or on back-country farms—the unskilled and uneducated often called an *underclass*—were not much better off than before.

Trends in American Intergroup Relations

A view of America that dates back to revolutionary days envisions the forming of a "new American," the product of various cultural ingredients. In the early twentieth century, Israel Zangwill gave a name to the process by which he thought this would occur—the "melting pot." Today many sociologists refer to the melting-pot idea as *amalgamation*. It involves the blending of peoples, a process that has always been more symbolic than real. As Nathan Glazer and Daniel Patrick Moynihan have written, "The point about the melting pot is that it did not happen. At least not in New York and . . . in those parts of America which resemble New York."

Another view dating back to the earliest days of settlement envisioned European immigrants as disappearing into the larger, established American culture. Social attitudes rather than laws set forth the standards of acceptability. George Washington, John Adams, and others welcomed European immigrants but urged that "they cast off the European skin never to resume it." In other words, the goal was *assimilation,* conformity to the folkways and mores of the dominant society.

What actually happened in America was that many ethnic groups became part of the wider society but continued to stand apart from it in various ways. Those whose appearance and attitudes were most similar to those of the dominant group were most apt to seek and gain acceptance. Those least similar, such as Native Americans, blacks, Asians, and Chicanos, remained most apart.

All groups, however, joined in accepting the basic values of American society, especially the ideals of freedom, equality, and justice, such as those expressed in the Bill of Rights. Thus, despite the bitterness of some, the vast majority of people saw themselves as Americans, though also Irish Americans, Polish Americans, Italian Americans, Jewish Americans, and so forth. On one side of the equation, they felt "American"; on the other, they remained "ethnic."

When applied to an entire society, this pattern is known as *pluralism*. It relates to the process of *accommodation,* an approach to the diverse groups in society that is characterized by a live-and-let-live attitude of mutual respect. Many scholars and community leaders see pluralism as the best alternative to assimilation. In any event, pluralism is a fact of American life and has been so since long before it ever became a sociological theory.

Politicians, certainly, have long recognized the full implications of ethnic "bloc power." They have often appealed to minority uniqueness and to each minority's desire for an independent voice in matters pertaining to its own affairs. Today minority groups often find that they have more power than they think they have. That power often influences business people and union leaders to listen more carefully to grievances about discrimination. It is also frequently used to press government to continue to honor the traditional values and norms of equality of opportunity.

REVIEW AND APPLICATION

1. *IDENTIFY:* Desegregation, underclass, amalgamation, assimilation, pluralism, accommodation.
2. What are some of the ways in which members of minorities withdraw from their minority status?
3. How do sociologists respond to attempts by minorities to imitate the dominate social group?
4. Which socioeconomic groups have achieved the most from affirmative-action programs? The least?

CRITICAL THINKING: Support the following comparison with passages from the text. "Both the civil-rights and black power movements were led by blacks for blacks, but their goals were widely different."

CHAPTER 14 REVIEW

In many modern societies, people are defined according to certain collective characteristics. One of these, race, has to do only with inherited physical traits but has often resulted in discrimination. Religion, at least in our society, has less often been a source of conflict. A third category, the ethnic group, gives its members a sense of identity but is also associated with ethnocentrism.

In multiethnic societies, harmony is often difficult to achieve. There is frequently a dominant group that controls subordinate groups, or minorities. Pluralistic societies may also exhibit ethnic stratification and conflicts among minorities. Prejudice and discrimination are closely related, although Americans vary from those having the attitudes of nonprejudiced nondiscriminators to those acting as prejudiced discriminators.

Social scientists have attributed prejudice to psychological factors, the cultural environment, and structural needs that make hierarchies useful.

Discriminatory actions run the gamut from name-calling to avoidance and segregation to violence. Those discriminated against may submit, withdraw, imitate the dominant group, or agitate for change. In the United States, blacks have resorted to a number of tactics: the civil-rights movement, the focus on black pride, and the attempt to mobilize black power.

Historically, the United States has progressed through several phases in intergroup relations. The concept of assimilation was followed by that of amalgamation and then by that of accommodation. The most recent emphasis has been on ethnic pride and cultural diversity.

Key Terms

Define the following:

intergroup conflict	apartheid	genocide
dominant group	institutional racism	desegregation
minority group	scapegoat theory	underclass
discrimination	authoritarian	amalgamation
prejudice	personality	assimilation
race	ethnic enclave	pluralism
ethnic group	segregation	accommodation
ethnocentrism	de facto segregation	
ethnicity	de jure segregation	

Applying Sociology

1. Obtain the names of those in your school's graduating class. Group them, as best you can, according to nationality. Is any one group represented in noticeably larger numbers? You might compare this with a list of graduates ten years ago that has been similarly grouped. Are the proportions of different nationalities much the same? What might account for any similarities or differences in the two lists?

2. Classify each of the following American groups as racial, religious, or national: (a) Japanese Americans; (b) American Indians; (c) Mormons; (d) American blacks; (e) Polish Americans; (i) Puerto Ricans; (j) Baptists. Which of these groups might also properly be called ethnic groups? Explain your reasons in each case. Add to your classification any other groups that occur to you.

3. Would the United States be better off if there were no ethnic divisions among us? Hold a class debate on the topic "Total assimilation of minority groups should be the goal of American society."

4. Since ours is a society that is already made up of many different peoples, how would you go about changing it, assuming you think it would be better not to have ethnic divisions? Write a paper describing the society you have in mind and the steps you would take.

5. Some high schools have adult evening courses in ethnic cooking, folk dancing, and the like. Does this further understanding of different cultures? Devise a model community-action plan that would use the school, the town library, and local activities to foster appreciation and toleration of ethnic differences.

6. If possible, hold an Ethnic Day program in which students bring from home or wear traditional items from their ancestral culture—flags, dashikis, mantillas, and the like. If it can be arranged, serve food that is native to the different cultures. In the event that your school has large representations of any particular ethnic groups, perhaps a similar day might honor them individually.

7. Write a paper dealing with the topic of ethnocentrism as a cause of war. You might select, as a focus for your composition, specific religious or nationality groups that have been in conflict, for example, Protestants and Catholics in Northern Ireland, Jews and Arabs, or other groups.

Extended Readings

David L. Evans, "Self-Help at Its Best," *Newsweek*, March, 16, 1987, p. 8.

1. According to the author, what is required to turn black inner city students into academic achievers?

2. How does the Education Par Excellence program motivate students?

William Greider, "The Heart of Everything That Is," *Rolling Stone*, May 7, 1987, pp. 37–64.

1. How does the author describe the lifestyle of the Indians on the reservation?
2. Why has it been so difficult for the Sioux to regain their land?

Gene Oishi, "The Anxiety of Being a Japanese-American," *New York Times Magazine*, April 28, 1985, p. 58–60, 65.

1. According to the article, what official forms of discrimination did Americans practice against Asian immigrants?
2. Why did the author have trouble testifying before the congressional commission?

Social Studies Skills

Writing a paragraph from an outline

Summarizing a large body of information requires that you identify the key points and their supporting facts. Organize the main ideas in Chapter 14 by completing the following outline. Then use the outline to write a short summary of the chapter.

Minorities and Discrimination
I. Groups of sociological minorities
   A.
   B.
   C.
II. Roots or prejudice
   A.
   B.
   C. Structural or institutional
III.
   A.
   B. Segregation
   C.

IV.
   A. Submission
   B.
   C.
   D.

Detecting prejudice in a statement

Even those people who have experienced discrimination may harbor prejudice against other minorities. What can you infer about the speaker's view of blacks from the following quote? " . . . if Negroes even object to my getting a house outside of Chinatown, how can I ever succeed in getting a place where no one objects."

Critical Thinking

Assessing Casual Reasoning: Look at the two graphs on page 346. What are the causes of this situation? Explain how these causes led to these effects.

15

Poverty

Chapter Preview

- **Before you read,** look up the following key terms in the glossary to become familiar with their definitions:

  ghetto

  technological
    unemployment

  subsistence level

  income

  underclass

- **As you read,** think about answers to the following questions:

  1. Do all Americans share in the American dream?
  2. What is the meaning of poverty?
  3. What groups of Americans live in poverty?
  4. What solutions are there to poverty in the U.S.?

Sections in this Chapter

1. The American Dream
2. The Meaning of Poverty
3. Groups in Poverty
4. Views of Poverty

Chapter Focus

Thumb through the advertising pages of a popular magazine such as *Time* or *Reader's Digest*. What impressions do the pictures give of American ways of life and standards of living? How true to American life are the ads? Clearly, a person whose idea of American life was taken from ads wouldn't know that this country had any poor people.

Who are the poor in the United States today? Do you define the poor as those without jobs or with low incomes? Are they people who have inadequate clothing and receive some form of welfare payments?

This chapter focuses on the problem of poverty and why hardship seems to fall more on some people than on others. It also discusses definitions of poverty and concludes with some conflicting opinions about the causes and extent of poverty in the United States.

Using Sociologists' Tools

- **Observe** how various neighborhoods in your community differ.
- **Describe** the apparent standard of living of the people in each of these neighborhoods.
- **Analyze** the positive and negative forces that might lead people to reside in a particular neighborhood.
- **Predict** what would happen to a working-class neighborhood if several homes were purchased by wealthy young families.

Not everyone has shared in the American dream. Poverty is a continuing problem in cities and rural regions throughout the nation.

1 The American Dream

During the late nineteenth and early twentieth centuries, a great wave of immigrants arrived in the United States. The following account of the Meleski family gives a picture of immigrant life. It describes the poverty of an earlier day and the dream that some people were able to realize:

When he decided to go to America, in 1907, Stefan Meleski was twenty-eight, son of a poor peasant in . . . Pomerania, then held by Prussia.

Stefan's personal problem—swinging mostly about his poverty and his love for Anna Przybylowicz—was typical of young Poles of his class and age at that time, when they were going to the United States by tens of thousands yearly. He could expect no help from his father or elder brother, who was in line to become the owner of the debt-ridden Meleski homestead. . . . As a carpenter, Stefan could do only the rough work, which was so ill paid in Pomerania that he could not get married on what he might earn. So he wrote to his youngest brother Pawel, who, three years before, at eighteen, had emigrated to evade military service and was now a miner in Coalville, Pennsylvania. Would Pawel send him the ticket? Pawel sent it. Then Stefan and Anna had a long tender talk about their future.

. . . Stefan and Anna agreed that he would send for her as soon as he had paid Pawel for his ticket and saved enough money to buy one for her. They did not know how long they might stay in America after she joined him. Possibly only till

355

they had enough to be able to return to Pomerania and acquire four or five acres on a sunward slope.

From Ellis Island, Stefan went directly to Pittsburgh. There Pawel awaited him, then took him twenty miles to Coalville, where about eight hundred miners—mostly Poles, Slovaks, Croatians, Slovenians, Ukrainians—were getting up trainloads of coal for the steel mills in Pittsburgh, Canton, and Youngstown.

Stefan's first name was promptly "Americanized" into Steve, as Pawel's had been into Paul. . . .

Steve's wages at the start were $2.08 for a ten-hour day, which in four months advanced to $2.76. They remained there for the rest of his time in Coalville. He could have become a miner and made as much as $3.62 a day, but he preferred to be a carpenter on the prop crew. . . .

Men talked of quitting coal mining as soon as they saved enough to buy a farm either in America or the old country, but Steve saw that most of them would never realize their dream. It was hard to save money, and when you did accumulate some, you usually developed the ambition to possess more; when you got a little more, along came illness, or an accident, or a strike, or some glib-tongued swindler. . . .

Toward the end of April, Steve and his gang were working in No. 6. Suddenly there was an explosion in No. 5, close by. Steve ordered his men to drop everything and get out. But it took several minutes before all were on the way. Meantime ex-

Before government social programs were introduced to help the poor, many immigrants to the United States suffered economic hardship. Those who lived in overcrowded tenements often turned to settlement houses for help in adjusting to their new land and its customs. In the long run, education provided the best route for immigrants to leave poverty behind them and achieve the American dream.

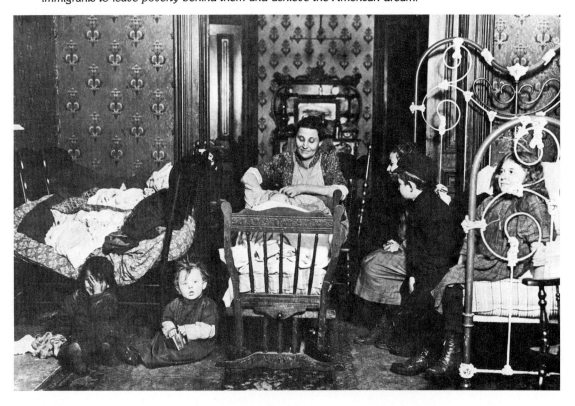

plosions in No. 5 and No. 6 followed in rapid succession. Fire. The timbers inside the pits burned for days, and 181 miners were trapped and perished. Steve lay in the overcrowded little hospital.

His mind was fixed on returning to Pomerania. He told Anna [who had joined him some time before] to get the tickets.

"Listen to me, Stefciu! You suffered so much, you are not yourself; you don't know what you are doing. You are desperate. Now I'll run this family for a while. Something tells me we will be sorry if we return to the old country. So we are not going. Our children were born here.

"We are going to Florida—on the land—to Paradise." . . .

When the Meleskis reached Parkersville, Florida, the place sizzled in the hot sun. She talked with Mr. Robinson, the local real estate man. Anna fell in love with the spot. Paradise indeed. But what could one do here in a practical way to make a living? Mr. Robinson said that, with all these acorns dropping throughout the year, the place was good for pigs.

Under the challenge of his new situation, Steve's strength returned quickly. He and Anna worked harder, and for longer hours, than ever before, but their toil carried with it more satisfaction than any previous effort of theirs. . . .

The pigs thrived on the acorns, and during the war Steve had no trouble selling them . . . and when, in the twenties, the Florida boom came along, Steve began to work as a carpenter in and around Tampa and Clearwater, making good money. . . .

By 1936 some of [Anna] and Steve's children were fairly on the way in life. In 1922, when Anthony had finished grade school, the Parkersville High School was built, and he attended it till 1926. Then, on the urging of a teacher, he went to the University of North Carolina. He graduated in 1931 and the next year got a position as a teacher of sociology in an Ohio college. Annie went through high school, then to a nursing institute, and found a job in a Tampa hospital. . . . In 1933 she married a young doctor of long Southern ancestry. . . .

In 1940, on the eve of World War II, Anna Meleski was asked again to describe her feelings about her old country. Then she said:

"I am more glad than I was ever before that we are here. God knows what is going to happen in Europe. . . . Maybe America is the hope of the world."

? Why did the Meleskis come to the United States? What was their dream? What kinds of struggles did they face? Do you think today's immigrants have an easier or a harder time of it? Explain your answer.

In many ways the Meleski's story typifies the American dream. Drawn by economic, political, and religious opportunities, people came by the thousands to take the many jobs that were available during the nineteenth and early twentieth centuries. Hard work, poverty, crowded living conditions, and despair met many of them in their search for a better life. Some were never able to overcome these obstacles. Others, especially immigrants belonging to certain groups, had children who later rose to positions of power and wealth.

As the United States, a nation of immigrants, expanded and became industrialized, which groups managed to overcome initial poverty and rise to success? Who achieved the American dream? How did this group manage to retain favorable circumstances from one generation to the next?

Research shows that white males born in the United States have had an advantage in gaining the high-pay, high-status occupations. Many of these men amassed their fortunes before the days of the income tax, during the late nineteenth century when industrialization transformed the American economy. Their children then became rich through inheritance, and they in turn passed on this wealth to their children. Once established as an upper class, members of these families were able to maintain their position through expensive and superior education.

During the latter part of the twentieth century, growth and change took place in this social elite, but for many years membership was restricted. For example, the professions of law and medicine, two prime avenues for upward mobility, were largely limited to this already established group. Social scientists have found that, until relatively recent times, patterns of discrimination against women, blacks, and other minority groups were the rule rather than the exception.

Of course, higher education and the professions have not been the only avenues to wealth. Marriage has been another route, although a rarer one. As you read in Chapter 5, special talents and abilities have always provided means by which some people could achieve their dreams. For the majority of the poor, however, it has been difficult to acquire the qualifications, contacts, help, and expertise necessary to rise in the social order.

REVIEW AND APPLICATION

1. What is the American dream? By what means might a person be able to fulfill this dream?
2. What group has been able to benefit the most from the American dream?
3. How has the upper class traditionally been able to maintain its position?

CRITICAL THINKING: Explain the cause-and-effect relationship between the industrialization of the economy during the late nineteenth century and upper class families today. How do these families maintain their position?

2 The Meaning of Poverty

The meaning of poverty is complex, and the concept of poverty is difficult to define. Poverty is partly a question of how people think of themselves. If you asked people whom you consider to be poor how they regard their economic condition, how do you think they would answer? In fact, poor people view their circumstances in a variety of ways. Some might say, "Yes, we are poor." Others in the same circumstances might think of themselves as much better off than their own parents during the Depression, when millions of Americans were out of work, bread lines were long, and government gave little public aid.

A third group might have strong faith in the future. They might define their situation as follows: "Sure, we don't have much money or much chance for a good job. But our kids are in school, and we have faith in them and what they can do to help the family when they grow up."

⁇ There are many other self-definitions that people of limited income might have. Can you think of any?

Definitions of Poverty

Defining who the poor are needs thought. Even the experts rarely agree on it. However, no matter how social analysts measure poverty—by income, by type of housing, or by the lack of certain basic necessities—almost all come to the conclusion that large numbers of people in the United States are poor.

According to the federal government, it took $9,287 to maintain a nonfarm family of four above the poverty level in 1981. This figure is considered a *subsistence-level income,* an income that gives a family enough money to survive. It does not leave them with extra money for unexpected expenses such as illness, losses from fire or theft, or loss of job. A family living below the poverty line does not have enough income to buy the basic necessities for survival—food, clothing, and housing.

As the standard of living has risen in the nation, the definition of subsistence has also changed. It takes into account that this is a very rich, industrialized country. Peasants in underindustrialized countries would probably define an adequate standard of living in more modest terms. They might not think that central heating, indoor toilets, or dental care are essential, as most of us would. Still, the figure used by the government is not very high.

The Extent of Poverty

Using the government poverty-line designation, approximately 33.1 million people, 14 percent of the population in the United States, are poor. This seems to be a large percentage, but actually the numbers living in poverty decreased substantially during the last two decades, when the government deliberately sponsored programs to help the poor. As the table at the top of this page indicates, however, more recent figures suggest that this trend is being reversed.

Given the American value of equality of opportunity, one might expect poor people to be randomly scattered throughout the population. In fact, however, a person's chance of living in poverty is largely determined by two ascribed factors. One is race. Although 15.2 percent of the overall population is poor, only 12.1 percent of the white population falls into this category, as compared with 28.4 percent of Hispanics and 35.7 percent of blacks. The other factor is sex. Over 30 percent of all households headed by females, including all races, fall below the poverty line.

When sex and race are combined, one finds the most vulnerable groups in American society. Native American, Eskimo, black, Puerto Rican, and Mexican American families headed by women are over five times as likely to be poor as are families headed by white men. Even families headed by white females are much more likely to be poor than are the families of majority males.

A study conducted by the Survey Research Center of the University of Michigan reinforced and added to these findings. It concluded that the families most likely to be living in poverty were those in which the head of the family was (1) sick or disabled, (2) a single head of household with children, (3) nonwhite, (4) temporarily jobless, or (5) a small farmer. Of course, sometimes a person fits into several of these categories,

PERCENTAGE OF U.S. POPULATION BELOW POVERTY LEVEL, 1962–1985

1962	19.0	1974	11.2
1963	17.3	1975	12.3
1964	15.7	1976	11.8
1965	14.7	1977	11.6
1966	14.2	1978	11.4
1967	12.8	1979	11.6
1968	12.1	1980	13.0
1969	12.6	1981	14.0
1970	12.5	1982	15.0
1971	11.9	1983	15.2
1972	11.9	1984	14.4
1973	11.6	1985	14.0

Source: U.S. Bureau of the Census

WHO ARE THE POOR?

Category	Percentage Who Are Poor[1]
All Americans	15.2
Whites	12.1
Blacks	35.7
People 65 and over	14.1
Families in central cities	19.8
Persons of Hispanic origin	28.4

[1] based on official U.S. government "poverty level"

Source: U.S. Bureau of the Census

CHART SKILL   According to these poverty figures, when was the poverty level highest? Lowest? Who forms the largest percentage of the poor? The smallest? Why might people 65 and over live below the poverty level?

FAMILIES BELOW POVERTY LEVEL IN THE UNITED STATES, 1986

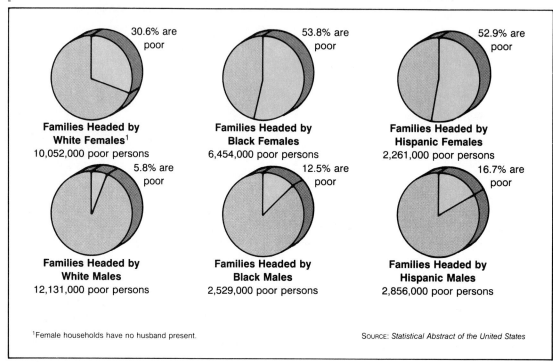

30.6% are poor

Families Headed by White Females[1]
10,052,000 poor persons

53.8% are poor

Families Headed by Black Females
6,454,000 poor persons

52.9% are poor

Families Headed by Hispanic Females
2,261,000 poor persons

5.8% are poor

Families Headed by White Males
12,131,000 poor persons

12.5% are poor

Families Headed by Black Males
2,529,000 poor persons

16.7% are poor

Families Headed by Hispanic Males
2,856,000 poor persons

[1]Female households have no husband present.

SOURCE: *Statistical Abstract of the United States*

GRAPH SKILL American families headed by women, particularly women from ethnic and racial minorities, account for many millions of the individuals living below the federal poverty level. Which family group has the lowest percentage of its people living in poverty? The highest?

Native Americans living on reservations comprise another ethnic group for whom living conditions are often harsh. This Navajo woman and her children are on welfare.

increasing the chance that the family faces poverty. For example, a nonwhite, female head of household with a large family who is unemployed, either because she is ill or because she wants to stay home to take care of her children, would probably be classified as poor.

Other experts have defined the poor as those kept from working by age, whether too young or too old; by disabilities, such as blindness or mental disorders; by discrimination; or by a lack of jobs in the area where they live, for example, in a rural farm community or in an inner-city area when the industry is in the suburbs. About two-thirds of the heads of household of poor families left school before the eighth grade. Few have gone beyond the educational levels of their fathers. Sometimes these families make up an "underclass" of the unskilled, unemployable, or frequently unemployed members of the labor force.

Thus, the statistics do not necessarily mean that the differences in income result from active discrimination against minority groups and women. Social scientists have employed statistical techniques to take into account variations in education, employment history, age, and other such factors. They found that, if past imbalances in education and opportunity could be erased, the figures would reveal some gain for disadvantaged groups in the 1960s and 1970s. However, these gains would not wipe out all differences. Race and sex would still put certain groups at a disadvantage. As you learned in Chapter 11, women earn only about 60 percent of what men earn, even when other factors are equal.

Poor people can be found in all areas of the country. Nationally, 60 percent of all poor people live in the metropolitan areas. Their living quarters are often overcrowded, which, by government standards, means having more than one person per room. Such homes tend to be noisy, to lack privacy, and to cause tension and attitudes of anger, rebelliousness, and despair.

Children in poverty suffer in many ways—from emotional neglect, from inadequate food and clothing, and blighted chances for the future. This little girl was photographed in her living room in Pittsburgh in 1982.

REVIEW AND APPLICATION

1. *IDENTIFY:* Subsistence-level income.
2. What are ways in which poverty can be measured?
3. The poverty standard for a nonfarm family of four in 1981 was $9,287 a year. The accompanying table shows some components that would make up a typical budget. Divide the total into monthly allotments and decide how much you would spend on each of the items. Now compare your budget with those of your classmates. How do you account for any differences?

CRITICAL THINKING: Consider the two factors which are the most significant in determining who are the poor. What are they? How might this change?

MONTHLY BUDGET

Item	Amount Allotted
Food	
Housing	
Clothing	
Transportation	
Medical	
Recreation	
Personal	
Life insurance	
Dues, gifts, contributions	
Social Security	
Income tax	
Total	

See question 3 at left.

3 Groups in Poverty

Although people differ in their views of their circumstances, certain objective criteria can be used to identify substandard conditions of life. This section examines those groups most likely to suffer from these disadvantages.

Nonwhites and Hispanics

American children born to nonwhite families or to Hispanic families, which are usually classified as nonwhite, have a greater chance of dying in infancy, of receiving poor health care, and of going to ill-equipped schools than do children born to white Americans. The nonwhite child is also more likely to drop out before graduating from high school and to have a difficult time finding a job.

Many such poor nonwhite families, comprising over half of the urban poor, are found in the ghettos of large cities. The term *ghetto* was used in the Middle Ages to describe an area of a medieval city where Jews lived. Today it refers to any section of a city where people of the same ethnic or racial group live.

The ghetto has unique cultural elements that give it liveliness and a special character. It sometimes includes working- and middle-class people as well as low-income families. But more and more ghetto areas are characterized by substandard housing, higher prices, and high unemployment. As a result, they also become breeding places for social problems, including high crime rates, illegitimacy, drug abuse, alcoholism, and family instability. Even with these conditions, the urban ghettos are for some an improvement

Among the groups hit hardest by poverty are the Spanish-speaking minorities— Mexican Americans, Puerto Ricans, Cubans, and those of other Hispanic national origins—who are recent arrivals in the United States.

over their former homes, as shown in this interview with a Puerto Rican immigrant:

> "Pobre?" the Puerto Rican woman exclaimed. "Ha! I'm not poor. I'm rich." "Rich" because she has food to eat. "Rich" because welfare pays her rent. "Rich" compared with her girlhood in Puerto Rico.
>
> Rosita P., forty-seven, was frying codfish cakes at the stove of her tiny kitchen (three feet by five feet) on New York City's Lower East Side. She had come to New York twelve years before.
>
> Rosita lives entirely on her welfare check. . . . Nearly half goes to the landlord as rent for their ill-lighted, overheated three-room flat in the basement of a dilapidated apartment building.
>
> With the rest, she buys food, secondhand clothing, an occasional item of furniture. An old television set and an equally aged record player provide entertainment.
>
> . . . Rosita never reached the eighth grade. Her children remain in school at fourteen and eleven, though, and when they finish, Rosita hopes to find a job. If she does, she can hope for little better than day after day of drudgery in a low-paying job.
>
> Rosita complains little; she and her children live more comfortably than they did in Puerto Rico. But she wonders about the day when "progress" will come to her neighborhood in the form of high-rise apartments: "Some day house go down," she says. "Then?" Then, she knows, she will have to pass progress by and search for another ill-lighted, overheated flat.

? Many people from Latin American countries are eager to migrate to the United States, some even illegally. From what you have read about such groups, what is their prime motivation? What living conditions do they find?

What substandard living conditions mean in concrete terms emerges clearly from a study by Carol B. Stack, who was a participant observer in a black community. In this community, the streets, many of which were

Most poor people want to find work in industries where they will be able to advance in income, knowledge, and skills.

unpaved, were always the last to be cleared by the city when it snowed. The homes were old, small, and almost always in need of major repairs. Health care in the community was inadequate. A free health clinic had recently opened, but many residents did not know of its services, and others were distrustful of its personnel. Infant mortality rates were double those of the white population, as were deaths from accidents.

Other studies present a different picture. Many suggest that black and other nonwhite

U.S. COLLEGE ENROLLMENTS, 1970–1983

	1970	1975	1980	1983	Percentage of Change Since 1970
Black	522,000	948,000	1,007,000	1,102,000	111.1%
White	6,759,000	8,516,000	8,875,000	9,242,000	36.7%
Hispanic	155,000	411,000	443,000	523,000	237.4%

Source: U.S. Bureau of the Census

PERSONS BELOW POVERTY LEVEL IN THE UNITED STATES, 1960–1985

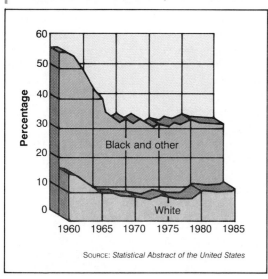

Source: *Statistical Abstract of the United States*

U.S. UNEMPLOYMENT RATES FOR WHITES AND NONWHITES, 1960–1986

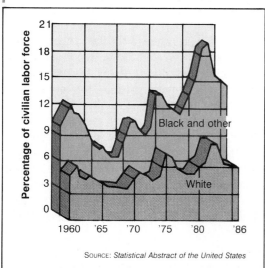

Source: *Statistical Abstract of the United States*

U.S. UNEMPLOYMENT RATES IN SELECTED CATEGORIES, 1981–1985

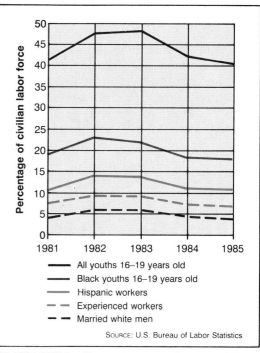

Source: U.S. Bureau of Labor Statistics

GRAPH SKILL   Poverty is a complex issue. Many social scientists disagree about the degree of poverty among blacks and Hispanics in the United States. Some say these groups are making little progress in their pursuit of equality with whites; others emphasize the strides that have been made. Using the graphs and tables, what generalizations can you make about the status of these minorities and the extent of poverty in general? What factors other than race and ethnicity are reflected here?

Americans made significant progress in the 1960s and 1970s. The levels of education and income of nonwhite groups rose, and greater numbers of their members joined unions, became skilled workers, and held white-collar jobs. Basing their conclusion on these factors, two statisticians, Ben Wattenberg and Richard Scammon, stated in the early 1970s that most black people could be considered members of the working and middle classes. They contended that many blacks, having put poverty behind them, were working in a vast array of jobs that ranged from bus driving and assembly-line work to teaching and supervisory positions.

Critics of Wattenberg and Scammon draw other conclusions. They acknowledge the progress made by some blacks but find the picture much less bright. They call attention to people left behind in the deteriorating inner cities. The critics also point to black unemployment, which is double that of white unemployment, and to the even greater employment discrepancy between teenage whites and blacks. They feel that much of the progress made by blacks in the 1960s and 1970s has been undone by automation and recession in the late 1970s and the 1980s. They point to Census Bureau figures that show that black college graduates have a lower median income than white high school graduates.

How can we put these contrasting positions in clearer perspective? Are they really so different? In reality, the viewpoints are not as contradictory as they may seem. Different aspects of the situation are stressed. Wattenberg and Scammon admit that a gap exists between whites and blacks, but they stress that blacks have made real progress in the last decade. Other social scientists place the emphasis on progress that still has to be made.

The Rural Poor

For many Americans, their role in the economic structure and their inability to use the new technology are the sources of their poverty. Nowhere is this so obvious as among farm workers. Successful competitive farming requires advanced machinery, chemical fertilizers, and sophisticated farming techniques. But this combination requires heavy capital investment, which most small farmers can ill afford. Even more financially insecure are migrant workers and sharecroppers, because they do not even own the land that they work or, usually, the tools that they use.

Migrant Workers Migrant workers move from place to place following the harvest seasons throughout the country. They often live in camps provided by growers, far from community stores, schools, and health services. Because of their low pay, they are generally ill fed and in debt to their crew bosses. Families often work from sunrise to sunset. Children attend school irregularly and thus are unable to achieve the skills that could improve their situation. A careful survey of migrant farm workers in the Northeast in the 1970s found substandard housing, health care, and education to be widespread.

In most states, migrant workers are not covered by minimum-wage laws, proper health and safety provisions, or guarantees of the right to collective bargaining through unions. The nature of their work prevents migrants from escaping from their economic insecurity and gaining political power. Moving from place to place makes it hard for them to vote in most elections or to form unions.

Even carefully planned legislative and social-service efforts to improve the working and living conditions of migrant workers may have effects nearly opposite those intended. For example, when minimum-wage laws and health codes force up growers' costs, human labor is often replaced by machines. Between 1965 and 1975, the number of migrant workers dropped about 50 percent.

Sharecroppers *Sharecroppers*, another disadvantaged rural group, farm land belonging to others in exchange for a place to live and a share of the crops. Sharecropper families generally live in abject poverty. In many ways, their lives resemble those of the serfs in feudal societies. The economic arrangement is overwhelmingly favorable to the landowners and harmful to the sharecroppers.

After a lifetime of sharecropping, a family may be evicted suddenly from the land. Many landowners have found that replacing sharecropping families with tractors and harvesters relieves them of responsibility and increases productivity and profit. Sometimes the federal government's soil-bank policy may make it more profitable to leave the land idle than to plant crops. In this case, too, sharecroppers are left to fend for themselves.

Many former sharecroppers have sought work in cities. Since their only skills are agricultural, there are few jobs they can fill in

Special problems affect American migrant workers, who follow the harvesting of different crops and therefore must deny their children the opportunity of attending school on a regular basis. Thus, it is difficult for the younger generation to break out of the poverty cycle.

an urban environment. Some find new work, but others are forced to go on welfare. They join masses of other unskilled workers whose jobs have been taken over by machines.

The Technologically Unemployed

Technological unemployment is a key problem in every industrial society. To put it simply, machines often replace human labor. Fewer workers are needed because machines can usually do the work of many men and women. This is true in many industries, from publishing to automobile production to the slaughtering of animals in meat-packing plants.

As a result, the issue of job security becomes a sensitive one. Labor unions always try to protect their members by bargaining with management to limit the introduction of new machinery. At times, a compromise is reached. Some workers lose their jobs, and others are kept on. Sometimes a revolution in technology makes a skill obsolete.

In the late 1970s, as a result of the energy crisis and the soaring costs of gas and oil, coal production experienced a revival. In the decades preceding the fuel shortage, however, coal mining declined in importance, and fewer workers were needed. Thousands of coal miners also lost their jobs to increased mechanization. The following is an excerpt from a classic study of unemployed miners. It reflects not just the problems miners faced during that period but those of other technologically unemployed workers as well. The speaker was brought into court for failing to send his children to school. He is responding to the judge's questions concerning this failure:

"I've been out of work now for four years. I've been all over this coalfield and over into Virginia and West Virginia looking for work. I've made trip after trip to Indianny, Ohio, and Michigan and I couldn't find a day's work anywhere. I drawed out my unemployment compensation over three years ago, and the only income I've had since has been just a day's work now and

Appalachia, a region encompassing parts of thirteen states from southern New York to eastern Mississippi, has been known for some time as a depressed area. In some sections, the main industry is coal mining. A recent revival of interest in coal as a fuel has inspired hope of eliminating some of Appalachia's pockets of poverty.

then doing farm work for somebody. I sold my old car, my shotgun, my radio, and even my watch to get money to feed my family. And now I don't have a thing in the world left that anybody would want. I'm dead broke and about ready to give up.

"I live over a mile from the schoolhouse and I simply don't have any money to buy my children shoes or clothes to wear. I own a little old four-room shanty of a house and twenty acres of wore-out hillside land. Last spring the coal company that owns the coal augured it and teetotally destroyed the land. I couldn't sell the whole piece for five hundred dollars if my life depended on it. Me and my oldest boy have one pair of shoes between us, and that's all. When he wears 'em I don't have any and when I wear 'em he don't have any.

"If it wasn't for these rations the gover'-ment gives us, I guess the whole family would of been starved to death long afore now. If you want to fine me I ain't got a penny to pay it with and I'll have to lay it out in jail. If you think puttin' me in jail

will help my young-uns any, then go ahead and do it and I'll be glad of it. If the county attorney or the truant officer will find me a job where I can work out something for my kids to wear I'll be much obliged to 'em as long as I live."

The judge mulled the problem over for a moment or two and then "filed away" the warrant. He explained that it was not being dismissed but was being continued upon the docket indefinitely. "If the case is ever set for trial again I will write you a letter well in advance of the trial date and tell you when to be here," he said. "In the meantime go home and do the best you possibly can to make enough money to educate your children. If they don't go to school they'll never be able to make a living and when they get grown they'll be in just as bad a fix as you are in now."

? If you had been the judge, how would you have ruled in the above case? If you had been the miner, would you have been able to come up with another solution to your problems? Explain.

Automation continues to be a problem for the working class. In the 1980s, for example, United States automobile workers were laid off by the thousands. Japanese imports, produced at much lower cost by robots and lower-salaried employees, have increased in popularity. Future technological changes in the auto and other assembly-line industries will continue to include a greater use of robot technology. Will robots in time replace the unskilled worker? Unfortunately, automation has already reduced the number of jobs open to the poor.

The labor market today requires more and more education. Even the need for semi-skilled workers is declining. Unlike the immigrant Meleskis, who were able to enter the work force, today's uneducated, particularly immigrants, find doors closed to them. Job opportunities today are mainly in the service fields, such as health care and educa-tion, which makes them unattainable to all but the educated. It would seem, then, that even with retraining of workers, the problem of poverty will remain for many people.

The Elderly

The problem of poverty is a serious one for many of the elderly. Many elderly people live in inferior housing, receive inadequate health care, and suffer from poor nutrition. Some have no choice but to turn to welfare funds and public nursing homes. The elderly poor who are hardest hit are the same groups that are most vulnerable during their working years: nonwhites and women.

Although many people over sixty-five still live in poverty, the situation of the aged has improved steadily over the years. Passage of the Social Security Act in the 1930s made 90 percent of Americans eligible for Old Age and Survivors Insurance. Most people are thus

Japan has the largest number of almost completely automated factories, in which giant machines work night and day with only a few human workers to guide them. Unlike traditional automation, robot performance is individualized; each machine is controlled by a computer that tells it what to do in accordance with an overall computerized production plan. Do you think the use of robots will increase in the United States? What sociological changes might result if industrial robots "took over"?

THE ROBOT POPULATION

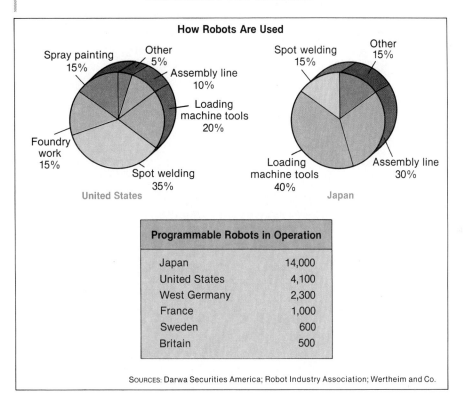

How Robots Are Used

United States

Spray painting 15%
Other 5%
Assembly line 10%
Loading machine tools 20%
Foundry work 15%
Spot welding 35%

Japan

Spot welding 15%
Other 15%
Assembly line 30%
Loading machine tools 40%

Programmable Robots in Operation	
Japan	14,000
United States	4,100
West Germany	2,300
France	1,000
Sweden	600
Britain	500

SOURCES: Darwa Securities America; Robot Industry Association; Wertheim and Co.

U.S. UNEMPLOYMENT RATE, 1947–1986

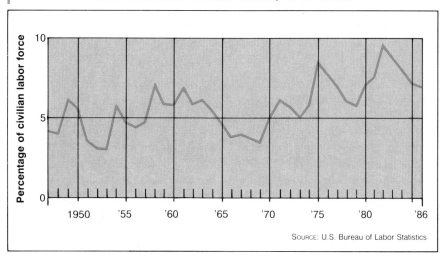

SOURCE: U.S. Bureau of Labor Statistics

GRAPH AND CHART SKILL   Unemployment has always been a major cause of poverty. In the early 1980s, a recession brought the unemployment level in the United States to 10 percent. The figures shown in the graph are averages for each period. While high interest rates and consumer resistance to high prices depressed major industries and helped cause unemployment, many jobs vanished because of automation. Why has the new element of technology loomed as an additional threat?

The position of the elderly in the United States has improved somewhat in recent years now that Medicare payments assist with medical bills and Social Security allotments include cost-of-living increases. Still, many old people live in or near poverty.

assured of some income after retirement. Medicare now provides additional health insurance. In the 1970s, legislation granted cost-of-living raises to recipients of Social Security and declared compulsory retirement at age sixty-five illegal. Increasing organization by the elderly has probably contributed to the general improvement in their condition.

Unfortunately, those who must depend on Social Security alone find that it does not give them enough to live on. What is worse, many retired people receive only partial benefits because they have not worked continuously long enough to have made the necessary contributions to the program. In contrast, old people who have personal assets or private pension plans or who can remain in the labor market past the age of sixty-five can usually manage quite well.

Social Security itself favors the well-to-do in certain of its provisions. For instance, retired people who earn more than $6,000 a year in wages lose a portion of their Social Security benefits. This is supposed to keep retired people out of the labor market and make room for younger workers. But income from stocks, bonds, or real estate is not counted. Retired people who receive this type of income can still receive full benefits.

Should older people be kept out of the labor market? Why or why not? How might increased public awareness of the plight of the elderly help to improve their circumstances overall?

REVIEW AND APPLICATION

1. *IDENTIFY:* Ghetto, sharecroppers, technological unemployment.
2. In which areas is the nonwhite child at a disadvantage when compared with the white child?
3. What were some of the observations made by Carol B. Stack in her study of a black community?
4. What conclusions did Wattenberg and Scammon draw about the socioeconomic gains made by blacks in the 1960s and 1970s? What conclusions did their critics draw?
5. Why is it so difficult for migrant workers and sharecroppers to improve their condition?
6. Why is it more difficult for uneducated workers today to find work than it was for uneducated people in the past?
7. What government programs have provided some safeguards against poverty in old age?
8. What solutions can you think of that might ease the problem of technological unemployment?

CRITICAL THINKING: You have read that the elderly who must depend on Social Security alone find that it does not give them enough to live. Many of these elderly live in inferior housing, receive inadequate health care, and suffer from poor nutrition. Compare their poverty with the poverty of the miner described on pages 366–367. What problems do the elderly poor and the miner share? How do their problems differ? Are the solutions to their particular plights different or the same? What options, if any, do the elderly poor and the miner have? Explain.

4 Views of Poverty

Opinions vary concerning poverty and the reasons for it, the extent of it, and the solutions for it. Sociologist Michael Lewis maintains that American attitudes and actions toward poverty have their roots deep in the past. The open frontier gave Americans the idea that any man—women were not considered—could achieve success by his own actions. Failure was to be met by willingness to move on to other spots where opportunity beckoned. These beliefs supported the free-enterprise system and put the major burden for failure on the individual. The closing of the frontier and, later, the loss of jobs during the Great Depression made it more difficult for people to rise through personal initiative.

Since the presidency of Franklin D. Roosevelt, whether the nation has been governed by Republicans or Democrats, liberals or conservatives, a major emphasis has been on upgrading the poor through a variety of government-sponsored programs. Why, then, do millions of Americans continue to live hand-to-mouth existences? The answer, says Lewis, is to be found in the ideology of the American dream itself. Since relatively few Americans can actually achieve great success, those who are only moderately successful need the poor and a criminal class to give themselves a psychological boost. Through this process, those who have achieved less than they hoped for can at least say that they have done far better than those people across town or those in the center city or the state prison. This kind of stratification system, asserts Lewis, allows the majority to feel less frustrated and more content.

Lewis's theory, as he himself has noted, is a controversial one. Some sociologists state that Lewis places too much emphasis on cultural factors. He doesn't consider the economic advantage for employers of having a labor force willing to work for low wages. These poor people also serve as a reminder to discontented workers that they can be replaced if their demands become too insistent. For example, in recent decades, hundreds of factories have moved from the North to the South, where workers are willing to work for lower wages.

Other analysts criticize Lewis for failing to emphasize the responsibility the poor have for themselves. These critics regard the efforts of the poor to rise, through education and hard work, as the best way to eliminate the poverty problem. Many of those who can't make the effort and who remain poor are unreachable because of personal problems or family disorganization. They comprise the group in the inner cities that is often called the *underclass*. As anthropologist

Oscar Lewis has observed, they live in an isolated "culture of poverty," where there is general hopelessness and little belief in the possibility of change.

Still another view is held by social theorists who believe that the entire issue of poverty in the United States has been exaggerated by what they call a "poverty cult." They reject the government figures on poverty as too sweeping, claiming that income alone does not measure whether a person is in the poverty class. Economics professor John Parrish writes:

> Let's take as an example a young married couple, the Smiths. They are attending college. They constitute a statistical household. Their annual income is [below the poverty line]. They are not being "hopelessly" shut out from the good things of life. They are, along with other American youth, enjoying a rate of access to higher education greater than the youth of any country, any time, any place. They enjoy electric lighting, refrigeration, adequate if not fancy food, and a secondhand automobile or motorcycle. They would like a new Cadillac but will manage without one. They aren't "poor" and need no crocodile tears shed in their behalf.

Some people who are called poor have resources that don't show up in government statistics. This ninety-one-year-old woman in Ashe County, North Carolina, owns her home and is able to supply some of her own food from her vegetable garden.

REVIEW AND APPLICATION

1. *IDENTIFY:* Underclass.
2. What are the main points of Michael Lewis's theory about the reasons for poverty in the United States? What are the criticisms of Lewis's theory?
3. What other sociological explanation has been given for poverty?
4. What does Professor Parrish mean by the term "poverty cult"? Why does the couple in the case he cites have incomes below the poverty line?

CRITICAL THINKING: Do you agree with Michael Lewis's explanation of why government-sponsored programs to aid the poor have failed? What other reasons might account for this?

Recap

The American dream dates back to the early days of immigration, when the country was hungry for workers and abounded in opportunities. An upper class arose during the period of rapid industrialization, maintaining its privileges through inheritance and education. Who became the poor is disputed even among the poor themselves. In terms of income, minority groups and women suffer disproportionately, as do inner-city dwellers. Infant mortality, poor health care, ill-equipped schools, and unemployment characterize the lives of many Hispanics and blacks. Despite these conditions, impressive numbers from both groups have managed to rise into the working and middle classes.

Farm workers, especially migrant laborers and sharecroppers, comprise another disadvantaged group. Their substandard living conditions and the nature of their work make upward mobility almost impossible. They have also been affected by technological advances, as have many urban workers. Technological unemployment particularly affects the unskilled and semiskilled. Further change, such as the use of robots, seems inevitable and offers further threats.

The aged, however, improved their situation once government provided Social Security and Medicare. But income distribution is uneven. The incomes of many of the elderly are below the poverty line.

Poverty has been viewed by some theorists as psychologically advantageous to the nonpoor, who may need to justify their own meager success. Other analysts emphasize the desirability, for employers, of a pool of people desperately in need of work. Some theorists place the responsibility for improving conditions on the poor themselves. Some even deny the extent of poverty as defined by government, claiming that conditions for many of the so-called poor are not as bad as statistics make them seem.

Key Terms

Define the following:

subsistence-level income
ghetto
sharecropper
technological unemployment
underclass

Applying Sociology

1. If possible, invite three community officials—possibly representatives of the welfare department, the housing authority, and the public health department—to discuss the problems of the poor in your community or area. Have questions prepared to find out if unemployment caused by the changing economy is a problem. What other kinds of poverty are present? What kinds of programs are under

way? What have been the successes and failures of past programs? What more could be done?

2. As a research project, have some members of the class find out from the local welfare agency the typical weekly food allowance for a family of four unable to find work. Ask how much aid the agency provides and what is available through food-stamp, surplus-food, and free-school-lunch programs. Now imagine that you must manage the weekly food shopping in this budget. Go to the local supermarket and make up a list that uses the money thriftily. Is it possible to buy enough food for a balanced diet?

3. Have members of the class visit as many governmental and private agencies working in the welfare and antipoverty fields as possible. Find out what programs seem to be working and what programs do not and why. Report to the class and use the data as the basis for a discussion of the scope, effectiveness, and problems of current programs.

4. Make a study of the want ads in your local paper over a period of a week or more. How many ads are there for jobs that do not require special skills? How many of the ads for unskilled labor appear day after day? Is this evidence that these are jobs that no one is willing to take? How many of the unskilled jobs are seasonal ones and how many appear to be perma-nent? Determine the answer to each of these questions and report your findings to the class.

5. Select an area of the country in which there is a great amount of poverty. Do some research into the history of that area and write an explanation of the historical reasons for poverty there.

6. Some theorists have argued that technological progress will eventually create more jobs than it eliminates. Do some research and list the arguments offered to support this point of view. Do you agree with it? Explain your answer fully.

7. List the characteristics some people have that would make it impossible for them to rise no matter how hard they tried. What do you think our country should do about these people?

8. Make up a relief program covering all the aspects of the poverty problem you can think of. Compare your suggestions with your classmates' and put together a class proposal to remedy poverty in the society.

9. Conduct a poll among students outside your class and then among a sample of adults in your community, asking whether they believe poverty is a serious problem in the United States today. Total the positive and negative responses given by each group. How do the totals compare? How would you explain this?

Extended Reading

David Whitman, "America's Hidden Poor," *U.S. News & World Report,* January 11, 1987, pp. 18–24.

1. What differences exist between the poor who accept welfare and the working poor?

2. Why has the government not tried to give more help to the working poor?

Stephen V. Monsma, "Should the Poor Earn Their Keep?," *Christianity Today*, June 12, 1987, pp. 28–31.

1. According to the author, what element must be involved in any attempt at welfare reform?
2. What are the main points of the author's proposed welfare reform program?

Jo McGowan, "The Poor Break Through," *Commonweal*, June 19, 1987, pp. 383–386.

1. What is the author's attitude toward the poor?
2. What does the quotation that the author cites mean?

Social Studies Skills

Making comparisons To reach their conclusions, what two groups did Wattenberg and Scammon compare? What two groups do the critics of Wattenberg and Scammon compare?

Drawing conclusions from government statistics The following conclusions are based upon the data given in the tables on page 359. On a separate sheet of paper, copy the letters to the left of the following conclusions. If the information on the chart at the top of page 359 supports the conclusion, write *s* after the letter. If the information conflicts with the conclusion, write *c*. If the information neither supports nor conflicts with the conclusion, write *n*. Write a statement to explain your answers.

(a) Fewer people in the United States were below the poverty level in 1974 than in any other year between 1962 and 1985.
(b) On the average, a larger part of the population was above the poverty level during the 1970s than the 1960s.
(c) A greater percentage of people were below the poverty level in 1958 than in any other year in U.S. history.
(d) Between 1964 and 1965, the percentage of Americans below the poverty level decreased more than during any other year from 1958 to 1981.

Critical Thinking

1. *Analyzing Comparisons:* Analyze this comparison argument: "Compared to whites, blacks have a much higher percentage of poverty. This shows that blacks aren't trying as hard as whites to get and keep good paying jobs."

2. *Recognizing Values:* What values are expressed in this argument? "Taxes should be raised on individuals with high incomes and the money should be used to increase welfare benefits for the less fortunate members of society."

CHAPTER

16 Crime

Chapter Preview

- **Before you read,** look up the following key terms in the glossary to become familiar with their definitions:

  white-collar crime   victimless crime
  halfway house   plea bargaining

- **As you read,** think about answers to the following questions:

  1. Why do people commit crimes?
  2. What is "white-collar" crime?
  3. Why is "organized crime" so difficult to stop?
  4. What reforms in the criminal justice system would curb crime?

Sections in this Chapter

1. What Is Crime?
2. White-Collar Crime
3. Organized Crime
4. "Victimless" Crimes
5. The Justice System

Chapter Focus

In the musical *West Side Story*, a confrontation takes place between a teenage gang and a policeman, Officer Krupke, in which the youths sing about explanations offered by judges, psychiatrists, and social workers of why people "go bad". They make excuses to Officer Krupke for their antisocial behavior. In its song, the gang offers specific causes that the experts have described: parental neglect, drug addiction, alcoholism, psychological disturbances, even adolescent confusion that leads to juvenile delinquency, and to adult deviant behavior.

Many theories have been offered to explain why crime exists. Some theorists blame the individuals, others blame the society. This chapter examines the nature and extent of crime in the U.S., considering some of the characteristics of criminals and crime itself.

Using Sociologists' Tools

- **Observe** the way a local capital crime is reported in the newspapers and on television.

- **Describe** the neighborhood in which the crime took place.

- **Analyze** the economic and social background of the criminal and the victim.

- **Predict** how people in your community would react to a person accused of embezzlement and to a teenager accused of stealing a car.

Prisons exist as a necessary part of our system of justice. Some critics have charged that prisons and jails are often, in fact, "manufacturers of crime."

1 What Is Crime?

Chapter 3 discussed deviance, or the failure to follow the norms of a society. You learned that societies vary markedly in what they consider to be right and proper. What is forbidden behavior in one culture may be perfectly acceptable in another.

In the United States, for example, a woman may wear a T-shirt and tight jeans. In many Muslim countries, such attire would be a clear violation of the mores. In Western societies, it is criminal to kill infants, but female infanticide is practiced in several non-Western societies where females are not valued. Even within a society, subcultural groups may differ widely in their attitudes toward what is acceptable behavior.

This section concentrates on those legally prohibited acts that involve serious wrongdoing—crimes. A *crime* is an action regarded as injurious to the public welfare or morals. Crimes are considered threats to the interests of the state.

Assessing the full extent of crime in the United States is difficult. Efficiency in collecting statistics on crime often varies. Nonetheless, there is a general consensus that crime has been increasing in recent decades. Fear of crime has become a major factor in the lives of many people.

"Ordinary" Crime

When people speak of crime, they are usually talking about street crime and crimes against property. Such criminal acts include assault, murder, rape, robbery, burglary, and vandalism. Despite the frightening statistics on the frequency of crime, surveys asking people whether they have been victims of a crime show that many victims do not notify the police. People may fear reprisals; wish to avoid humiliation, as in the case of rape; or have little confidence that the police can help them.

In one study, interviewers uncovered four times as much rape, three times as much burglary, and twice as much robbery and aggravated assault as was reported to the police. The survey did support the FBI figures on the relative frequency of crime in various regions of the country and on the greater prevalence of crime in large cities. Slums were shown to have the highest rates of both reported and unreported crime.

Statistics also reveal certain data about those arrested for crimes:

About five times as many males as females are arrested for violent crime. Males commit over 90 percent of all auto thefts, burglaries, and robberies. Women do, however, commit about one-third of all larcenies and about 15 percent of all murders. In ad-dition, during the last fifteen years there has been a substantial increase in the number of women arrested for assault and robberies.

Of those arrested, 72 percent are white and 25 percent are black. (Whites make up 87.5 percent of the population and blacks 12 percent.) These figures are difficult to interpret and are influenced by the social-class composition of the various races. Poorer blacks are most likely to be arrested, convicted, and given jail sentences.

Under 20 percent of those arrested are under eighteen. Those under twenty-one account for over 30 percent of all arrests.

In the early and mid-1980s, national rates of street crime increased, and the crime rate also rose in smaller cities, particularly in the Southwest. Since there was a decreasing percentage of people in the fifteen-to-twenty-four age group, experts had predicted that the rates of violence would subside in this period. So the increase was especially disturbing.

GRAPH SKILL Social scientists note that over a long-range period, homicide rates seem to be cyclical. When did the United States homicide rate reach its highest point? How would you describe the trend in the United States homicide rate from 1980 to 1987?

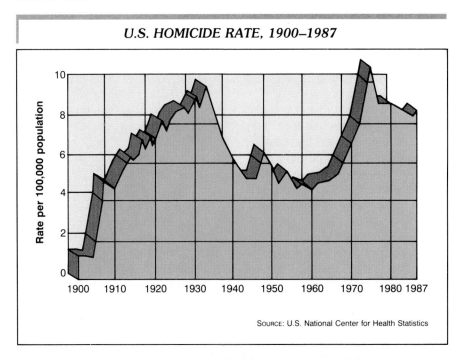

U.S. HOMICIDE RATE, 1900–1987

SOURCE: U.S. National Center for Health Statistics

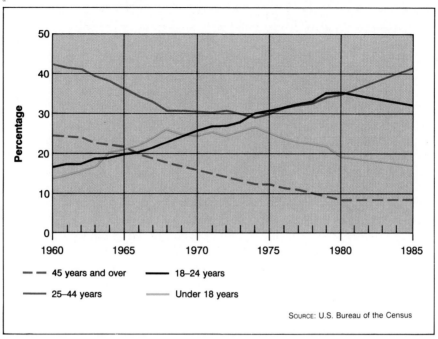

U.S. ARREST RATES, BY AGE, 1960–1985

Legend:
- – – – 45 years and over
- ——— 25–44 years
- ——— 18–24 years
- ——— Under 18 years

SOURCE: U.S. Bureau of the Census

GRAPH SKILL   In 1985, 18–24 year olds accounted for 32 percent of all arrests in the United States, compared to only 17 percent in 1960. During the same span, the percentage of those 45 and older arrested declined from about 25 percent to less than 10 percent. What factors do you think explain why 18–24 year olds represent an ever-larger percentage of the total number of Americans arrested?

Perhaps most troubling is that about 30 percent of households annually are hit by some kind of crime. Crime now affects all kinds of neighborhoods. One leading criminologist, Marvin Wolfgang, recently made the following observation about his own city: "I don't think I have a close friend in Philadelphia who has not been the victim of an auto theft or a residential burglary, or in some cases, a serious mugging. I think that's new."

GRAPH SKILL   It is difficult to assess accurately the amount of crime in a society. One reason offered for the apparent rise in the United States crime rate is that computers have made better record keeping possible. Because many people do not report crimes, however, this technological advance still leaves actual figures uncertain. What does this graph indicate about the crime index total in 1985?

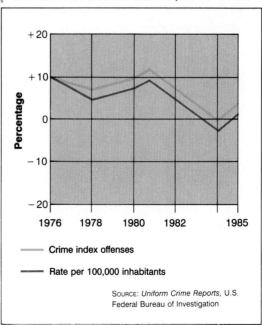

U.S. CRIME INDEX TOTAL, 1976–1985

Legend:
- ——— Crime index offenses
- ——— Rate per 100,000 inhabitants

SOURCE: *Uniform Crime Reports*, U.S. Federal Bureau of Investigation

Studies on crime have pointed out that the United States has had a long history of violence, due in part to the rough life on the frontiers. Some outlaws became folk heroes to people who admired their "daring." Here robbers hold up a stagecoach.

Suspiciousness, fear, and distrust are psychological consequences of crime. People try to defend themselves in many different ways. This woman wears an alarm around her neck in an effort to ward off would-be attackers.

Various analysts blame different factors, but many agree that crime will continue to plague the nation. After an intensive analysis, a national commission on crime in the United States wrote that American history has been full of violence. Some theorists believe that the lawlessness prevalent in America's early days has helped to create an approving atmosphere for personal gun ownership. Statistics show an astounding number of guns owned by citizens—approximately 100 million.

A main reason for the recent increase in firearms possession appears to be fear of crime. This fear is in turn related to other disturbing trends: the concentration of the poor and chronically unemployed in the central cities, and a loss of confidence that family, schools, religious organizations, and government agencies can provide the social controls necessary for protection.

Costs of Crime

The most visible consequences of street crime and crimes against property are injury or death and loss of property. Less visible are high insurance rates and the expense of maintaining an extensive criminal-justice system. The total cost of crime is difficult to estimate; certainly it is many billions of dollars. For example, the FBI *Uniform Crime Reports* states that crimes against property, such as robbery, burglary, and larceny, amounted to $5.8 billion in 1980.

Even more difficult to summarize are the psychological consequences suffered by victims and others close to them. People who live in or near high-crime areas are fearful of going out at night, unwilling to speak to strangers, and anxious to move to safer neighborhoods. People who have been assaulted or robbed suffer much greater trauma, ranging from shock, despair, shame, and humiliation to actual physical injury. During a severe heat wave in the summer of 1980, many elderly citizens perished in suffocating apartments; they refused to move into cooler public shelters for fear that their homes would be robbed while they were gone.

It is clear that crime cannot be measured only in dollars and cents or in damaged or stolen property. Victims suffer from the violation of their persons and from a continuing

The number of fires attributed to arson is increasing dramatically. Some areas are left so devastated that they resemble war zones. Arsonists may be mentally ill individuals, persons who are alienated or angry, or professionals paid by unscrupulous business people who hope to collect insurance on their failing enterprises.

dread that they may be attacked again. In many parts of the United States, the fear of crime is a constant companion.

REVIEW AND APPLICATION

1. *IDENTIFY:* Crime.
2. Which groups commit the most crimes?

3. What is the historical explanation offered for the high crime rate in the United States?
4. What are some of the costs of crime, both monetary and psychological?

CRITICAL THINKING: Do Wolfgang's close friends, discussed on page 379, make up a scientific sample of crime victims in Philadelphia? Why or why not?

---

2 White-Collar Crime

Less frightening than street crime but widespread and very costly is *white-collar crime,* which was first studied by criminologist Edwin Sutherland in the 1930s. White-collar crime is directed against the public and can be committed by individuals or corporations. Price fixing, bribery, stock manipulation, embezzlement, fraud, and the production of unsafe products all fall under this label.

Corporate Crime

The form of white-collar crime that is most costly to the public is the corporate criminal behavior of officials who seek to maximize profits through violations of the law. One example of corporate crime occurred when executives representing several major corporations in the electrical industry met secretly to fix prices. Price fixing assures that competition is eliminated and that each company receives a portion of the market and a percentage of the available profits. These executives, who were highly respectable in other aspects of their lives, acted in a cloak-and-dagger fashion, using codes and pseudonyms. When apprehended, they denied that they were criminals or that they had benefited personally from their illegal activities. Nonetheless, their well-publicized trials revealed that consumers had lost millions of dollars because of price fixing in that industry.

In another form of corporate crime, companies have secured a share of the overseas market by paying millions of dollars in bribes to foreign officials. Although bribery is condoned as a normal part of business in many countries, this type of behavior by United States corporations has been declared illegal by the United States government.

A third type of corporate crime is neglect of public safety. One example involved a tire company that produced a tire that came apart at high speeds. Although the company's director of development and the technical staff warned top management of the defect, the production continued. Over 24 million tires were sold, resulting in hundreds of injuries and even some deaths. As a consequence, lawsuits totaling millions of dollars were filed against the company.

In another example, workers in the asbestos industry were unknowingly exposed to the danger of asbestosis, a disease that is fatal unless it is diagnosed and treated early. The industry had been unaware of the danger for half a century, but even after it was discovered, some companies ignored the warnings of their medical consultants. To quote one study: "None of the company medical directors and physicians who found asbestosis in employee physical examinations blew the whistle publicly on company concealment of the findings from the employees or the suppression of medical trend data from the public."

From these cases, you can see that rapid correction of policies resulting in danger to employees or consumers is a responsibility that managers and professionals must assume for the public good.

? Are there any examples of alleged corporate crime featured in newspapers at the present time? If so, who are the plaintiffs and defendants? What accusations are being made and what defense is being offered?

Individual White-Collar Crime

An individual who would never commit a violent criminal act may fall into corrupt practices when tempted by "easy money" and the belief that there is little chance of being caught. This type of crime can range from relatively simple dishonest acts to highly complex computer fraud. In the following reading, an insurance claims agent, convicted of embezzlement, describes the process by which he became involved:

> Almost immediately after I got into this business I learned two things: first, the agents who got ahead with the company were the ones who made settlements at low figures and without taking cases into court; second, the settlements were generally made by collusion with the lawyers and doctors for the claimants. Most of the laywers for the claimants were ambulance chasers and were willing to make settlements because they got their fees without any work. The claims agent for the insurance company got a secret kickback out of the settlement. When I learned this was the way to get ahead in the casualty insurance business, I went in for it in a big way. Accidentally I left some papers loose in my office, from which it was discovered that I was "knocking down" on the settlements. The insurance company accused me of taking money which belonged to them, but actually I was taking money which belonged to the claimants.

? Do you think the agent was correct in his estimate of how to advance within the company? Might there have been another way to "get ahead"? In your opinion, was the agent any more guilty than the lawyers and doctors involved? How might a company discourage this type of dishonesty?

Embezzlement today can assume a new form. The explosive growth of computer technology has created a new white-collar menace: the computer criminal. Until recently,

As computer skills are acquired by ever-larger numbers of people, possibilities for white-collar crime increase. Computer experts are needed to develop safeguards against this new and highly sophisticated form of crime.

the high cost of personal computers put them far beyond the reach of most people. Now, however, lowered costs have helped spread them nationwide. In addition, many more students are studying computer technology, and more employees have access to computer terminals. Thus the potential for this sophisticated form of crime has been greatly increased.

In 1980, one bank was robbed by computer fraud of $21.3 million—more than half the total money lost through bank robberies in that year. Computers can tap into data-transmission lines to transfer money from one bank account to another. Each day more than $400 billion is transferred electronically by bank communication links. On a smaller scale, computer criminals, working within a corporation, can arrange to print out paychecks to fictitious persons or credit their charge accounts with large sums of money.

This new threat has created great pressure for the development of safeguards. Complicated codes, scrambled data, and special audit programs have been devised to assure computer security. Even so, protection devices to date lag behind the possibilities for crime.

Unlike criminals who are convicted of ordinary crime, white-collar criminals are often simply fined or sentenced to short terms in prison. Public outrage is generally lacking when illegal acts do not involve personal danger or loss. Then, too, corporations are often reluctant to publicize failures in their security systems, for fear of losing public confidence. As a result, many white-collar crimes are not revealed.

How can lawbreaking by executives and experts be explained? Sociologist Clifton D. Bryant writes:

> For ongoing commission of deviant behavior the individual must be able to acquire the necessary expertise, be strategically located to indulge in the behavior, be able to successfully disguise his actions and evade detection and sanction, encounter sympathetic and tolerant agents of social control, identify willing clients, victims, or co-perpetrators, and even if exposed, be able to enjoy a cushion for the resultant stigma and sanction. He must, in short, have *an opportunity structure* for deviant behavior, such as that often offered by his occupational specialty or the organizational work system in which he operates.

Thus while some criminal acts may be related to a person's limited ability to achieve goals, others may occur when opportunity offers illegal but comfortable means to success. The lack of ethical standards in individuals committing such crimes may be a personal failing, which is difficult to explain in sociological terms. The individuals' actions may also result from corporate policies that they feel helpless to resist.

REVIEW AND APPLICATION

1. IDENTIFY: White-collar crime.
2. In what ways does corporate crime affect the public? Can you give examples of such crime from the text or the news?

CRITICAL THINKING: Reread the account of the insurance agent on page 383. Which did the agent value more—success or honesty? Explain your choice.

3 Organized Crime

"The mob," "the syndicate," "the Mafia," "La Cosa Nostra"—all of these terms conjure up mental pictures of gun-toting racketeers planning gangland murders. Organized crime is indeed widespread, yet often much less dramatic. It is a "family" business organization, or group of organizations, and as such not only controls illicit enterprises such as drug dealing and gambling, but also has a hand in legal and often licensed industries, such as gambling casinos, sports complexes, and hotels. One study describes it this way:

> Organized crime has the unique distinction of being unlike any other criminal society. There is no question of impulse or insanity, nor ignorance of law or negligence. In organized enterprises each activity is preplanned and carefully prepared so as to avoid direct confrontation with law enforcement. Because of this nonconfrontation policy the public is not reminded of the millions of dollars that change hands as part of illegal activities. . . .
>
> A requisite of the organization has been the establishment of illegal enterprises to produce large profits, then convert these profits into channels of influence and legitimate enterprises.

Although the Mafia is frequently associated with organized crime, it does not monopolize it. The Mafia started in Sicily in 1282 as a patriotic and political organization and did not become directly involved with organized crime until the nineteenth century, when many of its members migrated to the United States to avoid persecution.

Today organized crime in America is made up of networks of about twenty-four different "families" and other groups. Among these differing groups, many internal power struggles take place for control of certain businesses and locations. Businesses such as bars and restaurants are likely targets for organized crime because it is relatively easy to manipulate their accounts and to invest in them without the funds being traced.

Organized crime has sometimes become involved with public agencies. For example, in one California county, organized crime, with the assistance of a local union, forced out independent hauling contractors who had negotiated an agreement with a big state highway project. The criminal interests then did millions of dollars worth of construction business.

In this instance, force was not necessary. It is not unusual, however, for a business that will not cooperate with the mob to find its deliveries cut off and its services curtailed. In more extreme cases, arson, bombings, beatings, kidnapping, and murder may be used to force a company to submit.

Organized crime continues to exist because of the ignorance or indifference of the participating public. Although thousands of men and women are involved in organized crime, there are relatively few convictions. This poor record results from people's fear of

"Crime does not pay at your level."

SOURCE: Drawing by Handelsman; © 1970 The New Yorker Magazine, Inc.

testifying and from the close connections of members with corrupt individuals in positions of power. Organized crime is hard to trace because its operations make up a network that crosses many cities and states.

REVIEW AND APPLICATION

1. What were the origins of the Mafia?
2. How does organized crime operate?

CRITICAL THINKING: Explain the cause-and-effect connection between people in powerful positions and the low conviction rate of organized crime members?

4 "Victimless" Crimes

At the other end of the continuum from organized crime are the so-called *victimless crimes.* Social problems such as alcoholism and drug addiction are not the results of antisocial acts committed by individuals against others. Rather, they represent problems of personal maladjustment. Stress, family difficulties, frustration, and tension may all be factors leading to maladjustment. Low intelligence, inability to compete successfully, or mental illness may be contributing factors. Most people believe that the causes of such deviance are multiple. Nor can specific problems be linked to specific individuals or groups. The afflicted are found at all social levels.

Some problems, however, are more common to particular groups. For example, the use of such drugs as heroin is prevalent in slum areas. Heroin has its distribution base among criminals living in areas of urban blight. They recruit teenagers looking for new "highs," usually young minority-group males. Many such young people have already been involved in crime. Their new habit perpetuates this tendency, as they frequently get money to buy drugs from shoplifting, auto theft, prostitution, burglary, and robbery.

Addiction has been defined as compulsive craving for habitual use of a substance. Although "escaping" into dependency on alcohol or other drugs is regarded by most people as deviant behavior, drinking alcohol and using drugs are a significant part of American culture. Social drinking is found almost everywhere. Similarly, although illegal drugs are rightfully condemned, Americans spend billions of dollars on doctors' prescriptions for barbiturates and various other mood-altering drugs.

Alcohol Abuse

Experts disagree on the exact definition of alcoholism. It is known, however, that alcohol alone accounts for approximately 24,000 traffic deaths annually. Excessive drinking also causes work absenteeism, accidents on the job, family disruption, poor health, and criminal behavior. Since there is much hidden and unreported alcoholism, analysts can only study samples of acknowledged drinkers. Although teenage drinking is an increasing problem today, findings indicate that the most severe alcohol abuse occurs in middle age.

"Skid Row" drunks form only a small percentage of these older alcoholics, but they have long been of interest to sociologists. Existing on welfare and by panhandling, Skid Row alcoholics are without jobs or homes. They have no traditional "social anchorages," such as family, friends, and religion, and they suffer from high rates of tuberculosis, venereal disease, pneumonia, and eye and teeth infections.

Sociologist Jacqueline Wiseman studied how the view of such people, predominantly men, toward themselves differs from the view held by those who try to help them. She found that people who work in jails, courts, Christian missions, and therapy clinics for alcoholics see the Skid Row alcoholic as depressed, apathetic, and overly dependent. This characterization leads to the view that the Skid Row alcoholic has been undersocialized. He is thought of as a "prime manifestation of social pathology." His apparent lack of commitment to family and job "is considered to be indicative of some flaw in his personality and upbringing." The Skid Row inhabitant himself, however, is more likely to attribute his state to conditions created by the society in which he lives.

Here a municipal court judge passes sentences on men convicted of being drunk and disorderly. It has been said that public drunkenness is a "victimless" crime because the only person hurt directly is the drinker. In what ways might society be considered a victim of drunkenness?

We Who Labor Here Seek Only Truth

Most people regard graffiti as an indication of social maladjustment. Some psychologists, however, view graffiti as a statement of identity and an effort at self-expression that may have positive psychological effects for the graffiti writer. Of course, society must pay the costs of the cleanup.

How does a person become a Skid Row alcoholic? According to one view, it is the result of a conscious decision. The alcoholic turns deliberately to drink and to Skid Row as "a solution to the tangible problems posed by poverty, transient status, and lack of family ties." Others suggest that social or psychological failure in the outside world causes a drinker who is already ignoring society's norms to sink gradually into the abyss.

CASE STUDY: *Manny, a Drug Addict*

"Drug abuse" commonly refers to the use of any drug to harmful excess or without proper medical supervision. Alcohol and nicotine are among the most widely abused drugs in the United States, and they are legal. Illegal and prescription drugs—such as the opiates, cocaine, marijuana, crack, barbiturates, and amphetamines—are also frequently abused. The opiates are derived from opium and include morphine, codeine, and heroin. They are often injected into the body, and they are considered physically addictive. The following case study, taken from a true account, reveals what opiate addiction can mean:

Most people don't really know what it is to be hooked on dope. I mean to be really sick. Like me and my brother Bobby in the Bronx back in the early sixties, after we were using for over a year. We were on a real heavy run. It was colder than the tail end of an iceberg, right in the dead of winter, and we're sleeping in the car parked out in the street because the cops were looking for me at my apartment. . . .

We have to fix; we have to get down. Not for the fun of getting loaded, but just to keep from getting sicker. So finally my brother says, "Okay, we'll go to a connection and score." This is two o'clock in the morning and it is in the middle of winter, and all I have on is a long-sleeved white shirt that I must have been wearing for over two weeks. No undershirt, no sweats, no coat. Just a thin, dirty, white shirt. . . .

I was hungry and I had no place to live, no place at all. I mean, nothin'! I had no friends. Y'know, I would con my own brother out of his shoes for a fix.

[Heroin] anesthetizes the whole . . . ugly world. All your troubles become forgotten memories, lost on another dimension, when you're in the nod. And you don't even consider that it will wear off and the gentle nod will turn into a screaming want. And the nose-dripping, crawling, wormy feeling of needing a fix always follows the mellowest nod. . . .

I had a lot of friends at one time. But I burned all my friends for dope. And that's not all, I'd of killed them too, for heroin, if that'd been necessary.

There is no consensus on the number of opiate addicts in the United States. Estimates range from 60,000 to 200,000. Most addicts are men. About half are under the age of thirty, and most are single and unemployed.

Opiate addiction can cause a multitude of problems. It is associated with criminal groups that import and distribute the drugs at very high prices. The cost forces many users to crime and other antisocial behavior to support their habits. Addiction can lead to health problems such as malnutrition and hepatitis. Overdoses may cause death. Although the individual user can suffer greatly, in the long run it is society that pays the price in needed community services.

REVIEW AND APPLICATION

1. *IDENTIFY:* Victimless crimes, addiction.
2. What did Jacqueline Wiseman observe about Skid Row alcoholics and the way others see them?

CRITICAL THINKING: What has opiate addiction meant to Manny?

5 The Justice System

Proposals for reducing crime often involve the justice system and almost always arouse strong feelings and controversy. Emotions arise because changes in social attitudes must take place before most proposals can be put into effect. Suggestions about how to handle crime and criminals usually fall under one of four categories: revising the law, changing the training and working conditions of the police, modifying the court system, and reforming the prisons.

Revise the Law?

Perhaps the most controversial suggestion concerning crime involves changing some of the legal definitions of what is criminal behavior and what is not. Many criminologists suggest "decriminalizing" victimless crimes like gambling, alcoholism, and narcotics use. Such a step would instantly decrease the workload of police as well as reduce the possibilities for corruption. It would also lighten clogged court schedules.

Decriminalization, moreover, would greatly lower the income of a major sponsor of these activities—organized crime. For example, if drug addiction were defined as a medical problem, the supply of drugs would be regulated by physicians. Organized crime would lose an important source of power and revenue. Addicts would not have to commit robberies and burglaries to support a very expensive habit. On the other hand, many people feel that this way of handling drug addiction would increase the number of addicts.

Because the results of the decriminalization of such crimes are unknown, it is unlikely that such legal changes will take place in this country. In any case, punishment is still regarded by many people as a deterrent and as the proper response to most deviant behavior.

Reform the Police and Courts?

Many reformers believe that making more money available to police and judicial systems would provide substantial help in handling the problem of crime. For example, more funding would make it possible to increase the size of police forces and to improve their training and efficiency. The presence of more officers in the streets has been shown to reduce crime. More modern equipment, such as computers, could facilitate record keeping. Higher pay might attract those with more education and would help retain police who find they cannot support a family on an officer's salary. More extensive training in human-relations skills would help police in their work with ghetto youth and with other groups in society whose customs and habits are unfamiliar to them.

Many social scientists feel that courts do not contribute as they should to deterring crime. The court system is now so jammed with cases that it is a serious question whether justice can be meted out. So much time can elapse before a case is resolved that witnesses may die or move away.

Those defendants who cannot afford bail often sit in jail for weeks or months. *Plea bargaining* has become an accepted way of dispensing justice. This is a system under which judges, prosecutors, defense attorneys, and defendants agree to allow the defendant to plead guilty to a lesser charge,

GRAPH SKILL *In many areas, crime is up, but arrests are down. Police consider shortage of personnel a major cause. In addition, many probation departments are too understaffed to properly supervise the lawbreakers in their custody. Since 1980, which has risen faster: criminal justice employment or expenditures? What is the percent of change for each?*

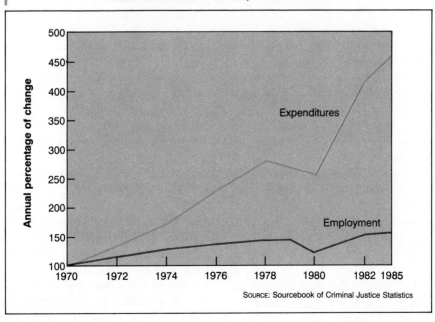

U.S. CRIMINAL-JUSTICE EMPLOYMENT AND EXPENDITURES, 1970–1985

SOURCE: Sourcebook of Criminal Justice Statistics

Should citizens rely on the police alone to fight crime? The Alliance of Guardian Angels, Inc., is an organization of young people formed to fight crime in the streets and on transportation systems. Active by 1982 in over twenty-two cities, the Guardian Angels learn karate, lifesaving techniques, and the legal requirements to make citizens' arrests. Some cities have welcomed their aid; in others, police and government officials have opposed them as "vigilantes" and questioned their value.

accept a lighter sentence, and thus avoid a lengthy and risky jury trial.

The appointment of judges has also come under scrutiny. Most judges are political appointees whose temperament and knowledge of the law have not been scrutinized. To get judges of the highest quality, some social scientists suggest, a local bar association could draw up lists of respected and competent candidates for appointment or election. In addition, these associations could help devise standards to assist judges in setting bail, sentencing criminals, and even conducting the trials.

? What steps might be taken to speed up the judicial process? Do you think the pres-ent system operates more to the advantage of criminals or against them? Explain your answer.

Reform the Prisons?

Prison is a controlled environment (see pages 64–65) for people who are considered threats to society. The welfare of prisoners is not the major concern. Like other controlled environments, prison forces inmates into a program of intensive resocialization. Policy is made by the warden and carried out be assistants and others in the hierarchy under his command. Prisoners are expected to follow the rules and routines all day and every day and to adapt to their new role.

Many studies have been made of prison life. All show prison to be a place where the inmates' lack of privacy and loss of a sense of self contribute to their dehumanization. If intensive resocialization forces prisoners into new roles, what will they be like when their jail terms are up? Does the need to control prisoners require guards to behave in a certain way?

An Experiment in Intensive Resocialization
To understand more about how guards and prisoners learn to play their roles, a group of social scientists set up a mock prison in the basement of a building at Stanford University as an experiment. Into this prison, they sent ten "prisoners" and eleven "guards." All the men were actually ordinary college students who had answered an advertisement offering them the chance to make fifteen dollars a day by participating in an experiment.

The people chosen to play the role of prisoner agreed to remain in the jail for two weeks, and each was arrested and booked by the local Stanford police, who cooperated in the experiment. Prisoners wore special smocks for uniforms and nylon stocking caps to imitate short haircuts. Guards were dressed in uniforms, and they carried billy clubs, whistles, and handcuffs. They wore sunglasses to avoid eye contact. They were told that they were responsible for maintaining law and order and that the situation was dangerous.

Prisoners were not allowed to write letters, smoke cigarettes, or go to the toilet without first obtaining permission. Roll call was held during each of three guard shifts, and prisoners were often awakened for special counts. Prisoners had to remain silent during rest periods, meals, and outdoor activities and after lights out. They could address each other only by ID numbers and were required to address guards as "Mr. Correctional Officer." The interaction between prisoners and guards was carefully recorded by hidden recorders and video cameras.

Consider the following three scenarios showing possible outcomes of the prison experiment. In scenario 1, although the guards and prisoners interacted within the prison setting, none of them could actually play the assigned roles. The guards did not treat the prisoners as inmates. Indeed, they were as kind to the prisoners as they were to their friends on the outside. All the guards were determined to be "good guys" and thus win the cooperation of the prisoners.

The prisoners didn't take their roles seriously. They knew they would be released in two weeks. They didn't feel afraid of the prison environment or the guards. The experiment showed that it is not possible to create a true prison atmosphere without the belief that prisoners have violated social norms and actually need resocializing.

In scenario 2, the prisoners played their role with great seriousness. The prison atmosphere, their uniforms, and their mock shaved heads all made them feel that they were actually "doing time." They followed the regulations carefully and did everything possible to cooperate with the guards. The prisoners seemed determined to show that they could maintain their dignity behind bars.

The guards also quickly stepped into an unfamiliar role. They had been told to keep order, and they did. They treated the prisoners with consideration, being careful not to abuse them. The guards decided that prisoners could be treated firmly but fairly. They

acted this out, and the prison ran smoothly. The experiment showed that the prisoner role could be played with dignity and that guards could control prisoners while treating them fairly as human beings.

In scenario 3, the prisoners panicked when they were arrested, searched, and locked up. They felt trapped by the bars, the guards' clubs, and the rules governing their behavior. They resented having to be told when they could smoke, use the toilet, or write a letter. They felt that the frequent prisoner counts, which even awakened them at night, were unnecessary.

Several prisoners could not adjust to the controlled setting. They quickly became depressed, cried constantly, and exhibited fits of rage. The authorities released them within the first few days, long before the scheduled

No society has been able to eliminate prisons, even though prisons seldom effect the changes in behavior hoped for. However, counseling can often be of value to first offenders and less hardened criminals, by helping them keep a sense of self-worth while they are in prison, and steering them toward a better life. Here a counselor discusses options with an inmate.

end of the experiment. Other prisoners rebelled and destroyed the furniture in their cells.

The guards quickly responded to the prisoners' actions. Guards felt threatened by the prisoners' hostility to their confinement. They decided that they could control the prisoners only by strict enforcement of rules. Prisoners were treated roughly and insulted on many occasions. A revolt was put down by spraying fire extinguishers at the prisoners. The guards punished all the rebellious prisoners and set aside a special cell for those who decided to cooperate.

? Which scenario do you think actually happened? Why?

Scenario 3 is correct. The experiment revealed that normal college students placed in a prison setting quickly assumed behavior that actual prisoners and guards display. When interviewed by the researchers, guards said how angry they became with prisoners who resisted their control. The guards enjoyed feeling the power they held over the prisoners and resented any attempt by the prisoners to stand up to them. One guard, for

Prisons have been called "warehouses of human degradation." Some prisons, however, make earnest efforts to separate "hard-core" criminals from those who have committed less serious crimes or who seem to be responsive to rehabilitation. This prisoner is an architect working in the prison's drafting shop.

example, told how he listened to a conversation a prisoner had with a visitor. The guard interrupted whenever he disagreed with anything the prisoner said. The guard reported that he relished the feeling of superiority, although he was deeply surprised by his own actions.

Most of the guards were sorry when the experiment ended. They did not like giving up the money they were making by participating in the experiment. But, even more important, they had really enjoyed their sense of power.

Prisoners, on the other hand, were glad when it was all over. In their cells they had talked almost constantly about the prison—food, their treatment, how they could escape. Prison had been a real and deeply troubling experience for them. They were afraid, hated their guards, and tried to rebel.

The experiment revealed that the prison affected the volunteers the way it does actual prisoners. The guards, too, responded much the way real guards do to hostile, threatening prisoners. It didn't matter that the subjects had individual personalities at the outset. Once put into their prison roles, they responded very similarly to others in those roles.

The researcher who led the experiment, Philip Zimbardo, concluded: "The prison situation, as presently arranged, is guaranteed to generate severe enough pathological reactions in both guards and prisoners as to debase their humanity, lower their feelings of self-worth and make it difficult for them to be a part of a society outside their prison."

Zimbardo's conclusion is supported by numerous official reports published over the years. Ramsey Clark, former attorney general of the United States, writes: "Jails and prisons in the United States today are more often than not manufacturers of crime. Of those who come to jail undecided, capable of either criminal conduct or lives free of crime, most are turned to crime. Prisons are usually little more than places to keep people—warehouses of human degradation. Ninety-five percent of all expenditures in the entire corrections effort of the nation is for custody—

iron bars, stone walls, guards. Five percent is for hope—health services, education, developing employment skills."

The Zimbardo material and other studies indicate that physical and verbal abuse by prison personnel produce only negative results. What are some changes reformers have suggested to make prisons more effective places for rehabilitation? Larger salaries would probably be necessary to attract administrators and professionals better qualified to provide teaching and counseling services. Since crowded quarters increase tension and the likelihood of violence and rebellion, more prisons seem to be needed. Overburdened staffs are unable to prepare inmates for productive work or to keep violence among prisoners under control.

Another approach advocates changing the characteristics of the corrective environment. Inmates, it is argued, should be brought into closer contact with the outside world. Although dangerous prisoners must be isolated from the rest of society, others should be taught employment skills. First offenders should be separated from the hardcore criminals. Model prisoners might be permitted to work in the community as part of their rehabilitation. Such work-release programs could also be associated with *halfway houses,* where prisoners who are soon to be released might live.

Efforts at rehabilitation such as these would face strong public opposition. More people accept reforms in theory than are willing to welcome prisoners or halfway houses into their neighborhoods. Where these suggestions have been implemented, they have shown some success. Yet there is strong resistance to programs that do not emphasize isolation and punishment.

In fact, some studies indicate that rehabilitation efforts are less effective than tough, assured penalties. As a consequence, it is unlikely that major changes will occur in our prison system. As long as we are threatened by criminals who attack us on the streets or break into our homes, we will continue to arrest, convict, and imprison increasing numbers of Americans. We have not yet found an

These Minnesota inmates are learning computer skills while serving their sentences.

effective public policy to deal with crime, its causes, and its punishments.

REVIEW AND APPLICATION

1. *IDENTIFY:* Plea bargaining, halfway house.
2. What is decriminalization and why has it been suggested?
3. How might police work be improved?
4. What were the conclusions Zimbardo drew from his experiment?

CRITICAL THINKING: Analyze the two approaches to prison reform discussed on page 393. Do you think work-release programs or better qualified teachers and counselers will make prisons more effective places for rehabilitation? Do you think halfway houses or more high-security prisons are needed? Explain your answers. After comparing the approaches, how would you recommend that the prison system be reformed?

Recap

Social norms define crime. That is, what is considered a crime in one society may be regarded as acceptable behavior in another. Violent crimes and crimes against property, however, are universally viewed as threats to society. In the United States, such "ordinary" crimes are on the increase.

White-collar crime is less visible and less frightening but still of great cost to society. Some corporate crime can be dangerous as well. Equally hidden from public view is organized crime, composed of "family" organizations that control vast fortunes in illicit enterprises. Preplanned operations, behind-the-scenes manipulations, and terrorist tactics have permitted organized crime to infiltrate many legitimate businesses as well.

Those involved in so-called victimless crimes are more obviously self-destructive than other criminals. However, the needs of alcoholics and other drug addicts can lead them to other criminal behavior, and the social costs of their problems are a public concern.

How to deal with crime and criminals, overloaded court schedules, and overcrowded "warehouse" prisons are unsolved problems for which many controversial solutions have been offered. Most social scientists agree that the justice system needs to be overhauled. One experiment in prison psychology revealed that the conditions of prison life have the opposite effect from the contrition and rehabilitation society desires and requires.

Key Terms

Define the following:

crime	victimless crime	plea bargaining
white-collar crime	addiction	halfway house

Applying Sociology

1. Which of the following suggested causes for the rise in crime rates seem most convincing to you? Explain your reasoning.

   Availability of weapons
   Racial discrimination

   Economic turndown
   Various revolutionary ideologies
   Loosening of social restraints as shown by more graphic violence and horror in the movies and television
   Deinstitutionalization of the mentally disturbed

Decline in religion

Emphasis on the self, on greed rather than service as a value

Desensitization through media contact with assassinations, hijackings, and so on

Hostility toward authority

Ineffectiveness of law-enforcement agencies

Ineffectual court procedures

2. Ramsey Clark states that prisons manufacture crime. Investigate some prison, such as Chino in California, that has attempted new policies in handling less hardened criminals. Describe these programs to the class.

3. Choose a theory or a combination of theories that seem particularly enlightening about the causes of crime. Write a composition using this theory to explain how persons become criminals.

4. Respondents to a poll were asked to identify some of the reasons that crime rates increase. The replies were as follows:

PUBLIC OPINION: RESPONSES TO THE QUESTION "WHAT DO YOU THINK IS RESPONSIBLE FOR INCREASES IN CRIME RATES?"

Cause	Percentage Naming Cause
Unemployment	33%
Court system too lenient	25%
No parental supervision	21%
Moral breakdown of society	14%
Drugs, alcohol	12%
Failure of police	8%
Not enough money in home	6%
No education	3%
No religion	3%
Feeling of hopelessness	2%
Increase in population	1%
Broken homes	1%

SOURCE: Adapted from the Gallup Organization survey conducted from November 2 to November 5, 1979.

The percentages listed here total more than 100 since many respondents gave more than one answer. Which combination of these possible causes do you feel would be most likely to contribute to increasing crime rates? Explain your reasoning.

5. Many observers of American life stress that people today often refuse to involve themselves in the affairs of their fellows. Several explanations have been offered:

   (a) The increasing anonymity of our urban life—very few people know many others on an intimate basis; it is not uncommon, for example, for apartment dwellers not to know who lives in the apartment next door to them
   (b) Fear that involvement will mean a considerable intrusion on one's own privacy
   (c) Being too busy with one's own affairs, resentment at the possibility of inconvenience
   (d) Basic dislike of other people
   (e) An underlying fear that involvement means exposing oneself and one's weaknesses to others, with the resultant possibility that one will be emotionally hurt in the process
   (f) Laziness
   (g) Fear of physical harm

   Which of these, if any, do you think is the most adequate explanation for this lack of involvement? Are there any indications of a change in this pattern?

6. Many authorities on crime feel there are two ways to reduce crime. One way is to head it off by working with young people to show them that nothing can be gained through a life of crime. One controversial program involved introducing students to "lifers," who described the horrors of the criminal life. Another way is to strengthen law-enforcement agencies to make it difficult for criminals to get away with crime. If you had to choose between these two ways, which one would you favor: trying to stop criminals before they begin or strengthening the police force to crack down on crime? Explain your reasons.

7. Respondents to a poll were asked how they would deal with a seventeen-year-old high school student from their own community who was caught stealing an automobile. They were told he had no previous record. Their responses were as follows, with (a) the response listed most often and (f) the response listed least often:

   (a) Give him another chance; be lenient.
   (b) Put him on probation; give him a suspended sentence.
   (c) Put him under the care of a psychiatrist or social worker.
   (d) Put him in an institution, such as jail or a reformatory.
   (e) Release him in the custody of his parents.
   (f) Punish his parents; fine them.

Do you disagree with this order? Explain why. Can you add any other suggestions to the list?

Jerome Brondfield, "Just for Kicks" *Reader's Digest*, August 1987, pp. 33–37.

1. What targets do vandals strike most often?
2. What are the costs of vandalism to our country?

Myron Peretz and Penina Migdal Glazer, "Whistle Blowing," *Psychology Today*, August 1986, pp. 36–43.

1. Why do some people feel they have to expose corruption in their company?
2. How did Vincent Laubach's superiors accept his revelation of departmental corruption?

John McCormick, "Chicago's Modern Mob: A Home in the Suburbs," *Newsweek*, May 11, 1987, p. 35.

1. Why did a group of organized crime bosses choose to make their homes in a rich Chicago suburb?
2. What barriers have the police encountered in attempting to stop the growth of organized crime in Du Page County?

Social Studies Skills

Adapting crime statistics from a bar graph to a circle graph The data from the graph on page 423 can also be presented on a circle graph. Draw a circle graph onto a separate piece of paper. Transfer the statistics regarding "Murder in the United States by Type of Weapon Used" onto the circle graph.

Completing a chart to compare types of crime

The various types of crime might differ in form and in their effect on society. Create a chart on a seperate piece of paper listing the various types of crime in one column and their effects on society in another. Complete the chart using facts from pages 377 to 385. Summarize your results.

Critical Thinking

Identifying Assumptions: What assumptions are made in this statement? "I knew he was from the worst part of town when I learned he was a convicted criminal."

CHAPTER

17

Problems of Mass Society

Chapter Preview

- **Before you read,** look up the following key terms in the glossary to become familiar with their definitions:

  mass society　　　　　　　　alienation　　　　　　anomie

- **As you read,** think about answers to the following questions:

1. What causes some cities to be overcrowded?
2. Why do many Americans prefer to live in single-family homes?
3. What are some solutions to industrial pollution?
4. What are the most important social conflicts in the U.S. today?

Chapter Focus

Mass society is a far cry from the traditional village described in Chapter 12. There everyone knows everyone else, transportation is limited, shopping is local, and personal interaction is highly prized.

Mass society does not just happen. It is the result of many factors, most important of which are the processes of urbanization and industrialization. As regional markets replace village squares, metropolitan centers begin to dominate cultural life. One of the principal lures of cities is their promise of new and exciting jobs. As more people hear of the wonders of city life, they break loose from the confines of farms and towns and set out for urban centers. Sometimes they find what they are after; more often they are faced with new problems to solve.

This chapter focuses on some of the problems that prevail today in mass societies, developed and developing, throughout the world. Many of the problems are products of social and geographic mobility, rapid growth, and poor planning.

Using Sociologists' Tools

- **Observe** the evening news for events reflecting problems of mass society such as hunger, disease, and overcrowding.
- **Describe** one particularly pressing problem in detail.
- **Analyze** the causes of that problem.
- **Predict** how the problem might be solved.

As population density rises in a given area, traffic congestion tends to worsen. Providing smooth transit for more people is one challenge facing urban planners.

1 Overcrowding

In Chapter 12, you read that population growth and movement can change a community. But the effects of population overcrowding go far beyond the community. Indeed, they create severe problems in all mass societies. A *mass society* is a society in which most people live in cities, crowded into small areas; physical contact with others is much greater than in small towns, but social contact is more impersonal. For example, think of a crowded elevator in an apartment complex or office building: the elevator riders know little about those against whom they are pressed every day. Similarly, crowded subways and buses carry strangers daily to their jobs in congested downtown areas.

Population Density

Density of population can vary greatly from city to city and even from neighborhood to neighborhood. Since *population density* is the number of people living in a given amount of space, it is not directly related to size of population. Even though San Francisco has a smaller population than Dallas, it has five times the population density of the larger city, as the table shows. In other words, although cities have an image as overcrowded places, some are not as tightly packed as others.

An extreme example of urban crowding is the city of Hong Kong. There, hundreds of thousands of people are crammed into housing that allows as little as twenty-four square feet of space (equal to four feet by six feet) per adult and only half that amount per child. A family of nine to twelve members might live in a single room of 120 square feet.

⁇ What effects might a lack of privacy have upon an individual? Do you think that close living quarters might make family members closer in other ways? Explain.

DENSITY OF SELECTED U.S. CITIES, 1984

Population per Square Mile

New York City	23,764	Detroit	8,031
Borough of Manhattan	65,590	Cleveland	6,918
		St. Louis	6,992
Paterson, N.J.	16,725	Oakland, Calif.	6,529
San Francisco	15,361	Seattle	5,843
Jersey City, N.J.	16,894	Honolulu	4,287
Chicago	13,119	Phoenix	2,208
Philadelphia	12,108	Dallas	2,940
Washington, D.C.	9,933	New Orleans	2,804

SOURCE: U.S. Bureau of the Census

CHART SKILL   *Population density figures are a more accurate measurement of overcrowding than population size figures. Which city, San Francisco or Cleveland, has a greater population density?*

Population Growth

Overcrowding has traditionally resulted from migration patterns in which large numbers of rural residents moved into the cities at about the same time. This was true in the United States throughout the nineteenth century, and, in some societies, this pattern continues today. In recent times, a lower urban death rate has caused further population growth that will lead to serious consequences if the economy cannot sustain the numbers being born. Only in industrial nations has the danger of overpopulation lessened.

One of the world's most crowded areas is Hong Kong, where poverty and housing shortages force thousands to live out their lives on boats in the harbor.

Problems that build up gradually, such as overpopulation, are not always foreseen at the outset. They often arise from direct or cumulative effects of acceptable norms and patterns of behavior. Sociologist Joseph Julian points out:

> Having many children has been a valued practice in many places for a long time, and for most of that time it was a real necessity. Throughout history, men and women have been producing offspring in great number, hoping that perhaps some of them might survive to adulthood. But now, because we have discovered ways of sustaining most human life, most societies suddenly have more than enough people. Certain countries, like India, have far more than they can feed properly. . . . In fact, many demographers predict that . . . by the year 2000 the earth will have more people than it can provide for.

Recently, other *demographers*—social scientists who study the relationship between population and social structures—have predicted that population growth will not be as extreme as many analysts have feared. For example, in 1981 the United Nations issued a report predicting that the world's population, then 4.4 billion, would stabilize at 10.5 billion by the year 2110. This assessment was based on a downward trend in population growth that began in 1965. That is, while population continued to "explode," the rate of increase had declined. The industrialized countries, which then accounted for 24 percent of the world's population, would account for only 13 percent in 2110, the UN report stated. And southern Africa and Asia would account for 60 percent of the earth's people.

What might this mean in terms of world social problems? No one, of course, can foresee possible events, such as war, that can radically throw off any projections. But barring cataclysms and unforeseen technological and agricultural advances, perhaps the main problem of the future will be world hunger.

WORLD POPULATION GROWTH

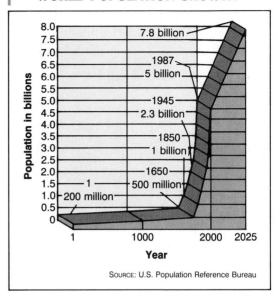

SOURCE: U.S. Population Reference Bureau

GRAPH SKILL   *Demographers estimate that approximately 50 billion people have lived since the beginning of human existence. If this is true, the 5.0 billion people alive today make up 10 percent of the total. If world population continues to increase at its present rate, current problems such as overcrowding and hunger will become even more acute. Some demographers, however, predict a leveling off of population by the year 2110. What technological, political, and social factors make such predictions tricky?*

In 1981, according to the UN report, about 10 percent of humanity went hungry. Thirty-six of the forty poorest and hungriest countries in the world exported raw materials or food to North America because they needed cash. As world population continues to grow, the political problems of equitable distribution will worsen. The ecological problems of depleted soil and dwindling amounts of land available for agriculture will make it difficult to produce sufficient food to feed the earth's billions.

The following reading is an excerpt from the diary of a woman who lived in a Brazilian slum, or *favela*, in the city of São Paulo, Brazil. She describes the pain and hunger she experienced. The author was more fortunate

WORLD POPULATION, 1987

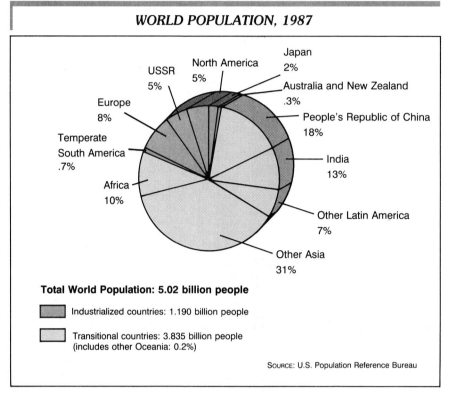

Japan 2%

USSR 5%

North America 5%

Australia and New Zealand .3%

Europe 8%

People's Republic of China 18%

Temperate South America .7%

India 13%

Africa 10%

Other Latin America 7%

Other Asia 31%

Total World Population: 5.02 billion people

Industrialized countries: 1.190 billion people

Transitional countries: 3.835 billion people (includes other Oceania: 0.2%)

SOURCE: U.S. Population Reference Bureau

GRAPH SKILL   *Birthrates in transitional societies are higher than those in industrialized countries. In 1987, the population of transitional countries was 3.835 billion. What percentage is this figure of the total world population?*

In the 1980s, hunger, a constant problem in transitional countries, was experienced for the first time by many in the industrialized countries as a result of worldwide inflation and unemployment. This Frenchman is searching for edible produce left in the trash.

than most slum dwellers, for the publication of this diary enabled her to improve the conditions of her life.

> I classify São Paulo this way: the Governor's Palace is the living room, the mayor's office is the dining room, and the city is the garden. And the *favela* is the back yard where they throw the garbage. . . .
> . . . How horrible it is to get up in the morning and not have anything to eat. I even thought of suicide. But I am killing myself now, by lack of food in the stomach. And unhappily I get up in the morning hungry.
> The boys got a few hard rolls, but they were covered with cockroach droppings. I threw them away and we just drank coffee. I put the last of the beans on to cook. I picked up my sack and went out, taking the children with me. I went to see Doña

Guilhermina, on Carlos de Campos Street. I asked her for a little rice. She gave me rice and macaroni. I stayed on to talk with her husband. He gave me some bottles to sell. And I picked up some scrap metal.

After getting a few things for the children to eat, I felt better. It calmed my spirit. I went to Senhor Manuel to sell the bottles. I got twenty-two *cruzeiros*. I spent ten on bread and a cup of coffee.

How horrible it is to see a child eat and ask, "Is there more?" This word "more" keeps ringing in the mother's head as she looks in the pot and doesn't have any more. . . .

All over the world, people in rural areas continue to migrate to cities, often finding only unemployment and squalid living conditions there. On the streets of Mexico City, one sees signs of both wealth and poverty. Given the conditions the text has described, which life, urban or rural, would you choose if you were a citizen of an industrializing country?

Most Brazilian cities have favelas, or slums, composed of shacks in areas without proper sanitation. These hillside buildings are in Rio de Janeiro.

When I first arrived from the Palace that is the city, my children ran to tell me that they had found some macaroni in the garbage. As the food supply was low I cooked some of the macaroni with beans. And my son João said to me, "Uh, huh. You told me we weren't going to eat any more things from the garbage."

The writer and her family had migrated to São Paulo from a rural area. Do you think they would have been better off if they had remained where they were? Why or why not?

Despite changes in the requirements of a society, people often continue to conform to once-legitimate societal expectations. For example, people may continue to have many children when society no longer needs large families. And despite the social ills in over-populated cities—hunger, crowding, and disease—people continue to flock to São Paulo, Hong Kong, Mexico City, Calcutta, and hundreds of other urban centers. They go there for many reasons, but most, of course, are searching for work and a better life.

Since social stratification, lack of job skills, and job scarcity all work together in most societies to limit work choices, few people are as fortunate as the diarist whose literary success changed her life. There is little social mobility in the world's transitional societies. Rich and poor stand in stark contrast, and the numbers of poor continue to multiply.

REVIEW AND APPLICATION

1. IDENTIFY: Mass society, population density, demographer, favela.

CRITICAL THINKING: "People often continue to conform to once-legitimate societal expectations .... [They] may continue to have many children when society no longer needs large families." What assumption about the reason people have children is implicit in the above statement? Do you think this assumption is valid? Why or why not?

2 Cities, Slums, and Suburbs

Overpopulation and population crowding in cities have caused a worldwide problem in housing. People need places to live, often as cheaply as possible. Because of a gradual decrease in the number of rural towns, in many countries most of the population lives in cities and suburbs. Inner-city slums in industrial countries share many conditions with slums thrown up on hillsides or even in cemeteries in transitional nations.

Case Study: Housing in a Transitional Country

Chile is one example of a country in transition. The two American students who wrote the letters in the following case study were traveling in Latin America some years ago. They wrote home about conditions in Santiago. As you read the case study, note the different types of housing mentioned and to whom they were available.

May 15

We've been in Santiago for two weeks now and have seen so much that we don't know what to tell first. Yesterday we rented a brand-new, lovely house in a fancy neighborhood where upper- and middle-class families are building homes. The house is brick, has a big living room, dining room, a study, one big bedroom, a small but modern and very clean kitchen, two bathrooms, a maid's room, a patio, and an unfinished back yard, where we'll have to plant some grass.

A young woman comes and helps with the laundry and cleaning two times a week. Most people here can't understand why we don't have a live-in maid. . . . Inez and her husband and young baby live nearby, along with many working-class families. Her husband is a construction worker earning two to three dollars per

A Saudi Arabian woman dressed in the traditional style for Moslem women stands out dramatically before a shop window filled with contemporary fashions.

day. They live in a wooden cottage (more like a little hut) on the building site. These houses are lean-tos occupied to make sure no one steals from the unfinished buildings—quite a contrast to the beautiful homes being built by business people and professionals here.

Nevertheless, Inez and her family are not completely down and out. She is the daughter of peasants who still live on a hacienda. She was brought to the city by a cousin of the owner to work as a maid when she was fourteen. Although she is still poor, she says she much prefers life in the city to the hacienda. In Santiago, she has more freedom. She hopes her children will get some schooling and be better off than she and her husband are now. . . .

June 1

. . . Today we took our first trip. We took the train to Valdivia, a medium-sized city in the south. We walked to the city's new university. The modern campus is quite pretty. The older universities in the main cities stress the older professions of law, medicine, engineering, and teaching. But this school has departments of forestry, agriculture, and other practical sciences. The children of the rich don't want to study these much-needed fields, but there is a large middle class who are slowly seeing how important these fields are.

We took the bus to a huge public housing project put up by the government. There are housing units for people of various levels. The lowest income units are very cheaply built and are becoming run-down quickly. Middle-class housing is better built. All the houses look alike, but they are pleasant places to live in and have all the modern conveniences which middle-class Chileans hope to own.

One thing here is very different. At home we have friends who are from fairly well-to-do families and some whose families are really struggling. Here, each social class seems to live in a separate world.

THE TEN MOST POPULOUS NATIONS, 1985

Rank and Country	Population in Millions
1. People's Republic of China	1,059
2. India	758
3. Soviet Union	278
4. United States	239
5. Indonesia	166
6. Brazil	135
7. Japan	120
8. Bangladesh	101
9. Pakistan	100
10. Nigeria	95

SOURCE: U.S. Bureau of the Census

CHART SKILL The table above shows the ten most populous countries in order of population size. As countries have become industrialized, their birthrates have dropped. What is the relationship?

The poor are only friendly with each other, and the same is true of middle-class and rich people. The little kids who live in the construction-site houses would never dream of playing with the kids in the fancy houses on the block. The gap between them is immense.

June 15

Last Saturday we took a bus to the end of the line, which was at the edge of the city. Mountains, fields, and a small group of shacks met our view. As we walked through, we saw these dwellings were made of scraps picked up anywhere and everywhere—wood, cardboard, tin, and anything else around. Of course, there is no indoor plumbing or electricity. The houses have dirt floors and are without windows.

It is clear that the people who live in these slums are the poorest people in the city. They've come from the countryside and have no marketable skills. Few have jobs. They try to sell gum or newspapers or collect and resell old bottles and shoes. The kids go begging from door-to-door or asking for odd household jobs. The government is trying to build *poblaciones*, small tracts of public housing, as fast as possible. But the task is enormous.

? What reasons are mentioned in the case study for migration to the cities? What aspects of mass society are indicated?

Sociologists who have studied poor communities in some transitional countries have found that slums such as those described here represent only one type of settlement. Migrants from the countryside sometimes band together, seize some empty government land, and go about the business of forming their own community. These people are known as squatters. The men work in the central city in factory and construction jobs, in service jobs such as bus driving, and in small workshops. Others run their own small retail and service businesses, such as shoe repair, specialty shops, and the like. Many women add to the family income by running small shops in their own communities or selling in other neighborhoods.

? What risks might people be taking by becoming squatters on government land? Do you think the benefits are worth the risk?

Housing in the United States

No cities in the United States suffer the population density of Hong Kong or the lack of facilities of the Brazilian *favelas* or the outskirts of Santiago, Chile. In fact, the American ideal of owning a single detached home continues to be the norm. Of all the housing units—houses, apartments, mobile homes—counted in the 1980 census, 62 percent were single-family detached homes.

Today's Households The 1980 census also showed fewer people living in each dwelling; the average household dropped from 3.1 persons to 2.8 in a decade. This happened despite the increase in housing costs, which far outstripped increases in household income. One indicator of the rising costs of home

A PROFILE OF AMERICAN HOME BUYERS

	1987	1983
WHO THEY WERE		
A Demographic Profile		
Median age	37.0 yrs.	34.4 yrs.
Unmarried	26.0%	25.8%
One- and two-person households	53.6%	51.3%
An Economic Profile		
Median income	$45,996	$35,987
Importance of second income*	54.5%	53.6%
First-time Buyers	35.1%	39.7%
WHAT THEY PURCHASED . . .		
Condominiums	13.5%	10.9%
New homes	24.8%	19.1%
Homes 25 or more years old	30.0%	34.2%
Median size of home (sq.ft.)	1,568	1,451
. . . and Its Cost		
Median purchase price	$95,000	$65,000
Median down payment	$19,850	$12,000
Median total monthly housing expense	$822	$709
Mortgage payment	$601	$524
Real estate taxes	$ 96	$ 65
Utilities	$100	$100
Hazard insurance	$ 25	$ 20
HOW THEY AFFORDED THEIR PURCHASE		
Less than 20% down payment	50.4%	55.1%
Housing expense exceeding 25% of household income	30.5%	40.4%

*Percentage of households with two adults in which income contributed by a second earner accounted for 10% or more of total household income.

SOURCE: U.S. League of Savings Associations

CHART SKILL   Many demographic trends as well as economic changes are revealed in this profile of the typical home buyer in 1983 and 1987. What generalizations about changes in American society can you make from this profile?

ownership was the increase in the number of mobile homes—up 84 percent since 1970. Mobile homes, of course, are much less expensive than conventional houses.

Many social trends have had an impact on American housing patterns: more single-parent families, more divorces, smaller families, the tendency of more young and elderly people to live alone. Thus, while population increased by 11 percent between 1970 and 1980, the number of households increased by 24 percent. Many Americans seem to prefer privacy, whatever the reason.

Still, some parts of our major urban areas are extremely congested. New York's Borough of Manhattan has nearly 65,000 people per square mile. The New York metropolitan area, which includes the five boroughs of New York City plus nearby regions of New York State, New Jersey, and Connecticut,

Congestion is an inevitable part of life in a major urban area.

contains more people than the combined populations of Alabama, Arizona, Delaware, Idaho, Massachusetts, Maine, Montana, Nevada, New Hampshire, New Mexico, North Dakota, South Dakota, Rhode Island, Utah, Vermont, and Wyoming. Despite current trends toward more households and fewer people per household, overcrowding is a problem in some of our cities.

New Urban Problems As is true of urban areas throughout the world, the poor in the United States tend to be concentrated in major cities. In Chapter 12, you read about the classic patterns of urban succession, in which immigrants from Europe, blacks from the rural South, and Puerto Ricans and other Hispanics congregated in the cities and then moved progressively outward.

Since the late 1950s, new patterns of urban succession have emerged in some areas—

The low incomes of the urban poor and the deteriorated housing of inner-city areas provide little tax revenue for American cities. Many people with the money to support city services have migrated to the suburbs.

patterns that threaten the economic survival of the city itself. While fewer people in the United States have moved from rural to urban areas, and fewer blacks have left the South for northern cities, many cities nevertheless have grown progressively poorer. This has happened because the middle and upper classes have increasingly abandoned the cities to the poor.

Poor city people must rely heavily on public services for transportation, medical care, hospitalization, and various other needs. Their limited incomes give them little buying power to keep city businesses going. Then, as businesses fail or leave, the tax revenues needed to maintain the city's many services decline. Income from property taxes also falls because neighborhoods deteriorate and property values go down.

The flight of industry has also contributed to the financial problems of urban areas in the United States. In many of the older industrial cities, major industries important to the economy have moved out in search of lower production costs, leaving unemployment and economic decay in their wake. This happened in such urban centers as Chicago, Detroit, New York, and Providence. The garment industry, for example, moved from northern to southern communities, where unions were weak or nonexistent and labor was cheaper. Similarly, the shoe and textile industries left New England and relocated not only in the South but also in other countries, such as Spain, Brazil, Taiwan, Korea, and the Philippines.

? In your opinion, is there any chance that the social classes with money to spend will move back into American cities? What might make them do so? Should people who work in a city but live elsewhere be required to support city services through taxation? Why or why not?

Growth of the Suburbs

Where do the middle and upper classes go when they abandon the cities? As everyone knows, they go to the suburbs. *Suburbs* have been defined as urbanized, residential communities that are outside the corporate

The majority of Americans prefer to own their own homes. Whether modest or luxurious, a home of one's own usually offers a yard and a sense of privacy that multiple dwellings fail to provide.

limits of a large central city but that are culturally and economically dependent upon the central city. One may further distinguish between "residential" and "employing" suburbs—those where people live and those where people live and work.

Suburbs are not a recent phenomenon. Large cities, such as New York and Chicago, had suburbs more than a hundred years ago, but the percentage of the population that lived in them was relatively small. The economic boom after World War II enabled thousands of middle-class city dwellers to buy their first piece of the American dream in suburbia: a home of their own; fresh air, space, and sunlight; clean, uncrowded schools for the children; friendly neighbors; a front lawn and a back yard. For many people, this approximation of the rural roots of our society had an irresistible appeal, and, by 1970, the population of the suburbs had surpassed that of the inner cities.

The economic boom that took place after World War II was only one cause of this phenomenal growth. Technology—the fuse for the urban population explosion of the last two centuries—played an important role. The prevalence of private automobiles and the availability of cheap gasoline spurred suburban growth. So did low-cost housing loans, government road-building projects, a rising birthrate, and a lack of housing in the central cities.

In 1950, the suburbs had less than 14 percent of the population; by 1970 they had over 37 percent. The figure continued to increase into the 1980s. As the flaws in city life motivated city dwellers to leave, so the seeming absence of these flaws in suburbia exerted a magnetic pull. City planner Edmund Bacon summed up the move this way:

> The rapid spread of this suburban image came about, I think, because valid dissatisfaction with life in the city led to acceptance of the idea that the . . . exact opposite was obviously the best thing achievable. So came the idea that low

density was good, therefore, lower density was better, and the more space around each home, the higher the state of culture it represented.

Suburban Problems There is little question that suburbs as well as cities face a number of problems in the 1990s. As a result of suburban growth, traffic arteries between cities and suburbs have become increasingly overloaded during rush hours and on weekends. Systems of mass transit have trouble attracting enough commuters to break even financially. This is partly because government appropriations tend to favor roads at the expense of public transportation. The effect is to jam cars together not only on commuter arteries but also on city streets, adding to congestion and air pollution in suburbs and city as well.

Originally, suburbia grew as young nuclear families moved in, assured that abundant gasoline was available for commuting to jobs. Now, suburban streets that once echoed with the sound of children are silent. The children have grown up and moved away, and the houses are too expensive to be purchased by most young families. Energy costs for heating and transportation have risen, and the energy supply seems to be much less guaranteed.

Rising gasoline prices have encouraged a movement of jobs from central cities to outlying regions. The number of white-collar positions, in particular, has expanded as corporate offices have moved away from city taxes and high rents. Overall, 70 percent of workers from suburban areas now work in the suburbs. But this change has brought new problems, too. Suburban land values have soared with the influx of corporate headquarters. As a result, housing costs have increased still further, and homeowning in suburbia is beyond the reach of many young families.

Recent statistics tell the story. Consider, for example, what is happening on suburban Long Island, near New York City. Demographers estimate that in 1990 the population under age fourteen will have dropped 40 per-

Commuting from the suburbs to jobs in the cities is a source of frustration for the millions of Americans whose cars clog major arteries.

cent from its 1970 total and the high school population will have been cut in half. Such figures don't just indicate school closings; they reflect a lower level of support for a major institution of suburban life. Parents whose children are adults are far less likely to accept high taxes to support education. The median age of suburban residents has thus risen sharply and will soon equal that of city dwellers.

Another major difference between suburbs and cities is also fast disappearing. As you read in Chapter 16, high crime rates drive people out of cities. But crime is now rising rapidly in the suburbs. In 1981, violent crime in some suburbs was up 20 percent over 1980, while the increase was about 9 percent nationwide.

The division of metropolitan areas into the central city, where most of the money in today's economy is earned, and the suburbs, where much of it is spent, has helped create a dilemma known as the "crisis of the cities." Many solutions have been proposed, but few have been tried, chiefly for lack of cooperation from the suburbs. Suburbs are not eager to share their wealth with cities voluntarily. However, if a workable solution is not found, central cities may decay to the point where traffic congestion, crime, slums, and other urban problems seriously threaten the well-being of city and suburb dweller alike.

Recent Trends In many American cities, real estate developers, large and small, have begun reclaiming deteriorated neighborhoods by restoring old apartment buildings for new condominiums. Couples also buy old houses for restoration, an increasingly popular venture among the middle classes. Rather than heading for the suburbs, some young two-paycheck families are restoring, buying, or renting in the city, where they find life convenient and interesting. This trend has been called gentrification.

While it often results in the rebirth of a dying area, gentrification has created problems for the poor and the elderly, who may be evicted from their center-city homes as their rental apartments are converted to condominiums or cooperatives that must be purchased.

Restoration of old houses, such as these in Wilmington, Delaware, is taking place in many American cities. This process of renewal has been called gentrification because it often involves the displacement of poor people by affluent working couples.

No one is certain how far this return of the middle classes to the cities will go. If it continues, it will probably result in many other changes in schools, businesses, and cultural facilities. It will also bring about new political alignments and unforeseen results.

REVIEW AND APPLICATION

1. *IDENTIFY:* Poblaciones, favelas, suburbs.
2. What is the character of housing in developing countries, as described in the case study of Santiago, Chile?

3. What social trends have influenced American housing patterns?
4. What are some reasons for the financial problems in American cities?
5. What factors have contributed to the growth of the suburbs?
6. What are some of the problems facing the suburbs today? What are some of the results of these problems?

CRITICAL THINKING: You have read that the return of the middle classes to the cities will result in changes in schools, businesses, and cultural facilities. What do you think these changes will be? Explain the connection between the return of the middle classes and each change you cite.

3 Pollution

Just as the increase in population, expansion of cities, and urban-suburban migrations were first viewed only in a positive

"So that's where it goes! Well, I'd like to thank you fellows for bringing this to my attention."

SOURCE: Drawing by Stevenson; © 1970 The New Yorker Magazine, Inc.

light, so, too, was the growth of technology and industry in modern society. Technological advances created the capacity to produce thousands of desirable products: air conditioners, easy-care synthetic fabrics, and microwave ovens, to name only a few. Resulting industrial expansion created jobs, satisfied consumer demand, and, by generating profits, formed the underpinning of a sound economy.

Yet there is a dark side, too. Such production can cause industrial pollution, which harms people and the environment. It often produces wastes that are difficult to get rid of, and sometimes it exposes workers to dangerous materials.

Although industrial pollution has existed for more than a century in our society, only since the 1950s has it aroused widespread concern among consumer and government organizations. But the efforts of these organizations to control pollution and eliminate health hazards have met with opposition. Many Americans fear that attempts to regulate industry may result in a loss of productivity, jobs, and profits. There has been serious conflict among various groups about whether to define pollution as a social problem and whether to commit resources to seek a solution.

One well-documented case of industrial pollution was exposed in the late 1970s. It was discovered that a chemical company had stored vast quantities of toxic waste materials in the Love Canal area near Niagara Falls, New York. Seepage of chemicals caused health problems and suffering among the residents of the region. A local reporter, Michael Brown, wrote about the situation:

When I walked on the Love Canal, I gasped for air as my lungs heaved in fits of wheezing. My eyes burned. There was a sour taste in my mouth. It seemed inconceivable that industry and government could have allowed this to happen, and yet there it was, an exposed cesspool of chemicals threatening not only those who lived nearby but, through its seepage, the viability of the very river my hometown was famous for. . . .

Nor was Niagara alone. Early in 1978, I had begun calling other regions of the country to see if they, too, had landfill problems. I [found] . . . that there were

indeed other dumpsites leaking their contents in a way that threatened human health.

Industrialization brings many advantages to a country, but the technology that accompanies industrialization causes problems, too. Waste products seem to accumulate faster than systems can be devised to get rid of them.

DRINKING WATER PROBLEM AREAS IN THE UNITED STATES

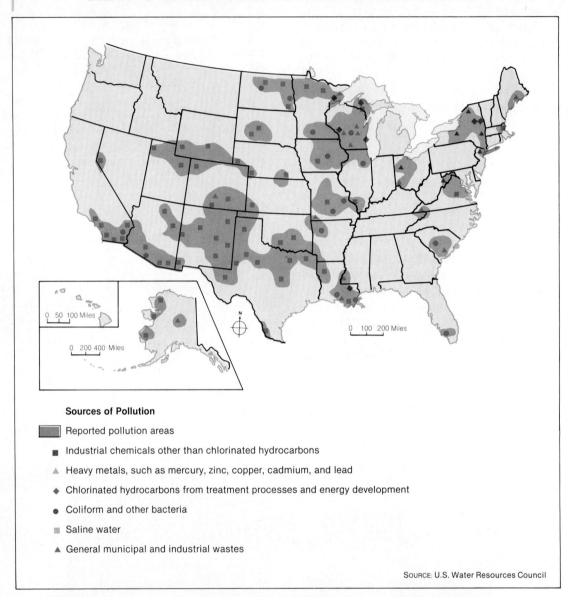

Sources of Pollution

- Reported pollution areas
- ■ Industrial chemicals other than chlorinated hydrocarbons
- ▲ Heavy metals, such as mercury, zinc, copper, cadmium, and lead
- ◆ Chlorinated hydrocarbons from treatment processes and energy development
- ● Coliform and other bacteria
- ▪ Saline water
- ▲ General municipal and industrial wastes

SOURCE: U.S. Water Resources Council

MAP SKILL The United States is fortunate in having ample supplies of clean water and little waterborne disease. But controversy surrounds the issue of water pollution, which has greatly increased in recent years. Science, industry, and government have yet to reach complete agreement on the technology and standards necessary to keep our water safe. The map indicates where federal and state or regional study teams have discovered specific water problems. Why are these areas so polluted?

Brown also discussed policies that might prevent similar problems, including the institution of safer procedures by industry, enforcement by government agencies, and the education of citizens to possible dangers. In the Love Canal situation, the state and federal governments finally relocated residents to safer areas. National exposure of this local disaster led to further study of toxic waste problems and to public consciousness of them. But how to handle toxic wastes remained a subject for research and debate.

REVIEW AND APPLICATION

1. What kind of pollution problem is exemplified by the Love Canal?
2. What are some advantages and some dis-

advantages of a highly industrialized society?

CRITICAL THINKING: Identify the results of industrial pollution at Love Canal alluded to in the following passage: "When I walked on the Love Canal, I gasped for air . . . an exposed cesspool of chemicals [was] threatening not only those who lived nearby but, through its seepage, the viability of the very river my hometown was famous for . . . ." What can be done to change the situation?

4 Alienation

How do residents of congested, decaying, polluted cities react to the pressures and inconveniences of their lives? Some social scientists claim that people living in mass society have different feelings about themselves and about other people than do residents of small towns. There is much evidence that one of the chief effects of urban living is a breakdown of group feelings. Lacking clear norms to guide behavior, people in cities may suffer from a widespread sense of loneliness. And many city residents—not merely the socially isolated—suffer from feelings of *alienation.*

Alienation is a feeling of not being involved in or a part of one's society or culture. To a person who is alienated, the values of the larger society seem meaningless. A sense of powerlessness prevails.

Many urban sociologists believe that the city fails to give its residents a feeling of security. For instance, Joseph Lyford called one large area on the West Side of Manhattan "an airtight cage" and described its inhabitants this way:

People convey the feeling that they have no community worth talking about. [An] attitude survey . . . reported that West Siders then had only the vaguest idea of where they would turn in case of need. They almost never mentioned political organizations, government agencies, or elected officials, and no single institution was mentioned more than a handful of times. . . .

The only people who talk about community as if they believe in it are the people who are paid to be community organizers.

The one [point of agreement] is that there is no community. The group that cuts across all class lines is the army of noninterferers who remain passive while violence is committed on another human being.

Lyford was talking about a section of New York City, but he might have been talking

Feelings of alienation are common in mass society, where people tend to be isolated and to lack a sense of community with others.

about any number of places marked by alienation and apathy. In such places, people are caught up in their own world. Because of high crime rates, city dwellers are often afraid to be friendly with strangers on the street or to come to the aid of others while crimes are in progress.

One example of fear conquering communal feeling is the well-publicized case of Kitty Genovese. This young New Yorker was attacked in the parking lot of her apartment building. Beaten and stabbed, she screamed for help. Many residents of the building heard her, but none went to her aid. Genovese died and her killer got away. An investigation of the crime showed that at least thirty-eight people had seen it. When they were asked why they didn't try to do something, they said, as if with one voice, "We didn't want to get involved."

What causes residents of big cities to feel alienated and uninvolved? Fear of becoming a crime victim is only part of the reason. According to urban sociologist Louis Wirth, the vast number of relationships that any city dweller must have makes formality, superficiality, and impersonality inevitable in human encounters. Because the informal social controls found in a community do not exist in a city, formal controls must be established: regulations, laws, and vigilant police departments.

Not knowing one's neighbors and not being known by them, perhaps, weakens the recognition and following of norms. And the diversity of values and norms in the city may also increase the distance between people. Perhaps, for some people it is not a decrease in caring for others that causes indifference or inaction. Rather, it is a belief that, with so many people around, someone else will step in to help when necessary.

The good and the bad in urban living are not felt equally by all people. The elderly living in inner-city areas are particularly affected by loneliness. They also suffer from the unwillingness of doctors to make house calls and the reluctance of cab drivers to venture into certain areas after dark. Even a city's pattern of ethnic enclaves may work against the elderly by increasing their sense of isolation. Alone in urban housing projects, old people may be attacked without restraint by muggers and purse-snatchers in deserted hallways. Fear and isolation create an alienation that may lead old people into mental deterioration.

REVIEW AND APPLICATION

1. *IDENTIFY:* Alienation.
2. Why did Joseph Lyford call an area of Manhattan "an airtight cage"?
3. What happened in the case of Kitty Genovese?
4. According to Louis Worth, what are the major causes of alienation? Which group is particularly affected by loneliness?

CRITICAL THINKING: What value does Joseph Lyford believe city people must acquire to eliminate alienation? Why?

5 Social Conflict

You have read how social life is possible because children are taught how to act and what to expect of others. The processes of socialization are central for preparing children, teenagers, single adults, parents, and the elderly to play appropriate roles. Sometimes situations arise, however, when people can no longer predict or control the behavior of others. At such times, the human density and potential for friction in mass society can produce social conflict.

People do not always agree on the extent of a problem or on the methods suitable for a solution. When a common understanding no longer exists about what is appropriate action, the result is social disorganization—the state called *anomie*. As you read in Chapter 12, this phenomenon was one result of the Buffalo Creek disaster, and it is a common phenomenon in mass society.

Even in situations in which the reactions of others are predictable, problems can arise

HIGH SCHOOL SENIORS REPORTING THEIR CONCERNS ABOUT SELECTED SOCIAL PROBLEMS, 1976–1985

	Class of 1976 (N[1] = 3,008)	Class of 1980 (N = 3,286)	Class of 1985 (N = 3,286)
Chance of nuclear war	42.2	67.4	64.5
Population growth	56.5	36.1	25.7
Crime and violence	89.0	81.2	82.3
Pollution	78.5	62.4	46.9
Energy shortages	70.7	83.9	33.7
Race relations	54.1	39.7	43.4
Hunger and poverty	63.7	52.8	69.7
Using open land for housing or industry	42.2	34.4	30.4
Urban decay	27.7	22.8	17.9
Economic problems	67.7	74.9	60.4
Drug abuse	67.4	63.3	69.1

[1]N represents number of respondents
SOURCE: Institute for Social Research, University of Michigan

CHART SKILL   Opinion polls reveal individual and group perspectives on issues facing society. The chart above reflects high school seniors' concerns about selected social problems. Study the changes from 1976 to 1985. How do you explain the most significant differences? Which of these issues are of concern to you?

when people disagree on what to think and how to behave. Instances of value conflict—serious disagreement over what is good and appropriate—abound in our society. Recent years have witnessed intense struggles over racial integration, abortion, gay rights, military spending, and the women's movement. In each instance, interest groups have appealed to American values—in the controversy over abortion, for example, the slogans "right to choose" and "right to life" reflect deeply held beliefs.

An analysis of the debate over nuclear energy shows how conflicting values lead to contradictory solutions. Because the United States is dependent on foreign oil for a sizable percentage of its energy needs, some groups maintain that Americans must build nuclear plants to assure sufficient energy output. The industry's safety record, they say, is unequaled in its protection of its workers, and they claim that no deaths have ever been traced to nuclear power plants.

Opposing groups believe that nuclear power plants are threats to people living in their vicinity and may also endanger future generations through genetic damage and contamination of soil and water. These groups advocate conservation and investment in solar power and other alternative energy sources. At times they have organized to prevent nuclear plant construction at various sites.

In 1979, an accident at Three Mile Island, Pennsylvania, intensified the debate over nuclear power. After a failure in the plant's cooling system, local residents were evacuated for several days. While many in the region anxiously awaited news about whether a major release of nuclear radiation had resulted, others were not concerned.

The debate over the dangers of nuclear plants intensified after the world's most serious nuclear disaster occurred in the Soviet Union on April 25, 1986. As a result of human and technical error, the core of the Chernobyl nuclear plant, located near the city of Kiev, melted down, spewing radioactive mist throughout the region and across much of Europe. Many of the workers in the immediate area were contaminated. Several died from radiation poisoning, and millions of Soviet and European citizens anxiously pondered the dangerous health effects of their exposure to the fall-out. Would there be a high rate of cancer and birth defects in years to come? What would be the consequences of radioactive material getting into the food chain, affecting plants and animals? For many, Chernobyl has come to symbolize the dangers to humanity of uncontrolled technology.

In Chapter 13, you read how social movements arise to represent both sides of every such value-laden social issue. In 1982, for example, a sharpened awareness of the dangers of nuclear war—including the possible destruction of the earth—created nearly worldwide disagreements between those who advocated nuclear weapons buildup and those who proposed a nuclear "freeze" or even nuclear disarmament.

At issue in the debate over nuclear weapons were several untestable questions: Can there be a "limited nuclear war," or is world conflagration inevitable once any nuclear weapons are employed? Will fear of annihilation force a superpower to make the "first strike"? Are the United States and the USSR about equal in nuclear strength, or does the USSR have an advantage? If the two countries are at parity, will this "balance of terror" continue to keep the peace, or is limitation or disarmament of nuclear weapons a better answer? Is disarmament even a realistic goal, given the distrust between nations?

Problems of world hunger, human congestion and conflict, and nuclear threat remain unsolved in the early 1980s. Mass society brought with it great technological achievements in energy, in space, and in the biological sciences. The ways in which these advances should be employed for the benefit of humanity continue to be concerns for moral debate.

REVIEW AND APPLICATION

1. *IDENTIFY:* Anomie.
2. What are some issues of value conflict prevalent to mass society in recent years?
3. What qualities of mass society produce social conflict?
4. What are the arguments given by nuclear power advocates? What arguments are given by their opponents?
5. What was the effect of the accident at Three Mile Island on the nuclear power debate? How did people living near the plant respond to the accident?
6. What are some of the questions that have arisen in the debate over nuclear weapons?

CRITICAL THINKING: Name a value that each of the following groups in the text is identified with: proponents of abortion, opponents of abortion, proponents of nuclear power, opponents of nuclear power, nuclear weapons advocates, nuclear disarmament advocates.

Recap

Social problems of the city and of modern industrial society go hand in hand. Modern cities are characterized by large size, housing density, and a great many poor people. In transitional countries, social stratification, few skills, and fewer opportunities condemn many to a degraded existence. Yet people continue to move to cities in search of a "better life."

In the United States, a highly industrialized economy has allowed the majority the luxury of private homes. Many central cities, however, have lost the tax base necessary to stem a downward slide when abandoned by businesses and the middle and upper classes. Transportation problems threaten the viability of suburbs themselves. In recent years, housing shortages and the deterioration of transit systems have affected both cities and suburbs. The changing urban scene has also led to new concepts of urban-suburban interdependence.

Some of the social problems associated with mass society are related to industrialization and advanced technology. Of paramount interest to certain groups are pollution concerns, which threaten worker health and safety. Mental health, too, is being challenged by the isolation that frequently produces alienation and anomie. Rather than withdrawing into themselves, some people respond to urban pressures by asserting their beliefs. Social conflict is common in mass society. Recently, nuclear energy and the possiblility of nuclear was have become issues that continue to cause concern.

Key Terms

Define the following:

mass society
population density
demographer

favela
suburb

alienation
anomie

Applying Sociology

1. Some countries, including France, Sweden, and Australia, have been concerned about underpopulation. Research one of these societies and write a brief composition on why that country wishes to counter its declining birthrate.
2. This text has viewed cities from a positive point of view, in Chapter 12, and from a negative point of view, in this chapter. Write your own view of cities. If you live in a city, tell why you plan to stay or to leave. If you don't live in a city, tell whether or not you plan to live in one someday and give your reasons.
3. Following is a list of words that have been used in describing cities. Number them from 1 to 15 in order of appropriateness, beginning with the most appropriate. Give reasons for your order.

dangerous
exciting

crowded
confusing
cruel
vibrant
dirty
stimulating
sick
frightening
cultured
hard
variegated
alive
indifferent

What other words can you add to the list?

4. Part of what makes a city a good or bad place to live is the habits of those who live there. Make a list of people's habits that make city living pleasant and a list of habits that make it undesirable. Is there any way the government of a city can change some of the harmful behavior of its inhabitants? Explain.

5. Form a committee to investigate your state pollution laws. After you find out what the laws are in your state, investigate court records or newspaper files to see how many charges have been made under the laws. Are the laws effective?

6. Make a list of all of the characteristics and pressures of mass society that you consider to be alienating. Are solutions to any of these pressures possible through personal efforts, government regulations, or group efforts? Make a matching column in which you give your suggestions for solutions.

7. Make a list of small indicators that seem to represent the depersonalization of mass society, for example, numbers instead of named telephone exchanges, plastic containers for cream rather than pitchers, or "fast food" in general. Would you eliminate these features if you could, or have you adapted to them as a consumer? Write a short paragraph to explain your thoughts.

8. Rank the following nine ways to reduce air pollution according to their feasibility and importance to good air quality, beginning with the most feasible and important:

(a) require the use of no-lead gasoline only

(b) ban diesel trucks and buses from city streets

(c) require industries to burn low-sulfur fuel

(d) require antipollution devices on all smokestacks

(e) ban all open burning within city limits

(f) ban airports within twenty miles of the city

(g) raise the tax on gasoline for use in private automobiles

(h) arrest drivers of automobiles that produce excessive smoke

(i) require antipollution devices on all automobiles

Are any of these laws in effect? What consequences, other than improving the air, might they have on the public?

9. If possible, invite a member of some group that advocates nonviolence and a representative of the armed forces or the National Guard to speak to the class on the question of disarmament versus nuclear deterrence as a way of avoiding war. Have the class prepare questions in advance to ask the speakers.

Martha Smiglis, "Hands Up and Butts Out!," *Time*, April 27, 1987, p. 78.

1. How do most smokers feel about the ban?
2. Why was the ban passed?

Lonnie Williamson, "A Deadly Rain," *Outdoor Life*, June 1987, pp. 47–48.

1. What effect does acid rain have on waterfowl?

2. What steps have been taken to stop acid rain pollution?

Clemens P. Work, "Jam Sessions," *U.S. News & World Report*, September 7, 1987, pp. 20–26.

1. How does the traffic problem affect the mental health of commuters?
2. What vision do planners have of American traffic in the 21st century?

Perceiving cause-and-effect relationships in complex social problems

Many problems facing society today are very complicated and have neither one cause or effect. Name at least two causes for each of the following effects:

(a) Many cities have grown progressively poorer. (See page 408.)
(b) By 1970, the population of the suburbs had surpassed that of the inner cities. (See page 409.)

Name at least two effects for each of the following causes:

(c) Suburban land values have soared with the influx of corporate headquarters. (See page 410.)

(d) Technological advances have expanded industry greatly. (See page 412.)

Negotiating to solve community problems

Would you want a nuclear power plant near your community? To help make a decision, use the following information. Add the arguments for and against each decision. Refer to page 417 for help.

ARGUMENTS FOR:
ARGUMENTS AGAINST:
POSSIBLE DECISIONS: Yes; No
PROBLEM: Would you want a nuclear power plant near your community?

Evaluating Samples: "The United States has a serious pollution problem." Which provides better evidence in support of this statement, the description of Love Canal on page 413 or the map of drinking water problems on page 414?

UNIT APPLICATION

The Problem of Crime

Crime is a topic for worldwide public concern, as indicated by the statistics in the table and graphs shown here. Study them and answer the questions on page 424.

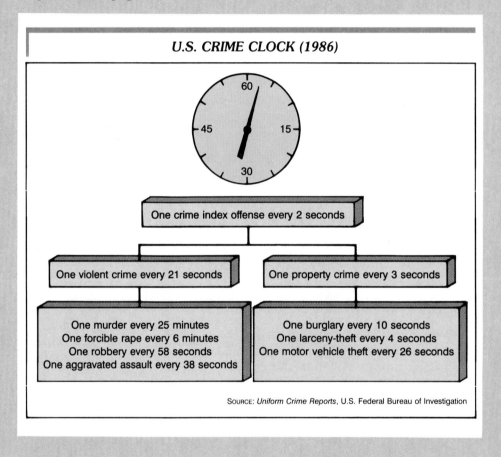

U.S. CRIME CLOCK (1986)

One crime index offense every 2 seconds

One violent crime every 21 seconds

One property crime every 3 seconds

One murder every 25 minutes
One forcible rape every 6 minutes
One robbery every 58 seconds
One aggravated assault every 38 seconds

One burglary every 10 seconds
One larceny-theft every 4 seconds
One motor vehicle theft every 26 seconds

SOURCE: *Uniform Crime Reports*, U.S. Federal Bureau of Investigation

HANDGUN DEATHS IN SELECTED COUNTRIES, 1980 AND 1985

	1980	1985
United States	10,728	8,985
Canada	52	73
Japan	48	129
Switzerland	34	58
Sweden	21	25
Great Britain	8	8

SOURCE: Department of Justice (INTERPOL)

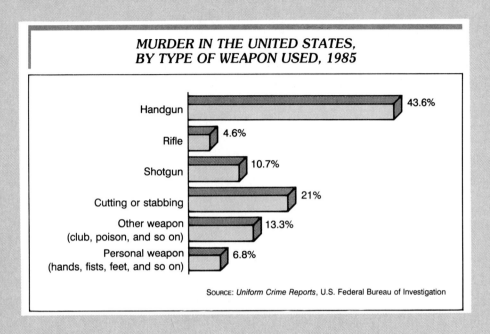

MURDER IN THE UNITED STATES, BY TYPE OF WEAPON USED, 1985

Handgun — 43.6%
Rifle — 4.6%
Shotgun — 10.7%
Cutting or stabbing — 21%
Other weapon (club, poison, and so on) — 13.3%
Personal weapon (hands, fists, feet, and so on) — 6.8%

SOURCE: *Uniform Crime Reports*, U.S. Federal Bureau of Investigation

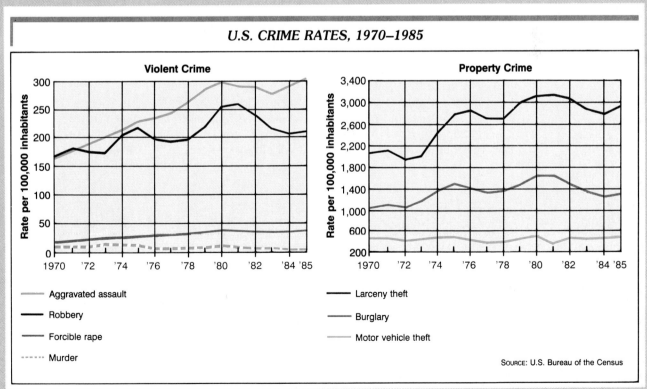

U.S. CRIME RATES, 1970–1985

Violent Crime
Property Crime

Aggravated assault
Robbery
Forcible rape
Murder

Larceny theft
Burglary
Motor vehicle theft

SOURCE: U.S. Bureau of the Census

Using and Analyzing Concepts

1. What generalizations about crime in the United States can you make from the table and graphs on pages 422 and 423?

2. Note the statistics on murder in the United States and elsewhere. Some people believe that the high rate of homicide in the United States is caused by the availability of handguns. Others feel that law-abiding citizens must be allowed guns for protection. Investigate the pros and cons of stricter gun-control laws and write a paper expressing your side of this controversy.

3. Do the necessary research and make a graph of crime in your community covering the last few years. Your police department can help.

   (a) Is the crime rate increasing or decreasing in your community or neighborhood? What types of offenses occur most frequently? Which crimes are increasing? Which are decreasing? What explanations can be offered for these increases or decreases?

   (b) Imagine that you are in charge of offering some solutions to your local crime problem. Devise a program that might result in reduced crime. What might stand in the way of your setting up your program? How would you answer criticisms or overcome objections?

4. There are many theories as to the cause of crime. Psychological theories state that crime is a result of emotional problems developed at an early age, mental retardation, or mental illness. Sociological theories state that crime is a result of association with or rebellion against certain groups, a byproduct of poverty, or an outgrowth of lower-class norms. Do some reading on crime and choose a sociological theory for further research. Include in your paper suggestions as to how this cause can be reduced or eliminated and thus help reduce crime.

The Problem of Pollution

Consider this scenario. For several years, a city government has been developing an industrial park in order to attract new industries to the community. The success of the park would result in new jobs and increased tax income for the city. A major political crisis develops when the local newspaper announces that the city has agreed to allow construction of a chemical plant in the industrial park. Citizens' groups begin protesting that such a plant would pollute the environment and be especially dangerous to workers directly exposed to hazardous chemicals. A public hearing is called to discuss the issue.

Using and Analyzing Concepts

1. Form a class committee to write a paper representing the views of the chemical industry and its supporters. The paper must present arguments explaining why the community should support plant construction.

2. Form another committee to write a paper representing environmental and citizens' interests. The paper must present arguments explaining why the community should oppose plant construction.

3. Let three students represent a team of sociologists who specialize in community development. They are called in as professional consultants to help resolve the issue. The team should compose questions they would ask about the community in order to make recommendations. After gathering information, the team should make proposals for resolving the conflict.

APPENDIX # The Research Process

Outline

You read in Chapter 1 how sociologists begin their research by making a hypothesis, or educated guess, about some behavior pattern or problem. These subjects include child-raising practices, voter behavior, population growth and control, crime and justice, religious feeling or its lack, role conflict, communication among workers in large corporations, and ethnic-group loyalties. Topics for sociological research are limitless.

Some sociologists work mainly in one area, such as crime, education, or population. Most, however, are able to do research in any area. This is because the ways of gathering and analyzing data are generally the same, regardless of the issues.

Most social research is done according to scientific methods. Such methods involve identifying problems, formulating hypotheses, and gathering and analyzing data. This appendix describes the research process used by sociologists, from their choice of research topics to the preparation of their reports.

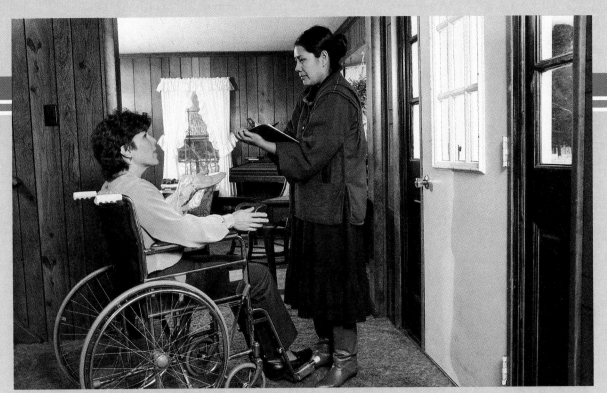

One way in which sociologists gather data is through the survey method. Here a pollster (standing, with clipboard) interviews a woman in her home.

1 Identifying Problems and Stating Hypotheses

Sociologists study the things they do for several reasons. One common reason is personal experience. A black person or Mexican American who has known discrimination may be drawn to do research in intergroup relations. Ex-soldiers may decide to study the army or navy. People who have grown up in rural villages and watched them become suburbs of growing cities might turn to the study of urban problems.

Public issues also offer subjects for research. Researchers may be concerned about rising crime rates, pollution, interracial busing, or political corruption. Many young sociologists interested in the state of public affairs want to learn more about these issues in hopes that their studies will lead to improvements.

In some cases, sociologists are invited to do a piece of research. Government, busi-

ness, labor unions, and various organizations hire people to study issues and problems. Some of this contract research deals with public issues. Some is market research, in which sociologists are asked to find out why people like or dislike a certain product or service. Contract research raises ethical questions because the findings must be turned over to the sponsor, who may misuse or distort them. Some people take part in contract research only if they can keep the right to publish their results in professional journals. They want their colleagues to know what they did and why.

Finally, there is required research. Every sociologist, as part of his or her training, must carry out a research project. Many doctoral dissertations have become famous studies. Two such studies are *Street Corner Society*, by William F. Whyte, and *Tally's*

Corner, by Elliot Liebow, which are mentioned elsewhere in this text. Both were written as required school research.

Of course, sociologists often do small projects. These can be done by anyone with interest and a willingness to follow certain simple rules. Identifying a problem is not hard. Deciding how to study it and what questions to ask is a good deal harder. Let's look at these matters next.

Asking Questions

Social scientists are curious. They want to know what makes the society, the community, and the group tick. They want to be able to describe the patterns of social relationships they study, to explain what is going on, and to predict what might happen in the future. Some social scientists also ask people what they think ought to happen: they ask them to prescribe solutions to problems.

To get this information, different types of questions are required:

1. A descriptive question asks for factual information: How many people went to the Billy Graham rally on October 31, 1981? What sorts of people join the Sierra Club?
2. An explanatory question asks why something happens: Why did black leadership shift the emphasis from civil rights to black power in the mid-1960s? Why do one out of every three American marriages end in divorce today?
3. A predictive question asks about what will happen: Given what you know at present, who will be the next president of the United States? What do you think will be the outcome of the Middle East dispute? A predictive question may be combined with an explanatory question: Why do you think so?
4. A prescriptive question asks people's opinions about what should be done: What should the school board do about the lack of funds for girls' sports? What should the local American Field Service chapter do to get more parents to open their homes to foreign students?

1. Look at the following questions and indicate which are (1) descriptive; (2) explanatory; (3) predictive; (4) prescriptive.
   (a) What do you think should be done to stop airplane hijacking?
   (b) Which house of Congress has power to impeach the president?
   (c) Why did the price of oil rise so sharply in the winter of 1974?
   (d) Who makes the financial decisions in the average American family?
   (e) When will there be a new election for president of your student body?
   (f) Why do reported crime rates seem to rise and fall?
   (g) Who are the three most influential people in your town?
   (h) Do you think poor people are more prone to become criminals than rich people?
   (i) Why is the burning of an American flag considered a crime?
2. Now make up two more questions of each of the four types.

In a later section, knowledge of these various types of questions will be applied to creating survey questionnaires.

Defining Key Terms

Often the questions that social scientists raise contain terms that need to be defined. For example, in item (d) of question 1 above, the term "financial decisions" may not mean the same thing to every person reading the question. A person studying the role of family members in making financial decisions would, at the start of the study, have to decide the meaning of this term. One might say that every time a person buys something, he or she is making a financial decision. But if we were to use this broad definition of financial decisions, it is clear that all family members who have any spending money are helping make "the financial decisions." For the study to be meaningful, the term would have to be defined much more narrowly.

Let's look at another question in the list. Item (h) has three terms that would have to be defined if one wanted to study the connections between wealth and criminal behavior: poor people, rich people, and criminals. Getting acceptable definitions of "rich" and "poor" would give some trouble. We could take the government definition of poverty to classify people as poor. But what income figure would we choose to classify people as rich?

Defining "criminal" might be even more troublesome. Try it. See if you can define "criminal." Here are some possible definitions: (1) a person who breaks the law; (2) a person convicted of committing any act defined by the state as a crime; (3) a person with two—or three or four—criminal convictions.

Clearly, the first definition is too vague. Persons who have never broken the law would be hard to find. And many people would not accept the label "criminal" for a person with a single conviction, perhaps for a "crime of passion" or one committed while drunk. They would reserve the term for those who show a pattern of criminal behavior. But how many incidents are required to show a pattern?

Another problem with using convictions as a measure of criminal behavior is that only a small number of all criminal acts lead to conviction. Many violators are never caught. Many others never come to trial. And then, of course, some innocent people are convicted.

An early task in social research, therefore, is to define key concepts in terms of the operations used in doing them. For example, suppose a key concept in a proposed experiment was "heavy coffee drinker." To qualify as a heavy coffee drinker in the study, a person must drink over eight cups of coffee daily. These are the operations that define the participant as a heavy coffee drinker. The concepts have been *operationalized* so that a researcher wishing to repeat an experiment and test its accuracy can know exactly how it was done the first time.

Using the same idea of operationalizing a concept, a social scientist might choose to define a criminal as a person with two or more criminal convictions. If this operational definition of criminal is clearly stated in the description of the experiment, any person reading it knows precisely what kinds of people were included in the study. The reader can then judge the experiment accordingly.

1. The following are two questions containing terms that need operational definition. Operationalize the terms in italics. Are high school *business-education students* in this state more likely to take a course in economics than are other students? Do college students coming from *small towns* get better grades than those from *big cities*?
2. Make up two more questions containing terms that need operationalizing in order to conduct social research. Then operationalize the terms.

Stating Hypotheses

The two preceding questions about business-education students and students from small towns and big cities ask about relationships that might exist between two or more things. The first question asks about the possible relationship between the number of people who sign up for economics courses and the number who enroll in the business-education curriculum. The second question asks about the relationship between college grade averages and the size of the students' home towns. Many of the questions asked by social scientists probe the way one aspect of society is related to another.

What relationships do the following questions ask about?
1. Are second marriages more likely than first marriages to end in divorce?
2. Are alcoholics more likely to have parents who are alcoholics than other people?

3. Does the crime rate go up during periods of high unemployment?
4. Are boys more likely to start conversations with girls who look them directly in the eye?

In doing research, scientists often turn questions about relationships into statements or hypotheses. For example, the question "Are poor people more likely than rich people to become criminals?" can be turned into three alternative statements, or hypotheses:

1. Poor people are more likely than rich people to become criminals.
2. Rich people are more likely than poor people to become criminals.
3. There is little or no difference in the likelihood of poor and rich persons to become criminals.

You noted in Chapter 1 that a hypothesis involves a relationship between two or more things. The task of the researcher is to test the hypothesis to see if the relationship proves true.

1. Take the four questions in the previous exercise and turn each one into a hypothesis.
2. Your first hypothesis asks about the relationship between divorce rates and first and second marriages. What relationships do your other hypotheses ask about?

The parts of the relationship that make up a hypothesis are called *variables*. The variables in the hypothesis "Poor people are more likely than rich people to become criminals" are wealth and criminality.

Something is a variable if it varies, or can assume two or more values. For example, wealth is a variable because people can be poor (one value), or rich (another value), or in between (another value). Criminal and noncriminal are two values of criminality. Three common values of social-class position are lower, middle, and upper. Sex has two values, male and female. Age has many values. So do religion, grades in school, residence, and all sorts of opinions.

2 Gathering Data

Social research requires a plan for gathering data and then sifting and analyzing them. The research design, or plan of action, that one chooses depends on many factors. Most important, of course, are the questions that have to be answered.

Choosing the Research Design

If, for example, you wanted to test a hypothesis about national attitudes toward political participation, face-to-face interviews wouldn't be practical. You would probably choose a questionnaire or survey to help you gather your data. If you were considering a historical hypothesis about colonial Americans, you would design a study relying heavily on library resources rather than on survey techniques.

In other research projects, in-depth interviews and observations of people might best fit your design. For example, a study of the impact of technology on Amish customs and values could best be approached by talking to Amish people about changes in their beliefs and by observing their life style. This information is not likely to be available in books, and Amish men and women might resent being asked to respond to a questionnaire on this topic. Thus, close observation might best meet the needs of your research design.

In short, depending on the type of question your hypothesis asks, you choose different techniques to help you answer it. After you have identified and operationalized the concepts, or variables, formulated a hypothesis, and decided on sources of information, you must gather data, or collect facts that may prove or disprove your "educated guess." There are a number of ways in which you can go about this task.

Using Library Resources

Almost all studies begin with a review of what others interested in the same problem have written before. Researchers examine "the literature" to find out what others learned—and what they didn't learn.

Reading the Literature Suppose you want to study the relationship between high school student governments and students' political attitudes. You might decide to compare students in schools with different sorts of student government, perhaps including some with no student government at all. Whatever your choices, you will want to ask students questions about their political beliefs and attitudes. Before completing your design, however, you ought to look at studies by others who have conducted research on this topic.

You might start with the *Readers' Guide to Periodical Literature,* which lists magazine articles. *Sociological Abstracts,* which offers brief summaries of articles, essays, and books on a variety of subjects, is another good source. Specialized journals of education and politics and such magazines as *Psychology Today* often carry useful articles for the social-science researcher.

Looking through the indexes of the *American Sociological Review* (the official journal of the American Sociological Association), the *American Journal of Sociology, Social Forces, Social Problems,* and *Sociology of Education* can provide additional help. *Contemporary Sociology,* a journal of book reviews, is especially helpful because it looks at recent books on students and politics. Of course, one would also check through the card catalog of the library to find other books on the topic. Help can also be found in collections of research studies in sociology, such as the *Handbook of Sociology.* The practice of "going to the literature" is both useful and important. One can often gain ideas, as well as save a good deal of time, by seeing what others have done.

Documents and Other Library Sources Some libraries have specialized collections on specific topics, such as prison reform, race relations, and education. A study of, say, the changing themes in the political writings of Margaret Sanger, one of the first champions of birth control and family planning, might well begin in the archives of the Nielson Library at Smith College. Here most of the Sanger papers are filed and stored. A review of civil-rights legislation, with special focus on the role of the National Association for the Advancement of Colored People (NAACP), might be carried out at the organization's headquarters in New York City. Besides "the literature" and written source materials, such as documents and back issues of newspapers, libraries may contain tapes, films, and recordings. For instance, a study of the humorous themes in the films of Charlie Chaplin might use a library film archive as a resource.

Such documents and resources are necessary to conduct two types of sociological analyses: *historical analysis* and *content analysis.* In historical analysis, the researcher studies records of the past to support or disprove a hypothesis, looking at the political leaflets, laws, newspapers, diaries, letters, business reports, and literature of all kinds from the time period being studied.

In content analysis, the researcher may use the same documents, but in this case he or she counts the number of times particular words or ideas appear. A sociologist interested in changes in attitudes toward women might do a content analysis of advertisements in women's magazines from 1920 to 1983, tracing the image of the female in these ads. Today computers aid sociologists in some types of content analysis.

Can you suggest a hypothesis for a content analysis of (1) daytime soap opera scripts, (2) army training manuals, (3) lyrics to current rock or pop music?

3 Observational Techniques

Much social research involves "people watching." Sometimes researchers are personally involved in what they are observing. This activity, *participant observation,* was the method used in the study of the blue-collar tavern in Chapter 4. Sometimes the researcher is an outside observer "looking in." This method is called *nonparticipant observation.*

Observing People in Social Situations

Suppose you are taking part in a project to determine patterns of leadership in high school. You decide that you want to look at informal relations between leaders and followers at a Friday night dance. You pick the school dance because you have noticed that at such social gatherings students tend to cluster around certain persons and to take behavior cues from them. For example, some students "follow the leader" on when to dance or not dance and when to leave. Because you are well known in your own school, you decide to conduct your "fieldwork" at a nearby high school.

One way to get information on the relationships among students during the dance would be to spend your evening mingling with students on the dance floor. You would try to get a sense of the atmosphere, of the sorts of things that were talked about, and especially of the kind of interaction that took place. You would be able to see who was drawn to whom, who was talked about in favorable or unfavorable terms, and who decided when the group would do what.

One problem with this approach is that you cannot be everywhere at once. On the crowded floor, you would probably tend to head toward one place and one group and stay put. Even if you moved around, you would not be able to take in the whole scene. You could not see the band and the dancers and the nondancers. But someone in the balcony could. You might have chosen to go there instead, as a nonparticipant observer.

In the balcony, you have the advantage of distance. You know that your presence will have no influence on the behavior of the people you are watching. The participant observer always takes the risk that people will act differently with an outsider in the group. In the balcony, you can watch all the action. You can even try to draw or plot patterns of interaction over a specific time period, such as ten minutes. Such a drawing will be data about the relationships of the individuals on the floor.

Of course, being a looker-on instead of a participant has its drawbacks. Without having everybody "bugged," it would be hard to get the true meaning of intense conversations, or laughter, or tears. You could only guess.

So one pays a price either way. When possible, sociologists combine techniques. Sometimes, however, it is impossible to enter a social situation unnoticed, and sometimes it is very hard to stay detached.

In the pages to follow, a wide range of observational techniques will be discussed, from direct involvement of the researcher in his or her study to the detached-onlooker role. However, observation most often calls for some of both detachment and involvement. Therefore, most research takes place in the area between the two extremes.

Concealed Participant Observation

At the school dance, you might have merged into the group easily without telling anyone that you were studying students' behavior. Investigators often conceal their identity from those being studied. This might be called concealed participant observation, in contrast to a more open form.

In concealed participant observation, the researcher is disguised as a member of the group in order to more closely observe the situation. To study soldiers, a sociologist might go through basic training disguised as a recruit. A researcher might join a Vermont commune or enter a mental hospital to observe the inner workings of these situations. Each would be using concealed-observation techniques.

An effective use of this technique was the experiment described in John Howard Griffin's study *Black Like Me*. Griffin, a newspaperman from Texas, had a single goal. He wanted to experience racial prejudice from the viewpoint of the southern black man. Reaching that goal was far from simple. Being white, he felt that he could never get black people to talk freely. Nor did he think he could really understand their plight without facing their sorts of problems. He decided to become black.

Griffin "became" a black man by shaving his head and altering the color of his skin through sunlamp treatments and the use of dyes. For many weeks, he moved, undetected, through the black world learning to see his two selves (the one white, the other black) in new lights. By hitchhiking, applying for jobs, and entering diners and hotels, he learned to know the stigma of a black skin in the South of the late 1950s. In time, as the deep tan began to fade, he would move between the two worlds, one day as a white man, the next (sometimes with the aid of a bit more dye) as a black.

His report, first published in *Sepia* magazine and later in his book, gave his fellow whites a glimpse of people that many of them thought they knew but really did not. Among blacks who read it, there were mixed reactions. Most reviews praised his effort and his motive. Some, however, felt that even such an experience could never give an outsider any real sense of what it meant to be black in white America.

Another example of concealed observation is Muzafer Sherif's study of a boys' camp. He reported his findings in the book *Groups in Harmony and Tension*. To study the interaction between campers, Sherif disguised himself as "Mr. Muzee," the handyman. As the handyman, he could see every part of camp life without arousing suspicion.

Suppose you wanted to study conditions in an institution for the retarded.
1. How would you get the information you needed?
2. Would you consider pretending you were retarded and having yourself signed in?
3. If so, what would you tell the other inmates? How would you identify yourself?

Sociologists wrestle with questions like these. Many feel that, no matter how effective, concealed observation is unfair. They argue that it is not so different from hiding a tape recorder in a committee meeting or wiretapping a telephone conversation. These are activities that, in this country, are against the law under most circumstances. Other sociologists disagree. They feel that the knowledge gained using these methods may be valuable in helping society understand itself—so valuable, in fact, that it justifies the methods used to get it.

Open Participant Observation

You might have answered the last question in the previous exercise by saying, "Well, I don't like complete disguise because it's sneaky. But I do see the importance of staying in the background." You might have added that the question itself may not be that important. In many cases, it is really impossible to disguise oneself effectively.

A partial solution to both problems is to go into a situation as a recognized and accepted outsider. In this method, the researcher takes part in the life of the community he or she is studying. But at the same time, the people being studied know the researcher's purpose for being there.

A number of excellent community studies mentioned in this book used this method. On page 269, you read how Arthur Vidich and Joseph Bensman's *Small Town in Mass*

Society reported on life in a village in upstate New York. And Elliot Liebow's study of the unskilled worker discussed on page 236 also used this method.

The study of an urban neighborhood by William F. Whyte is often cited as the best example of open observation. His book *Street Corner Society* describes a section of an Italian American neighborhood in Boston, which he observed in the 1940s. Whyte, a middle-class Protestant studying at Harvard, couldn't pass for a member of the community, so he didn't try. What he did was convince people of his sincerity to learn something about their community. He moved into the area. He learned some Italian. Most important, he made friends with "Doc," one of the leaders of the "Corner Boys." Doc became his guide, his informant, and his friend. With Doc, Whyte was able to move freely into what had been, to him, foreign territory.

To understand the social organization of "Cornerville," Whyte watched its people on the street, in their homes, in recreation halls, at political meetings, and in gambling houses. He kept mental notes of who spoke to whom, what was said, who were the leaders, and who were the followers. As soon as he got back to his room, he wrote up his notes and filed them under useful headings. When he was unclear about a point, he continued to watch and listen.

During his three years of research, Whyte became interested in the Cornerville Social and Athletic Club, which included a number of influential people. Whyte saw that there were two major groups in the club. He hoped to be able to tell which people sided with each faction so that he could later predict how people would line up on a major political issue. The following account by Whyte describes his methods for this kind of research:

Here I had a more complicated task than any I had faced before. The club had fifty members. Fortunately, only about thirty of them were frequent attenders, so that I could concentrate on that smaller number, but even that number presented a [major] problem.

I felt I would have to develop more formal and systematic procedures than I had used when I had been hanging on a street corner with a much smaller group of men. I began with positional mapmaking. Assuming that the men who associated together most closely socially would also be those who lined up together on the same side when decisions were to be made, I set about making a record of the groupings I observed each evening in the club. . . .

When evening activities were going full blast, I looked around the room to see which people were talking together, playing cards together, or otherwise interacting. I counted the number of men in the room, so as to know how many I would have to account for. Since I was familiar with the main physical objects of the club-room, it was not difficult to get a mental picture of the men in relation to tables, chairs, couches, radio, and so on. When individuals moved about or when there was some interaction between these groupings, I sought to retain that in mind. In the course of an evening, there might be a general reshuffling of positions. . . .

I managed to make a few notes on trips to the men's room, but most of the mapping was done from memory after I had gone home. At first, I went home once or twice for mapmaking during the evening, but, with practice, I got so that I . . . could do all of my notes at the end of the evening.

I found this an extremely rewarding method. . . . As I piled up these maps, it became evident just what the major social groupings were and what people [moved] between the two factions of the club. As issues arose within the club, I could predict who would stand where.

Nonparticipant Observation

William F. Whyte said that there were times when he tried to observe from afar. Looking out from behind the Venetian blinds, he tried to watch the comings and goings of various club members.

There are many times when participation is not practical. Earlier an example of nonparticipant observation—watching behavior on a dance floor from a balcony—was mentioned. Most of us carry on this kind of observation daily.

1. Go to a busy intersection with two of your friends. Stand six to ten feet apart and have each person record everything observed across the street for ten minutes. Compare notes. Do you agree on what each of you observed? Why or why not?
2. Now decide what you are all going to look at and for. Repeat the entire process. Compare your notes again.

More and more sociologists use videotape machines or tape recorders to observe and record various sorts of behavior. There is much controversy over the ethics of such "scientific snooping." One example of such a study took place in the early 1950s when researchers from the University of Chicago set out to study the American jury system. They wanted to know how the jury came to its decision after listening to the evidence given in court. After much debate, they decided that interviewing jury members or giving them questionnaires to fill out would not get the needed data. The researchers decided they had to record actual discussions among jury members without the jurors knowing they were being taped.

This turned out to be a difficult task. A number of judges had to be asked before one would agree to a project using a hidden recording device. Finally one judge agreed to cooperate. The team and the judge set up a system which ensured that the recordings could not harm any person on trial or get any jury member into trouble. Still, when the project became public knowledge some months later, many people criticized the taping. Members of the United States Senate accused the team of threatening the American right to privacy by eavesdropping on what had always been secret talks. The senators did not accept the argument that the team wanted to gather firsthand data to help improve the jury system.

1. Where do you stand on the use of hidden recording devices for such purposes as described here?
2. How do you feel about using the same techniques for studying alleged corruption in the office of a city treasurer or in other local agencies?

The answers are not easy. Many people approve of the technique in certain cases and only for certain purposes. Others say never. They feel that, although limits might be set on the use of such techniques, there will always be abuses. They state that the line between proper and improper use is not at all clear.

4 Using the Experimental Method

Sometimes sociologists conduct studies using the experimental method. These studies use two groups of subjects, an *experimental group,* which is exposed to a new idea or stimulus, and a *control group,* which is not. Except for the new idea or stimulus, the control group is identical in all ways to the experimental group. At the conclusion of a study, the researcher can compare both groups to make sure that changes in the experimental group are the result of the new idea or stimulus and are not changes that would have taken place anyway. Following is a summary of a study that shows how this method works.

Military recruits at many basic-training camps used to be housed in "open-bay" barracks, so called because they consisted of beds placed around the walls of one large room. At one such base, the commanding officers noticed that many of the young recruits seemed depressed and lonely. They also tended to go on sick call a good deal to escape work. The officers felt a change was needed.

Relying on Edward A. Shils's research on primary relations in the German army during World War II, one investigator suggested an experiment. In some of the large barracks, workmen would install partitions to divide the rooms into ten smaller cubicles having six beds each. This would reduce the amount of space in which the men spent most of their in-barracks time and might help to create a feeling of closeness among them. Recruits would be randomly assigned to the new "closed-bay barracks" or to the traditional open ones. Afterward, judgments would be made about their adjustment to army life and their morale.

The results of the study showed that changing a physical environment could affect the social structure. The men in the "closed-bay" barracks seemed to adjust more quickly to army life and to become friends more easily than those in the "open-bay" barracks. They seemed to become dependent on a small group of persons, often fellow members of their "room." Since the control-group recruits in the open barracks did not show similar improvements in morale, the researcher concluded that the factor causing the change was rearrangement of the barracks.

In other control-group experiments, there is a "before-and-after" test. For example, a researcher gives a group of students a questionnaire about racial prejudice. The group is divided in half at random, and half is shown a film or given a lecture showing what prejudice and discrimination can do to people. The other half does not see the film. Not surprisingly, when restudied (or "retested"), the experimental group, which has been shown the film, tends to show less prejudice than the control group.

1. Design a small experiment using two groups of your classmates. One group can serve as the control. You might wish to create a questionnaire asking students in both groups their attitudes toward such topics as the Arab-Israeli conflict or a local political issue. Then give the experimental group factual information on the topic you have chosen. Do not give the information to your control group. At the conclusion of the study, ask both groups to fill out the questionnaire again. Compare any changes.

2. You want to test the hypothesis that taking a driver-education course makes teenagers more concerned about safe driving. First create a questionnaire that asks a group of students about to take driver education their attitudes toward traffic safety. The control group taking the test could be made up of students with no present plans to take driver education. At the end of the driver-education course, both groups could be retested to measure any changes in attitudes.

5 The Sample Survey

To learn in some detail the attitudes, opinions, or beliefs of a large number of people, sociologists often use a sample survey. The method that they use is referred to as "sampling." Sampling is the selection of a small number of people to represent the views of the larger group.

When to Use a Sample Survey

Suppose you wanted to know whether attitudes toward a nuclear freeze had any relationship to the region of the country from which people came, to their religious beliefs, or to their social class. To get this information, you would want to question people from all parts of the country, making sure that you included people from many regions and social classes. You couldn't very well ask every adult in the nation for his or her views or, ordinarily, even all the adults in a single city. It would be too costly and time-consuming. Instead, you would take a randomly chosen sample of people from the total grouping. The total grouping is known as the *universe*.

The universe itself would vary from one study to another. If you wanted to know how the people in your community felt about a certain school bond issue, only local residents would be included in your universe. If you were interested in how Americans in general felt about the financing of public schooling, all citizens potentially would be part of your study. Your sample would be drawn from a national universe.

Sampling Techniques

The only truly representative sample is one chosen at random. In a *random sample,* every person in the total group—the universe—has an equal chance of being chosen. Suppose you want to ask citizens of your community their opinions about health care and welfare. Your town has 50,000 adults, all listed in a city directory. It would be too costly and time-consuming to poll them all. So instead you decide to use a sample of 500 from the 50,000, a 1 percent sample. Using the city directory as your guide, you might pick every hundredth name.

Or, for example, you might want to study the views of all students in the two high schools in that same community. Suppose there are 2,500 in the two schools, and you want a sample of 500. You might write all the names on slips of paper, put them in a big box, mix them thoroughly, and then pick out 500.

There are other ways, too. For example, a computer can select a sample at random from a list of numbers if programmed to do so. In actuality, the machine is doing the same sort of mixing and choosing that you would do in the big box.

Probability

Random samples represent perfectly the universe from which they are drawn. The reason is based on *probability theory.* The following example demonstrates this.

Pretend that you have a large container in front of you that holds a million marbles of equal size. Half of the marbles are red and half are green. You select randomly 100 marbles from the container. According to probability theory, you are very likely, within a 3 percent margin of error, to select 50 green marbles and 50 red marbles. According to probability theory, you are very likely to obtain the same results if you repeat this activity again and again.

This means that if you went back to the box with the 2,500 names of high school students, chose another 500 at random, and asked them the same questions, there would be the same divisions by sex and age and the same splits in responses in the second sample as in the first. And both would accurately reflect the total group of students.

Using lists of counties, cities, and larger areas as their basis, the Gallup Organization and similar polling organizations use samples of less than 2,000 individuals. Such a sample, randomly selected, is representative of all the adults in the United States.

Developing the Survey Instrument

After determining the universe and selecting a sample of respondents, researchers create the survey instrument. Usually this consists of either an interview guide or a questionnaire given either in person or by mail. Most interview guides and questionnaires ask the respondent a number of personal questions—age, sex, job, education, and the like—as well as inquire about the survey topic. Often questions are worded so that a single phrase or a check mark answers the question. Sometimes, however, the question calls for a longer reply. Certain rules of thumb are helpful when trying to get accurate information from respondents. The questions must be stated clearly and without bias.

Here are nine questions. Some are clear and unbiased. Others are confusing, misleading, or "loaded." See if you can pick out the unbiased questions and tell what is wrong with the others.

1. Where were you born?
2. Why do most delinquents come from broken homes?
3. How long does it take you to complete your paper route?
4. Are you male or female?
5. I hate television advertising, don't you?
6. Would you say you are more sympathetic, are less sympathetic, or feel about the same way you did a year ago on the issue of equal rights for women?
7. Do you agree or disagree that exculturation is inhibited by deprivation?
8. In general, how do you feel about the foreign policy of the president?
9. If it weren't for the Wright brothers, air congestion would never have become an issue. How do you feel about that?

One may get answers either face to face, in which case one visits the respondent and asks the questions directly, or by the use of a mailed questionnaire, which the person fills out and returns.

Face-to-face interviews ensure that the person you want to answer the questions is the one who does so. But they are costly in time and effort. For very large studies, they are rarely used, at least not as the only means of getting information. More commonly, researchers interview a subsample of the larger sample and contact the others by mail.

Face-to-face interviews have the advantage of allowing the investigator to probe or ask for further information. This is not possible in a mailed survey. If you are conducting an interview, the following rules are suggested:

How to Conduct an Interview

1. Introduce yourself. Tell the respondent why you are doing the research and that you would like to interview him or her.

2. Announce a time limit for the interview and stick to it. Say, "May I please have ten or fifteen minutes of your time?" Do not wear out your welcome.

3. Be courteous, be interested in what is being said, and really listen to the respondent. Be nonjudgmental or neutral about any beliefs or feelings the individual may express. Let the person explain his or her point of view without countering with your own.

4. Try to record answers to open-ended questions by using the respondent's own words. If an interviewer attempts to summarize what has been said, he or she may distort the meaning of the respondent's ideas or unconsciously take them out of context.

5. If you find you are holding up the interview by writing down the answers exactly, say, "I hope you don't mind the delay. I want to get the information you are giving exactly as you are saying it."

6. To help speed up your note taking, use abbreviations. Hash marks (////) may be used to show where further questions or explanations were asked of the respondent.

7. After the interview has been completed, read it over carefully to be sure you understand it clearly. See if you need to ask for any further information.

8. Ask the respondent whether you may use his or her name in presenting the results. If the respondent wishes to remain anonymous, be sure to respect this request and never to use or disclose the name.

Suppose you want to study the influence of parents' social class on the future plans of their children. You hypothesize that parents' position influences their children's goals. You would want to know (1) who the respondents and their parents are, (2) why they do what they do or believe what they believe, (3) what the children think their futures will be, and (4) what they would like to have happen to them.

Now suppose you have chosen a sample of 300 high school students from the two high schools in a given town. You have decided to interview 25 from each school and then send questionnaires to the other 250.

1. How would you select the sample and the subsample?
2. What questions would you ask?
3. Would you use the same questions for those being interviewed and those receiving the questionnaire? If not, how would they differ?

The following are two lists of survey questions used to get the same information. The first list is in the form of an interview guide. The second is a questionnaire.

An Interview Guide

Before you begin the interview, write down all the information you already know about the respondent, such as the person's address. Immediately after leaving, write down other key data, such as sex, approximate age (unless you are asking for this), race, and so on. Approach the person by saying that you are a sociology student doing a study of high school students and their plans for the future and that the respondent is one of a number of students randomly selected to participate.

Here are the sorts of questions you might ask:

1. Where were you born?
2. Where were your parents born?
3. Where, specifically, do you live now?
4. Have you lived there most of your life? (If the answer is no, ask: If not, where did you live?)
5. What is the name of your school?
6. What year are you in there?
7. What course—business, college entrance, home economics, and so on—are you taking?
8. Do you expect to graduate? If not, why not?
9. What do you expect to do when you leave school?

10. What about ten years from now? What do you expect to be then?
11. What are your parents' occupations?
12. How far did they go in school? (This might be a sensitive question that you would prefer to omit.)
13. What do you think your parents would like you to be?
14. What do you think they expect you to be?
15. How realistic do you think their expectations are?
16. Do you have any brothers or sisters? (If no, go on to the next question. If yes, ask: How old are they? What do the older ones do? What do you think will happen to the younger ones?)
17. In general, would you describe your parents as upper-class, middle-class, working-class, or lower-class?
18. Why would you place them in that particular category? (Be sure to write down the respondent's answer word for word.)
19. What about you? Do you think you are upper-class, middle-class, working-class, or lower-class?
20. Where do you think you will be placing yourself in twenty years?

Look over your interview sheets quickly and see if you have answers to all the questions posed. If you need more information, ask for it now. If not, thank the person for his or her time and leave.

A Mailed Questionnaire

Many of the same sorts of questions could be included in a questionnaire and mailed to the rest of the sample. Various methods are used to induce people to respond to such questionnaires. One of the most useful is to tell people, either in a "cover letter" that goes with the questionnaire or in person, that they are part of a carefully selected random sample and that everyone's response is needed for accurate results. Sometimes one can go further by stating, "We need your aid to help tell *your* story accurately."

Once drafted, the questionnaire should be pretested. That is, it should be tried out on a number of people before being sent to your sample. This is one way of finding out whether the questions are valid—that they measure the sorts of things they are supposed to measure. If not, revisions should be made and the new version tested.

To obtain data for a study, a researcher may use a questionnaire such as this one, which inquires about students' backgrounds and future plans.

QUESTIONNAIRE ON SOCIAL CLASS AND EDUCATIONAL PLANS

Name _____   Date _____

1. Where were you born?

    (a) _____ in this community

    (b) _____ elsewhere--please specify:

    _____

2. Where were your parents born?

    (a) father: _____

    (b) mother: _____

3. Where, specifically, do you live now?

    _____

    (street)   (city)

4. How long have you lived in your present house?

    (a) _____ less than a year

    (b) _____ one to three years

    (c) _____ more than three years

5. To which school do you go?

    (a) _____ East High School

    (b) _____ West High School

6. What year are you in there?

    (a) _____ freshman

    (b) _____ sophomore

    (c) _____ junior

    (d) _____ senior

    (e) _____ other--please specify:

    _____

7. What is your main course of study?

    (a) business administration

    (b) college entrance

    (c) home economics

    (d) secretarial science

    (e) mechanical or vocational

    (f) agricultural

    (g) other--please specify:

    _____

8. Do you expect to graduate from high school?

    (a) _____ yes

    (b) _____ no

    If not, why not?

    _____

    _____

    _____

9. What do you expect to do when you leave school?

    (a) _____ Go on to college. In what field?

    _____

    (b) _____ Go on to some other advanced training. In what field?

    _____

    (c) _____ Get a job. Doing what?

    _____

    (d) _____ other--please specify:

    _____

When the final version is ready, the next step is to send it to the chosen respondents. In this case, you would begin with a cover letter attached to the questionnaire, explaining that the person has been selected at random to take part in a study of high school students and their future plans. You might add that you hope the respondent will answer

page 2

10. What do you expect to be in ten years? (Please try to be as specific as you can, for example, a supervisor in an automobile factory, a surgeon, a bank teller, an officer in the Marines, a court stenographer.)

_____

11. What are your parents' occupations?

(a) father: _____

(b) mother: _____

12. How far did they go in school? (F = father; M = mother)

     F M

(a) ___ ___ less than eighth grade

(b) ___ ___ some high school

(c) ___ ___ high school diploma

(d) ___ ___ some college

(e) ___ ___ college degree

(f) ___ ___ some postgraduate study

(g) ___ ___ graduate degree

13. What do you think your parents would like you to be?

_____

14. What do you think they expect you to be?

_____

15. Do you have any brothers or sisters?

(a) _____ no

(b) _____ yes

If yes, how old are they, and what does each one do?

                  Age Occupation

(c) first brother: ____ _____

(d) second brother: ____ _____

(e) third brother: ____ _____

(f) fourth brother: ____ _____

                  Age Occupation

(g) fifth brother: ____ _____

(h) first sister: ____ _____

(i) second sister: ____ _____

(j) third sister: ____ _____

(k) fourth sister: ____ _____

(l) fifth sister: ____ _____

16. What is your family's social class?

(a) _____ upper class

(b) _____ middle class

(c) _____ working class

(d) _____ lower class

17. Why did you place them in the category you did? Please try to give as much detail as possible.

_____

_____

_____

18. What is your social class?

(a) _____ upper class

(b) _____ middle class

(c) _____ working class

(d) _____ lower class

19. What is your sex?

(a) _____ male

(b) _____ female

20. What is your racial background?

(a) _____ black

(b) _____ white

(c) _____ other--please specify:

_____

honestly and ask him or her not to sign the questionnaire. A stamped, addressed return envelope should be included for returning the survey. Identify yourself and the sponsoring agency—for example, the sociology class of North High School.

Tabulating the Responses

Once questionnaires have been returned—and any interviews completed if you are using this procedure to obtain a subsample—you are ready to start organizing the data, tabulating the results, and beginning the analysis. Today many questionnaires are precoded to allow the researchers to transfer the information to tapes or disks such as those used by computer firms. These tapes and disks are then fed into computers for accurate calculations. This procedure is essential in complex studies and very useful in all kinds of survey research.

In small sample surveys such as the one just discussed, computers are useful tools but not a necessity. To tally the results by hand, first you count the number of responses to each question. These are called "the marginals" because one usually writes them down on the side of a master copy of the questionnaire. For example, suppose you have 227 respondents from the total sample of 250 you asked to answer the survey, which would be an extremely high return. Let us look at the way the data from three of the questions you used are turned into useful information about our hypothesis. First the marginals are added together and shown as raw scores; then they are put into percentages.

What is your sex?

Sex	Number	Percentage
Male	152	67
Female	75	33
No answer	0	0
Total	227	100

To which school do you go?

School	Number	Percentage
East High School	122	54
West High School	103	45
No answer	2	1
Total	227	100

What is your family's social class?

Social Class	Number	Percentage
Upper class	21	9
Middle class	85	38
Working class	79	35
Lower class	37	16
No answer	5	2
Total	227	100

The percentages are based on the number of respondents to a given question. Since some respondents may skip certain questions, the number that a percentage represents will vary from question to question. In the first case, a result of 152 males from a total of 227 respondents is 67 percent. On another question, a smaller number may constitute 67 percent of the total respondents.

Now you are ready to begin some simple *cross tabulations,* comparing one item, or variable, such as sex, with another, such as plans after high school. You do this to find out what relationships between various categories of people or events are revealed by the answers to your questions.

In the study of 250 high school students, of which 227 (152 males and 75 females) finally responded, you might find a breakdown like the following:

Plans After Leaving School	Male (Number)	Female (Number)
Go to college	65	32
Get some other advanced training	34	15
Get a job	40	15
Other	13	13
Total	152	75

These raw figures are difficult to interpret since the bases, the totals in each column, are quite different. A glance at the first row across suggests that twice as many men as women plan to go to college after high school. But if the responses are put into percentages, the picture changes, as the following table shows:

Plans After Leaving School	Male		Female	
	f[1]	Percentage	f	Percentage
Go to college	65	43	32	43
Get some other advanced training	34	23	15	20
Get a job	40	26	15	20
Other	13	8	13	17
Total	152	100	75	100

[1]The symbol f is used to mean the frequency of response, or number answering the question.

If you compare the percentages, you see that an equal proportion of males and females who returned the questionnaires expect to go to college. How do the data on the category "other" change when raw figures and percentages are compared? In a report, this information would probably be presented in the following simplified table:

Plans After Leaving School	Male (152)[1]	Female (75)
Go to college	43%	43%
Get some other advanced training	23	20
Get a job	26	20
Other	8	17
Total	100%	100%

[1]The number in parentheses is the number of respondents.

Here's another cross tabulation drawn from the study of parental social class and student goals. Note that the total number of respondents here is 225, not 227. As noted above, two individuals did not identify their school.

Social Class of Parents (According to Respondent)	High School Attended	
	East High (122)	West High (103)
Upper class	5%	1%
Middle class	63	24
Working class	28	68
Lower class	4	7
Total	100%	100%

1. What percentage of the students attending East High considered their parents working-class? What percentage considered their parents lower-class?
2. Overall, do students at West High see their parents as higher or lower in social-class position than do students at East High?

In the previous tables, two variables were cross-tabulated. For example, in the second table, the variables were school attended and social class of parents. In the next table, there are three variables: school attended, social class of parents, and plans after leaving school. Note that the total number of respondents here is 222, not 227. As noted above, five individuals did not indicate their parents' social class.

HIGH SCHOOL ATTENDED AND SOCIAL CLASS OF PARENTS

Plans After Leaving School	East High (122)		West High (103)	
	Upper and Middle (83)	Working and Lower (36)	Upper and Middle (26)	Working and Lower (77)
Go to college	80%	32%	78%	13%
Get some other advanced training	8	30	14	25
Get a job	7	31	6	44
Other	5	7	2	18
Total	100%	100%	100%	100%

1. What percentage of upper- and middle-class students in each high school planned to attend college?
2. What percentage of East High's working- and lower-class students had college plans?
3. Does West High have more or fewer students of working- and lower-class families than East High who plan to go to college?
4. How might the differences between East High and West High working- and lower-class students on college plans be explained?

Analyzing the Data

The last two tables show a relationship between college attendance and social class of parents. They also show that East High has more middle- and upper-class students than West High does. It seems clear from the last table that there is a relationship between parents' social class, as seen by the student, and the student's future plans. In both schools, a high proportion of upper- and middle-class students plan to go to college.

The school appears to exert an influence on those students who see their families as working- and lower-class. Going to a largely middle-class high school seems to raise the expectations of working-class students. More of them intend to prepare for careers that offer upward social mobility. Of the East High students with working-class parents, 32 percent plant to attend college, whereas only 13 percent of West High's working-class students do.

The goal of the sociologist is to find causal connections. A causal connection is just what it sounds like: a relationship in which one event, or variable, causes or directly influences a second variable in a specific way. For example, as every dieter knows, there is a causal connection between the amount of food a person eats and how much the person weighs. In the table you just looked at, you might predict a causal relationship between parents' social class as seen by a student and the student's future plans.

Not all connections between variables are causal, however. *Correlation* is another relationship between two or more types of events. Suppose you observed that the overweight men in your study all had short hair. In that case, you could say that there was a correlation between short hair and overweight, or that these variables correlated, in your study.

However, the fact that two characteristics of the people in your study—short hair and overweight—correlated does not indicate a causal relationship between them. It is known that weight is not affected by hair length or vice versa; there is no causal connection between them. The two factors merely existed together in this study. Yet the correlation was almost perfect. Wherever one trait appeared, the researcher found the other.

In many studies, the correlation between two variables may be so high that the researcher may be tempted to think that one does indeed cause the other. There is a correlation, for example, between the amount of ice cream eaten at New York's largest beach, Coney Island, and the number of deaths by drowning on a given summer day. Is there a causal relationship as well? Remembering your mother's warning never to go swimming on a full stomach ("Wait at least one hour after you eat"), you might say, "Yes. It makes sense. If you eat ice cream and go into the water, you have a good chance of getting cramps and drowning."

Perhaps. But few doctors today believe that eating ice cream, which is easily digestible, causes cramps that lead to drowning. Behind the apparent causal connection lies the fact that both ice cream consumption and the number of people at the beach and in the water go up when it is hot. The temperature of the day is the principal factor accounting for a large attendance at the beach. And when it is hot, more people swim; therefore, more are exposed to drowning.

Correlation is not causation. It is simply the observed fact that two variables are related to one another. They may be related in one of two ways: positively or negatively. In a *positive correlation,* or direct relationship, as one variable increases or decreases, the other does the same. For example, think of the relationship between the size of a community and the amount of money needed to clean the streets, collect the garbage, and pay teachers. In a *negative correlation,* or inverse relationship, as one variable increases, the other decreases, and as one decreases, the other increases. For example, as the number of farms in the United States has decreased, the size of the average farm has increased. The variation in one variable can be predicted from knowledge about the other.

6 The Research Report

A researcher's work is not complete after the data have been analyzed. The research must still be recorded in its entirety, so that others—colleagues, sponsors, students, and the general public—can benefit from the researcher's efforts. This record is known as a research report. It may appear in a professional journal, in a full-length book, or perhaps as a statement for circulation among members of a government agency or private firm. The report usually contains an account of the nature of the problem; the available literature in the field; the major concepts and how they were operationalized; the hypotheses; the research design; the data collected, presented in tables, graphs, and other forms; the analysis; and the conclusions.

With this information, readers of the report are in a position to evaluate the importance of the research and its strengths and weaknesses. The researcher must carefully spell out particular problems in following the research design and how these difficulties were dealt with. If respondents were resistant, for example, the author of the report must say what percentage of the sample actually completed the interviews or questionnaires and how substitutions were made for those who could not be located or who declined to participate.

In this way, biases in the data can be evaluated not only by researchers themselves but also by the readers of the report. Serious researchers, therefore, often give potential critics sufficient evidence to "hang them." This is necessary as a built-in check on the research effort. Sociologists, after all, are presumably seeking to add to knowledge about society, not to make propaganda points. For this reason, any facts that might limit the validity of the research must be forthrightly published with the findings themselves.

7 Summary

Research is central to the work of sociologists. A researcher's choice of a subject for study may come from his or her own personal experiences. It may come from pressing public concern about an issue, from a contract offered by a government or private agency, or from the need to complete the requirements of a professional degree.

In setting up the research design, the sociologist must operationalize the key concepts contained in the question, or hypothesis. Then data must be collected. Methods include library research, such as historical and content analysis; participant observation; the experiment; and the sample survey, by questionnaire, interview, or both.

Some methods contain potential problems. A participant observer faces the ethical problem of violating the privacy of his or her subjects. A researcher using a sample survey must be sure that the sample is truly representative of the universe and that the universe is the right one for the problem. An interviewer must be careful not to question people in a way that may influence their answers.

The data collected must be organized, tabulated, and analyzed. Conclusions need to be drawn and perhaps applied in some way for the benefit of society. The research report detailing the study's methods and findings preserves the researcher's work and makes it possible for readers to evaluate its validity.

GLOSSARY

This glossary defines the key terms listed in the chapter reviews. The page numbers following the definitions refer to the pages on which the terms are introduced. More than one page number indicates that the term is defined in more than one chapter. The key terms appear in italics where they are defined in the text.

---

accommodation pluralism; a "live-and-let-live" attitude of mutual respect toward cultural differences, achieved through conscious effort (page 350)

achieved status a status that is earned by personal effort, such as that of judge, teacher, or astronaut (page 80)

addiction an extremely compulsive craving for habitual use of a substance (page 386)

adolescence the period between childhood and adulthood; the teenage years (page 213)

affirmative action preferential treatment, through admission and hiring policies, of minority-group members and women to compensate for past discrimination (pages 59, 251)

age-graded society society in which members participate in rites of passage at the same time as their age-mates throughout the life cycle (page 213)

agents of socialization parents, peers, teachers, and other people who teach one how to behave and what to believe; can also be a distant contact, such as television (page 193)

alienation the feeling of being alone and apart from one's society or culture; a sense of powerlessness and loss of purpose (page 415)

amalgamation the joining of groups from different cultures into one group (page 350)

anomie a condition in which there are no norms, or rules for behavior (pages 61, 416)

anticipatory socialization actions that prepare a person for future roles in life (pages 201, 416)

apartheid the policy of strict separation of races economically, socially, and politically as practiced in South Africa (page 338)

arbitrary communication communication that is deliberate and learned, such as words, sounds, and gestures (page 34)

archaeologist scientist who studies ancient life and culture by digging in ruins to uncover pots, bones, tools, weapons, and so on (page 27)

ascribed status a status that one is born to or that is assigned by society (page 80)

assimilation process in which a minority group replaces its own special traits with those of the group in power, thus losing its uniqueness (page 350)

assimilationist movement a social movement that seeks to improve conditions for a minority group through inclusion within the larger society (page 307)

authoritarian personality a stern, commanding type of person with conventional beliefs and little tolerance for differences (page 339)

---

bilateral descent ancestry traced through both parents (page 128)

biological differences variations in inherited physical characteristics, such as color of eyes, hair, or skin (page 21)

blue-collar work work performed manually, such as construction or mining; the term is derived from the blue work shirt worn by many manual laborers (page 236)

body language the movements, gestures, and facial expressions people make that convey their thoughts and feelings without words (page 34)

bureaucracy a formal organization that has a clear-cut chain of command from top to bottom; each group or person at each level is assigned a definite task (page 89)

---

capitalism the free-enterprise economic system (page 178)

caste system a system in which a person is born to a definite station in life and has no chance of changing his or her social position; caste divisions

448

may be supported by religion, as in India, but there are also similar systems based on racial discrimination (page 98)

charisma the persuasive force that a particular personality has over the members of a society (page 304)

charismatic authority authority based on exceptional personal appeal (pages 106, 171)

class a group of people considered as a unit because they share a certain economic and social position in society (page 101)

class consciousness an awareness of belonging to a particular class in a society; also, a feeling of solidarity with other members of the same class (page 100)

cognitive development the development of the ability to think, reason, and solve problems (page 197)

communism in a utopian state, a sharing according to need; property is publicly owned (page 179)

community people, usually in settlements, who share many similar feelings, attitudes, values, and goals; often based on national origin or religion (page 267)

compartmentalization separating competing or conflicting norms to allow oneself to feel comfortable when behaving in contradictory ways (page 83)

concentric-zone model a type of city growth in which cities grow in definite circular zones from the center outward, with each zone having its own characteristics (page 282)

conflict theory theory held by sociologists who view society as groups and classes in conflict, each seeking dominance (page 298)

content analysis a research method that studies documents to uncover information about a culture; the researcher counts the number of times that particular words or ideas appear (page 431)

control group a group that is identical to the experimental group in all ways but is not exposed to some new idea or stimulus (page 435)

controlled environment organization in which the individual is under the control of some powerful central authority, has little or no privacy, and performs most activities with other inmates (page 64)

correlation a connection between two sets of data or information (page 445)

cross tabulation comparing one variable, such as sex, with another, such as plans for after high school, to find relationships between various categories of people or events (page 442)

crowd a large group concentrated in one place in which there is little development of group values or norms (page 314)

cultural diffusion the spread of ideas and traits from one culture to another culture (page 278)

cultural item a material culture trait, which can be seen, handled, and used (page 28)

culture the sum of the ways in which a particular group of people lives; culture includes rules, ideas, and values as well as culture traits, such as dress, objects, gestures, inventions, and symbols (pages 22, 29)

culture trait the smallest element in a culture, either material, such as a pot, or nonmaterial, such as a belief (page 27)

de facto segregation the separation of races in fact but not by law (page 343)

de jure segregation the separation of the races by law, as in South Africa (page 343)

demographer social scientist who studies the relationship between population and social structure (page 401)

desegregation the removal of all legal and informal barriers to full integration and equality (page 348)

deviant a person whose behavior violates the norms of a society (page 60)

discrimination behavior that excludes members of a group or groups from the benefits of society; singling out certain groups for ill treatment (page 329)

dominant group the group in a society that sets the values, norms, and standards; members usually enjoy privileges that others in the society do not share (page 329)

ecology the study of the relationship of living things to their environments (page 281)

educational traditionalists those who see training in basic skills as the primary function of education (page 156)

ethnic enclave settlement of persons who share a unique social and cultural heritage different from that of the dominant group (page 342)

ethnic group a group whose members share a unique social and cultural heritage, often sharing patterns of family life, language, recreation, religion, and other customs (page 334)

ethnicity the sense of being different from other groups in a society by reason of cultural tradition, national origin, or religious belief (page 337)

ethnocentric given to believing in the superiority of one's own culture (page 32)

ethnocentrism the belief that one's group is superior to others in its moral standards, beliefs, or ways of behaving (page 334)

ethnologist scientist who studies groups of people to learn about their cultures—folkways, customs, beliefs, and so on (page 27)

evolutionary theory theory held by sociologists who believe that all societies progress from the simple to the complex, with increasing social and cultural differentiation (page 297)

experimental group a group that is treated in a particular way different from an entirely comparable group, called a control group; it is used to determine the effects of the introduction of some new idea or other stimulus (page 435)

extended family a family structure that includes many relatives or three or more generations, often living together or nearby (page 128)

favela a shantytown found in many of the cities of Latin America; poor people or recent poor immigrants to the city often make their homes in the *favela* (page 401)

felony a major crime, for which a statute provides a more severe punishment than for a misdemeanor (page 59)

feudal estate system a closed social system in which people are born to their position in life, social classes are sharply drawn, and it is very difficult to move from one class to another; wealth is heavily based on land ownership (page 98)

folkways preferences or customary ways of doing things; standards of behavior that are not strictly enforced (page 55)

formal organization a highly organized group with clear-cut roles and specific functions and goals (page 89)

functionalist theory the theory of society that emphasizes the integration of institutions and the consensus of values (page 299)

generalizing inferring or deriving a general rule from particular circumstances (page 196)

genocide the systematic murder of an entire people, who are considered racially or morally inferior by the group in power (page 344)

ghetto an area in which people of the same ethnic or racial group live (page 362)

glittering generalities a propaganda technique in which general, well-accepted terms are used in stressing the positive qualities of a person or thing (page 312)

halfway house place where persons are aided in readjusting to society after a period in prison or in a mental hospital (page 394)

historical analysis studying the records of the past, including leaflets, laws, letters, diaries, newspapers, and so on, to prove or disprove a hypothesis (page 431)

humanitarianism the philosophy that people are morally obligated to help those in need (page 49)

hypothesis an educated guess about how two or more things are related (page 19)

ideology a set of beliefs and values that justify or oppose social conditions (page 303)

imperialism the policy of forming an empire to get raw materials and markets by conquering other countries; also, the policy of dominating the economy of a weaker or less developed nation (page 273)

instinctive communication a natural reflex reaction, such as shielding one's eyes in a too-bright light (page 34)

institutional racism deeply embedded patterns of discrimination against a minority racial group, supported by all the institutions of a society (page 339)

institutionalized set into society's structure; said of patterns of behavior that are relatively permanent in a society (page 301)

intergroup conflict conflict among groups in society, which usually differ in certain traits (page 329)

internalizing the process of making the values of others, such as society or parents, a part of oneself (page 196)

labeling theory the theory that much deviance is a result of a person's being labeled as deviant by society (page 63)

legitimize for a job holder, to regard the status and requirements of the job as just, right, or reasonable (page 234)

looking-glass self the sense of self one develops in response to the imagined judgments of others (page 196)

mainstreaming bringing all children, including the handicapped, into regular classes (page 162)

mass as distinguished from a crowd, a group of people who have a shared object of attention but are not in one another's immediate vicinity (page 314)

mass society a society of strangers whose goals and interests are unknown or conflicting; most people live in cities, crowded into small areas (page 399)

matrilineal descent descent traced through the mother's family (page 128)

matrilocal residence pattern in which a newly married couple lives in the house or village of the wife's family (page 127)

meritocracy a social system in which a person's social position is supposed to depend solely on merit, or achievement (page 101)

metropolitan-area model a type of city growth; an extended city that has burst its boundaries and includes many smaller cities or suburbs (page 287)

minority group a subordinate group that differs culturally, socially, or religiously from the dominant group (page 329)

misdemeanor any minor offense for which a statute provides a lesser punishment than for a felony (page 59)

mixed economy an economic system having both public and private ownership of the means of production (page 179)

moral orientation a tendency to see the world in terms of right and wrong, or ethical and unethical (page 49)

mores the major essential rules of a society (page 55)

multiple-nuclei model a type of city growth in which cities grow by taking in outlying towns and villages (page 282)

name-calling a propaganda technique in which a negative label is placed on the opposition (page 312)

nationalism a feeling of loyalty and commitment to one's country (page 170)

negative correlation the observed fact that as one variable increases, the other decreases, and as one variable decreases, the other increases (page 446)

neolocal residence pattern in which a newly married couple establishes an independent household (page 127)

nonparticipant observation a research method in which the observer is not actively involved with the people being studied (page 432)

norms the rules that reflect the values of a society and govern the behavior of its members (page 47)

nuclear family a family made up of a mother, a father, and their unmarried children (page 129)

operationalize to define the key concepts of a study so that they may be measured; for example, "heavy drinker" means taking over four drinks daily (page 429)

participant observation a research method in which the observer is actively involved with the people or project being studied (pages 88, 432)

patrilineal descent lines of descent traced through the father's family (page 128)

patrilocal residence pattern in which a newly married couple lives in the house or village of the husband's family (page 127)

peer a friend and equal; person of equal rank (page 198)

pink-collar work jobs traditionally held by women, such as receptionist, clerk, and hairdresser (page 250)

plain-folks technique a propaganda technique employing a homespun approach and depicting ordinary people who might be neighbors and friends of the audience (page 313)

plea bargaining pleading guilty to a lesser charge in order to avoid a jury trial (page 389)

pluralism the sharing of power by competing groups (page 350)

pluralist movement a social movement that seeks to obtain recognition·for a minority group and to satisfy its needs without forcing it to change its traditions, beliefs, or values (page 307)

polyandry the practice of having two or more husbands at the same time (page 127)

polygamy the practice of having two or more wives or husbands at the same time; plural marriage (page 127)

polygyny the practice of having two or more wives at the same time (page 127)

population density the number of people living in a given amount of space (page 399)

positive correlation the observed fact that when one variable increases or decreases, the other does the same (page 446)

potlatch a ritual in which people lavish gifts upon others as a way of glorifying themselves and demonstrating their wealth (page 48)

prejudice an unfair or false belief about a person or group of people (page 329)

prescriptions rules stating what must be done (page 54)

primary deviance violating cultural norms without discovery; the primary deviant may consider himself or herself basically normal (page 63)

primary group a group made up of individuals who have close, informal relationships (page 87)

probability theory the theory that a random sample will perfectly represent the total group from which it is drawn, no matter how many times the experiment is repeated (page 437)

progressive education education that emphasizes "learning by doing" and the "education of the whole person" (page 156)

proscriptions rules forbidding certain behavior (page 54)

proxemics the study of social-spatial relationships, of "personal space" and how it is used (page 30)

puberty period of physical maturation, at which time reproduction becomes possible (page 215)

race biologically, a group of people who share certain inherited physical traits; socially, a group of people who share physical traits, are considered different from others because of this, and are treated differently (page 331)

random sample a sample in which every person in the universe, or total group, has an equal chance of being chosen (page 437)

rational-legal authority authority that resides in the position, not in the person; the presidency is an example (pages 106, 171)

reciprocal roles related roles, such as husband and wife, doctor and patient, or child and parent (page 82)

reference group the people by whose standards one judges oneself (page 201)

reformist movement a social movement that sets out to change some specific aspect of social life (page 308)

reinforcement strengthening a response by giving a reward, in positive reinforcement, or removing a restriction, in negative reinforcement (page 194)

religion a unified system of beliefs and practices relating to sacred things and uniting its practitioners into a community (page 147)

revolutionary movement a social movement seeking to make major, sweeping changes by assuming political power (page 309)

rites of passage ceremonies that mark the beginning of a new stage of growth or social acceptance (page 56)

role the part a person plays in relation to a group or society (page 81)

role conflict a situation in which the behavior that is expected of one role comes into conflict with the behavior expected of another role; or, conflicting expectations of the same role (page 83)

role loss the reduction or ending of a role that contributed to self-image, as happens with retirement (page 252)

role model a person whose behavior one imitates (page 201)

rumor an unconfirmed report in general circulation (page 315)

sacred related to religious mysteries; holy (page 147)

scapegoat theory the theory describing the process by which a person or group is assigned the blame for the errors of others (page 339)

secessionist movement a social movement in which the protesting group wants to leave the society rather than to change it (page 310)

secondary deviance behavior that results from labeling a person deviant (page 63)

secondary group a group in which relations are limited, specialized, and temporary (page 87)

sector model a type of city growth in which cities grow in parts, or sectors, often following the surface features of the land, such as hills, rivers, or valleys (page 282)

secular having values based on use and practicality rather than on faith or religion; worldly (page 214)

secularization a weakening of the influence of religion on people's lives (page 153)

segregation keeping two or more groups separate by law or by strict customs (page 342)

self-determination politically, the right of a people to set up their own government without outside influence (page 274)

sharecropper agricultural worker whose labor is exchanged for a place to live and a share of the crops (page 365)

significant other a person who has special impact on one's personality, often an agent of early socialization, such as a parent or teacher (page 193)

social category a collectivity of persons who play similar roles but who may or may not know one another (page 87)

social differences variations in ways of living among different societies (page 21)

social fact any social activity or situation that can be measured or observed (page 16)

social group a group of persons who interact in regular ways, share beliefs, values, and goals, and have a sense of belonging (page 87)

social mobility movement into a different stratum, or level, of society (page 98)

social movement a continuing, collective effort to promote or to resist social change (page 299)

social stratification the arrangement of a society into levels, called strata, based upon class, prestige, or power (page 97)

socialism an economic system based on public ownership of the means of production, with a regulated market (page 178)

socialization the process of learning the rules, beliefs, values, and acceptable ways of behaving in a culture or society (pages, 17, 191, 193)

sociology the study of society; the systematic study of human behavior (page 16)

sovereignty the supreme power embodied in the nation-state (page 170)

Standard Metropolitan Statistical Area (SMSA) a county or group of counties containing at least one central city of 50,000; or, a city of 25,000 that has adjoining areas making a combined total of 50,000, if the areas are part of the same economic community (page 288)

statistical aggregate a collectivity of persons who share certain traits but who may have no personal connection and may play dissimilar roles (page 87)

status the position or social standing one holds in an organization or society (pages 38, 77)

stereotype a set of oversimplified, exaggerated, and often unfavorable ideas about a group of people; it implies that all members of the group are exactly alike and does not take individual differences into account (page 223)

subculture a cultural group that shares certain traits with the larger society but has some different traits of its own (page 33)

subsistence-level income a government-defined figure that includes the bare necessities of life—food, clothing, and housing (page 358)

suburb a primarily residential community outside the corporate limits of a large central city but culturally and economically dependent upon the central city (page 408)

symbol a word, gesture, or other way of transmitting an idea (page 34)

symbolic communication the ways in which symbols—words, gestures, or signs—are used to transmit ideas (page 34)

systemic change a change that affects an entire social system (page 297)

---

terrorist a person who uses violence or the threat of violence to achieve a political aim (page 306)

testimonial a propaganda technique in which a well-liked famous person offers support for a product or candidate (page 312)

total environment another name for a controlled environment (page 64)

totalitarian characterized by a dictatorship in which the government regulates all aspects of life and in which no dissent is permitted (page 65)

totem a cultural item, usually an animal or natural object, that represents a particular family or group of people (page 40)

traditional authority authority based on the long-held beliefs of a society; the basis of legitimacy for an inherited office (pages 106, 171)

transfer a propaganda technique in which an association is made between an approved or appealing person or thing and an advocated person or thing (page 312)

transitional society a society in which there is a growing middle class and an expanding urban labor force, and in which chances for mobility exist but are limited (page 99)

underclass a group comprised of the unskilled, uneducated, or socially maladjusted who are unable to get or hold jobs (pages 349, 372)

universe in a sample survey, the total grouping from which a sample of people is chosen (page 437)

untouchable in India, person at the lowest level of the social system (page 98)

urban ecology the study of the relationship of humans to the urban setting (page 281)

urban succession the movement out of a city by one racial, ethnic, or economic group and its replacement by another (page 285)

values the ideas that a given group of people considers important (page 47)

variable in research, anything that can be measured and can change in a way that will affect the findings (page 430)

victimless crime a crime not directed against another person, such as alcoholism, drug addiction, or prostitution (page 385)

white-collar crime individual or corporate crime directed against the public (page 382)

white-collar work jobs involved in producing, recording, classifying, and storing information (page 242)

SOME SIGNIFICANT SOCIOLOGISTS

The works of many of the scholars listed here have had an influence upon the ideas and activities in this book. Among the sociologists whose names are included are some of the earliest contributors to the field as well as some who are contemporary and are still contributing. Each capsule biography lists one or more of the sociologist's major works.

Becker, Howard S. (1928–   ), the originator of "labeling theory" of deviant behavior. A frequent contributor of articles and photographs to *Society* and other journals, this Northwestern University sociologist is the author of *Boys in White, Outsiders, Social Problems, The Other Side*, and *Making the Grade*.

Bell, Daniel (1919–   ), Harvard-based specialist on political sociology and social policy. His books include *The End of Ideology, The Radical Right, Confrontation: The Student Rebellion and the Universities*, and *The Intellectual and the University*.

Berger, Peter L. (1929–   ), Vienna-born sociologist of religion, currently teaching at Rutgers University. His many books include *Invitation to Sociology, The Noise of Solemn Assemblies, The Precarious Vision, Facing Up to Modernity*, and *The Heretical Imperative*.

Bernard, Jessie (1903–   ), leading sociologist of the family whose many works include *The Future of Marriage*.

Blau, Peter (1918–   ), former president of the American Sociological Association. He is an authority on complex organizations. Professor Blau is the author of *Bureaucracy, Exchange and Power in Social Life, Inequality and Heterogeneity*, and *On the Nature of Organization* and the coauthor of *American Occupational Structure* and *The Dynamics of Bureaucracy*.

Blau, Zena Smith (1922–   ), specialist in adult socialization and gerontology—the study of the social consequences of aging. She has taught at many American universities and is the author of *Old Age in a Changing Society*.

Chinoy, Ely (1921–1975), industrial sociologist who taught at Smith College. He wrote *Automobile Workers and the American Dream, The Assembly Line, Sociological Perspective*, and *Society*.

Cohen, Albert (1918–   ), criminologist now teaching at the University of Connecticut who integrated functional theories and those of the "Chicago school" in *Delinquent Boys* and in *Prison Violence*.

Coleman, James (1926–   ), sociologist at the University of Chicago. His books include *The Adolescent Society, Adolescents and the Schools*, and *Community Conflict*.

Comte, Auguste (1778–1857), French philosopher and one of the founders of the discipline. He gave sociology its name and saw it as the new "positive religion."

Coser, Lewis A. (1913–   ), former president of the American Sociological Association taught at the State University of New York, Stony Brook. He is well known for such works as *The Functions of Social Conflict* and *Men of Ideas*.

Coser, Rose Laub (1916–   ), sociologist of family life and medicine. She is the author of *The Family: Its Structure and Functions* and *Life in the Ward*.

Daniels, Arlene Kaplan (1930–   ), member of the Northwestern University faculty. She is known for her writings on both field-research ethics and women's issues. Her most recent book is *Women and Work*, which she coedited.

Davis, Kingsley (1908–   ), author of the excellent text *Human Society*, papers on demography and sociological theory, and *The Population of India and Pakistan*.

Du Bois, W. E. B. (1868–1963), Atlanta University sociologist, one of the founders of the National Association for the Advancement of Colored People (NAACP), and famous black leader. His many books include *The Philadelphia Negro, The Souls of Black Folk*, and *Black Reconstruction in America*.

Durkheim, Emile (1858–1963), one of the founders of modern sociology. This French scholar was the author of four well-known books, *The Division of Labor in Society, The Rules of Sociological Method, Suicide,* and *The Elementary Forms of the Religious Life.*

Erikson, Kai T. (1932–), sociologist at Yale University. He is interested in the use of sociological approaches to the study of history and is the author of *Wayward Puritans* and *Everything in Its Path.*

Fox, Renée (1928–), professor who holds joint appointments in sociology and medicine at the University of Pennsylvania. Her books include *Experiment Perilous* and *The Courage to Fail.*

Frazier, E. Franklin (1894–1962), University of Chicago sociologist who conducted studies of black life in the United States, which are reported in *The Negro Family in the United States, Race and Culture Contacts in the Modern World,* and *Black Bourgeoisie.*

Gans, Herbert (1927–), urban sociologist based at Columbia University who is much concerned with the uses and abuses of social planning. His books include *The Urban Villagers, The Levittowners, People and Plans,* and *More Equality.*

Glazer, Nathan (1923–), historical and political sociologist now teaching at Harvard University. He is especially interested in ethnic groups in American life, as shown in his books *American Judaism, Beyond the Melting Pot,* and *Ethnicity* (the last two books with Daniel Patrick Moynihan).

Goffman, Erving (1922–1982), sociologist who expanded on Shakespeare's phrase "all the world's a stage" through his approach to the study of social interaction. He is the author of *The Presentation of Self in Everyday Life, Asylums, Encounters,* and *Interaction Rituals.*

Goode, William J. (1917–), Columbia University sociologist who is one of the world's leading authorities on the study of the family. His books include *After Divorce, The Family, Readings on Family and Society,* and *World Revolution and Family Patterns.*

Gordon, Milton M. (1918–), University of Massachusetts sociologist whose work is on social class and ethnic relations. He is the author of *Social Class in American Sociology, Assimilation in American Life,* and *Human Nature, Class, and Ethnicity.*

Horowitz, Irving Louis (1929–), editor of *Society,* a magazine of information on social science and social policy. This sociologist has written extensively on politics in this country and abroad, as seen in *The Rise and Fall of Project Camelot, Three Worlds of Development, Cuban Communism,* and *Genocide.*

Keller, Suzanne (1927–), Princeton sociologist who has conducted studies of marital and family relations, sex roles, and social stratification. She is the author of *Beyond the Ruling Class* and *Sociology* (with Donald Light).

Killian, Lewis M. (1919–), Chicago-trained student of social movements, regionalism, and race relations. Among his books are *Collective Behavior, The Racial Crisis in America, The Impossible Revolution,* and *White Southerners.*

Komarovsky, Mirra (1906–), Russian-born sociologist and former president of the American Sociological Association. She is the author of *Blue-Collar Marriage, Dilemmas of Masculinity,* and *The Unemployed Man and His Family.*

Lazarsfeld, Paul (1901–1976), Austrian-born sociologist who helped to found the Bureau of Applied Social Research at Columbia University. He was the author of numerous studies, including *Mathematical Thinking in the Social Sciences* and *Qualitative Analysis.*

Lenski, Gerhard (1924–), specialist in the study of social stratification and the sociology of religion. He is the author of *Power and Privilege* and *The Religious Factor.*

Lewis, Michael (1937–), teacher at the University of Massachusetts. His latest book, entitled *The Culture of Inequality,* focuses on the social costs of pursuing the American dream.

Lipset, Seymour Martin (1922–), sociologist who has concentrated on political behavior, social mobility, and comparative government. He is the author of *Political Man, The First New Nation, Passion and Politics,* and *Revolution and Counter-Revolution.*

Merton, Robert K. (1910–), Columbia University sociologist closely associated with functionalist tradition. His many books include *Social Theory and Social Structure, On the Shoulders of Giants,* and *The Student-Physician.*

Mills, C. Wright (1916–1962), leading critic of two tendencies in American sociology, "grand theory" and "abstract empiricism," as set forth in *The Sociological Imagination.* Other well-known works are *White Collar: The American Middle Classes* and *The Power Elite.*

Moore, Wilbert E. (1914–), specialist on industrialization and social change. His books include *Industrial Relations and the Social Order; Economy and Society; Man, Time and Society; The Professions;* and *Social Change.*

Moynihan, Daniel Patrick (1927–   ), former Harvard professor, former ambassador to India and to the United Nations, and social scientist who now serves as United States senator from New York. His many publications include *The Negro Family: A Case for National Action* and *Maximum Feasible Misunderstanding.*

Myrdal, Gunnar (1898–   ), Swedish economist and sociologist. He is the author of one of the most massive studies of race relations in the United States, *An American Dilemma.*

Nisbet, Robert (1913–   ), formerly Albert Schweitzer Professor of Sociology and History at Columbia University. He is an important commentator on both his discipline and his society. His many books include *The Sociological Tradition, Tradition and Revolt, Social Change and History, Man and Technics, The Social Bond,* and *Prejudices.*

Page, Charles H. (1909–   ), former editor of the American Sociological Review and professor of sociology at many American universities. He is the author of *Class and American Sociology: From Ward to Ross* and *Fifty Years in the Sociological Enterprise,* the coauthor of *Society, Freedom and Control in Modern Society,* and the coeditor of *Sport and Society.*

Park, Robert Ezra (1864–1944), journalist who became a sociologist. He was a guiding figure in the "Chicago school" of sociology, which produced many of America's best-known urban sociologists and social psychologists. He collaborated with a variety of authors, including Booker T. Washington (*The Man Farthest Down*) and Ernest Burgess (*Introduction to the Science of Society, Urban Sociology,* and *The City*).

Parsons, Talcott (1902–1980), founder of the famed Department of Social Relations at Harvard University. Parsons was often called "the dean of sociological theory" in America. His complex and controversial theories are presented in such volumes as *The Structure of Social Action, The Social System,* and *Social Structure and Personality.*

Riesman, David (1909–   ), lawyer who turned to social science and, after years at the University of Chicago, moved to Harvard. He is the coauthor of *The Lonely Crowd,* a study of American character, and the author of many books on American education.

Rossi, Alice K. (1922–   ), sociologist at the University of Massachusetts. She is one of the leading students of sex roles and family relations. She is best known for *The Feminist Papers,* which she edited.

Sennett, Richard (1943–   ), one of the liveliest and most inventive sociologists in America. His major works include *Classic Essays on the Culture of Cities, The Fall of the Public Man,* and *The Uses of Disorder.*

Shils, Edward (1911–   ) professor who holds joint appointments at the University of Chicago and Cambridge. His wide range of concerns are reflected in *Toward a General Theory of Action* (coauthored with Talcott Parsons), *The Torment of Secrecy,* and *The Political Development of New States.*

Simmel, Georg (1858–1918), German sociologist who had a profound and lasting effect upon modern sociology, particularly the study of human interaction and social conflict. A collection of his work, edited by Kurt H. Wolff, has been published as *The Sociology of Georg Simmel.*

Sorokin, Pitirim (1889–1969), Russian political refugee in the United States. He taught at Harvard University and wrote extensively about social conflict and social change in such books as *The Sociology of Revolution, Social Mobility,* and *Social and Cultural Dynamics.*

Spencer, Herbert (1820–1903), English social philosopher considered one of founding fathers of modern sociology, especially "structural functionalism," which views society as an organism. Among his influential works are *Social Statics* and *The Principles of Sociology.*

Sumner, William Graham (1840–1910), Yale sociologist whose theories reflected an orientation called social Darwinism, the view that in society, as in nature, there is a natural-selection process and that only the fittest survive. His book *Folkways* greatly influenced thinking about cultural differences.

Thomas, William Isaac (1863–1947), American sociologist who was interested in the relationship between individuals and their social worlds and the development of the self. His main thoughts are contained in *Self and Society* and *Primitive Behavior.*

Toennies, Ferdinand (1855–1936), German sociologist who, in his book *Community and Society,* presented the major concepts of *Gemeinschaft* (meaning community) and *Gesellschaft* (meaning secondary or impersonal association).

Tumin, Melvin M. (1919–   ), Princeton sociologist originally trained in anthropology. His books include *Caste in a Peasant Society, Patterns of Society,* and *Comparative Ethnic Relations.*

Warner, William Lloyd (1898–1970), anthropologist who became an influential sociologist of American society and culture. His many studies include the multivolume *Yankee City Series* and *Democracy in Jonesville.*

Weber, Max (1864–1920), German sociologist whose influence on theory construction and social research is evident in the works of most contemporary social scientists. He studied many aspects of society, including religion, economics, and bureaucratic organization. His many books include *The Protestant Ethic and the Spirit of Capitalism* and *Economy and Society.*

Whyte, William Foote (1914–   ), author of the famous study *Street Corner Society.* Whyte has also written and edited a number of books in industrial sociology, including *Industry and Society* and *Men at Work.*

Williams, Robin M., Jr. (1914–   ), Cornell University sociologist who has concentrated on the study of American values and social organization and on racial and ethnic relations. He is author of *American Society* and coauthor of *School in Transition* and *Strangers Next Door.*

Wilson, William J. (1935–   ), professor at the University of Chicago. He is the author of several volumes including the provocative *The Declining Significance of Race: Blacks and Changing American Institutions.*

Wirth, Louis (1897–1952), Chicago sociologist who was interested in minority problems and the character of city life. His major work is *The Ghetto,* a study of Jewish communities in Eastern Europe and in Chicago.

Yinger, J. Milton (1916–   ), past president of the American Sociological Association who teaches at Oberlin College. His interest in the sociology of religion and race relations is reflected in books such as *Religion in the Struggle for Power; Religion, Society and the Individual;* and *The Scientific Study of Religion.*

Znaniecki, Florian W. (1882–1958), teacher of sociology in his native Poland and at the University of Chicago and the University of Illinois. He conducted research with W. I. Thomas leading to their five-volume *The Polish Peasant in Europe and America.*

Zuckerman, Harriet (1937–   ), Columbia University sociologist who has written for many years on the sociology of science. Her published work includes *Scientific Elite: Nobel Laureates in the United States.*

CAREERS RELATED TO SOCIOLOGY

The careers related to the field of sociology are too numerous to mention, for a sociological perspective is important in almost every sphere of life and of work. A sociological viewpoint is useful in such government careers as public health officer, Peace Corps volunteer, police officer, Foreign Service officer, city manager, prison official, legislator, and judge. Sociology provides useful background for many careers related to community concerns: refugee worker, community organizer, consumer advocate, environmentalist, family counselor, and human-relations expert. Sociology is also useful in bringing a wider vision to such careers as architect, journalist, lawyer, college dean, psychologist, and teacher.

There are some vocations in which more than a sociological perspective is desirable and advanced training in sociological theory and research is required. Those who major in sociology in college often go on to become social studies teachers in secondary schools, probation officers and welfare workers, market researchers, statisticians, and demographers.

Those who continue in the field and receive master's degrees are frequently able to teach sociology in high schools and junior colleges or to work in government or industry as professional sociologists. Many people interested in applied sociology get their master's degrees in social work, education, counseling, and law.

The best-known sociologists—those who teach at universities, conduct major research projects, write textbooks, serve as heads of commissions, and work as consultants—have gone on to obtain the highest degree, a Ph.D. Many graduate schools offer courses leading to specialization in a subfield of the discipline, such as social theory, social research methods, criminology, family sociology, race relations, industrial sociology, the sociology of science, the sociology of the professions, and the sociology of art.

EDUCATIONAL REQUIREMENTS

Career	Degree	Career	Degree
Criminologist	Ph.D.	Social studies teacher	Bachelor's
Demographer	Bachelor's	Social worker	Master's
Family sociologist	Ph.D.	Sociology professor	Ph.D.
Industrial sociologist	Ph.D.	Sociology teacher	Master's
Market researcher	Bachelor's	Statistician	Bachelor's
Probation officer	Bachelor's	Welfare worker	Bachelor's

REFERENCES

No textbook is solely the work of its authors. The findings of many researchers are foundations upon which texts such as this are based. Listed here are the sources of the readings, quotations, excerpts, and research projects discussed in *Sociology: Understanding Society* and the page number on which each source is cited.

UNIT ONE

Page 16 Auguste Comte, *Positive Philosophy* (AMS Press).

Page 16 Emile Durkheim, *The Rules of Sociological Method* (Free Press).

Page 20 Erich Fromm, *Man for Himself* (Holt, Rinehart & Winston).

Page 29 Edward B. Tylor, *Primitive Culture* (Murray).

Page 30 Edward T. Hall, *The Hidden Dimension* (Doubleday).

Page 32 Henry Morgan, WNEW commentator, "OK, Tribesmen, Now Hear This."

Page 34 Nancy Henley, *Body Politics* (Prentice-Hall).

Page 38 Lance Morrow, "The Odd Practice of Neck Binding," *Time*.

Page 40 Ralph Linton, "Totemism and the A.E.F.," *American Anthropologist*.

Page 42 Elijah Muhammad, *Muslim Daily Prayers* (Univ. of Chicago Press).

Page 42 E. U. Essien-Udom, *Black Nationalism* (Univ. of Chicago Press).

Page 48 Ruth Benedict, *Patterns of Culture* (Houghton Mifflin).

Page 49 Robin Williams, *American Society*, 3rd ed. (Knopf).

Page 50 Horace Miner, "Body Ritual Among the Nacirema," *American Anthropologist*.

Page 52 Khin Myo Than, "From a Young Burmese Girl's Notebook," *UNESCO Courier*.

Page 56 Ruth Benedict, "Continuities and Discontinuities in Cultural Conditioning," *Psychiatry*.

Page 57 Oscar Lewis, *A Death in the Sanchez Family* (Random House).

Page 61 Emile Durkheim, *Suicide* (Free Press).

Page 61 Robert K. Merton, *Social Theory and Social Structure* (Free Press).

UNIT TWO

Page 75 Kingsley Davis, *Human Society* (Macmillan).

Page 79 Leonard Bickman, "Clothes Make the Person," *Psychology Today*.

Page 86 René Spitz, "Hospitalism: An Inquiry Into the Genesis of Psychiatric Conditions in Early Childhood," in *The Psychoanalytic Study of the Child*, edited by Anna Freud et al. (International Universities Press).

Page 86 Ely Chinoy, *Sociological Perspective*, 2nd ed. (Random House).

Page 88 E. E. LeMasters, *Blue-Collar Aristocrats* (Univ. of Wisconsin Press).

Page 92 Rafael Steinberg, *Man and the Organization* (Silver Burdett).

Page 108 C. Wright Mills, *The Power Elite* (Oxford Univ. Press).

Page 109 G. William Domhoff, *Fat Cats and Democrats* (Prentice-Hall).

Page 111 Peter Binzen, *Whitetown, U.S.A.* (Random House).

Page 112 Elliot Liebow, *Tally's Corner* (Little, Brown).

Page 113 Horatio Alger, Jr., *The Store Boy* (A. L. Burt Co.).

Page 116 Melvin M. Tumin, *Patterns of Society* (Little, Brown).

Page 118 Dwight Heath, Charles J. Erasmus, and Hans C. Buschler, *Land Reform and Social Revolution in Bolivia* (Praeger).

UNIT THREE

Page 131 Miriam Schneir, ed., *Feminism: The Essential Historical Writings* (Random House).

Page 132 Mirra Komarovsky, *Women in the Modern World* (Irvington).

Page 134 Alice S. Rossi, "Transition to Parenthood," in *Family in Transition*, edited by Arlene S. Skolnik and Jerome H. Skolnik (Little, Brown).

Page 135 Fred Davis, *Passage Through Crisis: Polio Victims and Their Families* (Bobbs-Merrill).

Page 136 René Spitz, "Hospitalism: An Inquiry Into the Genesis of Psychiatric Conditions in Early Childhood," in *The Psychoanalytic Study of the Child*, edited by Anna Freud et al. (International Universities Press).

Page 137 John Bowlby, *Attachment and Loss* (Hogarth Press and the Institute of Psychoanalysis).

Page 137 Alice S. Rossi, "A Biosocial Perspective on Parenting," *Daedalus, Journal of the American Academy of Arts and Sciences.*

Page 138 Urie Bronfenbrenner and Maureen Mahoney, eds., *Influences on Human Development* (Dryden Press).

Page 140 Robert S. Weiss, *Marital Separation* (Basic Books).

Page 142 Jessie Bernard, quoted in *Marital Separation,* by Robert Weiss (Basic Books).

Page 147 Emile Durkheim, *The Elementary Forms of the Religious Life* (Free Press).

Page 148 Gerhard Lenski, *Power and Privilege* (McGraw-Hill).

Page 149 Max Weber, *The Protestant Ethic and the Spirit of Capitalism* (Scribner's).

Page 152 Irving Howe, *World of Our Fathers* (Harcourt Brace Jovanovich).

Page 155 Mary C. Bredemeier and Harry Bredemeier, *Social Forces in Education: An Introduction to the Sociology of Education* (Alfred Publishing).

Page 158 Talcott Parsons, *The Social System* (Free Press).

Page 158 Richard Sennett and Jonathan Cobb, *The Hidden Injuries of Class* (Random House).

Page 159 James Coleman et al., *Equality of Educational Opportunity* (U.S. Office of Education).

Page 160 Robert Rosenthal and Lenore Jacobson, *Pygmalion in the Classroom* (Holt, Rinehart & Winston).

Page 160 Christopher Jencks et al., *Inequality: A Reassessment of the Effect of Family and Schooling in America* (Basic Books).

Page 160 William H. Sewell and Robert N. Hauser, *Education, Occupation, and Earnings* (Academic Press).

Page 162 Joseph Adelson, "The Political Imagination of the Young Adolescent," *Daedalus, Journal of the American Academy of Arts and Sciences.*

Page 164 Philip A. Cusick, *Inside High School* (Holt, Rinehart & Winston).

Page 171 Max Weber, *The Theory of Social and Economic Organization* (Oxford Univ. Press).

Page 181 Dwight D. Eisenhower, *Public Papers of the President* (General Services Administration).

UNIT FOUR

Page 196 Charles Horton Cooley, *Human Nature and the Social Order* (Shocken).

Page 196 Erik Erikson, *Childhood and Society* (W. W. Norton & Co.).

Page 197 Jean Piaget, *The Origin of Intelligence in Children* (International Universities Press).

Page 198 Robert Paul Smith, *"Where Did You Go?" "Out." "What Did You Do?" "Nothing"* (W. W. Norton & Co.).

Page 201 Peter Maas, *Serpico* (Viking).

Page 203 *Television and Growing Up: The Impact of Televised Violence* (National Institute of Mental Health).

Page 203 Bradley S. Greenberg, "British Children and Televised Violence," *Public Opinion Quarterly*.

Page 203 George Comstock et al., *Television and Human Behavior* (Columbia Univ. Press).

Page 204 John R. Seeley, R. Alexander Sim, and Elizabeth W. Lossley, *Crestwood Heights* (Univ. of Toronto Press).

Page 206 Herbert Gans, *The Urban Villagers: Group and Class in the Life of Italian-Americans* (Free Press).

Page 207 William Moore, Jr., *The Vertical Ghetto* (Random House).

Page 208 Lee Rainwater, "The Lessons of Pruitt-Igoe," *The Public Interest*.

Page 214 G. Stanley Hall, "The Moral and Religious Training of Children," *Princeton Review*.

Page 214 Ruth Benedict, *Patterns of Culture* (Houghton Mifflin).

Page 215 Roberta Simmons, Florence Rosenberg, and Morris Rosenberg, "Disturbances in the Self-image of Adolescence," *American Sociological Review*.

Page 216 Phyllis LaFarge, "An Uptight Adolescence," *Daedalus, Journal of the American Academy of Arts and Sciences*.

Page 216 Thomas Cottle, "The Connections of Adolescence," *Daedalus, Journal of the American Academy of Arts and Sciences*.

Page 216 Alice de Rivera, "On De-segregating Stuyvesant High," in *Sisterhood Is Powerful*, edited by Robin Morgan (Random House).

Page 218 Karen Durbin, "On Hating and Loving Being Single," *Mademoiselle*.

Page 219 Charlotte Leon Mayerson, *Two Blocks Apart* (Holt, Rinehart & Winston).

Page 220 Margaret Mead, *Sex and Temperament in Three Primitive Societies* (Morrow).

Page 222 Lenore Weitzman, "Sex-Role Specialization," in *Women: A Feminist Perspective*, edited by Jo Freeman (Mayfield).

Page 223 Ben Barker Benfield, "The Spermatic Economy: A Nineteenth Century View of Sexuality," in *The American Family in Social Historical Perspective*, edited by Michael Gordon (St. Martin's Press).

Page 223 *The Lady's Almanac* (1875).

Page 223 National Organization for Women (NOW) Central New Jersey Task Force, *Dick and Jane as Victims: Sex Stereotyping in Children's Readers*.

Page 223 Lenore Weitzman and Diane Rizzo, "Images of Males and Females in Elementary School Textbooks" (NOW Legal Defense and Education Fund).

Page 225   Terry Savo, Carol Nagy Jacklin, and Carol Kehr Tittle, "Sex Role Stereotyping in the Public Schools," *Harvard Educational Review.*

Page 225   Matina S. Horner, "Fail: Bright Women," *Psychology Today.*

Page 236   Elliot Liebow, *Tally's Corner* (Little, Brown).

Page 237   David Sudnow, *Passing On* (Prentice-Hall).

Page 238   Ely Chinoy, "Manning the Machines—The Assembly Line Worker," in *The Human Shape of Work,* edited by Peter Berger (Macmillan).

Page 239   John W. Haas, unpublished Ph.D. dissertation, Northwestern University.

Page 241   Robert M. Cook, "Work in the Construction Industry: A Report From the Field," in *Research in Social Problems and Public Policy,* edited by Michael Lewis (JAI Press).

Page 242   Martin Oppenheimer, "The Unionization of the Professional," *Social Policy.*

Page 243   Anthony Giddens, *The Class Structure of the Advanced Societies* (Harper & Row).

Page 243   Catherine Dracup, "The Secretary," in *Work,* vol. 2, edited by Ronald Fraser (Penguin).

Page 243   Robert Jackall, *Workers in a Labyrinth: Jobs and Survival* (Allanheld, Osmun and Co./University Books).

Page 244   William H. Whyte, Jr., *The Organization Man* (Doubleday).

Page 246   Rosabeth Kanter, *Men and Women of the Corporation* (Basic Books).

Page 253   Irving Rosow, *Socialization to Old Age* (Univ. of California Press).

Page 254   Kenneth Woodward, "Growing Old Happy," *Newsweek.*

Page 255   Judith Wax, "It's Like Your Own Home Here," *The New York Times Magazine.*

UNIT FIVE

Page 267   Earl C. Gottschalk, Jr., "A Place Apart," *The Wall Street Journal.*

Page 269   Arthur J. Vidich and Joseph Bensman, *Small Town in Mass Society: Class, Power and Religion* (Princeton Univ. Press).

Page 273   Kai T. Erikson, *Everything in Its Path* (Simon & Schuster).

Page 275   Lauriston Sharp, "Steel Axes for Stone Age Australians," in *Human Problems in Technology,* edited by Edward Spicer (Russell Sage Foundation).

Page 281   Robert E. Park, *The City* (Univ. of Chicago Press).

Page 288 Lewis Mumford, *The Culture of Cities* (Harcourt Brace Jovanovich).

Page 289 Louis Wirth, *The Ghetto* (Univ. of Chicago Press).

Page 289 Herbert Gans, *The Urban Villagers: Group and Class in the Life of Italian-Americans* (Free Press).

Page 291 Jane Jacobs, *The Death and Life of Great American Cities* (Random House).

Page 298 Ralf Dahrendorf, *Class and Conflict in Industrial Society* (Stanford Univ. Press).

Page 299 Talcott Parsons, *The Social System* (Free Press).

Page 309 Alex Inkeles, "The Great Social Experiment," in *The Soviet Experience,* edited by Daniel T. Brower (Holt, Rinehart & Winston).

Page 312 Alfred McClung Lee and Elizabeth Bryant Lee, *The Fine Art of Propaganda* (Octagon).

Page 314 John Lofland, "Collective Behavior: Elementary Forms and Processes," in *Social Psychology: Sociological Perspectives,* edited by Morris Rosenberg and Ralph Turner (Basic Books).

Page 317 Edward Jay Epstein, "Have You Ever Tried to Sell a Diamond?" *The Atlantic.*

Page 318 Neil J. Smelser, *Theory of Collective Behavior* (Free Press).

UNIT SIX

Page 331 Louis Wirth, "Problems of Minority Groups," in *The Science of Men and the World Crisis,* edited by Ralph Linton (Columbia Univ. Press).

Page 335 William Graham Sumner, *Folkways* (Ginn).

Page 335 Mary Roberts Coolidge, *Chinese Immigration* (Holt, Rinehart & Winston).

Page 337 Robert Coles and Jon Erikson, *The Middle Americans* (Little, Brown/Atlantic Monthly Press).

Page 339 Theodore W. Adorno et al., *The Authoritarian Personality* (Harper & Row).

Page 340 Stanley Rothman and Robert Lichter, *Radical Christians, Radical Jews* (Oxford Univ. Press).

Page 341 John Dollard, *Caste and Class in a Southern Town* (Yale Univ. Press).

Page 341 Robert K. Merton, "Discrimination and the American Creed," in *Discrimination and National Welfare,* edited by R. M. MacIver (Harper & Row).

Page 342 Robert Park et al., *The City* (Univ. of Chicago Press).

Page 343   Pierre van den Berghe, "Research in South Africa," in *Ethics, Politics, and Social Research,* edited by Gideon Sjoberg (Schenkman).

Page 345   Langston Hughes, "Dreams Deferred," in *Selected Poems* (Knopf).

Page 346   George Simpson and Milton Yinger, *Racial and Cultural Minorities* (Harper & Row).

Page 346   Peter Rose, *They and We,* 3rd ed. (Random House).

Page 348   William J. Wilson, *The Declining Significance of Race* (Univ. of Chicago Press).

Page 350   Nathan Glazer and Daniel Patrick Moynihan, *Beyond the Melting Pot* (MIT Press).

Page 350   Milton M. Gordon, *Assimilation in American Life* (Oxford Univ. Press).

Page 355   Louis Adamic, *From Many Lands* (Harper & Row).

Page 363   Lee Dirks, "The Poor Who Live Among Us," *The National Observer.*

Page 363   Carol B. Stack, *All Our Kin* (Harper & Row).

Page 365   Ben J. Wattenberg and Richard M. Scammon, "Black Progress and Liberal Rhetoric," *Commentary.*

Page 365   William H. Friedland and Dorothy Nelkin, *Migrant Agricultural Workers in America's Northeast* (Holt, Rinehart & Winston).

Page 366   Harry M. Caudill, *Night Comes to the Cumberlands: A Biography of a Depressed Area* (Little, Brown).

Page 371   Michael Lewis, *The Culture of Inequality* (Univ. of Massachusetts Press).

Page 372   John B. Parrish, "Is the United States Really Filled With Poverty?" *U.S. News and World Report.*

Page 378   National Commission on the Causes and Prevention of Crime, *To Establish Justice, to Insure Domestic Tranquility* (U.S. Government Printing Office).

Page 382   Edwin H. Sutherland, *White Collar Crime* (Holt, Rinehart & Winston).

Page 382   Alan F. Westin, ed., *Whistle-Blowing! Loyalty and Dissent in the Corporation* (McGraw-Hill).

Page 384   Clifton D. Bryant, *Social Problems Today* (Lippincott).

Page 384   Denny F. Pace and Jimmie C. Styles, *Organized Crime: Concepts and Control* (Prentice-Hall).

Page 386   Jacqueline P. Wiseman, *Stations of the Lost: The Treatment of Skid Row Alcoholics* (Prentice-Hall).

Page 387   Richard Rettig, Manuel Torres, and Gerald Garrett, *Manny: A Criminal Addict's Story* (Houghton Mifflin).

Page 390 Philip G. Zimbardo, W. Curtis Banks, Craig Haney, and David Jaffe, "A Pirandellian Prison," *The New York Times Magazine*.

Page 392 Philip G. Zimbardo, "Pathology of Imprisonment," *Society*.

Page 392 Ramsey Clark, *Crime in America* (Simon and Schuster).

Page 393 Bertram S. Griggs and Gary R. McCune, "Community Based Correction Programs: A Survey and Analysis," *Federal Probation*.

Page 401 Joseph Julian, *Social Problems*, 2nd ed. (Prentice-Hall).

Page 402 Carolina Maria de Jesus, *Child of the Dark: The Diary of Carolina Maria de Jesus*, translated by David St. Clair (Dutton).

Page 404 Penina Glazer and Myron Glazer, field notes.

Page 409 Edmund Bacon, lecture series "Cities and Suburbs," delivered at Goucher College.

Page 413 Michael Brown, *Laying Waste: The Poisoning of America by Toxic Chemicals* (Pantheon).

Page 415 Joseph Lyford, *The Airtight Cage* (Harper & Row).

APPENDIX

Page 434 William F. Whyte, *Street Corner Society* (Univ. of Chicago Press).

Associates; **71** Chuck Fishman/Woodfin Camp and Associates; **72** Ann Hagen Griffiths/Omni Photo; **75** Craig Aurness/Woodfin Camp and Associates; **76** David E. Dempster/Off-Shoot Stock; **77** UPI; **79** Bob Daemmrich; **80** (top) Joseph Nettis/Photo Researchers, Inc.; (bottom) Reininger/DPI; **81** Spencer Grant/The Picture Cube; **82** Bob Daemmrich; **85** (a) Michael Heron/Woodfin Camp and Associates; (b) David E. Dempster/Off-Shoot Stock; (c) Michael Abramson/Woodfin Camp and Associates; (d) Philippe Ledru/Sygma; (e) Suzanne Szasz/Photo Researchers, Inc.; **90** Nathan Benn/Woodfin Camp and Associates; **92** Jeff Lowenthal/Woodfin Camp and Associates; **93** Kurits/Liaison Agency; **98** (top) Mary Ellen Mark/Archive Pictures: (bottom) Ashvin Gatha/Leo de Wys; **99** (left) Alan Reininger/Contact Stock; (right) Alan Reininger/Contact Stock; **101** David E. Dempster/Off-Shoot Stock; (right) John Blaustein/Woodfin Camp and Associates; **105** Ann Hagen Griffiths/OPC; **108** Jerry Cooke/Photo Researchers, Inc.; **107** Robert Azzi/Woodfin Camp and Associates; **108** Anthony Howard/Woodfin Camp and Associates; **110** Bob Krist; **111** Michael Heron/Woodfin Camp and Associates; **112** (top) M. Bluestone/Stock Market (bottom) J. Menschenfreund/Stock Market **113** Andrew D. Bernstein/Focus on Sports; **120** David Forbert/Shostal Associates; **123** Peter Vachai/Stock Market; **124** The Granger Collection; **125** Michael Heron/Woodfin Camp and Associates; **126** Roy Morsch/Stock Market; **128** Nathan Bern/Woodfin Camp and Associates; **130** Klaut Lang/DPI; **131** Susanne Page; **132** Jeff Lowenthal/Woodfin Camp and Associates; **133** J. Barry O'Rourke/Stock Market; **134** Joel Gordon/DPI; **135** Charles Gupton/Stock Market; **136** Peter Vadnai/Editorial Photocolor Archives; **138** Nancy Kay/Leo de Wys; **142** Carol Lee/Click Chicago; **147** Charles Harbutt/Archive Pictures; **148** Goyla/Leo de Wys **150** J. Ales Langley/DPI; **151** New York Historical Society; **152** Stephanie Maze/Woodfin Camp and Associates; **153** (top) Mike Maple/Woodfin Camp and Associates; (bottom) Mike Maple/Woodfin Camp and Associates; **154** T. Fujihira/Monkmeyer; **155** The Granger Collection; **156** Brownie Harris/Stock Market; **157** Bruce Thomas/Nancy Palmer Associates; **158** Homer Sykes/Woodfin Camp and Associates; **160** Hugh Rogers/Monkmeyer; **162** Sepp Seitz/Woodfin Camp and Associates; **164** J. Gerard Smith; **169** Marty Heitman/The Picture Cube; **170** (top) William E. Smith/Off-Shoot Stock; (bottom) William E. Smith/Off-Shoot Stock; **171** Gabe Palmer/Stock Market; **172** Dilys Mehta/Contact Press; **176** David E. Dempster/Off-Shooot Stock; **179** Adam Woolfitt/Woodfin Camp and Associates; **180** Edward L. Miller/Stock Boston; **184** Michael L. Abramson/Woodfin Camp and Associates; **189** NASA; **190** William Hamilton/Shostal Associates; **193** J. Gerard Smith **194** Kay Reese and Associates/Editorial Photocolor Archives; (bottom) Michael Heron/Woodfin Camp and Associates; **195** (top) Adam Woolfitt/Woodfin Camp and Associates; (middle) Norman Mosallen/Click Chicago; (bottom) J. Menchenfreund/Taurus Photos; **196** Kim Massie/Rainbow; **198** (left) J. Gerard Smith; (right) Syd Avery/Shostal Associates; **199** F.B. Grunzweig/Photo Researchers, Inc.; **201** (top) Gabe Palmer/Stock Market; **202** Chuck Fishman/Woodfin Camp and Associates; **205** Michael Heron/Woodfin Camp and Associates; **206** Gail Greig/Shostal Associates; **208** C. Vargara/Photo Researchers, Inc.; **213** Eric Roth/The Picture Cube; **214** (top) Miro Vintoniv/The Picture Cube; (bottom) Culver Pictures; **216** Charles Gupton/Stock Market; **217** (top) Susan Lapides; (middle) Elizabeth Crews/Stock Boston; (bottom) Jeff Lowenthal/Woodfin Camp and Associates; **218** J. Gerard Smith; **219** Billy Grimes/Leo de Wys; **221** Suzanne L. Murphy/Click Chicago; **222** J. Gerard Smith; **225** David Strickler/The Picture Cube; **228** (topleft) Supreme Court;

(top right) Susan Steincamp/The Picture Group; (bottom left) Courtesy of Mayor's Office; (bottom right) Bettmann Newsphotos; **233** Jan Faul/DPI; **234** Erika Stone/Peter Arnold; **235** Miro Vintoniv/The Picture Cube; **236** Steve Hansen/Stock Boston; **238** Charles Harbutt/Archive Pictures; **239** (top) Ray Ellis/Kay Reese; (bottom) Sepp Seitz/Woodfin Camp and Associates; **240** Cynthia Johnson/Liason Agency; **241** David E. Dempster/Off-shoot Stock; **242** Rocky Weldon/Leo de Wys; **245** J. Alex Langley/DPI; **250** Camilla Smith/Rainbow; **252** Mark A. Millelman/Taurus Photos; **253** Brent C. Bolin/DPI; **255** Gabe Palmer/Stock Market; **257** Alan Reininger/Leo De Wys; **258** Sonya Jacobs/Stock Market; **264** William E. Smith/Off-shoot Stock; **267** Mark Haven/DPI; **268** Stephanie Maze/Woodfin Camp and Associates; **269** Thomas Ives; **270** (top) Evertt C. Johnson/Leo de Wys; (bottom) Robert Frerck/Woodfin Camp and Associates; **276** (left) Lois Vilota/Stock Market; (right) Laurence Schiller/Photo Researchers, Inc.; **277** Wide World; **278** Owen Franken/Stock Boston; **280** (top right) Mary D'Anella/Sygma; (top left) Bill Nation/Sygma; (bottom right) Randy Taylor/Sygma; (bottom left) Bettmann Newsphotos; **282** Moser/DPI; **284** (top) Roger Archibald/Woodfin Camp and Associates; (bottom) Roger Archibald/Woodfin Camp and Associates; **285** Cary Wolinsky/Stock Boston; **290** (top) Joel Gordon/DPI; (bottom) Freda Leinard/Monkmeyer; **291** (top) Suva/DPI; (bottom) Suyva/DPI; **297;** Stephanie Maze/Woodfin Camp and Associates; **298** Thomas Nebbia/Woodfin Camp and Associates; **301** Wide World; **303** Bettmann Newsphotos; **305** Jay Nadelson/Stock Market; **306** Anthony Succi/Black Star; **307** (left) Rick Smolan/Leo de Wys; (right) Bob Henning/Shostal Associates; **308** Medford Taylor/Black Star; **309** Jay Halaska/Photo Researchers, Inc.; **310** A. Isorlyvkevich/Sovfoto; **311** Culver Pictures; **313** Clifford W. Hautner/Leo de Wys; **315** (left) Stan Osolinski/Stock Market; **315** Van Parys/Sygma; **317** Roy Morsch/Stock Market; **324** Focus On Sports; **326** Danilo Boschung/Leo de Wys; **329** Jeff Lowenthal/Woodfin Camp and Associates; **331** William E. Smith/Off-shoot Stock; **332** Rocky Welder/Leo de Wys; **336** (top) Craig Aurness/Woodfin Camp and Associates; (bottom left) S. Reiss/Shostal Associates; (bottom right) Jerry Frank/DPI; **337** Chuck Fishman/Woodfin Camp and Associates; **340** Bettmann Newsphotos; **343** John Ficcra/Woodfin Camp and Associates; **345** Roy Morsch/Stock Market; **347** Frederick de Van/Nancy Palmer; **348** Spencer Grant/The Picture Cube; **349** Wide World; **349** Randy Duchaine/Stock Market; **350** Wide World; **355** Jack Hamilton/Shostal Associates; **356** Culver Pictures; **360** LeClair Bissell/Nancy Palmer **361** Wasyl Szkodzinsky/Photo Researchers, Inc.; **363** Mimi Forsyth/Monkmeyer; **366** Michael Heron/Monkmeyer; **367** (left) UPI; (right) James Theologos/Monkmeyer; **368** James Isreal/Shostal Associates; **370** J. Gerard Smith; **372** Kenneth Murray/Nancy Palmer; **377** J.P. Laffont/Sygma; **380** Brownie Harris/Stock Market; **381** Carl E. Kripp/Shostal Associates; **383** Barbara Alper/Stock Boston; **386** Michael Lloyd Carlebach/Nancy Palmer; **387** Rhoda Sidney/Leo de Wys; **390** Evertt C. Johnson/Leo de Wys; **391** Richard Falco/Black Star; **392** Nicholas Sahieha/Stock Boston; **393** (top) J.P. Laffont/Sygma; (bottom) J.P. Laffont/Sygma; **399** Willinger/Shostal Associates; **400** Tom Bross/Stock Boston; **402** J. Gerard Smith; **403** Eric Carle/Shostal Associates; (bottom) **405** Robert Azzi/Woodfin Camp and Associates; **407** Rogers/Monkmeyer; **408** Eric Kroll/Taurus Photos; **409** Michael Heron/Woodfin Camp and Associates; **410** Eric Carle/Shostal Associates; **411** Leslie Forbert/Shostal Associates; **413** Stacy Pick/Stock Boston; **415** Sepp Seitz/Woodfin Camp and Associates; **417** Stacy Pick/Stock Boston; **425** Dan J. McCoy/Rainbow; **427** Michael Heron/Woodfin Camp and Associates.

INDEX

Italic numbers refer to pages on which graphs, tables, charts, or photographs appear.